EARTHKEEPING
IN THE NINETIES

William B. Eerdmans Publishing Company
Grand Rapids, Michigan

EARTHKEEPING IN THE NINETIES

Stewardship of Creation

By the Fellows of the
Calvin Center for Christian Scholarship,
Calvin College

Peter De Vos
Calvin De Witt
Eugene Dykema
Vernon Ehlers
Loren Wilkinson

Revised Edition

William B. Eerdmans Publishing Company
Grand Rapids, Michigan

First edition copyright © 1980 by
Wm. B. Eerdmans Publishing Co.
255 Jefferson Ave. S.E., Grand Rapids, Mich. 49503

Revised edition copyright © 1991 by
Wm. B. Eerdmans Publishing Co.

Printed in the United States of America.
This book is printed on recycled paper.

Library of Congress Cataloging-in-Publication Data

Earthkeeping in the nineties: stewardship of creation /
by Peter De Vos . . . [et al.]. — Rev. ed.
p.   cm.
Rev. ed. of: Earthkeeping, Christian stewardship of natural resources. © 1980.
Includes index.
ISBN 0-8028-0534-5 (paper)
1. Natural resources. 2. Environmental protection. 3. Stewardship, Christian.
I. De Vos, Peter. II. Earthkeeping, Christian stewardship of natural resources.
HC55.E27   1991
261.8'5 — dc20   91-26874
CIP

Unless otherwise noted, biblical quotations are taken from the Revised Standard Version
of the Bible, copyrighted 1946, 1952, © 1971, 1973 by the Division of Christian Education of the National Council of the Churches of Christ in the U.S.A., and used by
permission.

Contents

Preface

THE ORIGINAL *EARTHKEEPING* WAS PUBLISHED IN 1980 (THOUGH MOST of the research on it was done in 1977-1978). In the decade that followed, it became an important resource for Christians concerned with the relationship between their faith and the planet's health.

From the beginning, the book's main strength was the breadth of its perspective, a result (thanks to the Calvin Center for Christian Scholarship) of its production by an unusual process of cooperation among Christian scholars in biology, physics, economics, literature, and philosophy. But inevitably, as the developments of the decade unfolded, and as a new wave of environmental awareness swept through the public and the church, it became somewhat out of date. So, in response to a growing general interest among Christians for careful, biblical thought on environmental problems, and in response to many requests for this book in particular, the team which produced it reconvened (in the spring of 1990) and determined to bring *Earthkeeping* up to date. Hence this greatly revised and augmented new edition.

Our purpose has not been to replace the original, but (where necessary) to correct, amplify, and update it. Much of what we wrote in 1978 still stands — especially those parts which deal with historical background and theological principle. Sometimes, though, the perspective has changed significantly, so we present the same material from a new angle of vision. For example, the photographs of the earth from space retain their breathtaking beauty and the importance they held in the seventies as reminders that we live on a planet. But in the nineties they have lost some of their innocence. For some they have taken on new significance as symbols for a troubling new religion of *Gaia*, goddess of the earth; for others they are subtle symbols of a technological arrogance which pull us away from the smells, tastes, sounds, and textures of our day-to-day life in a home-place.

Sometimes our changes deal with new information: we have added many things. In those additions we have tried to bring readers up-to-date with the twelve years since the first edition by (1) revising data (where that is necessary); (2) describing some of the significant objective changes in the state of the planet; (3) sketching some of the ways in which an awareness of our life in a dynamic, fragile, and limited ecosphere has moved from periphery to center; and (4) reflecting some of the many ways in which Christian thinkers have discovered, recovered, and (sometimes, we think) misinterpreted the meaning of the gospel for all of creation.

The decade has been filled with events and movements which require such updating. Here is a list of some of the things which have changed the world we are dealing with in this second edition of *Earth-keeping*:

- Measurable deterioration in the processes of planetary circulation and exchange, most notably in the ozone layer and the "greenhouse effect."
- Increasing problems with waste disposal (especially of toxic wastes).
- Rapid destruction of the rain forests, accompanied by accelerating species destruction.
- Several specific environmental catastrophes (the Valdez oil spill, the Chernobyl reactor failure, the Bhopal incident) which suggest that environmentalist fears are not unfounded.
- The popularization of the Gaia hypothesis, the anthropic principle, the Mandelbrodt set, and other indications of purpose in the universe which have encouraged religious (but usually not Christian) understandings of the cosmos.
- A growing conviction on the part of many — as in "Deep Ecology" and certain aspects of the "New Age movement" — that the crisis conditions of our age primarily require religious or spiritual solutions, rather than scientific or technical ones.
- A growing feminist concern for distinctively feminine ways for being on the earth — including serious attempts to recover goddess worship and *wicca* or witchcraft.

- Widespread exploration of religions which stress human unity with or subordination to "nature": paganism, animism, Taoism, etc.
- Increasingly vocal and activist movements criticizing human arrogance and "speciesism": e.g., Earth First, the Green Party, and animal rights movements.
- An increasingly explicit and outspoken criticism of the role of Christianity in environmental problems.
- A growing public acceptance of the word and concept "stewardship."
- In other circles, a rejection of the ideal of "stewardship" as a prime example of human arrogance.
- Public acceptance and support of recycling and conservation.
- A growing recognition that issues of environment and "development" are often different aspects of the same problem, and thus solutions need not be pitted against each other.
- Greater sophistication in including environmental concerns in economic theory.
- A remarkable increase in the number of both serious and popular studies of environmental issues.

Usually we have dealt with these issues by simply rewriting material in the first edition. Occasionally, when the developments since the first edition seem particularly significant, we refer specifically to the changes that have taken place since that edition. The phrase "in the last decade" usually indicates such an update.

No book — and certainly no revision — can be perfect. As we are aware of the first edition's imperfections, we are also aware of the limitations and incompleteness of the second edition. We would like to say much more about many more things. As it is, we have dropped (or drastically shortened) some sections of the first edition. Those omissions are most obvious in the material relating questions of justice and "third world" development to the broader concerns for stewardship. We have done this not because these are any less important considerations, but because, first of all, it is no longer as necessary as it was a decade ago to show that the well-being of men and women depends absolutely on the well-being of the land. "Environmental" concerns have never been just a rich man's luxury. The widely read and influential U.N. report *Our Common Future* (the subtitle significantly declares its purpose to discuss "Environment and Development") is only one significant study to make that point decisively. A growing literature on the relationship between development, environmental concerns, and justice suggested to us that it would be better not to try to deal with that dimension of the problem, but to focus more directly on understanding the nature of our stewardship of creation.

A word about the title. We hope this edition continues to make more familiar the rich word and concept "earthkeeping." It is intended to evoke "housekeeping" — and through the word "house" (which is *oikos* in Greek) the crucial connection between "economy" and "ecology." For it is the household or *oikoumene* of creation which we children of Adam are called to "keep" — with all the watchful care that the word can evoke.

But the passage of a decade has revealed problems with the book's original subtitle, *Christian Stewardship of Natural Resources*. For to the Christian the earth ought to be neither "Nature" (which suggests its elevation to divinity) nor "resources" (which implies its degradation to a mere stockpile of raw material awaiting the action of human industry). Nor is it simply the abstract "environment." It is rather "creation," a word which reminds us not only of the Creator, but also of our status as creatures and our task as stewards. The word "creation" has been diminished in recent years through being narrowed to apply only to the "how" and "when" of God's action. In this new edition, by using it more consistently to describe this vast, dynamic, beautiful, but suffering planet, we hope to contribute to a recovery and deepening of the full biblical doctrine of creation: that heaven and earth are the Lord's, the product of the Creator's ongoing love — a love which calls us, through creation and through Christ, back to our original task in creation, which is to be gardeners of the earth, stewards of what God has entrusted to us.

We also have dropped "Christian" from the subtitle, for it gave the impression that the sorts of actions we were proposing were incumbent only on Christians. The stewardship we are recommending is not only a Christian task, but belongs to all human creatures. We believe more than ever that only through the new life in Christ — the renewal of creation that begins with the renewing of the Creator's failed, flawed, willful stewards — will that stewardship of creation which more and more people are seeking to exercise ever be possible. But it is not only to Christians that the book is addressed. Rather, it is addressed to all stewards of creation.

ALL OF THE ORIGINAL FIVE SCHOLARS WERE INVOLVED IN THIS REVISION, though (without a luxury like our original funded year together) none of us was able to devote as much time to the revision as we would have liked. "Earthkeeping" continues to be a central concern for all of the authors, but the years since the first edition have brought important changes to all of them.

Peter De Vos, coordinator of the original project, fitted his work on the revision around his taking up of a new academic post as dean of Jordan College in Michigan. Eugene Dykema, still on the economics faculty at Calvin, was coordinator of the revision project, while also serving in his sixth year as chairman of the economics faculty. In fall of 1991 he assumed the position of director of the graduate business program at George Fox College in Newberg, Oregon. Vern Ehlers worked on the revision while campaigning for (and being reelected to) his third term as a Michigan state senator, where, for the past several years, he has been an important voice for environmental legislation.

Cal De Witt, still professor of environmental studies at the University of Wisconsin-Madison, has, for most of the time since the original *Earthkeeping* was published, also been director of the AuSable Institute of Environmental Studies in Mancelona, Michigan. Under his leadership the AuSable Institute (born about the same time as the original *Earthkeeping* study) has, for Christians all over the world, become an important center for reflection, research, and exchange of ideas about our use of creation. Many of the changes in this edition are the result of the encouragement and influence of the AuSable Institute, and the Institute's library was an important resource in the early stages of this revision project.

Loren Wilkinson, who served once again as editor and rewriter for this edition, has for the past ten years been professor of philosophy and interdisciplinary studies at Regent College, a graduate school of theology associated with the University of British Columbia in Vancouver, Canada. Student fellow Aileen Van Beilen (now Aileen Van Genkel) lives in Toronto, and though she was unable to be involved in the revision itself, she played a crucial role in getting the revision project underway.

The Calvin Center for Christian Scholarship once again made the project possible through funding for meetings, revisions, faxes, and phone calls; all who are interested in Christian stewardship — not only of creation, but of the Christian mind — owe the Center a great deal. For unlike the first *Earthkeeping* (which was the Center's first product) this new edition of *Earthkeeping* joins a long list of books and articles, on a variety of crucial issues, which the interdisciplinary research of the Center has made possible.

Preface to the First Edition

IN 1977 CALVIN COLLEGE BEGAN AN AMBITIOUS NEW ENTERPRISE: THE
establishment of the Calvin Center for Christian Scholarship. This
undertaking arose from a recognition that our calling as Christian scholars
and our responsibility as a Christian institution oblige us to contribute,
from within the vantage point of the Christian faith, to the solution of
the complex problems facing humankind today. The purpose of the Calvin
Center for Christian Scholarship is stated well in its constitution:

> The purpose of the Center is to promote rigorous, creative, and ar-
> ticulately Christian scholarship which is addressed to the solution of
> important theoretical and practical issues. More specifically, the
> scholarship promoted shall be of the sort:
>
> a. that goes beyond what is usually expected of an undergraduate
> faculty whose primary responsibility is to students;
>
> b. that goes beyond the specialized disciplinary research interests
> of individual members of the faculty;
>
> c. that can best be conducted by a group of Calvin College scholars
> working together, supplemented whenever feasible and desirable by
> scholars and others from outside the Calvin College community;
>
> d. that would be of benefit to a broad spectrum of the Calvin
> community and of the world beyond;
>
> e. that is focussed on areas of life and thought in which it is
> reasonable to expect that a distinctively Christian position can be
> worked out; and for which traditional Christian positions have been

too parochially expressed, too superficially developed, or too little in accord with the Christian faith.

The topic of study selected for the initial year of operation of the Calvin Center for Christian Scholarship was "Christian Stewardship and Natural Resources." Those scholars selected to participate in this study were: Peter De Vos, Professor of Philosophy, Calvin College; Calvin De Witt, Professor of Environmental Studies, University of Wisconsin-Madison; Eugene Dykema, Assistant Professor of Economics, Calvin College; Vernon Ehlers, Professor of Physics, Calvin College; and Loren Wilkinson, Professor of English, Seattle Pacific College (currently at the Oregon Extension of Trinity College, Deerfield, Illinois). In addition, two Student Fellows were selected: Derk Pereboom, philosophy major; and Aileen Van Beilen, history major. During the 1977-78 academic year this group actively studied the topic of Christian stewardship and natural resources.

However, the 1977-78 Fellows wished to do more than their assigned task of scholarship followed by the customary publication of their thought in scholarly articles and journals. It was also their desire to discuss, in a general yet scholarly way, the broad issues surrounding Christian stewardship of natural resources, and to do so at a level appropriate for the intelligent layperson. This book is the result of their study.

It was our desire to take a holistic approach to the problems discussed in this book, and not merely to produce an anthology which would deal with bits and pieces of them. This thrust us into an intensive project which entailed many group discussions and countless more individual conferences. We have attempted to bring to this enterprise the collective knowledge of our disciplines in a joint endeavor to address, in the broadest terms possible, the resource-use problems faced by the world today. We have not attempted to be so specific as to tell you what kind of car to buy, how to set your home thermostat, or what legislation your government must pass. Nor have we analyzed in detail which alternative energy approaches are best, least costly, or most environmentally suitable. There are others more capable of doing that. Furthermore, the value of this book, as we perceive it, is not that it is produced by a team of scholars from different disciplines, though the mutual insight and the correction of disciplinary narrowness generated by that combination is, we think, important. Nor is its strength that we have spent a year devoted specifically to understanding our use of resources; there are other think-tanks, with bigger budgets, which have done that. The distinctiveness of this book is rather that we have approached the problem in an in-depth and integrated way from within the framework provided by biblical principles. Thus, in this book we consider the enormously difficult and important problem of how human beings should use the world, guided by the knowledge that in the gospel of Christ, God shows people not only how to attain eternal life, but also how to care for the creation in which he has placed us as stewards.

The writing of this book has indeed been a joint endeavor, and no person can be singled out as having been the major driving force. However, it should be mentioned that Loren Wilkinson served as the principal writer, performing the Herculean task of taking six disparate writing styles and combining them into one. Aileen Van Beilen spent many hours writing, editing, and tending to the minutiae, such as footnotes and references, and Judy Nydam efficiently and unerringly converted illegible handwriting and garbled dictation into polished typewritten pages. Lastly, Vernon Ehlers served as editor-manager of the project.

꒰ꜝ   ꒰ꜝ

Humanity and the Earth: Two Futures

It was the best of times, it was the worst of times, it was the age of wisdom, it was the age of foolishness, it was the epoch of belief, it was the epoch of incredulity, it was the season of light, it was the season of darkness, it was the spring of hope, it was the winter of despair, we had everything before us, we had nothing before us. . . .

— Charles Dickens, *A Tale of Two Cities*

WE LIVE IN THE PRESENT. SHAPED BY THE PAST AND SHAPING THE future, it is nevertheless *now* that we make the choices that change our world. This has always been true for humans: for us, every point is a turning point. Nevertheless, some times seem more crucial than others, and we live in such a time.

For we have become profoundly aware of our future. This future orientation itself is an inescapable part of modernity and has been growing for several centuries. But for the first time in human history we are aware that when we say "our" future we are speaking of the whole planet: not only our region or our nation; not only humanity as a whole; not only living things; but the whole, vast network of earth, air, water, fire, plants, animals, and people which the photographs from space have shown us in such vivid and alarming beauty. That image of the round and cloud-wrapped planet has become for our time a central image of perfection.

In the biblical story of beginnings, the perfection of the Creator's work is symbolized by another emblem of wholeness, the number seven. In Christian reflection on creation we have often missed the main point of that story. For the overwhelming message of the Bible about creation is not its *how* or *how long*. It is rather that this vast and intricate cosmos — and especially this uniquely hospitable Eden of an earth — is the Creator's gift, upheld in every atom of its being by the Creator's costly love.

Likewise our principal task in creation is not figuring out how God did it (though bringing that silent history to voice is an honorable job of science, one of the ways we work out the gift of dominion). It is rather (in the words of Genesis 2:15) "to tend and keep it." *Earthkeeping* is our task. But too often (whether through ignorance or intent) earth-breaking has been our accomplishment.

Thus our sense of being at a turning point, a crisis. We have never been more aware of the beauty, intricacy, and goodness of our planetary home. But the more we learn of it, the more we learn also how the same civilization which has brought us knowledge of the earth also seems to threaten it. On the one hand our growing knowledge of creation has illuminated it — lifted it into the light of knowledge and wonder; on the other, our quest for ever unfolding knowledge, power, and well-being threatens to degrade the very earthly creation we are coming to know.

So we may well begin this exploration of biblical earthkeeping by reflecting briefly both on how we have illuminated creation and on how we have degraded it (willingly or not). For it is in this tension between sensitivity and power that our present crisis lies, and in such a crux we are called, by our Creator and Redeemer, to live.

Our treatment — for better and for worse — of creation may be recalled under seven ancient headings: air, earth, fire, and water; plants, animals, and human beings. The number is arbitrary, but not insignificant. The first four categories reflect both Greek and medieval notions of the cosmos; the remaining three are an inevitable and ancient way of describing the kinship of living things. Little is left out by these categories, and by a happy accident they add up to seven, that Hebrew sign of sabbath and perfection.

1. Gerard Manley Hopkins, "The Blessed Virgin Compared to the Air We Breathe," in *The Poems of Gerard Manley Hopkins*, ed. W. H. Gardner and N. H. MacKenzie (London: Oxford University Press, 1967), p. 93.

SEVEN ANCIENT DIVISIONS OF CREATION

Air

Of all the things which environ us, air (being invisible) is easiest to take for granted. Yet people have always marveled at the mysterious way in which air is intertwined with our life — so much so that from ancient times air, breath, wind, spirit, and life itself have been equated. Lines from that profoundly Christian — and profoundly ecological — poet Gerard Manley Hopkins express the mysterious, life-giving ubiquity of air:

> Wild air, world-mothering air,
> Nestling me everywhere,
> That each eyelash or hair
> Girdles; goes home betwixt
> The fleeciest, frailest-flixed
> Snowflake; that's fairly mixed
> With, riddles, and is rife
> In every least thing's life . . .[1]

In recent decades we have been learning how deep and complex is our dependence on air, not just for individual life, but for the life of the whole planet. Through the gases that we breathe we are in touch with all living things, for the winds ceaselessly mix and move their molecules around the globe. The needs of plants for carbon dioxide (CO_2) and of animals for oxygen are met by the atmosphere in a perfectly circulating balance which (as we are learning through comparison with the atmosphere of other planets) is not accidental. But an indirect result of the air's very mobility places the whole atmosphere at risk. By assuming that the winds will carry our pollutants away we have begun to hamper the life-giving work the atmosphere does. By rapidly increasing the gases which restrict the earth's re-radiation of the sun's energy back into space, we are warming the air as in a greenhouse. Of similar concern at the planetary level is destruction of the layer of stratospheric ozone which protects life from excessive ultraviolet radiation. Many of the chemicals released into the atmosphere as by-products of our industry — particularly the chloro-

---

1. Gerard Manley Hopkins, "The Blessed Virgin Compared to the Air We Breathe," in *The Poems of Gerard Manley Hopkins,* ed. W. H. Gardner and N. H. Mackenzie (London: Oxford University Press, 1967), p. 93.

fluorocarbons — have this effect. Since UV radiation is damaging to genetic material, we inadvertently (but now knowingly) are threatening the material through which the diverse miracle of life has been passed from generation to generation. Thus, just as we have illuminated the marvel of how the atmosphere functions to nourish life on the planet, so we have unwittingly degraded the atmosphere itself.

Earth

"Earth" is the planet, of course, but that view from space is a relatively new perspective. Traditionally, earth has been the opposite of air: it is *land*, the solid ground beneath our feet. More important, it is *soil*, whose continuing fertility produces our food. Most of us have shared Walt Whitman's astonishment at earth's ability to take corruption and turn it into health:

> Now I am terrified at the Earth, it is that calm and patient,
> It grows such sweet things out of such corruptions,
> . . . .
> It distills such exquisite winds out of such infused fetor,
> It renews with such unwitting looks its prodigal, annual,
>   sumptuous crops.
> It gives such divine materials to men, and accepts such leavings
>   from them at last.[2]

Over the centuries we have learned a great deal about how to enhance the fertility of the soil through terracing, draining, fertilizers, and irrigation. And our scientific understanding continues to give us insights into the astonishing mix of bacteria and microbes, living and nonliving things, which make up the vitality of the soil. But despite such knowledge, and the accumulated wisdom of many millennia of agriculture, in any given place the "earth" that grows our crops is, with only a few exceptions, far less fertile than it was when crops were first grown there. Time after time civilizations have failed to care for their topsoil — and now lie buried in drifting sand.

In the United States, on the average, we have lost half our topsoil

---

2. Walt Whitman, "This Compost," in *Leaves of Grass and Selected Prose*, ed. Sculley Bradley (New York: Holt, Rinehart & Winston, 1962), p. 307.

since agriculture began. And that is not all: we yearly remove one to three million acres of the best land from agricultural purposes. Early in our history we located farm communities where they could best serve agriculture. The early distribution of these agricultural service centers benignly freckled the landscape, but now those "freckles" have become a kind of cancer, each dot expanding to consume the very land by which it was once supported.

In other parts of the world degradation is of a different sort. Interest payments on debt to richer nations require cash crops, which take the best land, forcing people onto marginal land which soon becomes an eroded desert. Or else the people are forced into the cities, which swell to cover yet more farmland.

And in an attempt to compensate for the removal of the best land from agriculture, we often open new lands for farming by means of irrigation; but the rapid evaporation of water from the irrigated soil leaves behind salts, in many cases rendering the irrigated land unusable after a few years.

So although we grow more food than ever, we do so at a higher and higher price to the earth in which it grows. Modern culture does not sustain our agriculture.

Water

"All praise be yours, my Lord," wrote St. Francis, "through Sister Water, so useful, lowly, precious and pure." Unlike the air, water is visible, a living symbol of cleanliness, cool refreshment, fertility. It seeps in springs out of the earth, drips from moss, pours down mountains, and roars over falls; it sparkles in lakes; it circles, planet-wide, in the oceans' tides and currents. Like the air, water circulates freely and binds us in a community of living things. And, as is the case with air, that very ability to disperse and dissolve has led us to use rivers, lakes, and oceans as sewers and sinks for much of our waste. We are familiar with many of these degradations, for they are among the easiest to notice — and, perhaps, the easiest to repair. Less obvious, and harder to repair, is the increasing degradation of groundwater through injection wells and percolation through old dumps. We use water to cleanse ourselves and our world; we use it to power our turbines and carry our shipping. We know more today about the life it carries and sustains than we ever have before. But in the past few decades thousands

"We delayed and did nothing, in spite of one environmental warning after another — and now we're freezing over!"

From *The New Yorker*, May 8, 1989. Drawing by Ed Fisher;
© 1989 The New Yorker Magazine, Inc. Used by permission.

of northern lakes have become acid-rich and life-poor; with increasing frequency, oil fatally clogs the fur and feathers of sea life; water transports toxins into our homes. Despite our knowledge and skill, despite the sparkling abundance of water, we have degraded it as well.

Fire

Francis praised fire as well, but he recognized its ambivalence: "All praise be yours, my Lord, through Brother Fire, through whom you brighten up the night: how beautiful is he, how gay! Full of power and strength." Fire is the flickering symbol of energy; it has given us tremendous power over creation: from the cooking of food to the smelting of metals to the controlled "firing" of fuel in the harnessed chambers of our engines, some form of "fire" is involved in bringing about most of our well-being. But fire has an ominous side: it is by applying energy to creation that we change its forms. Through fire in its many forms we release the carbon of the forests, or synthesize dioxins, or distribute sulphur, lead, and mercury through the atmosphere. Burning derivatives of oil power our civilization — and pollute it. We have harnessed a sort of fire — the fire of thermonuclear reactions — to our benefit in hundreds of nuclear reactors around the world, but, unleashed (as at Chernobyl), it can blight the very genes of nearby living things. So we degrade *with* fire; but inevitably we also degrade fire (energy) itself, as we use it. This is unavoidable, a requirement of entropy, the second law of thermodynamics: energy must be degraded to accomplish work. But we have done so with blatant wastefulness in the construction of our engines, our buildings, and our industrial processes.

In Greek myth, Prometheus stole fire from the gods and gave it to mortals to lighten their load. But the living God has *given* us fire (as he has given us all things in creation) as a gift to use with stewardly care. We have used it to lighten our load immeasurably. But through careless use of the "fires" of energy, we have often not only degraded fire itself, but imposed a heavy burden on creation.

Plants

Green plants (fern, grass, oak, kelp, plankton) are one of the chief glories of creation: they color the continents and delight us in wilderness and garden alike. We have teased the seeds, stalks, roots, flowers, and leaves of plants into a million useful and nourishing things. We have even, through patience and careful breeding, changed the form of plants; now, through our growing capability to manipulate genetic material directly, we stand on the threshold of being able to use them even more for our benefit.

Through plants, the air, water, and soil are kept and circulated for the planet's nourishment. Yet for our short-term gain we are inexorably degrading the largest and most complex communities of plants. This is most obvious in the degradation of the rain forests, both temperate and tropical. In the tropics alone a forest area the size of Michigan is destroyed each year. The purpose of this destruction is a quick conversion of forests into marketable products and farmable land. But this is a rapid and wasteful use of creation's riches, which have taken thousands of years to become established: it is a harvesting where there has not been sowing, a reaping where there has not been cultivation or care. The result is a degraded forest, still green with weedy vegetation, but with severely diminished numbers of species, soil nutrients, and diversity. At present rates of degradation, by the year 2000 at least half of all tropical forests will be lost, with most of the rest following in the next three decades. And with the loss of the forest, the degradation of soil, air, and water can only accelerate. Through the silent miracle of photosynthesis plants have poured out their bounty for us: our civilization is based on their sun-trapping chemistry. But that same civilization threatens to destroy much of that wild bounty from which it has drawn nourishment.

Animals

With animals we come close to ourselves: their very shapes declare both our kinship and our difference. We have lived in a long ambivalence to the world of animals, making them our pets — and our slaves; our symbols — and our food. The Bible reflects this ambivalence, showing us Noah (a kind of human savior) surrounded by beasts — and telling us that

> the fear and dread of you will fall upon all the beasts of the earth and all the birds of the air, upon every creature that moves along the ground, and upon all the fish of the sea; they are given into your hands. (Gen. 9:2, NIV)

Though we have, across human history, often treated animals with kindness and love, often bringing them into the circle of our world, we have more often simply regarded them as raw material to do our work or provide our protein, leather, and fur. We need not agree with those who say that it is inappropriate ever to use animals for food or research, but all too often we use them only as machines for the production of protein, leather, and fur, with no sense that they are fellow creatures. Though it may be appropriate to use animals to increase our well-being, it is a solemn thing to do, demanding attitudes of husbandry and stewardship which are (for the most part) no longer present. And even more tragically, our civilization, through default, is acting as though animals for which we have discovered no use are irrelevant, so we destroy their habitat and send them into extinction: we *daily* lose many species of insects, fish, birds, and animals. Among these are many that we do not know, for far fewer than half of the earth's living things have even been given names. Yet destruction and pollution of habitats is accelerating everywhere — and not only in some remote rain forest. In the developed world, animal habitat is rapidly being lost to poorly planned suburban and agricultural growth; wetland, estuarine, and coastal habitat are being degraded by urban and industrial wastes and by draining and filling. Human activity is like a new deluge threatening the beasts. And though our concern for the fate of animals has never been greater, we are painfully unable to change their situation.

Human Beings

We men and women were shaped by our Creator in a long process that links us wonderfully to the rest of creation. And the story of human civilization, for all its pain, cruelty, and degradation, is also the story of men and women carefully tending creation and offering it back in thanks to the Creator. Thus the various cultures of the world have matched, in their colorful and creative diversity, the diversity of the creation which they tend.

Yet we seem to be rapidly losing a sense of what it means to be an image bearer of the Creator in a creation entrusted to our care. Before the onslaught of a technical, secularized, worldwide civilization, culture after culture is losing its uniqueness, its awareness of the root meaning of culture, which is the tending of creation.

One such cultural degradation is the loss or marginalization of groups of people who have learned to live sustainably on the earth. These range from traditional subsistence farmers in temperate regions to the rapidly diminishing tribes of the rain forest. Such groups have learned, over centuries and millennia, how to live rich lives in a sustainable relationship with complex ecosystems. With the disappearance of the tribal cultures goes a priceless store of information about human uses of plants and animals for food, fiber, and medicine.

Another kind of cultural degradation is closer to home: it is the worldwide emergence of an urban culture whose people — from childhood on — have no direct contact with creation. They live in an entirely human world. Many children growing up in cities have never seen the stars, have never seen a forest or a clean, free-flowing river. Yet the tragedy is that more and more people think such a life is normal. So we are losing our ancient sense of being the articulate caretakers of earth, air, fire, water, plants, and beasts.

WE CONFESS THESE DEGRADATIONS OF CREATION, YET THEY BEWILDER US. None of them came about out of malice. They are rather the result of carelessness: literally a lack of care for creation, a willingness to go about the legitimate business of building a human world without noticing the cost to God's earth. Yet in recent years we *have* noticed. The same gifts of wisdom and power — our science and technology — which have created many of the problems have also opened our eyes to the accompanying degradation. So our civilization is in a quandary. Some argue that what we are experiencing now is simply the pain of growth and maturing; we need to forge ahead and consolidate our growing control over creation. Consider these words:

> 200 years ago almost everywhere human beings were comparatively few, poor and at the mercy of the forces of nature, and 200 years from now, we expect, almost everywhere they will be numerous, rich and in control of the forces of nature.[3]

Others feel that our increasing control over creation has brought us close to racial, if not planetary, death. Thus Robert Heilbroner, considering just a few of the degradations we have considered, observes accurately:

> There is a question in the air, more sensed than seen, like the invisible approach of a distant storm, a question that I would hesitate to ask aloud did I not believe it existed unvoiced in the minds of many: "Is there hope for man?"[4]

We may merely be suffering from what one futurist called "future shock" — the too-rapid approach of the future and the changes it brings — but in any case, we are obsessed with the total shadow which our present actions cast across the future. A handful of typical concerns illustrates this compulsive "tomorrow-mindedness":

----

3. Herman Kahn, *The Next Two Hundred Years* (New York: William Morrow, 1976), p. 1.

4. Robert Heilbroner, *An Inquiry into the Human Prospect* (New York: W. W. Norton, 1975), p. 13.

- We live (though by now it has become almost a cliché to say it) under the "shadow of the mushroom." The mere possibility of nuclear war keeps us aware that everything we take for granted might be canceled by the radiant zero of thermonuclear explosion. Though the conscious fear of nuclear war may have receded somewhat in the decades since Hiroshima — and especially since the sudden ending of the Cold War — it is unlikely that we will ever again live in a world free of nuclear terror. The number of nations with nuclear weapons, as well as the number of nuclear power plants (each a potential Chernobyl), continues to increase. And with each increase the burden on the future grows greater.
- For the first time ever, large numbers of people have become concerned with the health of the atmosphere. "Greenhouse effect" and "ozone layer" have become (literally) household words. Household habits, national policies, and international accords have been shaped by concern over things which *might* happen: the consequences of a warming planet and a thinning ozone shield, though dire, are at this point only anticipated.
- Something like a new religious movement has, in the past decade or so, grown out of the faith that (despite appearances to the contrary) humanity is on the threshold of a "New Age" in which it will begin to take control of its own evolution and the guidance of "spaceship earth."
- A vocal minority of North Americans have changed their way of life at the prospect of various kinds of future chaos: a "population explosion" that might threaten our well-being; a worldwide famine that would starve millions; the melting of the polar ice caps (from too much air pollution); the destruction of the ozone layers (from too many aerosol cans). In addition to those who have made some sort of token attempt to avoid such an assortment of catastrophes, millions more live unchanged lives, but do so in a vague uneasiness of approaching calamity.

Individuals have been at a turning point before. But, for the first time in history, large numbers of people are beginning to see that — for better or worse — what we do affects not only ourselves, but the whole earth. We have unwittingly been degrading creation for a long time, but now we are increasingly aware of those degradations — and increasingly unwilling to let them continue. Phrases like "planetary health," "global awareness," and "the ecosphere" were strange a generation ago; now they are common vocabulary. And whether these new words issue in new actions is not, perhaps, as important as the new awareness that they point to. Like it or not, we now know that we are involved with the planet's life — with the health of an Ethiopian child, the dwindling population of the blue whale, the thickness of the polar ice caps, the composition of the atmosphere.

Appropriately, this new planetary awareness is the gift (or curse) of those who have the greatest ability to actually affect the earth. The hungry child in Ethiopia knows far less about his or her involvement in the world community than does the American businessperson; but such a child will also have far less chance to change it. Thus our new knowledge is bitter: the more we understand that we are managers of the planet, the more we recognize that we have not managed it well. Our obsession with the future, then, is a painful consequence of the consciousness of our involvement in the life of the earth.

This growing awareness of our obligation to the earth (particularly in the wealthy West, where we are haunted by both consciousness and conscience) places Christians in a difficult position. On the one hand, we affirm that God made the earth, called it good, and directs its course. And we believe that God continues to care for it. The word translated "world" in the New Testament is usually *kosmos,* which means, in its broadest sense, "cosmos," the universe. When Christians affirm that God loved the world and that Christ died for the life of the world, they are speaking not just of humanity, but of the whole planet — indeed, the whole created universe. Thus, of all people, Christians should be concerned for the future health of the planet — both for the narrow "world" of humankind and the broader "earth" of a complex and living ecosphere.

And yet (with a few important exceptions) Western Christendom has not shown much concern for the world's health. For the emphasis in Christian thought has been much more on personal than on cosmic salvation. Indeed, one narrow use of the word *world* is in declarations that Christians have been saved *out of* the world. That idea has been interpreted by many to be a sort of license to neglect the world in order to care for the soul. This interpretation, when combined with a radically individualistic trend in Western thought, has produced the prevailing mood among Christians with regard to their involvement in the planetary environment: we are concerned first of all with the relevance of the gospel for our own salvation; second, with its relevance for the salvation of the rest of humankind. But for most, the concern stops there; that vital human center is also the circumference of any feeling of responsibility for the rest of creation. Human degradation we are sensitive to — but we have been largely blind to the degradation of creation. We have seen the rest of the world merely as background for the human drama of salvation.

We simply cannot escape from our embeddedness in creation: we are creatures. And an even more startling fact is that the earth cannot escape from us. It can only wait for us to exercise our stewardship.

At this point the bewilderment for the thoughtful Christian increases. For there are, in our time, plenty of non-Christian thinkers who are quick to see humans as lords or saviors of nature. Yet their ideas are difficult for the Christian to affirm. At one extreme, we find those who regard nature merely as raw material for the building of human civilization, the perfecting of human comfort.

Such a picture of human mastery is provided by the late Buckminster Fuller, whose argument is that it is our destiny to do increasingly more and more with less and less. Thus we steadily increase our control over nature, and by doing so, free our mental powers for the unique sort of management we can give to the processes of the planet. Fuller's viewpoint is perhaps best suggested in the title of one of his books: *Operating Manual for Spaceship Earth.*

But that popular modern picture of the earth as a spaceship, though it expresses a much-needed recognition of the unity of the planet, is in some ways inappropriate. As one contemporary historian puts it, "The metaphor is, in fact, ecologically terrifying. A spaceship is completely a human artifact, designed to sustain human life and for no other purpose."[5] The Christian knows that the earth is the Lord's, not ours; thus, sustaining human life is not its only purpose.

There is in that body of truth at the center of the Christian's faith justification for both views — the view that humanity is bound for destructive crisis, and the view that it is growing toward an Edenic utopia.

In support of the first view, Christians have it on high authority that humans are destructively wicked creatures. From Eden on, we have tried to make ourselves gods, and in the attempt we have consistently misused creation (from Eve's fruit to Cain's club to Babel's bricks). We have always brought pain or death to other persons, and we have as often

---

5. Lynn White, "Continuing the Conversation," in *Western Man and Environmental Ethics,* ed. Ian Barbour (Reading, MA: Addison-Wesley, 1973), p. 63.

brought destruction to the wider world — whether in flood sent to punish the human race or in fire that fell on Sodom. But of course we do not have to look to biblical history to find evidence of humanity's destructive sinfulness; any place or period of our past is filled with examples of such dead-end malignancy: Roman soldiers salting the fields of conquered enemies, Nazis cremating millions of Jews, Americans slaughtering billions of passenger pigeons, the scorched-earth policies of a thousand petty tyrants. The contemporary Christian finds in these episodes good reason to despair at the present state of human stewardship and the future prospects for humanity. Anxiety would seem to be the only response to a future governed by such a creature, whose heart is "deceitful above all things, and desperately wicked" (Jer. 17:9, KJV).

But there is another biblical picture of human possibility and the earth's future. Men and women are not solely evil: we were made good in God's image, and the twisted path of our goodness is made straight in Christ. Great portraits of *shalom*, peace, abound in the Bible. They present humans as living in harmony with each other, with the world, and with God. Such is the ideal picture of Psalm 104, in which God is portrayed as causing

> . . . the grass to grow for the cattle,
>   and plants for man to cultivate,
> that he may bring forth food from the earth,
>   and wine to gladden the heart of man,
> oil to make his face shine,
>   and bread to strengthen man's heart.
> The trees of the LORD are watered abundantly,
>   the cedars of Lebanon which he planted.
> In them the birds build their nests;
>   the stork has her home in the fir trees.
>
> (Ps. 104:14-17)

We find such a picture of harmony between people and their environment in the apocalyptic future of Isaiah, in which they

> shall plant vineyards and eat their fruit. . . .
> They shall not labor in vain,
> or bear children for calamity. . . .
> The wolf and the lamb shall feed together. . . .
> They shall not hurt or destroy in all my holy mountain.
>
> (Isa. 65:21, 23, 25)

Thus Christians ought to understand the greed, the voraciousness, the evil that seems to be turning the world toward destruction; but we also ought to understand the possibility of a redeemed — and redemptive — humanity, at peace in a garden earth.

How then should the Christian think and act? This book is an attempt to answer that question by looking carefully and thoroughly at the nature of the problems which face us, at the nature of humanity itself, and at the significance of the gospel of Christ for Christians who seek to live wisely in the present and carefully for the world's future.

Should the Christian side with the doomsayers or with the utopians? What kind of tomorrow should the Christian work toward? How should Christians live their lives in the face of the obvious needs of their fellow creatures — both human and nonhuman?

There have been two main answers in the history of Christendom. One has stressed the separation of the church from the world — and even from the earth. From Tertullian to Ellul, those who have held this position have asserted the tension between Athens and Jerusalem. They have maintained that the wisdom, powers, and techniques of corrupt humankind can only lead to slavery and destruction, and that any attempt to build a future on human foundations will produce Babel, Babylon, or Sodom — but not Zion. Today, those who hold this view stress the evil of technology, the corruption of the political process, and the need for Christians to live in radical tension with the fallen order — if necessary, letting it destroy them to thus reveal its fallenness.

The other response to the dilemma is made by those who see the institutions and abilities of humans as gifts of God, redeemable along with humankind. From Justin Martyr through Calvin and the Eastern Orthodox tradition to many contemporary Reformed or Sacramental thinkers, these have maintained in various ways that for Christians to build the city of man, however haltingly, in an awareness of God's working in the world is to build Zion and that ultimate kingdom of peace.

The consequences of these traditional answers are magnified today by the enormous forces which humans have learned to exercise. The extent of those human powers seems to confirm those who give the first answer, for they are clearly powers misused. We see their misuse in exploitative trade relationships, destructive mining, devastation of the habitat of nonhuman creatures. But that enormous human power also confirms those who give the second answer: they see in it, in the very technology which can be so destructive, a potential to care for, to *steward*, the earth.

We need to recognize too that often when, with the best of intentions, we have tried to build the New Jerusalem, we have ended up by constructing another Babel. Ultimately, not only is the earth the Lord's, but the future is his as well. But that very recognition that we are *not* gods ought to give us some freedom to act as the Creator's stewards.

How then should Christians live on the earth? In these pages we seek to give information which will help to answer that question. The answers are at times complex and difficult, and to find them we will explore many paths, both in the contemporary affairs of humanity and nature and in that complex past which has shaped human thought and action. But there are answers; of this we are confident. This book develops the possibility of a careful Christian stewardship of creation.

We began by speaking of seven ancient divisions of creation and of our own troubled and troubling relationship to them. In the Genesis story the culmination of creation — the seventh day — is the sabbath: the Creator's resting in the goodness of all his works. Throughout our long history of failings and degradations God keeps recalling us to the sabbath, to the vision of a creation in perfect harmony with itself and with the Creator, a creation in which men and women offer it all back in thankfulness to God. It is in the hope of such a planetary sabbath that this book is written.

SECTION I

THE STATE OF THE PLANET

CHAPTER 1

❧   ❧

The Land Entrusted to Us

The Lord has a charge to bring against you who live in the land: There is no faithfulness, no love, no acknowledgment of God in the land. . . . Because of this the land mourns and all who live in it waste away; the beasts of the field and the birds of the air and the fish of the sea are dying.

— Hosea 4:1, 3, NIV

IN DECEMBER 1977, THE VOYAGER I SPACE PROBE, OUTWARD BOUND ON a journey that would take it past Jupiter, Saturn, Uranus, and finally out of the solar system entirely, sent back a photograph. From seven million miles out, the picture shows the earth and the moon hanging like twin planets against the black backdrop of space. From that distance the difference in size is not appreciable. The remarkable difference, however, is in the colors: the moon shows bone white and dead, while the earth is a living jewel of blues, whites, and greens, and its whites, unlike those of the sun-blasted, meteor-scoured face of the moon, are the whites of shifting mist.

Voyager was launched at about the time we started work on the first edition of *Earthkeeping,* and that particular distant view of the earth and moon together became an emblem of the uniqueness of the planet which is our home.

19

Now, after nearly a decade and a half, the goals of the Voyager space probes have been met spectacularly. We have seen colored clouds larger than the earth eddy around Jovian hurricanes; we have watched sulphur volcanoes erupting on Io and have traced curving, planet-long ridges of ice on Europa. The solar system has kept on surprising us; but none of the wonders we have seen match the miracle evident in that last lonely look back at the earth.

Seeing the earth and moon together, small but whole, emphasized then what we have suspected for some time and the marvels revealed by Voyager have only confirmed: the earth's life is unique in the solar system, and perhaps in the universe. In the years of Voyager's revelations (which have been roughly the years between editions of *Earthkeeping*), we have watched this awareness of the fragility of life on the planet grow from a minority concern to a planet-wide priority. The image of the cloud-wrapped living planet has become something like a religious symbol for our increasingly secular age: "Mother Gaia," some call it in awe. For we increasingly understand this blue, white, and green sphere to be a highly ordered system in which more than five million species of living things are maintained by the sun-powered cycling of liquid, solid, and gas.

Those processes which support the earth's life take place in a thin film of land, water, and air: the biosphere. Every living creature lives within this biosphere and draws from it the materials necessary for its life. And whether those resources are used for shelter, food, or other basic needs, they are, after being used, returned to the biosphere for use by others in a complex and perpetual cycling of materials.

Even when we study the biosphere, most of this life-sustaining cycling of resources is not very evident. Some of those processes have been discovered only recently, and more are unknown or uncomprehended. Only recently, for example, have we learned of the strong likelihood that the earth's oxygen-rich atmosphere not only makes life possible but is itself made by life, specifically by the photosynthesis, over many years, of green plants. Without that continual renewal and cleansing of the air, the atmosphere would be a lethal mixture of methane and carbon dioxide.

We are learning slowly how the biosphere is made and maintained. In the pages that follow, we would like to review some of the fragile features of that biosphere. To begin such a study, it will be helpful first to consider the meanings of a few terms. The most important is *ecosystem*. An ecosystem is any set of interacting plants, animals, and nonliving things (such as earth, water, wind) which can be viewed as a functioning unit. Thus a

lake, a marsh, a forest, or a stream can be viewed as an ecosystem. So also can the entire biosphere — that envelope of all living things and their sustaining environment.

In any given ecosystem, the interacting set of plant and animal species is called a *biotic community*, or simply a *community*. The forests of northeastern North America contain the beech-maple community, an intricate system of plants and animals such as beech trees, sugar maples, box turtles, and jacks-in-the-pulpit. All are living parts of that forest ecosystem.

One way to explore the design of ecosystems is to look in detail at several of them. Such in-depth consideration is quite possible: major studies have been made on such large ecosystems as the lakes, grasslands, and eastern deciduous forests of North America. The result of such studies is a detailed understanding of the way the sun's energy flows through an ecosystem. In general, the energy is caught and stored by the photosynthesizing plants, which are eaten by herbivores, which are eaten in turn by carnivores, which may be eaten by yet larger carnivores. And even those top carnivores — eagle, grizzly, or human — are broken back down into soil by microscopic organisms which specialize in decomposition. Such ecosystem studies also show how nonliving substances — water, oxygen, carbon dioxide, carbon, phosphorus, iron — are caught up and cycled by the network of life.

But from such a study one learns not only the contents of the ecosystem; one also learns about what is even more important: the relationships. Those relationships, among the living things and between them and the nonliving environment, are highly complex. Relationships and interactions are essential to the perpetuation of the health and beauty of ecosystems. When disturbed by drastic environmental change — fire, floods, or destructive storms — most healthy ecosystems are resilient enough to restore themselves. Their complex design tends to be self-sustaining.

In this ability to sustain itself over a long period of time, an ecosystem has some of the characteristics of an individual organism. But however large the ecosystems are, they, like organisms, are nevertheless *finite*. When we see from outer space the thin blue haze at the margins of the earth, we realize how finite the total of those ecosystems are in comparison to the extent of the universe, the solar system, or even earth itself. From both that distant vision provided by space flight and our own study of ecosystems, we know that living things live and move within definite limits. In no way can they use more energy, more food, and more nutrients than are available. They must "live within their means." And, of course, they do.

But the very fact that creatures live within those limits says much about the design of the biosphere. For living things rarely exploit their resources to the limits, collapsing after futile attempts to live beyond them. If this were the case, we would expect to see weak and hungry animals. But normally we do not — starving animals are rare in nature, except perhaps during an especially severe winter. Most of us have probably never seen a starving robin, rabbit, or squirrel. The design of animal social systems is such that resources usually are *not* exploited to the limit. They have the potential to reproduce themselves so abundantly that within a few years, or a few decades, they could cover the earth. But, in fact, they do not. Their high potential for reproduction is normally not realized. Rather than pressing the limits of needed resources by increasing their number, populations are usually kept well below those limits. The cardinal singing in the backyard usually has more food than it needs. So it is with other organisms. Consequently, organisms in nature are normally healthy and vigorous.

This regulation is accomplished by many different means. The availability of food may affect the number of eggs laid; the sight or sound of an increasingly dense population may diminish the number of breeding animals; the disturbance of a large population may affect fertility; predation may keep population down; and so forth. But, for the purpose of our study of human use of the earth, it is mainly important to understand not the mechanism itself, but the *fact* that population size among animals is successfully controlled. Other creatures tend to stay within the limits set by their resources. And with very few exceptions, starvation is normally *not* one of those means. We do not see a starving and emaciated natural world. We see something much more like the bounty described by the Psalmist:

> He makes springs pour water into the ravines;
>   it flows between the mountains.
> They give water to all the beasts of the field;
>   the wild donkeys quench their thirst.
> The birds of the air nest by the waters;
>   they sing among the branches . . .
>   the earth is satisfied by the fruit of his work.
>   (Ps. 104:10-13, NIV)

As we understand more of the balanced intricacy of the biosphere, fewer and fewer people are willing to consider it all a meaningless accident; in the past decade it has become increasingly common for people to speak of the earth in terms of some mysterious purpose, whether it is understood half-mythologically as "Gaia" or half-scientifically as "Evolution" with a direction and a goal. Once again, in stumbling ways, creation is turning us toward the Creator. For this balance in the ecosystem is, to the Christian, an indication of a Creator who does all things well. The life-sustaining beauty of the created earth declares the glory of God, as God declares its goodness. Thus the more we understand of the intricacy of a healthy ecosystem, the more we learn of the Creator. Nevertheless, that intricacy reminds us of our creatureliness, for, despite the fact that starvation does not generally occur within ecosystems, the balance is maintained by death. And death — of a plant, an animal, or another person — reminds us that we too are creatures. We are a part of that biosphere.

HUMANITY'S DUAL NATURE

Men and women are also creatures. It is true that we have a personal relationship with God, we are "made in his image" (though what that means continues to be debated and misunderstood), and thus we stand apart in some ways from the rest of creation. But it is also clear that God has created us as he has all other creatures. We, too, are organisms, living within a rich but limited world. We share with all creatures fundamental biological needs: the need for energy and minerals, for food, air, and water. We can now get so far away from the earth that we can see earth and moon as two small spheres against blackness; nevertheless, we are bound to earth, still enmeshed in its cycles of life. The life of the earth is *our* life, and we depend upon it. Thus the Christian respect for creation has a twofold source: believers delight in it as God's work and respect it as they respect their own bodies — for in a sense the biosphere is our extended body.

This dual nature of human respect for creation suggests that there are two ways in which we can study human use of it. First of all, a human is another organism in the ecosystem: a large, omnivorous mammal. Thus we can study the human organism as a part of the biosphere. But men and women, made in the image of God, can also — in their imagination, in their reason, and above all, in their relationship of responsibility to the Creator — be more than simply another part of the biosphere. We can, therefore, study the modifications we make in the biosphere, modifications of a different sort than those made by other creatures who use creation.

Humans as Parts of Ecosystems

In the distant past, all humans were part of natural ecosystems (this is still true today for a few remote human communities). Such early humans harvested animals from the naturally occurring food chains, and, while sometimes planting a tree here or there to provide convenient food and liquid along a trail, made little effort to cultivate the plants they used as food. We have called them "hunters and gatherers." They harvested and ate only the food provided by the natural functioning of the ecosystem. Uneaten food and body wastes were returned to the soil not far from their origin. Under these circumstances, humans meshed well with their ecosystems, fitting into natural flows of energy and materials. They affected those cycles no more than would any large mammal. They were mainly non-manipulative parts of the ecosystem, taking their places within it without altering its major processes or parts.

Humans as Modifiers of Ecosystems

It seems to have been possible at one time for humans to function harmoniously in an ecosystem without deliberate manipulation. But that is no longer an alternative for most of us. For thousands of years, most people have been living in tension with their supporting ecosystems. From their beginning, humans have been able to manipulate the natural world to a degree that no other animals have achieved. It is likely, for example, that the extinction of many large mammals at the end of the last ice age is the result of human hunters.

Often such changes have been to the benefit of human populations, resulting in improved conditions and better living — for humans. Unfortunately, human modification of natural ecosystems has seldom, if ever, improved the condition of the ecosystem itself. Sometimes, human disruption of ecosystems has resulted in the lowering of the quality of life even for humans. All too often throughout history, well-functioning ecosystems have been converted into deserts, dust bowls, and cesspools. Clearly, though people may once have been simply a part of the biosphere, and though they still depend upon it, they are capable of altering it drastically. There is something different about our species. The anthropologist Loren Eiseley sums up the grim side of that difference:

> It is with the coming of man that a vast hole seems to open in nature,
> a vast black whirlpool spinning faster and faster, consuming flesh,
> stones, soil, minerals, sucking down the lightning, wrenching power
> from the atom, until the ancient sounds of nature are drowned in the

cacophony of something which is no longer nature, something instead which is loose and knocking at the world's heart, something demonic and no longer planned — escaped, it may be — spewed out of nature, contending in a final giant's game against its master.[1]

Though the Christian is not likely to agree completely with the picture of universal chaos which Eiseley's words present, it is nevertheless important to understand the nature of those increasing disruptions of the ecosystem. And one of the greatest comes from our manipulation of ecosystems in order to grow food efficiently.

Agro-ecosystems

Humankind has largely replaced prairie and forest ecosystems with systems of its own design: the "agro-systems" of our farmlands, and the urban complexes of our towns and cities. This replacement of naturally balanced systems by systems under human management has, in some cases, been successful.[2] Soils have been maintained, and harvests have been sustained over centuries. Much of Europe and Japan has traditionally been farmed this way. Most of the plants and animals are under human care and control, but the resulting system is fertile and stable, without the need for large amounts of commercial fertilizers or fossil fuels.

But more often, our attempts at replacing natural ecosystems with

---

1. Loren Eiseley, *The Firmament of Time* (New York: Atheneum Publishers, 1971), pp. 123-24.

2. At least from a human point of view. But usually the cost of such balanced agro-ecosystems is a drastic reduction in the diversity of living things. Thus advocates of wilderness argue that even a completely stable human population in a balanced and productive agro-ecosystem would be a great loss. Thus Roderick Nash, in the concluding section of his third edition of *Wilderness and the American Mind*, laments the future which many anticipate as a utopia. It is what he calls the "garden scenario," which ends wilderness, but beneficently rather than destructively: "In a garden earth the fertility of the soil is not only maintained, but enhanced. Fruit trees support songbirds. Carefully managed streams run pure and clear. The air is unpolluted. Forests provide an endless supply of wood. Large cities are rare as people decentralize into the hinterland. Many live on self-sufficient family farms. The animals permitted to exist are safe and useful. A softer variety of technology enables man to live gracefully and gratefully as part of the natural community." But, continues Nash, "wilderness is just as dead in the garden as it is in the concrete wasteland," for "there are simply too many people on the planet to decentralize into garden environments and still have significant amounts of wilderness" (Roderick Nash, *Wilderness and the American Mind*, 3rd ed. [New Haven: Yale University Press, 1982], pp. 380-81).

synthetic ones end in failure. This is depressingly true of the current highly mechanized agriculture in North America. Increasingly, the principles which sustain the productivity of a natural ecosystem are largely ignored. They are replaced instead by an agriculture which draws largely on a diminishing supply of fossil fuel in order to produce crops more cheaply. As a result, nutrients once returned to the fields are now lost to creeks and rivers. As contour farming is abandoned, soils are exposed to wind and rain — a problem furthered when protective fencerows and windbreaks are removed to allow for more efficient mechanized farming. The traditional farm, which produced a variety of crops and maintained a variety of animals, is now replaced by farms which grow only one crop in great amounts.

In the United States, we have already learned the painful consequences of carelessly replacing natural ecosystems with synthetic ones. But those lessons learned in the dust bowl days of the 1930s are being set aside once more in an attempt to produce ever more food with ever less labor. Increasing costs of labor and a steadily growing human population seem to justify such short-term measures. But the long-term costs are the declining fertility and stability of the soil.

This gradual decline in the productivity of agricultural land is worldwide. On marginal land good only for grazing — which makes up eight billion acres of the earth's thirty-two billion acres of land — overgrazing is rapidly transforming pasture into desert. And our record with the four to five billion acres of land most suitable for agriculture has not been much better. About 3.6 billion acres of such land are already under cultivation. The rest could be cultivated only at very high cost, largely because of the need for drainage and irrigation (see Figure 1.1).

In our replacement of natural with agricultural systems we have shown little concern for stability, longevity, and sustainability. The land has been cleared of its natural vegetation and planted with crops which leave soils exposed to wind and rain. In order to make up for the resulting loss of nutrients, we have had to use fertilizers on an increasingly large scale. The result, almost without exception, is that we have replaced ecosystems which had a yearly gain in topsoil with systems which have a yearly loss in topsoil. The complex natural system made up of many plants and animals has been replaced by simple systems with only one or two components. Self-regulating features have thus been destroyed; vital nutrients no longer recycle within the system but escape to rivers, lakes, oceans, and the atmosphere.

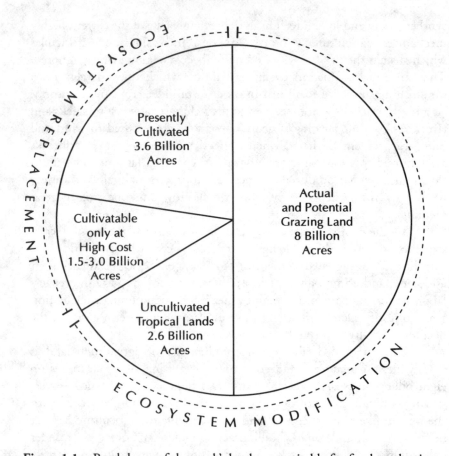

Figure 1.1. Breakdown of the earth's land areas suitable for food production. An area of 3.6 billion acres is presently cultivated, up only 0.1 billion acres from ten years ago. All indications are that we are approaching the limits of replacing natural ecosystems with synthetic ones. Based upon data from G. Tyler Miller, Jr., *Living in the Environment* (Belmont, CA: Wadsworth, 1975), and the National Academy of Sciences, *Resources and Man* (San Francisco: W. H. Freeman, 1969).

This is not an overstatement of the situation. The United States, which as a result of the dust bowl years has been more sensitive to erosion than many other nations, still loses an average of twelve tons of topsoil per acre each year, while the annual rate of soil formation, under normal conditions, is only one and a half tons per acre. Consequently, some fifty million tons of plant nutrients — nitrogen, phosphorus, potassium — are

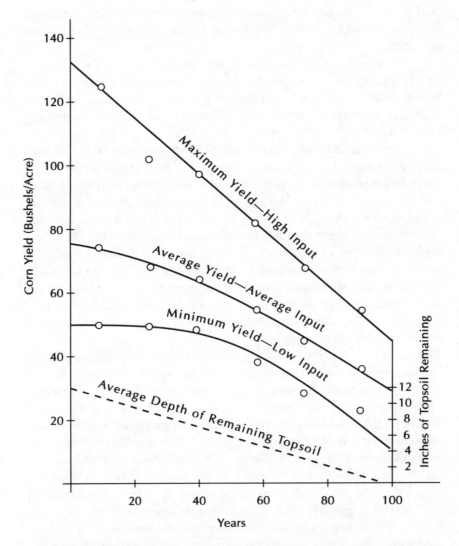

Figure 1.2. Decline of corn yields and topsoil under three different levels of management: high fertilizer and other technology, low fertilizer and other technology, and an intermediate case. Graph constructed on the basis of (1) data for corn yields as a function of topsoil depth and technology input and (2) data on acreage loss of U.S. topsoil. Based upon data compiled by David Pimental et al., "Land Degradation: Effects on Food and Energy Resources," *Science* 194 (1976): 149-55.

lost each year from U.S. cropland. And that loss of nutrients from the land produces too much fertility in the water: lakes become increasingly eutrophic through excessive fertilization and become choked with plant growth.

In any one year, the loss of topsoil does not result in a very significant crop loss. Thus people with short-term interests in land (some bankers, land speculators, and tenant farmers, for instance) may not notice the continuous erosion of the cultivated soil, and may do nothing to stop it.

This loss in a corn field amounts to about a half bushel of corn per acre — worth less than one percent of the total production cost and insignificant relative to the total. In time, however, those continuing losses add up. Figure 1.2, which is based on data from field studies, shows that a field of corn with a typical twenty ton per acre soil loss decreases steadily in yield, so that after a century the yield is only half. Whether the farmer applies large or small amounts of fertilizer, yield still decreases. For those who have only a short-term interest in the land, these decreases are unimportant. Persons who expect to pass the farm on to their children, on the other hand, are likely to take better care of the soil — but by doing so, they will not be able to compete with those who farm the land for maximum short-term yield.

There is, however, a way of farming which sustains the soil's productivity — thus duplicating the effect of the natural ecosystem. If corn is grown only twice during a five-year period, as part of a corn-corn-oats-pasture-pasture sequence, the result is a slight *increase* in topsoil (Figure 1.3). The middle curve in the diagram, which describes continuous corn-cropping and declining yields, appears to be most feasible, but in the long run it represents very poor management of resources. Even poorer is the intensive cultivation represented by the bottom curve. Yet for those who hold land near a city, expecting to sell it soon for industrial or residential development, such destructive agriculture is all too common. Reinforcing the trend is the fact that the poorer the land becomes for food production, the more reasonable it seems to convert it to urban uses.

Recently *sustainable agriculture* has emerged as a way in which to address the problem of deteriorating land. The goal of this approach is no net loss of soil and soil fertility. As part of this new effort to live more in accord with the regenerative processes of the soil and vegetation, *rotational* grazing is getting increased attention and is being reintroduced. Its approach is to move grazing animals from paddock to paddock, allowing

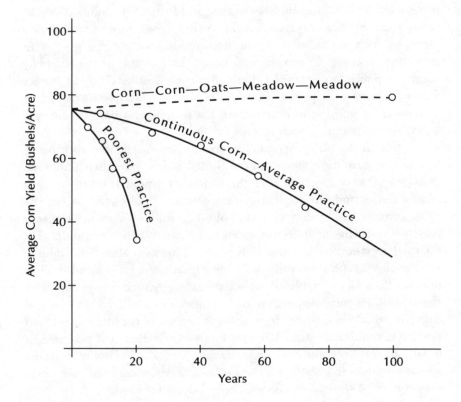

Figure 1.3. Corn yield under three management programs. Based upon data compiled by Pimental et al., "Land Degradation," pp. 149-55.

land and grasses time to regenerate between grazings. Such an approach has become standard practice in New Zealand, for example, with spectacular results both in productivity and in land health. (Perhaps the awareness of limits which is so much a part of an island society like New Zealand's contributes to such wise practices: if so, we need to recognize how much the whole earth is a limited island of life.)

An even more radical approach to maintaining the health of agricultural land is evident in various forms of *minimum-tillage* agriculture, which are exploring ways to avoid the periodic break-up of the stabilizing (and moisture-retaining) root structure which has been an essential feature of traditional agriculture. The most thoroughgoing of such approaches is represented by Wes Jackson, head of the Land Institute in Salinas, Kansas. Jackson and his students have sought to study and restore native prairie plants in such a way as to enhance their food value. The goal is an agriculture that meets human food needs through use of the naturally occurring prairie ecosystem.[3] (Many rain-forest "gardens" in the tropics follow the same principles, and one of the ways in which we are degrading creation is by pushing into extinction the people who have the ancient knowledge to maintain such forest gardens.)

But on the whole, agriculture remains non-sustainable, continuing a trend that is, in most regions of the United States, more than a hundred years old. The average depth of the American topsoil is seven or eight inches, down from an original average of more than twelve inches. By 1935, erosion had already ruined about 100 million acres of cropland, some of which has now been restored to forests. When we consider that the total present cropland area in the United States is about 400 million acres, such vast and continuing losses give great cause for worry. It is clear that we have largely replaced self-perpetuating natural ecosystems with short-term, destructive human ones. Our agriculture still operates, by and large, on principles different from those of the rest of the biosphere. Good stewardship, although practiced, is still rare. And where it is practiced, it usually requires economic sacrifice, because the farm economy generally operates within too short a time horizon to encourage the long-term preservation of those very soils we depend upon for food.

The Threat of Urban Expansion

Thus far we have spoken of the *quality* of the land entrusted to us. And, whether we speak of the disruption of natural ecosystems or of the declining productivity of agricultural land, it is clear that human activity has affected that quality adversely. But the *quantity* of productive land is also threatened, particularly by the expansion of cities — and their accompanying suburbs, roads, factories, power stations, and garbage dumps — onto agricultural land. It will be helpful to review briefly the pressures cities place upon productive land. We will do so by concentrating on the

---

3. The best introduction to Jackson's vision is in Evan Eisenberg, "Back to Eden," *Atlanta Monthly*, Nov. 1989, pp. 57-89. See also *Meeting the Expectations of the Land: Essays in Sustainable Agriculture and Stewardship*, ed. Wes Jackson, Wendell Berry, and Bruce Coleman (San Francisco: North Point Press, 1984).

situation in America — though similar pressures are present all over the world.

The towns and villages of the American Midwest — the world's most productive agricultural area — were built to serve agriculture. The farmers of the great plains and the newly cleared forest lands of the Midwest needed places at which they could sell their harvests, buy provisions, seeds, and implements, and attend church. Thus as farms spread across the Midwest, villages sprang up, spaced about a day's wagon journey apart and usually arranged along the major routes from the farmland to the marketplaces of large cities. Where agriculture is limited, by poor soil or low rainfall (as is the case further west), towns and villages are sparse.

But the towns that once served agriculture exclusively have since diversified. With the coming of labor-saving farm machinery, fewer people were needed to work the farms. Instead, new industries and new jobs were created in town. As these commercial and industrial enterprises grew, new residential areas grew to serve their employees. Towns that were once placed on agricultural land in order to serve the farmers have turned away from agriculture, spreading out over the adjacent fertile soil which once nourished a farm town. So it is that often the finest agricultural land in America is the first to be consumed by the growth of the cities. Though this pattern is most evident in the Midwest, it is characteristic of most American cities. Around Seattle, for example, the only Class I soil in the county is long since buried under a shopping center. Much of the richest agricultural area of southern California now survives only in names like "Orange County."

The pattern of consuming cropland near cities was intensified by the invention of the automobile: the resulting cheap transportation has put most of the best U.S. cropland within commuting range of large cities. And since most Americans want to live in a suburban or rural setting, the spreading suburbs are rapidly devouring good farmland.

Other factors encourage this rapid conversion of farms to cities. Although the rate of U.S. population growth has declined, the amount of land used per family for residential purposes is steadily increasing. Young cities reveal this fact by their low population densities; cities which grew large before the automobile have a much higher density. And within the commuting zone of any large city the trend is clearly evident: lot sizes grow progressively larger as one moves from the city to the suburbs. In most cases, that increased space is bought at the price of decreased farmland.

At least one other factor affects this rapid conversion of agricultural land to urban purposes: the number of households. Though the average family size in the United States is indeed declining, the demand for housing does not decline proportionately. Each family, whether it has eight members or two, needs a place to live. The increasing number of single-parent families — and single people who choose not to marry, but want a house of their own — only exacerbates this tendency. Thus the demand for housing remains very high. And since most people prefer to live on the fringes of the cities, that growing fringe is devouring farmland. The result of this growing demand for residential land is the estimated yearly displacement of between one million and three million acres of the best cropland from a base of about 400 million acres.

In some communities (for example, the town of Dunn in Dane County, Wisconsin) a halt to the consumption of agricultural land has been implemented through the use of a land stewardship plan and agricultural conservancy zoning. In others (as in some of the agricultural lands of western Washington, threatened by housing pressure from nearby urban centers) development rights to agricultural land have been bought with county, state, or federal funds in order to insure the perpetuation of agriculture. But in most communities there is a continuous yielding to pressures to use more and more land for low-density urban growth.

Obviously, such pressure on farmland ultimately threatens our base for food production. But it is indirectly responsible for another problem. We are compensating for disappearing farmland by putting new lands into production. This new farmland comes from draining marshes, irrigating the dry soil of the West, clearing still more forests, and putting marginal lands into production. In most cases the expansion of agriculture into these new areas means less room for dwindling wildlife. And in all cases it means greater expenditure in dollars and energy for transporting, irrigating, and fertilizing, often resulting in higher food prices.

How long can such a trend continue? In the United States lands remain that could be converted for agricultural use, but such conversion would be at the expense of pastureland, forests, and wetlands. The value of forests and wetlands in maintaining the quality of soil, water, and wildlife is so great that the acceptability of such losses must be seriously questioned. So too must the advisability of using marginal lands which were, in many cases, removed from production in the first place because of erosion problems.

Our record of learning from the structure of divinely created ecosystems is not a good one. Natural ecosystems are characterized by diversity; but we replace them with systems containing only a single species. Natural ecosystems match gains with losses; our agro-ecosystems lose more than they gain and make little use of recycled materials. Natural ecosystems continue over centuries; our replacement ecosystems are short-lived.

The solution to these problems is not to give up agriculture. It is rather to develop enough humility to learn from the functioning of the created world. And we must have the economic foresight and courage to apply responsibly what we learn.

CHAPTER 2

❧　　❧

The Creatures under Our Care

Yet may you teach a man a necessary thing to know,
Which has to do of the strict conformity that creaturehood entails.
And constitutes the prime commitment all things share.
For God has given you the imponderable grace to be His verification,
Outside the mulled incertitude of our forensic choices;
That you, our lessers in the rich hegemony of Being,
May serve as testament to what a creature is,
And what creation owes.

— William Everson, "Canticle to the Waterbirds"

IN THE FOREGOING CHAPTER WE CONSIDERED MAINLY THE LAND — OR, more precisely, the biosphere. There our concern was with the overall health of ecosystems, from the stable complexity of a forest to the precarious simplicity of a wheat field. In either case, the emphasis thus far has been on the whole pattern, not on individual parts of it. In these next two chapters, however, we will narrow our consideration to the particular creatures supported by that biosphere and to the effects of human activity on those creatures. There are two chapters in this discussion of the earth's creatures because there are inevitably from the human viewpoint two sorts of creatures: humans on the one hand, and plants and animals on the other.

By dividing creation in this way we do not at all wish to imply that we humans are not creatures — quite the contrary. But we *are* a very peculiar sort of creature: as the foregoing survey of our uses of the land suggests, we humans have not hesitated to shove other creatures aside when we feed at the planet's wealth; indeed, we have regarded all other creatures strictly *as* our wealth. So at this point we are considering *nonhuman creatures*. (Later in the book we consider the reasons for — and the danger of — thus viewing humans as unique.) In this chapter, then, we will consider the health of nonhuman creatures on an increasingly human-dominated planet. And in the following chapter we will consider the physical welfare of humanity itself on the planet which — for better or for worse — we have dominated.

We began the previous chapter by recalling the now-familiar sight of the earth from space. Those photos are a good way to reflect on the marvel of the planet's life. But, in one sense, that distant blue-green vision of vitality is misleading. Despite the obvious symbolic power and near-religious use of the photographs of the earth from space, we can perhaps dwell on them too much. Though it is wise to keep in mind that we live on a planet, in a biosphere, the photographs of the whole do a certain violence to our experience of the parts — which is all the experience we ever have. Consider the words of Yaakov Jerome Garv:

> there is a certain psychological flattening and impoverishment of understanding that occurs when a narrative and mythic Earth imagery is replaced by this static and literal photographic image. That is, the whole Earth image relies on sight alone to inform us about our planet. The smell of redwoods, the warmth of summer breezes, the sound of crickets at night (and even the unthinkable cold and silence of space — the location from which this image derives) are, quite literally, not part of the picture.[1]

The view from space is all too likely to persuade us that all is well on the home planet, for the sizable human disruptions of the ecosystem are invisible from a distance. Had there been observers on the moon for the thousands of years of human history, they might not have known we were here. To such observers, the colors of the planet would still be blue, green,

---

1. Yaakov Jerome Garv, "Musings on Contemporary Earth Imagery," in *Reweaving the World: The Emergence of Ecofeminism,* ed. Irene Diamond and Gloria Feman Orenstein (San Francisco: Sierra Club Books, 1990), p. 267.

and shifting white; the seasons would still tint the continents; the great
white spirals of storms would still move slowly across the surface; and the
edges of the crescent earth would be smudged, now as ten thousand years
ago, with the blur of atmosphere. Despite many millennia of agriculture
and two centuries of industry, the main features of our biosphere are
unchanged. Despite erosion, smog, and creeping cities, the planet is still
green and living — at least from a distance. Even from a low earth orbit
— say, a hundred miles up — the difference between natural and agricultural systems is hard to notice.

In the previous chapter we cataloged some of the consequences of
our alterations to the biosphere, more visible to us than to an observer on
the moon: the substitution of wheat fields for prairies, for example, or
lawns and shrubs for beech-maple forests. But apart from some unpleasant
economic consequences (like higher prices for food), the differences between a natural ecosystem and a farm, or between a soil-sustaining farm
and a soil-destroying one, are (at least for a little while) increasingly
inconsequential to those humans for whom the biosphere is mainly irrelevant background. So long as we have air, water, and food, the changes
in the biosphere over the last ten thousand years — and especially over
the last century — are hardly more visible to us than they would be to an
observer on the moon. The fine points of the biosphere are too often not
our concern.

In the same way, the average dwellers in London or Paris see that
all is well on the skyline of their city. It is only the eccentric or the specialist
who notices that the saints and gargoyles of the cathedrals have, in the
past few decades, dissolved like leprous flesh in the automotive air. It is
just as difficult, at first, to notice the changes in the great cathedral of
creation. The outline is the same; the ecosystems still function. But in the
niches and cornices of the biosphere, the fine work blurs and crumbles.
Whole species dwindle and vanish. And though the outline of the system
may be roughly the same, creation, like a cathedral in the city, becomes
more and more like a vast hollow shell, degraded and diminished in its
intricacy.

Indeed, cathedrals, like planets, need to be seen close up *and* from
far off. In his illuminating book on "love of Place" entitled *Topophilia,* Yi
Fu Tuan has this to say about cathedrals:

> Outside the cathedral, the modern tourist may be able to get a good
> picture of the total structure from a distance. But in mediaeval times

this was seldom possible. . . . Moreover, to see the cathedral from a distance would diminish its impact of bulk and verticality. The details of its facade would no longer be visible. The mediaeval cathedral was meant to be experienced; it was a dense text to be read with devout attention and not an architectural form to be merely seen. In fact, some figures and decorations could not be seen at all. They were made for the eyes of God.[2]

Creation is likewise a "dense text." The profound distant view of the cathedral of creation (whether provided by science or satellite) should never keep us from "seeing" it as a child sees: with nose, tongue, ears, and fingertips.

It is our purpose in this chapter, then, to move beyond the main features of the biosphere and to look at some details, particularly at some instances of the threatened and dwindling diversity of those million species of living things that fill the niches of this temple, the earth.

What the Psalmist exclaimed about himself is true of all creatures: they are "fearfully and wonderfully made" (Ps. 139:14, KJV). Indeed (as we will see in a later chapter), God answers Job's complaints about his management by pointing out the intricacy and strangeness of the world he made. He says of the hippopotamus (or "behemoth"):

> Behold, Behemoth,
>   which I made as I made you;
>   he eats grass like an ox.
> Behold, his strength in his loins,
>   and his power in the muscles of his belly.
> He makes his tail stiff like a cedar;
>   the sinews of his thighs are knit together.
> His bones are tubes of bronze,
>   his limbs like bars of iron.
> He is the first of the works of God;
>   let him who made him bring near his sword!
>   (Job 40:15-19)

And speaking of this creature's ecological setting God goes on to exclaim:

---

2. Yi Fu Tuan, *Topophilia* (Englewood Cliffs, NJ: Prentice-Hall, 1974), cited in Garv, "Musings on Contemporary Earth Imagery," p. 266.

The hills bring him their produce,
  and all the wild animals play nearby.
Under the lotus plants he lies,
  hidden among the reeds in the marsh.
The lotuses conceal him in their shadow;
  the poplars by the stream surround him.

                    (Job 40:20-22, NIV)

Whether or not we have marveled thus at a hippopotamus, the principle is clear: cedars, whales, dragonflies — and hippopotami — are of value for themselves and for what they declare of the Creator. Their use to humans is not particularly important, and it oftentimes is difficult to describe their importance to the creation as a whole. They are exultantly unique and individual but also wondrously integrated with their habitats. They are works of God, which only their Maker is allowed to destroy. But we have used our own might and power to destroy the creatures, and when we destroy the last individuals of a species, we cannot re-create them. The splendor of creation as a whole is diminished; we empoverish creation's ability to bring God praise.

To be sure, extinction is a natural process; that is, it takes place apart from human influence, with perhaps one species becoming extinct per century. For creation is a continuing process, and it involves change not only in the physical environment, but in the creatures who live in that environment. And if creation is a dynamic and changing work of divine art — like a song — Christians should not understand their task to be stopping the music at one particular point. Yet neither should we accelerate the song to cacophony by eliminating habitat for cranes, hunting pigeons to extinction, or rendering all remaining sea mammals into oil. All of these things we have done, or are in the process of doing. For the pressing demands of the human population for food, minerals, energy, and living space are inexorably reducing the chances for life of most other creatures on the planet.

There is a strong biblical reason for developing a way of life which treats the rest of creation with great care: obedience to our Creator, in the pattern of service set for us by the "New Adam," Jesus. That should be enough for any Christian. But quite apart from duty and love, there are more practical, utilitarian reasons for good earthkeeping.

One such reason, quite apart from those which Christians ought to follow because of a personal relationship with the Creator, is that the

*"I think it's a very worthy cause, but I've already
responded to a phone solicitation."*

From *The New Yorker*, October 30, 1989. Drawing by Lorenz;
© 1989 The New Yorker Magazine, Inc. Used by permission.

diversity of creation may be humanly useful in yet undisclosed ways. We
ought to cherish the full diversity of created things, not only for their own
sake, but because those things make up an irreplaceable genetic reservoir
from which we may draw new sources of food and other materials in the
years to come.

The utilitarian wisdom of such a strategy is undeniable. Consider
an example cited in the 1987 U.N. report of the World Commission on
Environment and Development, *Our Common Future:*

The US maize [corn] crop suffered a severe setback in 1970, when a leaf fungus blighted croplands, causing losses to farmers worth more than $2 billion. Then fungus-resistant genetic material was found in genetic stocks that had originated in Mexico. More recently, a primitive species of maize was discovered in a montane forest of south-central Mexico. This wild plant is the most primitive known relative of modern maize and was surviving in only three tiny patches covering a mere four hectares in an area threatened with destruction by farmers and loggers. The wild species is a perennial; all other forms of maize are annuals. Its cross-breeding with commercial varieties of maize opens up the prospect that farmers [and the land itself!] could be spared the annual expense of ploughing and sowing, since the plant would grow again yearly of its own accord. The genetic benefits of this wild plant, discovered when not more than a few thousand last stalks remained, could total several thousand million dollars a year.[3]

The editors of *Our Common Future* go on to point out that "Wild species likewise contribute to medicine. Half of all prescriptions dispensed have their origins in wild organisms."[4] As these examples suggest, if we should succeed in eliminating from the earth all life except what we have an immediate use for, the tragedy would not be only for that other life and a few "nature lovers" or "earthkeepers." For in so doing we would eliminate most of that source of living potential which enables us to breed new plants and animals.

One source of hope (suggested by the Mexican maize experience) in an otherwise discouraging long-range outlook for world food production is the improvement and diversification of food crops for greater productivity, more resistance to disease and drought, higher food value, and so forth. For example, the hunger organization ECHO, in Fort Myers, Florida, searches out and produces seed for little-used species and varieties to improve the ability of the poor in the world to live sustainably. Other organizations search out undiscovered, undomesticated species to increase the genetic resources from which human food crops can be improved.

A second utilitarian reason for maintaining plant and animal diversity is that such a variety allows us to gain knowledge of our own bodily functions — particularly through study of creatures in which those func-

---

3. *Our Common Future: The World Commission on Environment and Development* (Oxford: Oxford University Press, 1987), p. 155.
4. Ibid.

tions are exaggerated through response to a particular environment. For example, the function of the kidney in desert kangaroo rats, adapted as they are to the scarcity of water in desert environments, has contributed much to our knowledge of the functioning of the normal human kidney. In the same way, the giant nerve cells of seagoing squids provide an excellent tool for understanding the function of human nerves.

There are many other human-centered reasons for preserving various forms of life: possible new drugs such as quinine and antibiotics; biological pest control; a fuller understanding of how ecosystems function

"For your own good I'm telling you that I'm loaded with pesticides."

From *Audubon.* Used by permission of Jan van Wessum.

in order to maintain the livability of increasingly manipulated systems; and so on. And, of course, there is wide interest in preserving species on aesthetic grounds.

Despite the merit of all these reasons for preserving animal and plant life, for the Christian the fundamental reason is still unselfish: humans are called to be stewards, or guardians, over creation. And today we, like Noah, are presented with a threat to the earth's life and are given the task of preserving it.

On the whole, we have done poorly at that task, and there is little to indicate that the Christian vision has improved the generally destructive human attitude toward the rest of creation. Humankind has exploited much life to extinction, or near it. The catalog of examples is not a pleasant perspective on human history. In North America, the list of endangered animals is long and depressing. There are very few grizzly bears and timber wolves left in the United States. (They are still relatively abundant in Canada.) Despite their important role as "top carnivores" in the food chain, they have been regarded as "varmints" through most of our history — "critters," not creatures.

The Atlantic salmon, which once thronged up pure Eastern rivers, is rarely seen. The great ivory-billed woodpecker — once hunted for food and feathers — is extinct or on the verge of extinction. Elsewhere, the once-expansive forests we know as the cedars of Lebanon have been reduced to twelve small and scattered groves. And even these few remaining stands would have perished if it had not been for the stewardly care given the species by a few monks who preserved the trees near their chapels. An even grimmer story is that of the whale. There are only a few hundred blue whales — the largest of all animals — left in the oceans. And in our eagerness to catch large quantities of fish from the sea we are killing dolphins and sea turtles — air-breathing creatures that are entrapped in fish nets and drown.

The extinction or near extinction of whales, wolves, great auks, bison, and passenger pigeons is something we should all abhor. It was for the most part blatant and deliberate, and the animals were attacked directly. But such conscious exploitation is only a small part of the problem. Much more serious than such direct actions is the destruction of the animals' habitat. And for such destruction we are all responsible: in our increasing use of land for homes, in our increasingly "efficient" agriculture, in our mining and processing of mineral resources, we are diminishing the living space of nonhuman creatures.

In building homes, we alter the landscape. Some of the land is covered with buildings; rainwater runoff increases, due to large areas of impervious materials on rooftops and roadways. Homeowners in wooded areas remove trees to allow sunlight to reach lawns; plants and animals are thus left with no habitat, and die. Drainage patterns are altered to remove unpleasant wetness; creeks are replaced with storm sewers, and moisture-dependent species are eliminated. Gradual marsh borders are replaced with sharp, neat banks, destroying the moisture gradient on which a complex of plants and animals depend — each with its slightly different water-level requirements. Thus herons no longer have a place to fish. And mosquitoes multiply in the absence of dragonflies, which depend on marsh-edge vegetation for metamorphosis from aquatic nymphs into flying, mosquito-eating adults.

Threats to natural habitats occur on every continent, especially in those areas of heavy rain forests where an incredible diversity of nature is manifested. The variety of woody plant species growing on the slopes of a single volcano in the Philippines is greater than that of the entire United States. The Amazon Basin, with Southeast Asia close behind, contains millions of plant and animal species. Such areas are biologically the richest regions on earth. Yet an area of tropical rain forest equal in size to the state of Michigan is destroyed each year and another area of about the same size is seriously degraded.[5] That rate has accelerated by at least 50 percent in the past decade: in that period an area of tropical forest roughly equal in size to the state of Alaska has been lost. But such abstractions convey none of the deep tragedy of the loss of thousands of kinds of creatures — fish, mammals, insects, flowers, trees — many of them never seen, known, or named by any man or woman, which have left behind not even a memory. One regional example — from a globe-wide gallery of such barely noticed tragedies — focuses the picture somewhat. Till 1950, the relatively small island of Madagascar had over 12,000 species of plant and 190,000 species of animal. Over 60 percent of them were unique to Madagascar. But in the few decades since 1950, 93 percent of Madagascar's forest has disappeared and with that habitat at least half (over 100,000) of the original species.[6]

---

5. See Erik Eckholm, *Disappearing Species: The Social Challenge* (Washington, DC: Worldwatch Institute, 1978). This book decries the alarming losses that result from continued human expansion.

6. See *Our Common Future*, p. 149.

The destruction of rain forest habitat is not only a tropical and "Third-World" problem. A similar crisis exists in the northwest corner of North America, where once-vast coastal forests of redwood, Douglas fir, Sitka spruce, and red cedar have been reduced to a small fraction of their original extent. Though this area on our western coast is not as diverse in sheer numbers of species as rain forests in the tropics, pound for pound its sheer mass of living matter is seven times as great. Though large tracts of first, second, and third growth forest remain, the old growth — that is, the original, intact ecosystem — is almost gone. In Canada and the United States, an increasing need for wood — for lumber, paper, and fuel, and for export dollars — has placed steadily greater pressure on old growth forests, which have been labelled "decadent" or "over-mature" to justify cutting. Old policies of selective cutting have been abandoned — especially in the West — in place of "even-age management." Such practices turn forests into tree farms. The danger in such a move is not in the concept of farming — and hence, harvesting — trees, but rather, that some of the destructively single-purpose methods of modern agriculture are being applied to forest management, with the same grim consequences for the diversity and health of the ecosystem. Increasingly, tree farms are planting one species of tree, which is bred for maximum wood production in a short period of time. There is no room in such "forests" for trees which grow slowly or produce unusable wood. Underbrush is discouraged. Nothing is done to encourage nonusable wildlife, and it is tolerated only if it does no damage. (Black bears, for example, are a nuisance in the tree farms of the West because they tend to destroy seedlings. Where possible, the bears are being removed.) Obviously, the consequences of such a utilitarian silviculture leave little room for nonuseful species. Yet there are more subtle effects. Since all of a tree is viewed as a crop, dead and rotting trees or fallen, unused limbs are seen as waste. No wood should be wasted — that is, nothing should rot. But that rotting, as we saw in the previous chapter, is the first stage in a process that supports not only the health of the very soil, but also the worms and insects which are the foundation of the whole complex pyramid of an ecosystem. It is little wonder, then, that the habitat for creatures for which we have no immediate use is rapidly diminishing.

Slowly the logging industry is making the difficult transition from thinking of growing trees to thinking about maintaining forests. But the transition may come too late. Rowe Findley, in a recent *National Geographic* article on our coastal rain forest, put the crisis eloquently:

While we pursue hopeful visions, our options shrink daily, and somewhere in what remains there stands a tree of no return. It is not a
specific spruce or fir but a specific number in the sequence of cutting,
beyond which the remaining old growth will have shrunk below what
natural processes can repair. Then creatures and plants dependent on
the ancient woodland's moist multilayered canopies and rich ground
covers, on the shelter and nurture bequeathed by its fallen patriarchs,
will limp towards extinction amid the once great forest's crazy-quilt
vestiges.[7]

In providing for our needs for lumber — and export dollars (for
many of the best trees are shipped overseas) — we have substituted one-
species tree farms for forest diversity. The same is true on our farms. In
providing for our food needs, we have replaced prairies and deciduous
forests with agriculture, in the process moving many creatures near extinction by taking away their habitat. As the pressures for more efficient food
production increase, semi-natural areas on the farm become more costly
to maintain; consequently, fencerows, marshes, and woodlots are removed.
And the removal each year of vast acreages for roads and suburbs (in the
U.S. alone, it amounts to an area about 50 miles on a side) places ever
greater pressure on remaining wild areas; woods are eliminated, marshes
are drained, and arid lands are irrigated for crops.

The wealth of mineral resources — coal, peat, sand, metal ores, and
so forth — has become as crucial to human needs as food itself. Yet the
extraction of these materials also places pressures on living space for nonhuman life. In many places such materials are strip-mined. And in order
to get at the deposit, the "overburden" must be removed. "Overburden"
is a conveniently vague term, for it includes not only "worthless" rock,
but also the soil, the bacteria, the plants, and the animals living there. In
short, to remove the "overburden" is to remove a piece of the ecosystem.
In some cases, a kind of ecosystem has been established in an area after it
has been mined. But even in these rare cases, the life that was there before
was incomparably more complex and resilient than the agriculturally managed replacement.

There are many of these trade-off situations: marshes and swamps
are being seen as valuable tertiary sewage treatment plants; sand dunes,
with their vibrant cover of life, are seen as raw material for making glass;

---

7. Rowe Findley, "Will We Save our Endangered Forests?" *National Geographic*
178, 3 (Sept. 1990): 136.

*"We just ran a test on your river water, . . . it will support life,
in fact, you can walk on it."*

From *Industrial Research*, January 1971.
© 1971, *Industrial Research*. Used by permission.

and trees, from cedars of Lebanon to redwoods, are understood as lumber
in the rough. In none of these solutions to human problems is there any
room for the creature — bird, beast, tree, or flower — which has no value
as a crop.

There are, of course, some exceptions. The Endangered Species Act
in the United States prohibits destruction of the environment of an endangered species. This admirable law has enraged and amused many
people, having halted a power plant in the Northeast for threatening the
furbish lousewort and a similar project in the Southeast for threatening
the snail darter. In the Pacific Northwest, the spotted owl has recently
been named to the endangered species list, to the rage of some loggers and
businesspeople whose livelihood seems to depend on access to the old-
growth stands which are the only place the bird can live. In all these
examples, the crucial thing is not, however, the single threatened species,
but the fact that its threatened extinction is a kind of thermometer regis-
tering the health of the whole ecosystem which supports it.

Such situations present us with a real dilemma. How much right
does a species have to live? A dam may (through flood control) save
hundreds of human lives, and it may also provide jobs and power for
human well-being and happiness. What if the only price of such a project
is the loss from the planet of the spotted owl? Would it not be worth it?

What if our own life were at stake, or our children's? Would we not choose their lives over the perpetuation of a small fish? We may justly criticize the destruction of ecosystems and the dwindling or extinction of animal life. But our own standard of living — at least in Western society — has risen as the vigor of many species has declined. Does the benefit to us outweigh the cost to nonhuman creatures? These are difficult questions, and we will not attempt to answer them until we have looked at the situation from several other perspectives. But one thing is clear: the dynamics of human civilization leave little room for plants and animals for which we have no use.

The impact of our activity on natural ecosystems is often not very obvious, however. As we noted at the beginning of this chapter, an observer from the moon would see the earth as green now as it was a thousand years ago. But again, it is the *quality* of the life which has diminished. This is particularly obvious when one considers the kinds of creatures that surround the average North American dwelling place. On the farm, they are corn, wheat, rice, sheep, and cattle. In suburbs and on farms there may be dandelions, chickweed, plantains, cats, rats, cockroaches, European house sparrows, European rock doves, and European starlings. Such plants and animals — wanted or not — form part of a human "ethno-ecosystem," a pattern of life which accompanies human settlement, and which, in our case, has followed us to the New World from Europe and Asia.

Now European dandelions are as worthy a flower as an American relative — say, a common sunflower. Likewise, a starling is a bird as interesting and worthy as a red-winged blackbird.[8] The problem is not that alien species — be they weeds, trees, or songbirds — are inferior; rather, what is of concern is the displacement of native species. The more their living space is taken over by alien species, the more likely we are to see a diminishing of the carefully designed harmony of the biosphere. Sometimes, as on the disturbed floodplains of rivers (a preferred location for many American towns), we use native trees: American elm, or sycamore, or silver maple. Some native birds and animals have prospered,

---

8. The starling got its start on this continent when a wealthy American developed a hobby of introducing into the country all the birds mentioned in Shakespeare's plays. Nightingales and cuckoos, alas, did not prosper. But the starlings thrived so much that they have become a colossal nuisance, requiring large-scale efforts at extermination. Millions at a time have been killed by spraying on the birds a mixture which renders them susceptible to cold.

too, especially those which like the continuous edge between trees and lawn — robins, cardinals, and squirrels — or those which like human garbage — raccoons, for example. But in the majority of cases, native species diminish rather than prosper as human civilization brings with it the plants and animals which have made a more successful adaptation to the activities of the human steward.

But this diminishing of all life that does not fit in with human activity is tragically poor stewardship of the Creator's bounty. From the perspective of nonhuman life, human activity is beginning to look like a new deluge. What should be our attitude toward that inexorable flooding of the human population? To that difficult question we turn in the next chapter.

CHAPTER 3

❧   ❧

The Human Deluge

"Be fruitful and increase in number; fill the earth and subdue it."

— Genesis 1:28, NIV

"Woe to those who add house to house and join field to field till no space is left and you live alone in the land."

— Isaiah 5:8, NIV

T HE RELATIONSHIP BETWEEN THE SPIRITUAL HEALTH OF PEOPLE AND the health of the land they dwell in is as old as Eden. But in the past, the earth was vast enough and humans scarce enough that poor human stewardship of creation did not seem very consequential. At worst a people could always move to undisturbed land and start over. This ancient illusion of endless resources was given new life by the first three centuries of North American experience in the New World.

But the vast increase in human population in recent years has suddenly brought the limits of the earth's productivity — as well as the decline in the earth's environmental health — home to us with startling suddenness. There are now 5.2 billion people on the earth — an increase of some 2 billion beyond the population just 35 years ago, and 800 million in the past decade. But it is not only the unprecedented increase in population which threatens the continuing health of the planet. It is also that the human use of machines and fossil fuels has enormously multiplied our ability to dominate the earth. It is now common for a single person to wield the power of a hundred. Though it is true that only a relatively small percentage of the earth's population have such power available, so spectacular have the consequences of that power been that the rest of the earth's peoples both fear it and seek it. Today when we speak of "development" in the Third World, we frequently mean development that will give individuals of other nations a power over creation equivalent to our own. (In view of the increasing number and intensity of degradations of creation occurring in "developed" societies, it's clear that *development* — which means moving toward wholeness — is not the best word for the ideal of progress which we have been exporting.)

The result of the recent dramatic increase both in the number of humans and in the power available to them is (as we saw in the previous chapters) a great increase in demands for land, food, and other resources. The demands for land have resulted in human expansion into almost every habitable area — usually at the expense of the biosphere. Grazing of marginal arid land in Africa and the attempted clearing of the Brazilian jungle are two large-scale instances of this expansion. Demands for food and forest resources result in drastic alteration of ecosystems and threats to the stability of the whole natural order; alien species are introduced, and native species are diminished, replaced, and destroyed.

Thus it is necessary for us to consider the increasing human impact on the biosphere as a consequence of our increasing population and our increasing technology. And it is necessary to consider the worldwide demand for that basic human necessity, food. For it is our need for food that causes much of the pressure we apply to the fabric of the earth's ecosystems.

BASIC HUMAN FOOD NEEDS

Apart from superficial differences owing to physical size and level of activity, adult humans all over the world require about the same amount of food. We need that food for two reasons: to provide the energy necessary for work, and to provide materials to build, maintain, and repair our bodies.

"*Give us this day our daily meat. . . .*"

The need for energy is measured in Calories. A Calorie (actually a "kilocalorie," 1000 "small calories") is the amount of heat needed to raise the temperature of a kilogram of water one degree Celsius. Ultimately, then, the world food need is an energy problem. Food is fuel, "burned" in the organic furnace of our bodies. Each person in the world needs, on the average, about 2200 Calories a day of that organic fuel, food.

The other food need — materials for growth and maintenance — is measured in weight units: grams, milligrams, ounces. Of these materials, proteins are of particular interest. These complex substances, derived from animals and plants, are essential for human life. Proteins are made up of amino acids. Some of these amino acids can be synthesized from other substances, but others cannot be made by our bodies and must therefore be part of our diet. The body's need for protein is not related to how active we are, as is our caloric need. Rather, these needs are a result of the biological demands for raw materials needed for growth, maintenance, or repair. Persons who have a particular need for protein, therefore, are growing children, nursing mothers, and those undergoing healing processes.

Proteins vary in quality — that is, in suitability for the body's needs. Thus, in addition to differences in people's need for protein, there are differences in the capacity of various foods to meet those needs. Animal protein is more accessible to the body's metabolism than is most plant protein; therefore, it is usually necessary to eat more plant protein than animal protein to provide the same amount for the body. There are exceptions, however, since some kinds of plant protein, when combined with others, complement each other and are adequate substitutes for meat. For example, a diet of rice provides inadequate protein, as does a diet of beans, but a diet of rice and beans *eaten together* will provide the amino acids necessary for the body's needs. On the average, the body needs about seventy grams, or 2.5 ounces, of protein per day.

Food Needs Per Person

The immediate reason for inadequate food in the world is the lack of the resources — money, land, and so forth — for obtaining food. The ability to purchase food increases as the standard of living rises. As a country becomes wealthier, the per-person demand for food increases. Unfortunately, however, that *demand* for food often exceeds — by large margins — those basic minimal *requirements* for Calories and protein.

One result of this excessive food demand on the part of the wealthier countries is simply that people eat too much — overweight is a major problem in North America. A more serious problem, however, is not that people demand extra helpings of things, but rather that they demand high-quality protein. To meet the world's protein needs we could use our land to grow protein-rich crops, which, when eaten in the proper combination, would provide the bulk of our protein requirements. Instead, we use a large percentage of our cropland in North America to grow feed for livestock. Ultimately we eat the livestock, but by the time grain gets converted into beef, about 90 percent of the energy content of the food has been lost.

This is not to say, of course, that it is wrong to eat meat.[1] Nor does

---

1. In making this statement, we clearly are taking sides in a debate which has become more intense since the first edition of *Earthkeeping:* that is, the growing conviction on the part of many (sometimes they are referred to as the "animal rights movement") that it is arrogant of us to think that we have the right to use any animal for any purpose: research, labor, skins, or food. Though we do not agree with all of the premises or the conclusions of those who make such arguments, they are serious and important. We consider them in greater depth in chapters 14 and 16.

it imply that it is wrong to raise animals for food. Much land can grow no other crops besides those suitable for grazing. But for millions of acres of cropland in North America we have the choice: do we grow crops for food or crops for feed?

Obviously, when human food needs are met by eating the protein-rich crops directly, instead of by eating the animals to which they are usually fed, a given amount of land can feed many more people. One result is less pressure on those dwindling wild areas we discussed in the previous chapter; another is more food for the steadily growing human population. It is important not to oversimplify the problem here. In some situations, it is a good thing to maintain a population of grazing animals. They can be maintained as a kind of buffer, such that excess grain can be fed to cattle in "fat" years, and those cattle can be killed and eaten in "lean" years. Agricultural societies have operated this way for centuries. Nevertheless, it is clear that the demand of affluent countries for a high-meat diet is a drain on the availability of both food for other humans and habitat for the earth's nonhuman creatures. Figure 3.1 provides a good summary of the impact of different diets on the amount of real food eaten. The consumption of animal products, as shown in the shaded area, has an impact on the food-producing system many times greater than if the land producing feed were used instead to produce food directly for humans. Though it is not possible for a person to sustain a food consumption rate of 10,000 Calories per day, we effectively do so when we eat a high-meat diet, for we are eating animals fed from land which could feed people.

Pointing out the intrinsic wastefulness of a high-meat diet is likely to make most of us uncomfortable about our eating habits. And it probably should. But at this point, we are not concerned with arousing feelings of guilt over last night's dinner or the contents of our refrigerator. Our purpose is rather to provide an understanding of the worldwide need for adequate food and of the pressure that demand places on natural ecosystems and the earth's productivity. About one-eighth of the world's 5.2 billion people have an inadequate food supply — they are either severely malnourished or starving. At least that many more people are barely able to eat enough to supply their basic bodily needs. These people lack food because they lack money. An increase in monetary resources would multiply their demand for food, but it would place even greater pressure both on our food supplies and on the dwindling natural ecosystems of the earth. Even if there were no further increase in world population (and there unavoidably will be a great increase, as the last part of this chapter makes

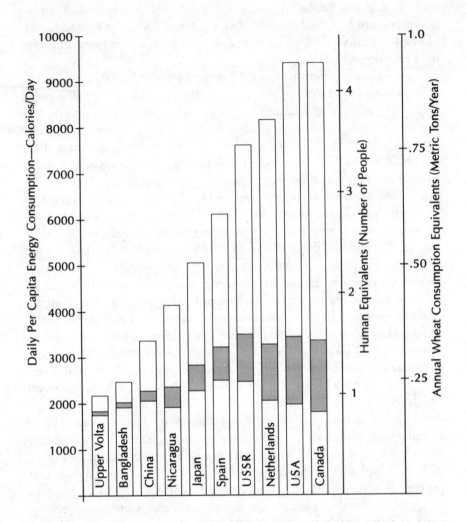

Figure 3.1. Food consumption per person for various nations, showing the effects of consumption of grain-based animal products. The length of the clear area containing the name of the nation indicates the daily per-capita consumption of non-animal foods, while the shaded area represents the consumption of animal-product Calories. The total length of each bar represents the total equivalent Calorie consumption of each nation, based on the conservative assumption that the average Calorie input in grain fed to animals is five times greater than the number of Calories delivered as usable animal-derived food. Data from various U.N. sources.

plain), to bring all people in the world to our level of diet would require a fourfold increase in the land's productivity. It is questionable — in view of the destructive tendencies of modern agriculture outlined in an earlier chapter — whether humanly managed ecosystems could survive such an increase even if it were possible. (As chapter 1 makes clear, we are already exceeding the limits of sustainability in much modern food production.) Clearly, then, a concern both for the world's poor and for the maintenance of the healthy diversity of the biosphere suggests that large-scale changes are needed in the diet to which most North Americans have become accustomed. Are we willing to reduce our own personal impact on the food production system? For reasons of economic and political survival, we, or our children, might *have* to. But for reasons of compassion, love, and stewardly responsibility — not to mention for reasons of personal health — we might *want* to reduce our consumption. In either case, some sort of change in diet seems inevitable for North Americans in the near future. As Christians, we must determine whether that change will be forced upon us, or whether we will be leaders in effecting it.[2]

HUMAN POPULATION GROWTH

A cloud on the horizon of any discussion of our use of creation is the awesome, inexorable increase in human population. All of the problems we have discussed thus far — whether we speak of energy needs, mineral needs, food needs, or impact on the biosphere — are already problems under present levels of population. But the increase in population means that the problems can only become more severe. And that increase is magnified in turn by the efforts of poorer nations to achieve the scale of consumption established as a model by the industrialized world, particularly by North America.

Despite all that has been said in books and newspapers and on television, not many of the world's burgeoning billions understand the

---

2. Here once again it is important not to oversimplify either the problem or the solution. A change in our diet will make little difference in the well-being of a malnourished child elsewhere in the world. Complex changes in economic relationships among nations — and even more subtle changes in such things as *attitude* toward food — need to accompany any such change in diet if it is to make any difference.

"Their breeding rate is incredible."

From the *Grand Rapids Press,* April 4, 1969.
Used by permission of Bill Mauldin and Wil-Jo Associates, Inc.

unprecedented scale or danger of the current population increase. In 1950, a time well within the memory of many readers of this book, there were 2,600,000,000 fewer people on earth than there are today. When we consider that this number is (for example) 538 times greater than the population of the entire state of Wisconsin, ten and a half times the population of the United States, and two and a half times the population of China, we begin to realize the magnitude and speed of the increase. The number of people added to the world in the last decade is equal to three and one-third times the population of the United States — on average a new U.S. every three years! What does it take to support the United States' population? Can the world provide the support necessary to support a new United States over the next three years? And still another one in the following three years? And so on? (The growth rate is even faster than this because population growth rate is still increasing exponentially.)

We have spoken in the previous chapter of the impact of expanding agricultural land on the remaining natural ecosystems. Population growth figures make us see that the destructive expansion is understandable, if not inevitable. For if we allow the bare minimum of one acre (208 feet by 208 feet) for the production of each person's food needs, the amount of land needed to feed that increase from 1950 to 1980 would require more than four times the area of existing U.S. cropland. Another area twice that size would be required to support the population added from 1980 to 1990.

This enormous increase in population is disturbing enough. It took all of human history — from the beginning of humanity to about 1940 — to reach the first 2 billion people. The next 2 billion was added in a scant 35 years. If our present rate of increase continues, the third 2 billion will be added in the 25 years between 1975 and 2000.

The current time taken for the human population to double in size is about 39 years. (We can take some slight comfort in the fact that this doubling time has slowed, in a decade, from 38 to 39 years. The population growth rate is declining, but far too slowly.) Thus a population of 5 billion becomes 10 billion in 39 years; in the succeeding 39 years it becomes 20 billion. This rate of increase is remarkably high for any human population at any time in human history. One can readily test this by beginning with an estimated population of 8.6 billion people in the year 2020 and halving it time and time again, as is shown in Table 1. It takes only 32 "halvings" to go from 8.6 billion people to 2 people. Put the other way around, a population of 2 people produces 8.6 billion people in only 32 doubling times.

If we assume that each of those previous doublings of the human

Table 1 Population Levels for 32 Doublings

The population figures shown below were produced by halving the estimated 2020 population time after time, rounding off appropriately, until an initial population of two persons was reached. The column labeled "Year" gives the date for each doubling, using the present doubling time of 39 years. Note that if population had always increased at its present rate, Adam and Eve would have to have been created in A.D. 772!

Doubling Period	Year	Population
32	2020	8,600,000,000
31	1981	4,300,000,000
30	1942	2,150,000,000
29	1903	1,075,000,000
28	1864	537,500,000
27	1825	268,750,000
26	1786	134,375,000
25	1747	67,187,500
24	1708	33,593,750
23	1669	16,796,875
22	1630	8,398,437
21	1591	4,199,218
20	1552	2,099,609
19	1513	1,049,804
18	1474	524,902
17	1435	262,451
16	1396	131,225
15	1357	65,612
14	1318	32,806
13	1279	16,403
12	1240	8,201
11	1201	4,100
10	1162	2,050
9	1123	1,025
8	1084	512
7	1045	256
6	1006	128
5	967	64
4	928	32
3	889	16
2	850	8
1	811	4
0	772	2

population took place at our current doubling time of 39 years, and that the 8.6 billion level is reached in the year 2020, we find the date of Adam and Eve to be A.D. 772! Even if we take a doubling time of 100 years, we press the beginning of humanity back to only 1180 B.C., 3200 years ago.

Obviously, humanity has been around much longer than 2 or 3 thousand years. This exercise is only a way of illustrating that the present doubling time of 39 years — or less — is highly unusual. It has not long been in effect in the past, and it cannot be in effect very long in the future. For all practical purposes, then, zero population growth, an idea that seems radical to many today, was the norm throughout most of human history, with birth rates nearly equal to death rates.

At least in the developed, industrialized nations, there has been an implicit recognition of this problem of population increase, and in those countries moves to control it are meeting with some success. But the most serious problem is in the developing countries (see Table 2). In these areas, even though agricultural production is (by a variety of means, some of them destructive and expensive) steadily increasing, that increase is only enough to maintain the already low level of food per person. In those countries, tremendous efforts are necessary simply to keep on feeding the

Table 2 Regional Populations, Doubling Times, and Birth and Death Rates (from 1990 World Population Data Sheet, Population Reference Bureau, Washington, DC)

	Population Estimate (millions)	Doubling Time (years)	Population Projection to Year 2000	Births per Woman	Infant Mortality Rate (per 1000 live births first year)	Per Capita GNP
Africa	661	24	884	6.2	109	600
Asia	3116	37	3718	3.5	74	1430
North America	278	93	298	2.0	9	19490
Latin America	447	33	535	3.5	54	1930
Europe	501	266	515	1.7	12	12170
U.S.S.R.	291	80	312	2.5	29	—
Oceania	27	57	31	2.6	26	9550
World	5321	39	6292	3.5	73	3470

people at the same low level — in some cases at a starvation level. The increase in population means that the number of tilled acres per person in these countries will inevitably be reduced to one-half the present area in less than a lifetime. A further consequence of that population growth is that even the gross national product (GNP) per person will, despite large increases in the country's total GNP, show little increase — a fact which reflects the diminishing resources available to each person for obtaining food.

Why is it that the less-developed countries have such explosive rates of population growth when compared to industrialized nations like the United States and Japan? Without going into the immediate personal reasons for why people choose to have a certain number of children, we can find a helpful explanation simply by looking at the relationship of the birth rate to the death rate. In the developed countries, largely as a result of various applications of medical and food-producing technology, both death rates and birth rates have shown significant declines in the past hundred years. A hundred years ago the number of children born to each American mother was close to the 6.2 which is the current African average. But in America both birth and death rates have fallen slowly, giving our cultural expectations time to change with them.

In the less-developed countries, on the other hand, as the result of the sudden introduction of modern medical technology, death rates have dropped abruptly in less than a generation. But birth rates — which are affected by much more subtle factors than death rates — have inevitably lagged behind.

Of course, what a healthy planet requires is not simply declining birth and death rates; what is required is that the birth rate and the death rate at least be balanced — as they appear to have been throughout most of human history. (In fact, it is probably the case that a healthy biosphere requires a somewhat smaller human population.) In any case, the sheer limitations of the biosphere will impose such a balance (or even reduction) sooner or later, and all humans would like to avoid the most likely means for achieving that stability: war, starvation, and disease. Yet already, through the starvation of millions of people in countries with high birth rates and low death rates, we can watch that deadly type of equalization beginning to take place. Certainly a task arising from the Christian gospel is to bring about such stability, and to do it through means other than starvation and warfare. Those tasks are our Christian obligation, not only for the sake of other humans, but also for the sake of this Eden of a planet placed in our trust. For it clearly will become a kind of man-made desert unless we can control the exploding population, and the exploding demands, of the people of the planet.

Prospects for the Populations of Developing Countries

In this matter of the increasing demands that come with progress (automobiles, electrification, a high-meat diet, convenient throwaway packaging, etc.) we in the "developed" nations bear a high degree of responsibility for the ultimate impact on the earth of rapid human population growth. For we have not only assumed that our own happiness and well-being depend on such conveniences; we have assumed that everyone will want them and have advertised them as measures of the good life, of "development." With readily available radio, TV, and video, few people on earth are beyond the reach of such images of "the good life" which our medias make available. Unfortunately, that "good life" shows little concern for the impact on the earth; rather, it reflects a thoughtless consumerism.

It is fairly clear that people do reduce their population as their standard of living increases. Our terrible liability in the West is to have built up a worldwide ideal of a standard of living which — though many envy it — is destructive of the biosphere. We have assumed that imitating such a standard is the sort of "development" all other peoples seek, and we have hypocritically lamented the impact of such development on the biosphere without seriously questioning its consequences in our own society.

Even if affluence does overtake population, North American society (and the image of it which the media projects worldwide) is an embarrassing example of the fact that increasing wealth causes our demands for food — and other resources — to rise far beyond the level needed for a comfortable existence. In fact, we are, in North America, the world's most spectacular example of the principle that increasing affluence increases waste. Simply increasing affluence in hopes that it will decrease the birth rate does not seem a wise choice. It is more important to get at the reasons for high and low birth rates, and to change them without destroying the worth and freedom of individual persons. Such a solution requires more wisdom than most members of affluent countries have been able to exercise. More important, it requires the kind of understanding love which Christians ought to demonstrate.

Ultimately, the goal of population control must be to prevent population size from exceeding the carrying capacity of the environment. It is very difficult to determine what the carrying capacity of an environment is, particularly when we are speaking of the whole biosphere as the environment of humans and millions of other species. But the preceding chapters have shown that the carrying capacity at which we arrive must leave room for the diversity and intricacy of the rest of creation. The reasons for that accommodation are both selfish, for we know we cannot survive apart from the supporting life of a healthy biosphere, and stewardly, for it is the human responsibility to care for creation.

In some cases, even when the carrying capacity is understood, arriving at a stable population will not be enough. For, in places adversely affected by climatic change (which is probably going to accelerate), or by the lingering effects of human overuse (as in the dry areas of the world being taken over by deserts), it may even be necessary to *reduce* the population size by letting the birth rate fall below the death rate.

A number of nations have already achieved zero population growth. They have usually done so by slowly recognizing the limits to their continued growth. In nations such as the United States, however, that change in attitude took place very slowly. But in the developing nations it must take place much more rapidly. One indication of the rapidity with which such a realization is coming to other nations is the fact that even if birth rates were to equal death rates — that is, if each couple were to have, on the average, only two children — there would still be a sizable increase in population in those nations.

This is largely due to the ages of the people within those various populations. Developing countries, due to the suddenness with which modern medical technology has been introduced, have a very large proportion of young people. This youthful age structure is reflected in the pyramidal shape of the age-structure diagram for developing countries shown in Figure 3.2. Contrasts are revealing. In North America only 22 percent of the people are under age 15; in Western Europe, only 18 percent. But in Latin America, 38 percent of the people are under the age of 15, in Southeast Asia, 38 percent, and in Africa, 45 percent.

A hidden consequence of this youthful population in developing countries is that, even if the number of children per family were steadily and dramatically reduced, the size of the population would continue to increase as those who are now children approach child-bearing age. The long delay in humans between birth and reproduction builds a lag into

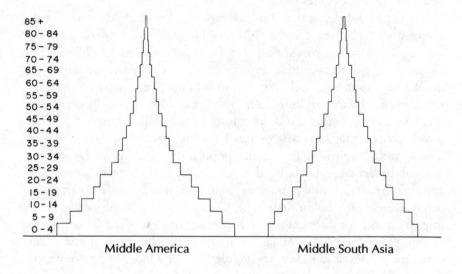

85 +	
80 – 84	
75 – 79	
70 – 74	
65 – 69	
60 – 64	
55 – 59	
50 – 54	
45 – 49	
40 – 44	
35 – 39	
30 – 34	
25 – 29	
20 – 24	
15 – 19	
10 – 14	
5 – 9	
0 – 4	

Middle America   Middle South Asia

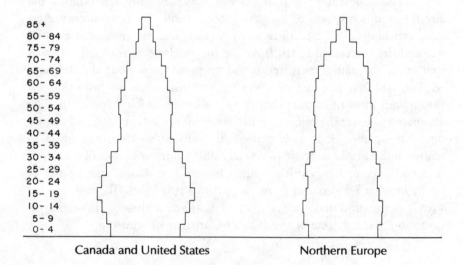

85 +	
80 – 84	
75 – 79	
70 – 74	
65 – 69	
60 – 64	
55 – 59	
50 – 54	
45 – 49	
40 – 44	
35 – 39	
30 – 34	
25 – 29	
20 – 24	
15 – 19	
10 – 14	
5 – 9	
0 – 4	

Canada and United States   Northern Europe

Figure 3.2. Age structures of various populations showing those with prospects for continuing explosive growth (pyramid form) and those with prospects for relatively stable levels (steep-sided form). Based upon data compiled from the *Demographic Yearbook* of the United Nations (1977, 1978).

population dynamics, so that the effects of changes in birth rates are still being felt several decades later.

Figure 3.3 shows that if the average number of children per family dropped to replacement levels (NRR — Natural Replacement Rate) by the year 2000 (which means dropping from 2.6 down to 2.1 children per family in developed countries, and from 5.7 to 2.7 children per family in developing countries), world population would still increase from its present level of 5 billion to 5.8 billion in the year 2000. It would eventually stabilize, shortly before 2100, at a level of 8.2 billion (curve C). That possibility is perhaps the best we can hope for, given the present ethos of Third-World countries. But if the population in developed countries reached replacement levels by the year 2000, and those of developing countries by 2045, world population would not stabilize until about 2145, at a level near 15.5 billion (curve B). Curves D and A (both of which are impossible, but for different reasons) show the context of the consequences of our present actions. Population momentum due to a youthful age structure will result in increasing populations for a long time to come, no matter what we do to slow population growth.

The problem of a youthful age structure only compounds the already serious problem of increasing population. We have already exercised our abilities to control death. It is clear that we must also exercise our abilities to control birth. If we are to exercise care for each other, as well as for the planet entrusted to us, we must temper our abilities with wisdom and love in order to achieve consciously what has been the case throughout most of human history — a relatively stable population. The alternative is to let the blind destructiveness of starvation, war, and disease do what we should do as a matter of careful stewardship. In order to maintain the planet as home to several million different kinds of creatures, it is necessary to have both a limited human population and a sense of limits in what we demand from the earth to sustain us. To work toward such a population and such a sense of fulfillment through limited consumption is clearly one of the tasks of Christian stewardship.

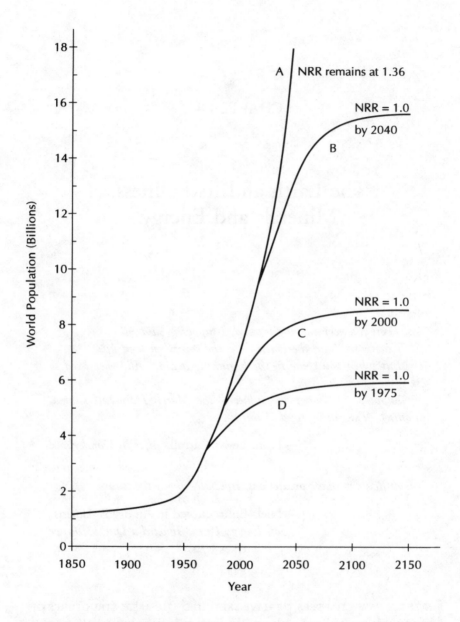

Figure 3.3. World population past and future, under various assumptions (see text). Generated from a computer model based upon data from T. Frejka, *The Future of Population Growth* (New York: John Wiley & Sons, 1973), and estimates of past populations by A. M. Carr-Saunders, *World Population: Past Growth and Present Trends* (London: Frank Cass & Co., 1964).

CHAPTER 4

❦　　❦

The Earth and Its Fullness:
Minerals and Energy

"Then you keep moving around, I suppose?" said Alice.

"Exactly so," said the Hatter, "As the things get used up."

"But when you come to the beginning again?" Alice ventured to ask.

"Suppose we change the subject," the March Hare interrupted, yawning. "I'm getting tired of this. . . ."

— From Lewis Carroll, *Alice in Wonderland*

It is difficult to make predictions, especially about the future.

— Niels Bohr, quoted in Amory B. Lovins,
Soft Energy Paths: Toward a Durable Peace

IN THESE PAST CHAPTERS WE HAVE SKETCHED THE BASIC STRUCTURES OF life on this great gift of a planet. We have seen first the complexity and delicacy of the relationships between plants, animals, and humans. We have seen also the serious ways in which those relationships, and the organisms themselves, have been disrupted by human activity.

But underlying all this activity, from the industry of fungi breaking a fallen tree into soil to the industry of humans breaking a mountain down into coal, are two basic nonliving resources: minerals and energy. When we consider the world of God's creation we are likely to think first not of this, but of the world of living things — perhaps because we are living things ourselves. But without the energy of the sun, and without carbon, calcium, nitrogen, oxygen, iron, all those substances which we first encounter in the blossoming flesh of the planet — none of that life would live.

Likewise, apart from the energies of sun and atom and our own abilities to apply those energies to the bedrock of creation — coal, iron, copper, oil — all our civilization, and human life itself, would cease. Thus it is our purpose in this chapter to consider the state of those nonliving resources on which both human and nonhuman life depend so totally. We are not concerned now with the complex and marvelous ways in which the plant world turns earth and energy into the food which sustains all life; rather, we are concerned with *human* use of earth and energy. In this sense, our discussion is one step removed from the previous chapters, for we are not discussing the operation of the planet as it takes place in creation apart from human intervention. Rather, we are considering the *human* use of creation. And though we, like plants and animals, use energy to transform minerals for our own purposes, our energy use is different. First of all, it differs in scale: no other creature has the ability to change the earth so radically and quickly. Nor does any other creature have the ability to turn so many things to its own use. For this reason, the analysis of our resource use in the future is particularly difficult. For what is not a resource today may become one tomorrow. Likewise, today's hotly contested resources may someday dwindle to insignificance.

A modern fable describes a man condemned by fate — like the Wandering Jew or the Flying Dutchman — to carry through the ages a rock from a mountain. He had to carry the rock until a use was discovered for it. It (and the mountain of its origin) was useless stone for millennia; but in the twentieth century the man's quest ended, for the process of nuclear fission was discovered, and the rock was found to be from a deposit of uranium ore.

The same sort of story could be told of coal, oil, and iron ore. The earth is a storehouse of wealth, but until we learn to use it, it is worthless: part of what makes it "wealth" is human knowledge. Applying that knowledge in order to use the earth's treasure is a legitimate human activity. Unfortunately, in many cases we have not managed the storehouse well;

we have regarded it *only* as a storehouse, raided it unwisely and indiscriminately, and often used its treasure carelessly.

By the middle of this century, uranium had become a treasure — but it had also become an object of dread. The same sort of thing has taken place with other resources. For large areas of the Appalachian mountains, for example, we have determined that the treasure of coal is greater than the treasure of the soil, its life, and the human culture it supports. So for many decades we have been stripping away the soil (which has become "overburden") to get at the treasure beneath. Likewise a treasure of oil was discovered on the north slope of Alaska — but to use it we threaten not only the fragile arctic ecosystem beneath which it lies, but also the incomparably fertile world of Pacific estuaries and islands through which it must be transported.

It is our purpose in this chapter to take a close look at these ambiguous treasures of energy and minerals, at the way in which we have used them (and may yet use them), and the implications of our use for the human task of stewardship.

We have divided our discussion of these resources into two categories: "energy" and "minerals." But this is not a very precise distinction. For example, we use 95 percent of all petroleum and natural gas for fuel, but the other 5 percent is our main source of raw materials for petrochemicals. However, though many have argued that it is unwise to burn up a mineral treasure like petroleum on our freeways and in our furnaces, we will nevertheless consider resources under their principal current use. Thus, in our discussion, petroleum is an energy resource.

IN TRYING TO GET AN OVERALL PICTURE OF OUR MINERAL AND ENERGY resources, it might be helpful to look at the planet's wealth by analogy with the wealth of an individual. People ordinarily have three sources of wealth: *income, savings,* and *inheritance.* By analogy, in the earth's resources we have only one source of *income:* the vast but neglected flood of solar energy. We also have *savings:* a fraction of that solar income, caught by plants through the marvelous process of photosynthesis and stored in food, wood, coal, oil, and natural gas. Most of the energy we currently use, both in our bodies and in industry, comes from these solar savings. Finally, we have an *inheritance:* the nonliving planet itself — the heat of the earth's core, and its rock and mineral wealth, of which radioactive ores are particularly important for energy.

In the human use of natural resources, just as in an individual's use of financial resources, it is wise to live within one's income, though for a short time that income may be supplemented by drawing on savings and inheritance. The wealth of personal savings and inheritance may be either wasted or invested in order to yield a return. In the same way we may waste our savings of fossil fuels and our inheritance of mineral wealth, or we may use them so as to yield a return. A useful, long-term principle for resource use is that our inheritance of mineral wealth should be recycled; we should live within our solar energy income, and draw cautiously on the savings of fossil fuels or the inheritance of nuclear energy (which can only be used once). We ought to use our savings and inheritance only to set up better ways of using our energy income or of recycling our mineral inheritance. When we reflect on the way in which the ecosystems described in chapter 1 operate, we see that such a pattern is implicit in the nonhuman world. The rest of creation lives within its income of available food or sunlight. And eventually the savings of fiber or protein are "recycled" in the earth or taken up into the food web. But ultimately, nothing is wasted, except the unused energy that is radiated back into space.

ENERGY RESOURCES

Against this background of personal and "natural" finance, let us consider energy, our energy resources, and the use we make of them. First, we must understand what energy *is*.

Energy is unique among natural resources. It has properties which no other resource has. These characteristics underline why energy is our most important resource, why it is so important in contemporary human civilization, and why the "energy crisis" is of such great concern.

We can summarize these unique characteristics of energy very simply by saying that energy
  • is intangible;
  • is the capacity to do work;
  • is the most basic natural resource;
  • is the only nonrecyclable resource;
  • is the biggest factor in changing how we live.
Let us consider why each of these claims is true.

Energy is intangible. Despite the abundance of talk about energy, few people understand what it is — and no one has seen it or touched it. We have all seen the *effects* of energy or the *sources* of energy, but never the energy itself. When we lie in the sun on a warm day, we can see the source of the energy — the sun — and feel the effect of the energy — the sun's warmth on the skin — but we do not experience the energy itself as it is transmitted between the sun and the body. For energy itself is intangible.

Energy is the capacity to do work. Energy's great importance to us comes from its ability to do work; humans have always tried to minimize the work they do. In earlier days, this was done by animals, or slaves; today it is done by machines — but both slaves and machines apply energy to a particular job. Likewise, for millennia people have realized that heat energy is useful and have used fire for heating and cooking. It took them much longer to recognize that other forms of energy — particularly mechanical energy — could also be useful. Once this discovery was made, the industrial revolution was upon us. Today, most people in industrialized societies live lives of relative leisure, because energy-consuming machines do their work for them.

Energy is our most basic natural resource. This claim might at first seem extravagant, but consider the following: if we wish to make an object out of iron, whether it be an automobile or a can, we must first mine the iron ore, then transport it to a smelter, smelt it, form an ingot, transport the ingot to a rolling mill, roll the steel, transport it to a factory, and then make the car or the can, which must finally be transported to the consumer. Energy is required at every step. Without energy, we could not dig the iron ore out of the ground, smelt it, form an ingot, transport it, roll it, or form an end product. This is the reason energy is the most basic natural resource, for without it we could not use our other natural resources. Until we learned how to use nonanimal sources of energy effectively, we were unable to tap most mineral resources. And many other mineral resources such as oil shale or the uranium in granite are at this time effectively inaccessible to us because of the tremendous energy which would be needed to process them.

Energy is our only nonrecyclable resource. Most material resources — plastics, for example — can, with the right kind of effort, be recycled. We have not done so much in the past, but in principle there is nothing to prevent us from doing so. The same could be said of most of our nonfuel mineral resources. But energy is different. Even if we wanted to recycle it, we could not; it is impossible. The second law of thermodynamics states that any transformation of energy results in a lower quality of energy — that is, in energy which can do less useful work. Energy is degraded in all natural processes. Furthermore, virtually all energy used or transformed is eventually converted into heat energy, which ultimately is radiated into space, never to be recovered. There is no way of stopping this. The more energy we use, the more energy we radiate outward. This necessary and irrevocable loss makes energy intrinsically nonrecyclable. (The fact that energy is nonrecyclable does not at all preclude its being used with much greater efficiency: as we shall see, energy conservation is our most important energy resource.)

Energy is the biggest factor in modifying our lifestyle. Because energy is the capacity to do work, the application of energy for our own purposes means that we have less work to do, or at least a different kind of work. Energy's ability to do work affects even what we call play — as when we use a golf cart to move us around a golf course, or a power boat to pull a water-skier.

The consequences of the application of energy to necessary tasks have been so great in the last century as to almost totally transform the shape of everyday life. We have no way of knowing, therefore, what changes energy use will produce in our future. But there is one thing of which we can be certain: energy has a price. We pay that price in two ways. The first is the depletion of solar "savings" in coal and oil and the "inheritance" of nuclear fuels. The resulting scarcity brings higher costs. The second price is that both our extraction and our use of energy degrade the fabric of creation. A grim collection of modern worries — smog, acid rain, oil spills, the greenhouse effect, and nuclear wastes — all describe some of the environmental costs of our use of energy. We will not be able to pay these prices — economic or environmental — indefinitely. On the other hand, a change in our pattern of energy use would result in profound changes in our way of life — particularly in North America, where that life has been transformed so thoroughly by cheap energy.

The "Energy Crisis," Large and Small

So much for what energy is. We must now consider the availability of energy. Is there an energy shortage? An energy crisis? In absolute terms, no: there is no energy shortage, and until the sun dies there will be none. Each *day* the sun pours onto the earth more energy than is stored in *all* the remaining reserves of coal and oil.[1] But as long as our energy-hungry civilization is tied closely to scarce and dwindling fossil fuel reserves, there will continue to be shortages and crises. A survey of recent history makes this clear.

"Crisis" language first appeared in the early seventies, as a result of increasing American dependence on Middle Eastern oil. In 1973, out of disapproval of American support of Israel in the "Yom Kippur" war, the Arabs declared an oil embargo. The result was an immediate shortage of petroleum products in the United States, which meant that Americans had to wait in line for gas at service stations and sometimes could not get gas at all. But that 1973 shortage of oil was not absolute; it was artificially contrived. The Arabs turned off the valve, and our gas stations ran dry. The oil was still under the ground, however, waiting to be pumped up and distributed. When the political problems were worked out, the valves were opened, and oil from Arabia flowed again to the U.S. In fact, though America was importing less than 25 percent of its oil before that first temporary crisis, by the end of the decade (1980) it was importing nearly 50 percent, and thus was much more vulnerable to the same sort of politically motivated cutoff. We have not reduced that percentage of import; under present energy policy, it will only increase. The hard lesson of our vulnerability was taught (though probably not learned) again in 1979 as a result of Iranian political unrest. It was taught once again a decade later in 1990 when Iraq invaded Kuwait and the price of crude oil doubled.

To each of these short-term crises North Americans responded with some attempts to reduce energy consumption. But when the immediate crisis ended, cheap oil came pouring back (along with words like "glut" and "surplus"). Increased use makes the shallowness of our response evident and shows that we are unaware of the *real* energy crisis.

That crisis, approaching inexorably, refers to the time when most of the oil will have been pumped out and used. That real energy crisis has not yet begun — but by all indications, it is not far off. Our recurring, politically induced shortages only serve to remind us of our dependence on oil and the consequences of its coming depletion.

The reasons for this approaching *real* energy crisis are all around us. At any supermarket, for example, we can look in the parking lot and notice rows and rows of 3000-pound automobiles which have been driven

---

1. According to a recent *National Geographic* calculation, the planet receives in a year 15,000 times the amount of energy stored in remaining fossil fuels.

there by 150-pound persons to pick up ten pounds of groceries. It takes very little energy to transport ten pounds of groceries from the store to the home. It does not even take much energy to carry a person from his or her home to a store — most people could walk it without much trouble. But it takes a great deal of energy to transport a 3000-pound automobile to and from the store. A little experiment can dramatize the difference. On your next trip to the store, instead of driving your car, try pushing it!

Such an experiment might cause us to reflect on the history of our use of energy. When Abraham was wandering about the Near East, he used very little energy: wood for heating and cooking, and pasture for his camels and horses. His own personal use probably amounted to about 2500 Calories per day. This basic human energy consumption — the food it takes to keep an active person healthy — is indicated on the accompanying chart (Figure 4.1).

Already in Abraham's day, some civilizations were making the transition from an economy based on nomadic existence to one based on agriculture. But this agricultural revolution did not succeed until domesticated animals were used to work the fields. In other words, it was not until humanity learned to harness energy other than its own that the effects of the agricultural revolution became permanent. Cities came into being and the capacity of the earth to support humans increased dramatically. The first major revolution in our use of energy had a major impact on human history. The typical agricultural person used (or uses — there are still some agricultural societies) approximately 20,000 Calories of energy per day, as we have shown on the accompanying chart. The added 17,500 Calories were consumed not by the person directly, but by the animals whose muscles he had used to assist him in his work.

The next major increase in our use of energy occurred in the industrial revolution. When we learned how to tap nonanimal sources of energy and to develop machines to use it, both energy use and our way of life changed more dramatically than ever. At the beginning of the industrial revolution, when we were burning mainly wood and coal, the energy consumption per person rose to about 75,000 Calories per day. It was then that we began to draw heavily on the "savings" of solar energy in fossil fuels. Today, in North America, we use approximately 250,000 Calories per person per day.

The figures on this chart illustrate the point we made earlier: energy use is the major factor in changing our way of life. The two greatest changes in the way humanity has lived on the earth were the agricultural revolution

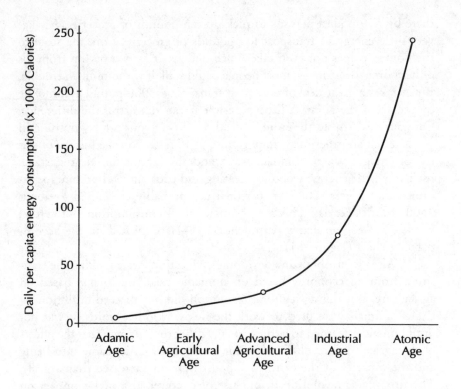

Figure 4.1. Daily per capita consumption of energy at different stages of development of civilization. The energy consumed by primitive civilizations consisted only of the food necessary to sustain life. As people began using wood and other fuels, as well as animal energy, energy consumption increased. Today vast quantities of energy are used in transportation, heating and cooling, and industrial production. Adapted from Earl Cook, "The Flow of Energy in an Industrial Society," *Scientific American* 224 (Sept. 1971): 136, with additional data from *EBASCO: 1977 Business and Economic Charts* (New York: Ebasco Services, 1978).

and the industrial revolution. In both cases, these revolutions were the result of changes in our ability to use energy. With each change, the amount of energy use increased manyfold. As a result, each of us in North America uses approximately 100 times the amount of energy per day that a person of Abraham's time would have consumed. Because energy represents the capacity to do work, the effect is like having 100 slaves working for each of us.

This increase in energy consumption per person is magnified by the growing number of people using that energy. To be sure, the bulk of that population increase is occurring in nations which have a relatively low consumption of energy per person. But that fact only suggests two other unpleasant realities. One is that we already use far more than our share of the earth's resources. The other is that our excessive use has been adopted as a model for the developing world; the Third-World countries are trying, as rapidly as they can, to catch up with our number of "energy slaves." All our policies and attitudes reinforce the idea that it is only through such high rates of energy use that we can achieve happiness. The consequence is that the exponentially rising world population, multiplied by the exponentially rising per-person energy use, is placing a very great strain both on our energy resources and on the systems of earth, air, and water which absorb the wastes from our energy use. The demand for energy is being met almost entirely out of energy savings and inheritance — very little out of energy income. There is a very real possibility that we may use up those great reserves of fossil fuels before we are forced to develop means of effectively harnessing energy income — and by that time, we may not have sufficient energy resources to do so. There is danger too that in our rapid burning of fossil fuels we are changing the chemistry of the atmosphere more rapidly than the biosphere can respond.

Such predictions may seem unnecessarily alarming. With regard to availability, there is still much oil in the Middle East, and new discoveries are being made elsewhere every year. But simply because we have plenty of oil now does not mean that we will have plenty in the future. We have a glut of oil now, but we can foresee severe shortages in fifteen years and a real crisis in thirty. And with regard to wastes, though it is not *completely* certain that the planet is warming up as the result of increased CO_2 in the atmosphere, the rise of CO_2 is measured and inexorable, the resultant warming is inevitable, and by the time we are certain of its consequences, it will be too late to reverse them. So "crisis" language is appropriate.

We seem, then, to be nearing the end of an era. Our desire for energy, particularly for the cheap energy of solar "savings," is likely to surpass our ability to fulfill it before the end of the century. And even if we could fulfill all our energy desires, it is probable that the planet's life-support system would be seriously degraded.

Not one, therefore, but two energy crises confront us. The first has to do with availability and supply: how will we supply the energy needs of an increasingly energy-hungry human world? The second is perhaps more serious: how do we keep our use of energy from continuing to degrade the biosphere that supports us? We will consider first the simpler problem of supply.

Can We Increase Our Supply of Energy?

In considering a diminishing energy supply, we have only two alternatives: we must either increase our energy supply or reduce our demand. What are the possibilities of increasing supply? Only three sources of energy are available to us: the sun, which provides our energy income and is the source of those fossil fuel savings which have been so important in the past hundred years; the moon, which (through the tides) produces a small energy income; and the earth, whose heat and minerals make up our energy inheritance.

Energy Income: The Sun

Of these three, through all of history, virtually all energy used has come from the sun. We have used its energy from the beginning to fuel our bodies, to keep us warm, to enable us to work. By means of photosynthesis, plants are able to transform and to store in themselves the radiant energy of the sun. Our most immediate way of using these energy savings is to eat and digest the food; the plant's stored chemical energy is released in heat energy and in the movements of our muscles. In addition to providing our food energy in this way, the sun heats our entire planet, enabling it to support life. Thus our very existence depends on the sun's incoming energy.

Even when we begin using energy other than food, we find that it still comes from the sun. Whether we harness the energy of animals or burn wood to cook our food, we are releasing, either as work or as heat, the photosynthetically stored energy of the sun. Since the industrial revolution and the massive use of fossil fuels that accompanied it, we have increasingly turned away from using the short-term savings of wood and food to the long-term savings of coal and oil; but still we are using the energy of the sun. This ancient solar energy, stored for eons in the hydrocarbons of old jungles and river deltas, has fueled the industrial revolution. But, as we have already seen, our coal- and oil-dependent society faces two huge problems. One is the fact that we are "living on savings" to fuel our society, and the savings are running out. The second is that we have released into the atmosphere (in the space of a century or two) hundreds of billions of tons of carbon (in the form of carbon dioxide), and the likely effect is going to be a rapid warming of the planet. (Later in this chapter we will consider the consequences of this disruption.)

Solar Savings: How Much Is Left?

We will consider first the problem of availability. The planet's "savings" in fossil fuels are not inexhaustible, and we must seriously ask what will happen to our industrial society when that ancient stored sunlight is so scarce that we can no longer afford to find and use it. The accompanying graph (Figure 4.2) is a production curve typical for all fossil fuels, although this particular curve describes only petroleum. As the curve shows, production begins slowly. As persons demand more and more energy, new production facilities are built, and use and production increase. At some point, however, the supply of fuel is depleted to the point that production must decrease — because no savings account is infinite.

The most startling feature of this graph is its prediction (based on the most reliable data available) that by the year 2000 we will have reached the peak of the petroleum production curve. Thereafter, despite all our efforts, petroleum production will decrease. And, as the graph shows, even if optimistic predictions about the amount in the fuel reserves are correct, the increased supplies will make little difference in the time when the peak in production is reached and must begin declining.

The curve for natural gas, in Figure 4.3, is even less comforting; at current rates of usage, we are likely to run out of natural gas even before we run out of petroleum.

The curve for coal (Figure 4.4), on the other hand, is considerably more comforting: the great forests of the Carboniferous era trapped and stored vast amounts of sunlight, now buried in veins of coal. But serious problems are connected with the large-scale use of coal. To begin with, mining is a problem, particularly strip-mining. Furthermore, coal is inconvenient for individual use. This problem could be solved if proposals to liquefy and gasify coal were successful, but such processes consume energy and would have the likely net result of making the whole process more inefficient. Burning coal releases into the air large amounts of sulphur dioxide, which forms an acidic and destructive rain. Coal-burning also produces much particulate matter.

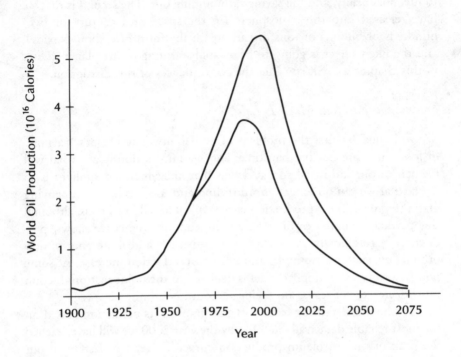

Figure 4.2. Actual and projected world oil production as a function of time. The upper line is based upon an optimistic estimate of the earth's total oil reserves; the bottom line reflects a pessimistic estimate. Adapted from M. K. Hubbert, "The Energy Resources of the Earth," *Scientific American* 224 (Sept. 1971): 69.

But by far the most serious problem with burning coal is that doing so will continue to build up atmospheric CO_2 till global warming (and consequent sea-level rise) will be catastrophic. In a century or two we will have restored to the atmosphere CO_2 that was removed over millions of years; the likely result, in the next century or two, will be a climate like that of the Carboniferous era.

A quite different but ultimately very important reason to be conservative in our use of the fossil fuels is that coal, oil, and natural gas are chemical treasures and our main source of synthetic materials. To burn them is foolish if there are alternatives to doing so. Future generations will

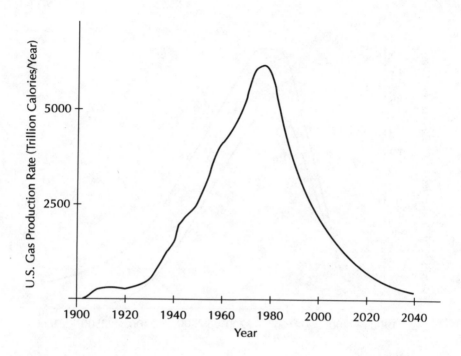

Figure 4.3. Actual and projected United States natural gas production as a function of time. Note that, although world natural gas production is still increasing, United States natural gas production has already begun to decline. Based on information in Roger F. Naill, *Managing the Energy Transition* (Cambridge, MA: Ballinger, 1977), p. 54, and Samuel M. Dix, *Energy: A Critical Decision for the United States Economy* (Grand Rapids: Energy Education Publishers [Dix and Associates], 1977), p. 24.

be grateful for our conserving oil and coal — not for fuel, but for use in producing synthetics, and for other, better uses that we don't know of yet.

We have not yet considered the large reserves of petroleum contained in oil shales or tar sands. However, their extraction would take large amounts of energy and (especially in the case of oil shale) would probably leave large amounts of waste. In any case, the use of these low-grade energy reserves would only increase by another few decades the time until the oil is effectively depleted.

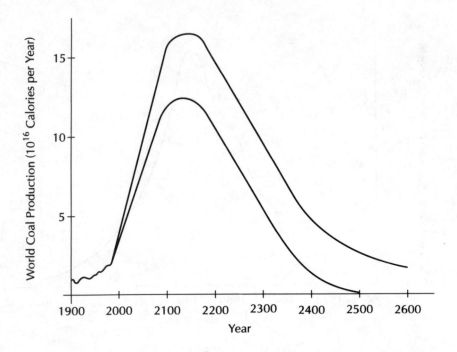

Figure 4.4. Actual and projected world coal production as a function of time. The upper curve reflects an optimistic estimate of the supply of mineable coal; the bottom curve reflects a pessimistic estimate. Adapted from Hubbert, "The Energy Resources of the Earth," p. 69.

No matter how wealthy one is, one cannot draw indefinitely on a savings account. The main problem with our use of fossil fuels is that we are drawing on savings which were deposited over millions of years, but which we are burning up in a few centuries (see Figure 4.5). Obviously, such a pattern cannot continue; yet the majority of the world's people act as though it will do so indefinitely.

Some Alternatives: Using Solar Income

The "solar savings" of fossil fuels have been cheap and relatively available, but like all savings, they are limited. As they become scarce they will

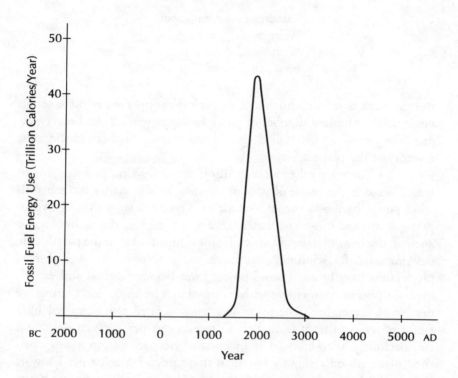

Figure 4.5. Total fossil fuel use, showing the relatively short time fossil fuels play an important role compared to the history of humankind. Adapted from M. K. Hubbert, "Energy Resources," in *Resources and Man,* National Academy of Sciences (San Francisco: W. H. Freeman, 1969), p. 206.

increase in cost; in addition, as we become more aware of the environmental damage they bring, greater efforts to use them cleanly will add to their cost. So we are already being driven to consider the only long-term alternative: using the incoming energy of the sun.

We tap solar energy in many ways. One of the simplest and cleanest is to hold water behind dams, releasing it to spin the turbines of electric generators on its way back to the sea. By doing this we are capturing solar energy, for it was the sun which first evaporated the water from the seas and lifted it into the sky, from where it fell again on the high watersheds behind the dam. The elegance of such a method is suggested in a poem by Wendell Berry called "Falling Asleep":

Raindrops on the tin roof.
What do they say?
We have all
been here before.

But excellent as it is, hydroelectric power can't supply many more of our needs. Only a limited number of good dam sites remain. And every new dam site floods a valley filled with living things, further reducing the diversity of the planet's life.

But there are other ways of using the sun. Wind power is one of these. Wind is the result of unequal heating of the earth's surface; thus wind power harnesses sun-moved air in ways analogous to how hydropower harnesses sun-lifted water. Like water power, the technology is ancient, unchanged in basic principles for centuries. Yet in the past decade new materials for windmills, computerized control of rotors, and mass production have brought wind power from being marginal and experimental to being competitive with conventional technologies. During the decade of the eighties the price of wind-generated electricity fell by a factor of ten, so that it is now about seven cents per kilowatt hour, and still declining. (Per–kilowatt hour costs of electricity from a new coal-fired plant are only slightly less than that, around 5 cents per kilowatt hour.) Wind-generated electrical capacity of over 1600 megawatt hours (equivalent to nearly two large coal or nuclear power stations) was installed in the eighties, and the 1990 *Worldwatch* report suggests that 10 percent of the world's electricity could reasonably be generated at competitive costs by 2030. Though the intermittent nature of the wind requires that wind-generated electricity not be the sole source on which a region depends, it is nevertheless a very promising complement to other sources.

One such source is electrical generation from direct solar radiation. This takes two forms: one is the use of the sun's heat to vaporize a liquid and turn a turbine to produce electricity; the other, photovoltaic, is more elegant: it produces electrical current from the light of the sun with no pollution and no moving parts. There have been remarkable advances in both technologies during the past decade. Turbine generation of electricity from solar energy has profited (like wind power) from new materials, technology, modular production, and computerized control. As a result, "solar farms" in high sunlight areas are much closer to economic viability than they were a decade ago. In California a series of 80 megawatt plants, modularly constructed in 9 months (as opposed to 6-12 years for conventional plants) began producing power in 1988. The cost per kilowatt hour was about 10 cents, which will certainly come down with subsequent construction.

Advances in photovoltaic construction are even more promising. Thirty years ago this was an exotic technology, so expensive that its first applications were only on satellites where expense was no object. In 1970, photovoltaic energy cost $60 per kilowatt hour to produce. By 1980, costs had fallen to $1 per kilowatt hour, and they are now at 20-30 cents per kilowatt hour, already very competitive in remote locations. It seems likely that the day when rooftop photovoltaic cells can provide most of the electrical needs for a household is approaching rapidly. There are yet other promising solar technologies. One whose contribution has increased considerably in the last decade is biomass, in which forest or agricultural waste products are burnt to run turbines, or fermented to provide ethanol, a gasoline substitute. (A serious drawback to biomass technologies, however, is that they are polluting, producing some of the same waste gases as fossil fuels.) Another likely future source of energy from the sun involves using electricity generated by wind, photovoltism, or more exotic means (such as the tapping of differences in ocean temperatures between the surface and the depths) to break water down into hydrogen and oxygen. Hydrogen is a fuel which can be used like natural gas, and whose combustion with air produces no CO_2 (it does, however, produce nitrous oxides, so it is not completely pollution-free). This method has the added advantage of providing a transportable substitute for gasoline, which makes it suitable for remote sites, and for filling gaps resulting from the intermittent nature of solar energy.

Thus far we have been talking about "active" uses of solar income, mainly useful for the production of electricity. Just as promising are more "passive" uses of solar energy, which can help meet our great need for low-temperature heat for buildings, hot water, and drying. Since in North America heating (and cooling) of buildings is currently the largest single user of energy (over 1/3 of our total energy use goes for heating and cooling), a small savings here can make a large difference. Solar hot water heaters (or pre-heaters) have been used for several decades. New materials and modular construction continue to improve these options. Great strides have been made in improving the insulating value of windows, especially through a "low emissivity" (low-E) coating applied to the inside. Such windows provide a means for retaining the energy of sunlight absorbed (a *positive* "greenhouse effect"). A 1990 *Scientific American* study makes clear the enormous savings available here:

> The average low-E coating plant costs $5 million to build, yet the windows it produces each day will save 10,000 barrels of oil, an amount equivalent to a 10,000 barrel-a-day offshore drilling platform, which costs 100 times more — $500 million — to build.[2]

Other passive strategies for using the sun are careful siting of buildings, use of porches and awnings that admit sun in winter and keep it out in summer, and a more careful use of reflective and absorptive colors of paint.

As these developments make clear, ways of tapping the inexhaustible solar *income* — not just the limited and polluting solar savings in coal and oil — are on the verge of becoming a major source of energy. But solar energy (whether "income" or "savings") is not our only option.

We mentioned earlier that the sun, moon, and earth are our only basic sources of energy. We do not normally consider the moon as an energy source; it neither radiates nor generates energy. But, if we could tap it, the energy stored in its relative motion around the earth would provide the earth's energy needs for a billion years, at our present rate of consumption. Tidal energy is the one way in which we can make use of this kinetic energy, for the energy in the tides comes from the energy of the moon's motion. The mouth of the Rance River in France is one place where tidal energy is being used. However, since the type of site required — a large bay, a narrow inlet, and a great difference between high and low tide levels — is not abundant, it is unlikely that we will be able to tap the moon's kinetic energy to any large extent.

Energy Inheritance: Planetary Heat and Radioactivity

The other probable source of energy is that major part of our inheritance, the earth itself. The earth contains (besides coal, oil, and natural gas, the stored solar energy we mentioned earlier) only two known sources of energy: geothermal and nuclear. Geothermal energy is the heat energy stored in the earth's interior. Hot springs, geysers, and volcanoes are

---

2. *Scientific American* 263, 3 (Sept. 1990): 82. Much of the detail on contemporary alternative energy developments in this chapter is taken from articles in this special issue on "Energy for Planet Earth."

manifestations of this hot center; anyone who has observed a lava flow must be impressed with the rock-melting potential of the earth's inner heat. However, though the heat energy is there, it is very difficult to use. In most places, the very hot material is too far below the surface to be readily accessible. Only in a few thermally active areas does the hot magma come close enough to the surface to be used for energy generation. One such area is Geyserville, California, a valley where many steam vents dot the landscape. Pacific Gas and Electric Company has built a large power plant there to make use of the steam escaping from the ground. That plant produces as much energy as a very large coal or nuclear power plant.

Even in areas where steam or hot water does not come directly to the surface, the energy of the earth's interior may be used if the hot material is not too deep. There are a number of proposals for doing so, such as pumping water down until it is heated by the hot rock. Although there is considerable promise in such energy sites, their uneven distribution and their frequent association with scenic areas, as in Yellowstone, suggests that geothermal power will only be a relatively small part of the solution to the energy problem.

The other source of energy in the earth is nuclear. Einstein's famous equation $E = mc^2$ expressed the concept that matter itself is a form of energy and is theoretically capable of being transformed into useful energy. However, methods for converting one into the other — nuclear fission or nuclear fusion — are neither obvious nor simple. Unfortunately, we first experienced these forms of energy (apart from the fusion which provides the sun's energy) in weapons. Thus the best-known example of fission is the nuclear (atomic) bomb, while the hydrogen bomb provides a grim example of nuclear fusion. Obviously, we do not wish to obtain our energy from such uncontrolled explosions, and we have found it possible to build a nuclear reactor which uses the fission process to obtain usable energy. By assembling a large quantity of uranium (or plutonium) inside a reactor, a controllable chain reaction takes place which can release a considerable amount of heat energy over a long period of time. This heat can be used to generate steam, which can then drive turbines to generate electricity. As in all large thermal plants, the whole process is relatively inefficient. But since nuclear reactions release far more energy (that is, convert more mass to energy) per reaction than chemical ones do, the total amount of fuel consumed in a nuclear reactor is still quite small compared to the amount of coal burned in an ordinary coal-fired power plant. And therein lies the beauty of the nuclear reactor.

If we use uranium-235 fuel only, we have enough uranium to supply our electrical energy needs for a century or more. If, instead, we develop breeder reactors, which use plutonium fuel made from the more abundant uranium-238 isotope, we should be able to meet our needs for a few millennia.

There are serious problems associated with nuclear power plants. In part, these problems are the results of an unwarranted (but understandable) linking in the public mind of all nuclear energy with the destructive power of nuclear weapons. But apart from that fearsome association, there are other problems. These are primarily (1) the disposal of radioactive wastes; (2) the possibility of an explosion or a meltdown, resulting in dangerous release of radioactive material into the atmosphere (this came close to happening in 1980 in the Three Mile Island incident, and happened at Chernobyl in 1986, causing dozens of deaths immediately from fire and radioactivity and threatening the well-being of people in a wide area for generations to come); (3) diversion of nuclear material for use as weapons material by terrorist groups or nation-states; and (4) the relative scarcity of uranium, the most common fuel stock for nuclear reactors. These problems have been widely and hotly debated and are, as yet, unsolved. We can summarize the prospects and problems of nuclear energy in the words of Alvin Weinberg, former director of Oak Ridge National Laboratories: "We nuclear people have made a Faustian compact with society: we offer . . . an inexhaustible energy source . . . tainted with potential side effects that, if uncontrolled, could spell disaster."[3]

In some ways, the nuclear fusion process shows more promise. The fuel supply, deuterium (a hydrogen isotope), is abundant in the ocean, replacing the ordinary hydrogen atoms in one out of every 5000 gallons of seawater. Even though (in our present knowledge of fusion) the process would draw on "inherited" energy sources, the fuel is so abundant that we would not have to worry about depletion for thousands of years. Also, the problem of radioactive waste appears to be much less with fusion. However, though the hydrogen bomb has proved that the fusion process does, indeed, release enormous amounts of energy, we have not yet succeeded in slowing the reaction down to a point where it can be controlled and usable energy can be released. Much research is being done on

---

3. Alvin Weinberg, cited in Allen L. Hammond, William D. Metz, and Thomas H. Maugh III, *Energy and the Future* (Washington, DC: American Association for the Advancement of Science, 1973), p. 30.

fusion power, but each problem resolved suggests more which need to be solved. We are unlikely to have a fusion reactor which shows a net energy gain before the year 2000, or a working power plant before 2025, and perhaps not for a long time after that. So the promise of inexhaustible power from nuclear fusion is a very uncertain one.

Till quite recently, the combination of expense, worries about accidents, and slowness of deployment seemed to spell the end of nuclear energy in North America. This suspicion increased after the serious accident at Chernobyl. But as evidence of the greenhouse effect and worry over the consequences of global warming have increased, nuclear power is emerging again as the lesser of two evils. The argument has been: better a possible (though unlikely) catastrophe (as in nuclear energy) than one which is certain (as in unabated use of fossil fuels). The logic is hard to fault, and it may well be that the best medium-term solution to our energy needs is the construction of more nuclear power plants. But safety and containment designs must be better than they have been so far. And we should not be rushed into a false choice. Sometimes we are presented with the choice between coal and nuclear power as if that were the only one. But a persuasive case has been made that we can meet future energy needs through a combination of conservation and solar-income strategies. In the period between 1970 and 1990 the U.S. increased its economic output by 40 percent — but held its energy use constant. This was accomplished mainly through more efficient use, an option which we should continue to explore before we rush into building either more coal-fired power plants or more nuclear plants.

As this short summary has shown, there are a variety of possible ways of increasing our energy resources. But all of them are deficient in one way or another. Thus it seems clear that energy costs are likely to rise substantially in the future. These rising costs and dwindling energy supplies will inevitably affect the way we live and the way our industrial processes are carried out. These changes will, in turn, have great economic and political consequences. No alternative to our limited supply of fossil fuels shows much promise for enabling us to maintain the way of life we now know.

There is, however, an alternative to increasing our supply of energy. It is one which Christians, in particular, should act on, for reasons which will become clearer later in the book. That alternative is to use less energy: this we can do by conserving energy or by using it more efficiently. The energy we do use should come, where possible, from income, not from savings or inheritance resources. Historically, in our use of energy, at least, we have been prodigal; we have "wasted our substance in riotous living," and need to take better care of a rich inheritance.

The Other Energy Crisis: Impact on the Biosphere

In the past decade, air pollution has moved from a primarily cosmetic concern to a deep worry over the long-range health of the planet. So long as air pollution was seen as mainly an offense to aesthetic sensibilities, it was understood as inconsequential. We might not like the sight of smog or the smell of sulphur dioxide. But (so it was said) it is the smell of money, or of progress, and we can get used to it. So it was easy to dismiss — or in some cases even to welcome — significant amounts of pollution.

Recently, however, it has become evident that air pollution is not just an offense to the fastidious; rather, it may be a matter of planetary life or death. The poor health of the atmosphere is evident in three grim phenomena: acid rain, ozone depletion, and the "greenhouse effect."

Acid Rain

All over the northern hemisphere, where forests grow downwind from major industrial areas, trees are dying and lakes have turned ominously clear. The culprit is acid rain, sometimes transported hundreds of miles from its point of origin — usually the smokestack of a coal-burning factory or power plant. Airborne compounds of sulphur mix with tiny water droplets and produce a mild sulphuric acid which, in thousands of lakes in Canada's Northeast and New York's Adirondacks, is nevertheless of sufficient strength to wipe out not only the fish and frogs from high on the food chain, but even the microscopic plants and animals that support them: the result is a lake that is crystalline-clear — and largely dead.

Whole forests are dying as well. Germany's Black Forest has been particularly hard hit, as have forests in the Swiss Alps. Birch trees northeast of Lake Superior are leafless in mid-summer. We simply do not know enough about the subtle chemistry of soils or lakes to be absolutely certain about the causes of these deaths, a fact which has led governments to stall for more time, more certainty, before taking measures to reduce airborne pollution. But there is little real doubt that the problems are related to increased acidity from atmospheric pollution.

Ozone Depletion

For a long time we have known that a thin layer of ozone in the upper atmosphere protects living things from destructive ultraviolet radiation. And for almost twenty years we have known that some of the chemicals we release into the atmosphere might have a damaging effect on that protective ozone shield. Some chemical evidence was so clear that in 1978 the U.S. banned most fluorocarbons (used mainly as propellants in aerosol cans). But even then actual damage to the ozone layer was still only a theoretical concern, one of a number of anxieties about an indefinite future. But in the last few years the level of concern has accelerated rapidly. Excerpts from the 1989 *State of the World* report tell the story eloquently:

> When British scientists reported in 1985 that a hole in the ozone layer over Antarctica had been occurring each year since 1979, the news came as a complete surprise. . . . By the Antarctic spring of 1987, the average ozone concentration over the South Pole was down 50 percent. In isolated spots it had essentially disappeared . . . a scientific report issued in March 1988 . . . reported that the ozone layer around the globe was eroding much faster than any model had predicted. Between 1969 and 1986, the average global concentration of ozone in the stratosphere had fallen by approximately 2 percent.[4]

Though the chemistry and likely extent of the hole in the ozone are not completely understood, apparently chlorine monoxide molecules act as a sort of catalyst, breaking down ozone molecules but remaining unaffected themselves. Unique antarctic weather conditions (especially in the spring) make it the center for ozone destruction, but the circulating atmosphere makes it certain that the problem is planet-wide. In the heavily populated temperate zones of North America, Europe, and the Soviet Union, for example, average decline has been measured at about 3 percent. What will this mean? Certainly one result will be an increase in cataracts and skin cancer in human beings — especially Caucasians, whose skin is more sensitive to the sun. It will probably have an impact on plant photosynthesis; one of the most chilling facts yet discovered is that the microscopic plants of the ocean would be 30 percent less productive of oxygen if the ozone layer were decreased by 25 percent.

---

4. Cynthia Pollock Shea, "Protecting the Ozone Layer," in Lester Brown et al., *State of the World 1989* (New York: W. W. Norton, 1988), p. 86.

The chlorine-based compounds in aerosols, foam insulation, solvents, and refrigeration are the chief culprits, and reducing or eliminating these sources of the problem, though possible, will not be easy. A depressing fact about the problem is that it takes several years for the chemicals to migrate to the upper atmosphere, and that once there they might remain active for a century. So even if we immediately stopped using all the offending chemicals, the problem would worsen — and persist — for many decades.

The response of the world community to the crisis has been unusually swift. In September 1987, twenty-four countries signed the Montreal Accord, a historic agreement to reduce the use of chlorofluorocarbons. (The number of signatories to the accord continues to grow.) But encouraging as this international response is, it will only slow the worsening of the problem, not solve it.

(An ironic and confusing feature of ozone is that at the surface it is a noxious gas that is destructive to plants, an irritant in smog, and likely to increase as ultraviolet radiation increases, so the less we have in the stratosphere the more we will get at the surface — and both facts are damaging.)

The Greenhouse Effect: Global Warming

Enough has been said and written in recent years about global warming and the greenhouse effect that we will not go into great detail here. Unlike the destruction of the ozone layer, which is incontrovertibly connected to the presence in the upper atmosphere of man-made chemicals, global warming is mainly an acceleration of "natural" processes, affecting naturally occurring components of the atmosphere. This fact, in addition to normal fluctuation in climate patterns, has, until quite recently, made it hard to say beyond doubt that human activity is affecting climate in significant ways. Throughout the eighties, some governments used this difficulty as an excuse to do nothing (an approach perfected somewhat earlier in disputes over acid rain). But now, in the nineties, there is widespread public, political, and scientific acceptance of the present reality and future acceleration of a significant planetary warming trend.

The relevant facts are these:

- Several naturally occurring atmospheric gases (mainly CO_2, methane, and nitrous oxide), as well as the man-made chlorofluorocarbons, act in such a way that they allow sunlight to penetrate, but inhibit re-radiated heat. The result is a warming like that in a greenhouse or a closed car on a sunny day. This effect is mainly beneficial and is one of several which keep the earth's surface so friendly to life.

- The percentage of these gases in the atmosphere has increased measurably in the last century or so. CO_2 is up 25 percent from pre-industrial levels, nitrous oxide 19 percent, and methane 100 percent.[5] In sheer volume the increase in CO_2 is enormous: in 1988, 5.66 billion tons of carbon were consumed, and for each ton 3.7 tons of carbon dioxide entered the atmosphere.

- There have been significant signs already of global warming, but they are minor compared to the rapid increase in temperature expected to take place in the next century: estimates range from 5 to 10 degrees.

Why is such a rise in temperature cause for concern? There may well be some local benefits — greater warmth in the north, more rain in some areas, less in others. But because we are tinkering with something so vast as the atmosphere of a whole planet, the more likely consequence is that we will do far more damage than good. When (and if) such fluctuations have taken place in the past they have done so over great periods of time. This change will be sudden. Rising sea levels (from melting glaciers), more violent storms, and catastrophic changes in precipitation patterns are likely to occur. Even more serious, in the long run, is the fact that plants and animals which have had long periods of time to adjust to their environment will be forced to shift their range very rapidly — hence adding to the spectre of species extinction, for many will simply not be able to make the change.

Governments are finally responding with programs — usually inadequate — for reducing carbon emissions. A more creative approach is to plant large tracts of forest to offset those being cut for fuel or lumber. But none of these is likely to alter the fact that the earth is changing because of what the human world has done to the atmosphere.

---

5. Christopher Flavin, "Slowing Global Warming," in Lester Brown et al., *State of the World 1990* (New York: W. W. Norton, 1990), p. 17.

MINERAL RESOURCES

As the preceding discussion of energy has made clear, we are really approaching two crises: the first is one of supply; the second is one of pollution — unwanted side-effects from our use of energy. Ultimately, though, pollution — evident in such effects as acid rain and greenhouse effect — is the more serious problem. For as long as the sun lasts, our supply of energy is inexhaustible.

When we turn to mineral resources, the matter is different: much more depends upon our "inheritance." Apart from a few large meteorites, there is no mineral income similar to the energy income from the sun. There are, to be sure, slow processes of concentration taking place in seabed rifts. But these processes take place over eons. We must, for practical purposes, consider the supply of minerals unchanging — they are an inheritance, not income. What this indicates, of course, is that one of the ways in which we should use our energy income is to set up means for ensuring that our mineral inheritance will be recycled and not wasted. Unfortunately, we have — with the exception of a few rare and very precious metals like gold — done very little to conserve and recycle mineral resources. But the need for doing so should be obvious from a brief discussion of the mineral wealth of the earth.

Traditionally, we have extracted most minerals from the land, but recently it has become apparent that there are substantial resources on the seabed as well. In this section we will briefly examine our mineral resources on both land and sea, review the known reserves and patterns of our usage, and then consider some of the effects of that usage on the earth's energy supply and on the earth's life. Finally, we will consider a neglected but essential approach to our need for all non-energy resources: recycling.

Land Resources

From early in history, people have extracted minerals and metals from the earth to make tools and implements. This early mining was mainly for gold, iron, silver, and copper, and it took place near the surface. As the human race gained technical knowledge, the mining and use of minerals became increasingly sophisticated. In today's industrialized world, mining is a major industry, and mines descend ever deeper into the earth. Furthermore, increasingly sophisticated materials and alloys are being developed from the various minerals we extract.

However, most minerals do not occur abundantly, and mining is economical only where there is a substantial concentration of a specific material. With continued use, the high quality reserves are disappearing. Thus we must continually improve our mining practices as we search for new deposits. This is particularly true in North America: the United States has only 6 percent of the world's population but consumes approximately one-third of all the world's resources. If we continue our exponential increase in the use of the world's resources, or if the remainder of the world even begins to approach our level of resource consumption, we are likely to face shortages of minerals very soon.

How much is yet available for our use? The answer to this difficult question depends on many factors. As reserves of a particular material become depleted, the price tends to rise. This rise in price naturally slows down the rate at which the material is used. Furthermore, the increase in price encourages recycling or the development of substitute resources.

The best estimates of resource depletion are obtained by analyzing current usage patterns, making reasonable predictions about future usage and discovery of resources, and plotting resource depletion curves like those shown earlier in this chapter for petroleum and natural gas (see Figures 4.2 and 4.3). Because depletion curves approach zero as time goes on (but reach it only in infinity), it is impossible to say that one ever really "runs out" of a resource. Use simply decreases as availability decreases, the difficulty of recovery increases, and prices rise. A useful way of measuring the effective size of the reserves is to calculate the estimated number of years until 80 percent depletion occurs. If we make the modest assumption that usage will increase at 2.5 percent per year, we find that the majority of our known mineral resources will reach that 80 percent depletion level in the next half century. Even if we assume a fivefold increase in the amount of reserves discovered, we will extend our depletion times at most only to the year 2100.

Thus our situation with mineral resources appears little better than with fossil fuel resources. In other words, the "energy crisis" of today may be replaced by a "minerals crisis" during the next century. But the problem with mineral resources is actually much more severe than with energy resources, for minerals are part of an irreplaceable inheritance. We have no mineral income.

Seabed Resources

Because of the newly discovered wealth of the seabed, this picture of future mineral reserves is not as bleak as it might appear. We have known for some time that there are substantial amounts of minerals in ocean water, but they are extremely diffuse and in most cases it is not economically feasible to recover them. Recently we have learned, however, that the spreading of plates in the earth's crust allows mineral-rich waters to well up from below the ocean floor and to create layers of minerals near continental rifts. Scattered about the ocean floor in a number of different places are manganese nodules, which contain not only manganese, but also numerous other important metals such as copper, iron, aluminum, nickel, and magnesium. These nodules and seafloor deposits represent a most important resource to us. Table 1 indicates that if we consider these seafloor resources, the depletion time for many key minerals should be expressed not in centuries, but in millennia.

From these figures one might get the impression that the problem of mineral resources is solved; however, several words of caution must be inserted here. First, the chart shows depletion times which are calculated strictly by taking present consumption levels and extending them at the same rate. But our use of most minerals, as we saw earlier, is increasing exponentially. Figured on the basis of that increase, the chart would yield appreciably shorter depletion times. Second, there are many unsolved problems involved in mining the deep seabed, and these must be overcome. Third, the environmental effects of deep seabed mining are unknown at this point and deserve very careful study. Present proposals involve dredging the ocean bottom with large suction dredges. This would involve sucking up many ocean plants and animals, as well as sediment, and redistributing them in the process, unless extreme care were exercised. This disruption would have major environmental consequences. A fourth unknown at this point is the international legal situation with respect to mining. The law of the seas has historically assumed the ocean to be a common heritage of all humankind. There has been considerable controversy during the past several years regarding deep seabed mining and its relationship to the law of the seas. Some people believe that any nation with the technological ability should be free to begin mining the ocean bottom. But many others believe that mining should be carried out by international consortia, or that, at the very least, the profits of mining

Table 1 Reserves of Metals in Manganese Nodules of the Pacific Ocean

Element	Amount of elements in nodules (billions of tons)[a]	Reserves in nodules at consumption rate of 1960[b] (years)	U.S. rate of consumption of element in 1960[c] (millions of tons per year)	Ratio of (world consumption) (U.S. consumption)
Magnesium	25	600,000	0.04	2.5
Aluminum	43	20,000	2.0	2.0
Titanium	9.9	2,000,000	.30	4.0
Vanadium	0.8	400,000	.002	4.0
Manganese	358	400,000	.8	8.0
Iron	207	2,000	100.	2.5
Cobalt	5.2	200,000	.008	2.0
Nickel	14.7	150,000	.11	3.0
Copper	7.9	6,000	1.2	4.0
Zinc	.7	1,000	.9	3.5
Gallium	.015	150,000	.001	—
Zirconium	.93	+100,000	.0013	—
Molybdenum	.77	30,000	0.25	2.0
Silver	.001	100	.006	—
Lead	1.3	1,000	1.0	2.5

a. All tonnages in metric units.
b. Amount available in the nodules divided by the consumption rate.
c. Calculated as the element in metric tons.
(From J. L. Mero, "Potential Economic Value of Ocean-Floor Manganese Nodule Deposits," in *Ferromanganese Deposits on the Ocean Floor,* ed. D. R. Horn, IDOE, National Science Foundation, Washington, DC, 1972: 191-203.)

should be distributed to all nations equitably. After more than a decade of wrangling, these legal problems appear no closer to a solution.

In summary, although the ocean appears to offer substantial mineral resources for our use, it is unclear at this point what the economic, political, and environmental effects of deep seabed mining will be. Some who were originally optimistic about deep sea mining are now pessimistic. It is too early to say that we have solved the problem of mineral resources.

Resource Recovery

Even if seabed mining should be as good as its most enthusiastic and optimistic supporters claim, we still would not have solved the basic issues; we would simply have extended the depletion times. But as we have mentioned, the earth's minerals are an inheritance for humankind and for the planet. Even if we had enough of them to supply all our needs for one or two thousand years, our current usage levels and patterns would be difficult to justify. We do not know what the future will bring, but we must take into consideration the needs of future generations, as well as the impact of materials recovery (such as strip mining or open pit mining) upon the planet these generations will inherit. For this reason, we should use such inherited resources conservingly. In fact, the ideal situation would be to recycle all materials for which we have no income. Such recycling would allow the mineral resources in the earth or on the ocean floor to continually circulate from one use to another. It is ironic that in today's world we transport iron ores from Europe to Japan for smelting, transport the steel from Japan to the United States for manufacture, and then throw the product into a landfill after we finish with it! Some of our landfills have an iron content as high as some natural iron ore deposits currently being mined. Yet governments persist in subsidizing mining operations and (till recently) have been reluctant to support recycling efforts. In addition, regulated freight rates are often preferentially weighted toward virgin materials rather than recycled materials. As a result, it is economically more advantageous to bury our steel cans in a landfill than to recycle them.

Clearly this practice must be reversed. There are encouraging signs in industry: many companies are now making major efforts to recycle as many of their waste products as possible, and the burgeoning scrap iron and steel industry today insures that more portions of automobiles are recycled than are put into landfills. In recent years more and more states and municipalities have passed or are considering passing legislation making recycling of many materials mandatory. The year 1989 appeared to mark a turning point in people's attitudes towards recycling, with a wave of new recycling programs building across North America.

At present, the biggest offender is still the average homeowner. Thus it becomes absolutely essential for all of us to recycle as many materials as possible. Glass bottles, steel and aluminum cans, and even yard wastes or other organic wastes should be separated and recycled. Such work takes

*"As far as we can make out, there's a small, heavy core,
and then it's all polystyrene foam."*

little time or effort on the part of the individual homeowner, but it can accomplish a great deal of good. In future years our trash may be our best resource.

Three things are essential if recycling and full-scale resource recovery are to take place. First, there must be a change of public attitude. Why, for example, should waste baskets be called "waste" baskets? Should they not be called something like "resource" baskets? To call what one puts into a basket "waste" means that it is worthless. But to call it a "resource" is to think of its possible uses. Such subtle changes in language and attitude are essential if we are to develop a recycling attitude and overcome the biases our culture has built into us.

A second essential is the development of markets for recycled products. It does no good to recycle newsprint, beverage cans, and other materials if there is no market to buy them and they end up being dumped in a landfill in their separated state. The scrap iron and steel industry has served as a model for recyclers, and we must expand that industry — and its offspring — as rapidly as possible. Once again, this will require a change in basic attitudes and practices. If a purchasing agent refuses to buy recycled paper because it jams in photocopiers, the solution is to have that same purchasing agent require that all photocopiers purchased be able to use recycled paper! A third essential for development of a recycling economy is to make recycling as convenient as possible for the typical homeowner. In our current system, if people want to recycle their goods they must separate them, store them in boxes in the garage, and periodically bring them to a recycling center. But if they want to throw the materials into a landfill, they only have to place them on the curb (or in the alley) and a truck will come by and take them out of sight. Once again, a basic change in attitude is necessary. We should simply reverse the process: we should have curbside pickup of recyclable material and require that people take their own nonrecyclable garbage to a "garbage center." Such a policy would bring about a change in behavior — very quickly.

In recent years a new aspect of resource recovery has emerged. Many communities are turning to incineration as a means of recovering not material resources but energy from our wastes. Energy cannot be recovered, of course, from the noncombustible fraction — the glasses, metals, and other materials — but only from the combustible part. And since most combustible materials originally obtained their intrinsic energy from the sun, incineration becomes yet another way of using solar energy. Moreover, since the noncombustible portion of our waste lends itself to source-separation and recycling, the combination of a good curbside recycling program with a waste-to-energy plant is an attractive option for many municipalities.

Environmental Effects

An important part of our analysis of mineral resources and their use must be our concern with the impact on the health and integrity of creation. Pollution is usually a misplaced, poorly used resource. If we could re-use what we are used to throwing "away" (one of the prime laws of ecology is that there *is* no "away"), seeking to minimize environmental effects, we would go far toward solving present or future resource shortages, and at the same time we would minimize pollution.

This has become increasingly apparent during the last two decades. Perhaps the single most severe environmental problem facing industrialized nations is the toxic waste leaching out of old landfills, polluting our groundwater, and eventually draining into surface waters. Through its "Superfund" legislation the U.S. is spending billions of dollars to clean up these old landfills, which now serve only as sources of toxic contaminants of our environment. Every region in the industrialized world faces similar problems. We not only need to ensure proper handling and disposal of waste materials; we also need to atone for the sins of the past by requiring that all old dumps or landfills be cleaned up or contained. In many communities, the cost of such a cleanup is heavy, and companies and municipalities must bear a staggering burden as they seek to rectify the degradations of creation brought about through our waste.

Thus a strong argument for the ideal of recycling *everything* is environmental. In the largest sense, it is a matter of earthkeeping: wise stewardship of creation. But the Christian has an even stronger argument. By keeping materials out of landfills we are restoring to them a place and a purpose: consciously or not, we are honoring them and the Creator by saving them, giving them a new life. Language of salvation and new birth is not entirely inappropriate here — even for minerals. By re-using things, by finding new uses for them, we keep offering God's good gifts back to him in thankfulness and service. And by giving some parts of creation a new life, we are preserving other parts of creation from contamination.

In some ways, we in the industrialized nations are barely emerging from barbarism in our handling of the "waste" stream. A useful comparison is between the development of waste handling and the development of sewage treatment plants. A bare hundred years ago, most of our sewage flowed directly from homes and factories into the sewers, and thence directly into the rivers, lakes, or the ocean. Most (but not all!) communities in North America have decided that this is intolerable and have built treatment plants to process the sewage before it reaches the river. With time, these plants have become increasingly sophisticated, and today it is common to provide not only secondary treatment of sewage, but even tertiary treatment in order to remove all contaminants, both biological and chemical.

In the same way, society's initial handling of solid waste was simply to dump it on the ground, just as we once dumped sewage directly into the rivers. These "dumps" were common in every part of the land, near every municipality, large or small. As time went on, these dumps were required to have a daily cover of earth to prevent rat and fly propagation. Then we began, euphemistically, to call them "sanitary landfills." Only recently has our generation begun to learn that we must process our waste, exactly as we learned a century ago that we must process our sewage. Thus today there is a strong thrust toward waste treatment in many forms.

The best approach is a comprehensive one, encompassing the three "Rs," plus incineration and (as a last resort) putting in a well-designed landfill. The first "R" is to *reduce* our use of material resources as much as possible, perhaps through eliminating excessive packaging, the amount of materials wasted in products, and other ways. The next "R" is *re-use* of materials, through using returnable containers, or turning styrofoam cups into plant starters and egg cartons into children's art projects! The third "R" refers to *recycling,* the process of keeping used materials separate and returning them to manufacturers for remanufacture into other products. Recycling also includes composting of yard clippings, leaves, and other organic materials and returning them directly to the soil as an enriching medium.

The next step in a comprehensive system of dealing with waste involves incineration with extraction of energy. There is some legitimate concern about the contaminants issuing from the stacks of incinerators, or ending up in the ash residue. But these contaminants must be compared with the environmental damage caused by similar effluents in the air and ash created by the coal-burning power plants which the incinerators supplement or replace. Furthermore, if comprehensive recycling does take place, very few toxic materials will find their way into the incinerators.

Clearly, incineration without energy recovery is not environmentally desirable, but incineration *with* energy recovery may often be the most stewardly way of treating wastes.

The last resort for disposing of our waste remains the landfill, whether we use it for nonrecyclable, noncombustible waste or for the ash from incinerators. Landfills will be needed for some time to come, but our goal must be to reduce their use and their contents as much as possible. Furthermore, through proper engineering, and through "design for recycling" of new products, we can certainly reduce the amount of materials which must still be put into a landfill.

The Role of Energy

As we pointed out earlier in this chapter, energy plays a crucial role in our handling of materials. Ultimately we can't separate our stewardship of energy from our stewardship of materials. All our use of mineral resources depends upon the availability of sources of energy: that flow of energy is essential if we are to insure the flow of materials. However, materials are recyclable and energy is not.

Fortunately, God has provided his creation with a continuous energy income. So if we are to live according to the pattern set forth in creation, in the future our energy must come primarily from the sun, with a supplement from our "inheritance" of nuclear and geothermal energy. This energy should be used, among other things, to maintain the flow of mineral resources from one capital stock to another, in a continual closed-loop recycling pattern, similar to the flow of materials and energy in the whole ecosphere. Because we are only beginning to think of our use of energy and materials on a worldwide scale, we have not yet established such a pattern for recycling. But we need to model it after the way in which creation itself cycles matter and energy through its intricate web of life. We need then to bring our industry and our individual way of life into conformity with that pattern of "living within income" which is established by the economy of creation.

What is needed in handling material resources is not only research in developing new resources and new methods of using, re-using, and treating those resources, but also — and especially — a transformation of our attitudes. Fundamentally, we need to think of resources — in their origin, their use, and their destiny — as *creatures,* not just processed raw material. We must leave behind the attitude that proper use of creation simply involves digging materials out of a hole in the ground, using them, and throwing them back into a hole. Above all, in our use of both energy and minerals, we need to recover our responsibility as *stewards* of creation and all its resources.

❧   ❧   ❧

So that, briefly, is the state of the planet. These first four chapters have given us some understanding of the wealth in the minerals, fuels, animals, and soil of this rich earth. They have also sketched how we are using — and misusing — that wealth.

But we opened this book by recalling the degradations of creation: not only its wealth but its peril. We *do* live in the midst of creation's incomparable treasure, and it is to our shame that we are turned so easily from wonder to calculation. Yet in a sense this is the human dilemma: to be suspended between wonder and wealth-making. For it is in turning the wonder of creation into *our* wealth (personally and collectively) that we have degraded it. Yet paradoxically, our appreciation of its beauty and complexity has advanced along with our degradation of it, a situation which lends both urgency and hope to our present dilemma.

Thus far we have been looking primarily at the *earth* and what we have done with it. In the chapters that follow, we will be shifting our attention to the human *world* of attitudes which have, across history, both degraded the earth and elevated it into an object of wonder and concern. Let us look again, in summary, at the earth which we keep so imperfectly in the worlds we make of it.

First, there is the nonliving stuff of the earth: that planetary given of rock, water, and air around a core of hidden heat. And though we call that mineral sphere nonliving, it changes with a dynamism that suggests life: tides pull its oceans daily around a basalt crust; and that crust itself, we are learning, shifts and flows in a vast, slow cycle that brings metal-rich rock from the molten core, shifts and lifts it across seafloor and continent, and, after unimaginable time, conveys it down again to the planet's heart. We have quite literally only scratched the surface of that mineral sphere, and of its total resources we know very little.

A second kind of wealth is the steady flood of energy through which our planet moves. We circle a star that every second transforms more than four million tons of its mass into energy and beams it into space. Turning in this torrent of radiance, the earth receives only about a billionth of the total, yet so great is that earth-impinging energy that, if it could be harnessed, each person on earth would have for his or her personal use over 3000 times the energy consumption of each citizen of the United States; the total solar energy striking the earth in only one day is greater than the energy contained in all the oil, coal, and natural gas ever stored in the earth. That great wealth of energy moves the currents of the sea and brings a vast (and often violent) movement to the atmosphere. As the surface of the world turns steadily from its shadow into light, the unevenly heated air circles and flows in breezes, gusts, and hurricanes; each day the sun's energy in the atmosphere causes thousands of thunderstorms, each with the energy of many atomic bombs. More importantly, each day the sun's heat evaporates and condenses billions of gallons of water into clouds, which rain down on the land and flow from it in a great wealth of waterfalls and rivers. And, most important of all, the daily turning of the planet into the sun's light drives the silent chemistry of photosynthesis. Thus the sun is the physical source of our life.

Then there is the third great kind of treasure on our planet: that fecund wealth of living cells, ordered in patterns that we call cedar, spider, trillium . . . and human being. Catching the sunlight in chemical nets, trillions of organisms breathe, eat, multiply, and die; the very breathability of the atmosphere is a result of countless sun-catching lives; so also is that stored intensity of sunlight in oil and coal. The soil in forests and fields owes its fertility to living things, as we owe the food which sustains us to that life-supported, and life-supporting, fertility. What that intricate interdependence recalls for us, lest we forget, is that we too are organisms. Not only do we depend on this tissue of life, but we are also part of it — not simply because we affect other life, and life affects us, but because we *share* its life. Such thoroughness of participation in the natural world is disturbing: how can such coinherence of nature and ourselves be understood as *wealth?* But it is disturbing only if we are chauvinistic about our distinctness from nature.

If we understand that our bodies are inseparable from the rest of organic life, and that we can only say, with the Psalmist, "I am fearfully and wonderfully made," if we include the fox, the paramecium, and the oak tree, then we will have learned an essential lesson about how to live on the planet. We will have understood that the intricate diversity of organic life is our own diversity. Every time we eat or breathe we participate in that created network of sun-catching life which is fertile, tough, resilient, and which its Creator — and ours — calls good.

And yet, we are more than that life. To the mineral wealth of the planet, the torrent of energy which bathes it, and the rich diversity of organic life in which our bodies are enmeshed, we must add the fourth and (apart from our knowledge of God) greatest kind of wealth we have: that is, our own ability to stand apart (in our consciousness) from the planet — to know it, to name it, to use it, and to see it whole. Nothing better symbolizes that ability than the photographs of the earth from space. They not only reveal the earth as a rich and vulnerable planet, but also demonstrate our ability to use the planet's wealth to transcend it. Ultimately, then, it is that human capability to *know*, and to create new things and methods with that knowledge, which is our greatest resource. Without it, none of the planet's other wealth — its mineral capital, its stored and incoming solar energy, its blooming and beautiful life — is wealth at all. The greatest resource is humanity itself, and the capabilities to know, structure, create, and accomplish which seem to distinguish humanity from the rest of creation.

As this quick summary of our resources suggests, there is cause for joy in being human at this difficult time — joy at simply being present, alive, responsive, and responsible in this diverse kingdom of a planet. There is cause for joy, too, in the task which was given to the unfallen Adam, but which is no less ours: to *cultivate* the fertile earth — somehow to use and serve its great wealth.

And yet there is also cause for despair. For though the planet's wealth is undeniably great, its greatest wealth — the human capacity to know, change, and manipulate — is also the planet's greatest danger. For all of the degradations referred to in the earlier chapters — the forced urbanization, the wasting of energy, the loss of our topsoil, the human starvation, the decline of wildlife — are the consequences of that great gift of intelligence and creativity. Clearly it is that wealth of manipulative and reflective ability which enables us to use the rest of the world's wealth. But clearly, too, that manipulative ability is monstrous — even suicidal — unless it is guided and controlled. For, as the problems of the planet show, the values that guide our humanity and that inform our structures of use and exploitation need redeeming. And such redemption comes not from the earth, for all its wealth and beauty; it comes from beyond it, from its Creator.

If, then, we are to choose among different ways of using the planet's wealth, we must, as Christians, consider more broadly the consequences of that salvation which we have understood too often as a private and otherworldly gift. For we are saved not only *from* the consequences of our sinning, but *for* that continued task of stewardship once given to Adam. Unless our understanding of redemption extends to our stewardship of the earth, it is incomplete; and without redeemed persons, humanity will only destroy the rich and beautiful planet it inhabits.

It is not easy for us to think of the relevance of Christianity for our treatment of creation — in part because we see it only as "resources" and are blind to it as creation. There are clear historical and structural reasons for that blindness which we will consider in the next section; in the section following it, we will explore the biblical bases of a concern for the planet and its wealth. But a brief reflection on a familiar biblical story, from a perspective provided by the foregoing material, may serve as a good intro- duction to a consideration of our *attitudes* toward the earth. To see the relevance of the story we must digress briefly.

It could be objected that a concern for the whole planet's life, an attempt to apply human intelligence and creativity to the development of the whole earth and its resources, is a task for God, not humankind. The last edition of that counter-cultural bible, *The Whole Earth Catalogue,* had as a preface the declaration, "We *are* as gods and might as well get good at it." Such a confident declaration of our powers sounds blasphemous. It does express the same astonishment at human capacity which the Psalmist voices in Psalm 8: "You made him [humanity] a little lower than God." But those words are addressed to the Creator. When we marvel at our creative powers outside of our dependence on God, the result is dangerous indeed. The consequences, for both the human world and the created earth, of the full use of the unredeemed manipulative powers of humanity are likely to be disastrous. This potential tragedy has been seen clearly by many thoughtful Christians. C. S. Lewis, for example, in a novel that explores the problems of an unregenerate human power over the earth, writes of a time and situation much like our own, when

> dreams of the far future destiny of man were dragging up from its shallow and unquiet grave the old dream of Man as God. . . . There was now at last a real chance for fallen Man to shake off that limitation of his powers which mercy has imposed upon him as a protection from the full results of [his] fall. If this succeeded . . . Nature, all over the globe of Tellus, would become [his] slave; and of that dominion no end, before the end of time itself, could be certainly foreseen.[6]

---

6. C. S. Lewis, *That Hideous Strength* (New York: Macmillan, 1947), pp. 234-35.

The story of Babel is one record of the consequences of that "old dream of Man as God." Impelled by their efficiency, the cleverness of their hands, and their power over nature, people said, "Come, let us build ourselves a city, and a tower with its top in the heavens, and let us make a name for ourselves, lest we be scattered abroad upon the face of the whole earth" (Gen. 11:4). Certainly there are today many equally clever schemes for applying ever greater skill and efficiency to our power over both humanity and nature. Indeed, any awareness of the need — and ability — to master the earth and its wealth could easily become a Babel-like hubris.

God's response to this example of human creativity and endeavor has seemed to many to make of God a sort of anti-Promethean killjoy: ". . . this is only the beginning of what they will do; and nothing that they propose to do will now be impossible for them. Come, let us go down, and there confuse their language, that they may not understand one another's speech" (Gen. 11:6-7). But that response should not be taken as divine timidity, nor should it discourage Christians from exercising godlike powers in their care and use of the planet's wealth. For it is not the divine intention to limit human endeavor or accomplishment. The Psalmist does speak of humanity as "a little lower than God," and a frequently repeated New Testament teaching is that redeemed men and women are to be "fellow heirs" with Christ — Christ, the sustaining *logos* of the world, in whom all things consist. The idea that humanity — redeemed humanity — is to share in that "creatorly" task is clearly the implication of Romans 8:19, in which Paul writes that "the creation waits with eager longing for the revealing of the sons of God."

There are, as we shall see in the chapters that follow, great longings in men and women to restore the foundations of Babel, to make themselves masters on their own terms. Such unredeemed mastery would indeed be the occasion for despair. But there are also, as we shall see in subsequent chapters, good reasons for Christians to care for creation as Christ cares for it. And the consequence of that kind of mastery is one at which the very trees will clap their hands, and the mountains and hills shout with joy.

SECTION II

THE EARTH KEEPERS

Part A

❧   ❧

Historical Roots

W<small>E BEGAN THIS INTRODUCTION TO EARTHKEEPING BY RECALLING</small>
seven aspects of creation, and the way men and women have both
enhanced and degraded it. We have examined six of those aspects of
creation in the previous chapters: earth, air, water, fire, plants, and animals.
These are aspects of the physical, measurable world: the interactions of
minerals, energy, and biological life. But we have yet to consider humanity
itself. For ultimately, of course, "environmental" problems are human
problems. They have their origin in the rationality, creativity, and will
which enable us to *use* — and misuse — the earth.

Thus, increasingly in the last decade, above the cacophony of our
misuse of creation there have come many calls for people to change not
simply their behavior, but their attitudes and beliefs. These calls for change
have been directed not only toward the *actions* of people and nations; we
have also been urged to consider the springs of those actions. For without
a change in those impelling sources of action, the action itself is not likely
to change significantly (except through coercion, or the threat of it — and
that implies a change in attitude on the part of the coercers).

The purpose of this next section is to determine what, in fact, those
springs of action are. What views of creation have shaped our use of it in
the Western world? In the chapters which follow we are going to consider
in some detail the many ideas and beliefs which, apart from the Christian
gospel, have shaped the mind of Western people, and which the gospel is
intended to clarify or transform. That transformation has seldom been
complete. What many have pointed to as the destructive influence of

111

Christianity is, usually, the destructive influence of pre-Christian ideas, imperfectly transformed by the gospel, and too often mistaken for the gospel itself. So in Section III we will turn to an exposition of what, indeed, that Christian teaching concerning the human use of creation is. But let us look first at the history of our ideas about "nature."

CHAPTER 5

⁂   ⁂

The Contribution of the Greeks

Plato thought nature but a spume that plays
Upon a ghostly paradigm of things . . .

— William Butler Yeats,
"Among School Children"

THE CHRISTIAN GOSPEL WAS FIRST PROCLAIMED IN A WORLD PERMEATED with Greek thought. The earliest, and at that time the most influential, Christian thinkers explained the gospel in terms of Greek philosophy. Thus it is to Greek ideas that we must first turn in determining the main influences on those "springs of action" which have motivated Christendom's treatment of nature. And it is worth pointing out at the outset that one of the most enduring — and unfortunate — Greek influences on Christian thought was the substitution of the concept of "nature" for the concept of "creation." It is the Latin-based word for that Greek concept — the word *nature* — that we will normally use throughout this chapter. But we are still speaking of creation.

Four more or less distinct views of nature emerged in that Hellenistic thought which, for many centuries, shaped the worldview of the peoples around the Mediterranean. We will refer to them henceforth as the Platonic, Aristotelian, Epicurean, and Stoic views of nature, with the warning, however, that this brief summary contains only the dominant themes,

113

without much regard for the refinements and niceties of individual thinkers. However, since it is those dominant themes which have exerted the greatest influence on views of nature, these summaries should not be misleading.

PLATONIC VIEWS OF NATURE

For the Platonists, the most obvious and important characteristic of nature is that it keeps changing. Things come into being and pass away, are subject to the everlasting cycles of birth, growth, decay, and death, move here and there, and constantly change their character. The world of nature is the world revealed through the senses, and what the senses sense is a world full of motion and change, a world in which nothing is stable and nothing is eternal.

This ceaseless mutability of the sensible world is abhorrent to the Platonists. For them, change is a mark of imperfection; only that which is immutable, eternal, and wholly orderly is perfect. Thus, insofar as the world of nature is a changing world, it is an imperfect one.

But nature is not entirely imperfect. It does display *some* order and stability. Even the constant change, in itself a sign of imperfection, can be orderly and harmonious. Since some perfection may be found, even in this imperfect world, nature is both orderly and disorderly — not wholly perfect, but not wholly imperfect either.

To explain these contradictions, the Platonists maintain that the orderliness in nature results from its participation in the Forms of a transcendent, perfect world, one not apprehended by the senses at all. These eternal Forms are unchanging and perfect, and they are the source of whatever beauty or stability nature has. This world is perceived only by the intellect and it is the only legitimate focus of a good person's attention, for it alone is the source of truth, beauty, and perfection.

Thus the Platonic world is dualistic, split between a changeable, transient world of matter known by the senses and an eternal world of ideal Forms known only by the intellect. We, however, belong to neither world — or more precisely, to both. The soul, which is the seat of the intellect, is forced to reside in a body, and the body is a part of mutable nature. The soul is therefore distracted from its true end: communion with that transnatural world of the Forms. As a venerable Greek pun puts it, the body, *soma*, is the tomb, *sema*, of the soul.

In this Platonic doctrine of the body as the tomb of the soul we find the source of an influential element in the Western treatment of nature. It is sometimes referred to as *contemptus mundi,* contempt for the world, and it issues in an attitude of flight from any dealings with the world which are not absolutely necessary for bodily survival. The body, and all of nature, is seen as something foreign to the essence of a person, a distraction from the soul's proper task. Nature itself is but a pale shadow of what is truly good and beautiful; it is not worthy of our serious involvement. This is one important consequence of the Platonic view of nature. And it is clearly a negative one, so far as any positive human treatment of the earth is concerned.

There is, however, a more positive and constructive Platonic view of the proper relationship between persons and nature, and it stands in some tension with the otherworldly Platonism we have just outlined. For some of the Platonists — including Plato himself — believed that humans have a task with regard to nature. That task is, so far as possible, to bring order into nature itself.

The first place where we are to bring order is the body; the pleasures, pains, drives, and yearnings that distract it from its true task are to be brought under control. But the duty to bring order extends beyond the self. All good human actions consist of bringing form to the formless: the woodcarver imposes order on wood; the shoemaker imposes order on leather; the politician imposes order on the state. It is thus that the artisan, the craftsman, and the politician fulfill their duty as embodied souls.

To impose order is to follow the example of the master craftsman who first formed nature, and who maintains its order. In the creation story in Plato's *Timaeus,* that master craftsman encounters a nature in complete disarray, and, because of his goodness, imposes order upon it. Said Plato:

> He was good; and in the good no jealousy in any matter can ever arise. So, being without jealousy, he desired that all things should come as near as possible to being like himself. . . . Desiring, then, that all things should be good and, so far as might be, nothing imperfect, the god took over all that is visible — not at rest, but in discordant and un-ordered motion — and brought it from disorder into order, since he judged that order was in every way the better.[1]

---

1. Plato, *Timaeus* (29E-30A), trans. F. M. Cornford, in *Plato's Cosmology* (Atlantic Highlands, NJ: Humanities Press, and London: Routledge & Kegan Paul, 1952).

But it is clear that no one, not even the god, can completely overcome the recalcitrance of the material with which he has to work; nature is inherently disorderly, and neither god nor humanity can bring order past what is allowed by the material itself. Nature can never be perfect. Three aspects of significance for subsequent views of nature should be noted about this Platonic view of humans as orderers.

First, it reverses the emphasis on flight from the world which is an inevitable consequence of seeing nature as an impediment to the soul's attainment of the ideal. Indeed, were it not for this ordering element in Platonic thought, we would expect the Hellenistic heritage to be solely one of inward-looking mysticism, rather than the glorious collection of shaped marble, metrical language, and symmetrical architecture that has been preserved.

Second, though such artifacts clearly show that there is in Platonism an impetus for working with nature, it is clear that the order is imposed on nature. It is not that the ordering craftsman, through his work, somehow allows nature to reveal itself. To the Platonist, a revealed nature is simply chaos. All the order comes from the intellect, which alone is capable of perceiving the transcendent and thoroughly nonnatural Forms. Thus the thinking behind the humans-as-orderers Platonism is not fundamentally different from that other kind of Platonism which can easily result in "contempt for the world."

Third, it is clear (even in the brief passage from the *Timaeus* quoted above) that the action of the ordering craftsman is admirable not because of any benefit which appears in nature itself, for it is order which is good, not nature.

One more feature of Platonism deserves mention. There is no room in it for the idea that nature is divine. Though the Olympian religion has a pantheon of gods who are clearly present in nature, Platonists take great care to disassociate themselves from that religion, at least in any form which would confuse God and nature. It was not the presence of the gods in the natural world which was the great Greek influence on Christian thought, but the separation of the *good* from the natural world. One cannot look to Platonic sources for nourishment of any kind of reverence for nature.

In reviewing these two aspects of Platonism, we see that though the idea of humans as craftsmen does encourage an involvement with nature, there is little concern for nature itself. The source of goodness and order is always beyond nature, which remains a chaos in need of shaping.

Thus, though the otherworldly concern of Platonism does not explicitly encourage ruthlessness toward nature, there is no room in it for anything in nature which would discourage such ruthlessness, no equivalent, for example, of the repeated declaration in the biblical creation story that this physical world is good — very good. But there are other traditions in Greek thought.

ARISTOTELIAN VIEWS OF NATURE

The most influential of those other traditions is the Aristotelian. Though Aristotle was a pupil of Plato, his thought in many ways opposes Platonism. Together, Plato and Aristotle represent two frequently encountered poles in the relationship between humans and nature. As one historian of philosophy put it:

> Like the Gilbert and Sullivan Englishman who is born either a Liberal or a Conservative, it has been remarked that everyone is born either a Platonist or an Aristotelian. Plato and Aristotle, that is, represent two different attitudes toward the world. Plato was a perfectionist whose inclination . . . was always toward a utopian solution that was impractical precisely because the perfect is never realized in this world. Where Plato was otherworldly and idealistic, Aristotle was practical and empirical.[2]

Whereas in Platonism the true form of a thing is beyond nature, in Aristotelianism it is *in* nature. One need not leave the world of the senses to learn what a thing in reality *is*. Likewise, where Platonism tends to stress the desirability for all things to be unified in one transcendent whole, a fundamental feature of the Aristotelian world picture is that it is composed of countless diverse things: stones, trees, animals, humans, and so forth.

These "things" are substances; they are capable of existing independently of other things — at least to a degree. Thus a stone is a substance, but its grayish color is not, for the color of the stone is not sufficiently independent of the stone to qualify as a substance. Substances, in turn,

---

2. W. T. Jones, "The Classical Mind," in *A History of Western Philosophy*, 2nd ed. (New York: Harcourt Brace Jovanovich, 1970), pp. 217-18.

are composed of two parts: matter and form. The form of a substance is the property (or properties) which makes the substance what it is — the form of a horse, for example, is what makes a horse a horse and not a chair. The matter of a substance, on the other hand, is what receives the form; it is that on which the form is impressed.

We may notice at this point at least an important similarity to Platonic thought: the distinction between the matter of which a thing is composed and the principle of intelligibility which makes it accessible to the mind. What is "matter" to Aristotle is to Plato the unformed chaos of nature. And "form" in Aristotle's conception of substance is that ordering principle which, in Platonic thought, resides in the changeless and eternal realm, and can only be imperfectly imposed upon a recalcitrant nature. Though there is a superficial similarity between the two conceptions, there is an all-important difference: for Aristotle, there is no transcendent realm of the forms, no way of encountering in nature a form apart from matter. The way to knowledge is, therefore, not through insight into the ideal realm; it is through the senses. Thus there is in Aristotle more recognition of the ability of nature to be a vehicle for truth, and potentially a much higher view of nature itself.

In Aristotelian thought, the substances that make up the world can be grouped into natural kinds, depending upon the sort of essential form they share. For example, all individual horses share an essential form — that which makes them horses — and thus they form a kind. Within that kind, the *best* horse is the one which most thoroughly receives the imprint of what a horse is: the best horse is the horsiest horse. Every substance is a member of some natural kind, and these natural kinds are not the imposition of human categories on nature. Nature, in itself, is divided into kinds.

These natural kinds, in turn, form natural groups or kingdoms of kinds. Agates are of a kind in the mineral kingdom; maples are of a kind in the vegetable kingdom; horses are of a kind in the animal kingdom; humans are of a kind in the rational kingdom.

These kinds and kingdoms are marvelously interrelated; indeed, they form a continuous hierarchy. Consider, for example, an agate. It is a member of the mineral kingdom. Accordingly, it has a certain form imposed upon its matter which makes it spatial, solid, and organized. Now consider a maple. In addition to all the qualities of the mineral kingdom (which it shares with stones) it has other characteristics: the ability to grow and to multiply itself. This additional form makes it a member of the vegetable kingdom. In the same way, a horse has the characteristics of the mineral kingdom and the vegetable kingdom, but it also has other forms which make it a member of the animal kingdom: the ability to move, to sense things, and to work toward goals. Thus the horse, and any other animal, shares form with the vegetable and mineral kingdoms, but it is more than anything else in these kingdoms; it is a sensing, self-moving, "mineral-vegetable" substance.

In the same way, humans share form with the mineral, vegetable, and animal kingdoms, but also have more: the ability to think things out prudentially and scientifically. This thinking ability means that humankind transcends the other kingdoms. But it also includes them; in addition to being rational, people are also fully animals, vegetables, and minerals. Thus humans are embedded in nature and share completely in its character.

The familiar Aristotelian definition of humans as rational animals thus contains far more information than is commonly realized. For it tells us our place in the whole continuity and hierarchy of nature; indeed, in the Aristotelian scheme there is a place for everything, and everything is in its place. To understand humans is to see their place in the unity and diversity of the world. (In the past decade we have witnessed a strong critique of modern utilitarian notions of value, a critique which draws on an Aristotelian picture of final cause. The most important work in this connection is Alasdair MacIntyre's *After Virtue.*)

The contrast with Plato's view of nature is clear. For Plato, nature is intrinsically disordered, and it receives order only through the imposition of ideal Forms which are alien to it and can never be fully realized within its stubborn materiality. For Aristotle, nature is intricately and intrinsically ordered.

The place of humans in nature is likewise radically different in Aristotle. The soul, in Platonic thought, exists distinct from the body and is always in some tension with the body. Humanity is thus, for Plato, essentially an alien presence in nature. Aristotle, however, though he speaks of a soul, does not mean by it something distinct from the mineral-vegetable-animal human body; rather, it is that which is unique about persons: the form which humans possess but which all things below humans lack. Accordingly, the Aristotelians also spoke of animal and vegetable souls, but they meant only that form which made vegetable substances different from mineral, or animal substances different from vegetable.

Another important aspect of the Aristotelian view of nature is the idea of purpose. Nature, said Aristotle in *On the Heavens,* does nothing in vain, nothing superfluous. There is a purpose for every substance, every characteristic, every change. However, these purposes are not decreed by some craftsman-god, as in Plato; rather, they are to be found in the substances themselves. The purposes we seek — and find — in nature are not the product of any mind; they are unpurposed purposes, undesigned designs. The universe, for Aristotle, appears to be a great work of craftsmanship — but with no craftsman.

(Interestingly, however, in one passage in the *Politics* Aristotle seems to reverse this teaching on purpose by declaring that the purposes in nature are ultimately centered in humanity: plants are for animals, and animals are for humans. Says Aristotle [or perhaps Aristotle's confused student, since the passage is so counter to the rest of Aristotelian teaching]: "If nature makes nothing incomplete, and nothing in vain, the inference must be that she has made all animals for the sake of man" [*Politics,* I, 8].)

In contrast to Plato, whose overriding suspicion of the physical world causes him to speak often of the need either to transcend or to impose order on it, Aristotle gives no clear teaching on our duty with regard to nature. He states clearly, in the *Ethics* and elsewhere, that the duty of a good person is to fulfill his or her function in the scheme of things. For humans, this would be to fully realize their distinctiveness from the animal kingdom — namely, being rational. However, given Aristotle's teaching on the human relationship to nature, that teaching could have two consequences. Since humans are in fact also mineral, vegetable, and animal, their rational capacity could be understood as simply the capacity to wonder about, study, and classify the other natural kingdoms. In such a view, humans would be the *consciousness* of nature, and thus would have the same attitude of respect and care toward it that a person would have toward his or her own body.

Another consequence of Aristotle's teaching on nature — concentrating especially on the idea that all things are for human use — is that since all things are to have a purpose, and since all purposes seem to be directed toward humans, the rational animals, then humans are justified in using all the rest of nature to fulfill their own purpose.

Actually, both ideas have shaped subsequent thought. For the most part, though, despite Aristotle's insistence that matter and form are inseparable, Christian and non-Christian interpreters of him have tended to emphasize the ideal rather than the empirical (sense knowledge), and have perpetuated a more idealistic, less empirical kind of Aristotelianism. This was particularly true in the time right before the downfall of Aristotelian science. Thus, we will further consider Aristotle's effect on views of nature when we look at the scientific revolution.

STOIC VIEWS OF NATURE

Stoicism, which arose in Greece after the time of Plato and Aristotle, has not had the abiding philosophical influence of those two thinkers, but — perhaps because it became more of a religion than either Platonism or Aristotelianism, and because its greatest popularity corresponded with the greatest power and influence of the Roman Empire — a few Stoic ideas have nevertheless contributed substantially to subsequent views of nature.

The basic Stoic doctrine is that there is in the universe a dynamic ordering principle which is the source, pattern, and goal of all things, including humans. The Stoics called this ordering principle by a variety of names: God, Zeus, creative fire, ether, the law of nature, providence, soul of the world, Word, and so forth. For the Stoic, the universe was like an orderly, spherical animal, held together by the divine ordering *logos.* Though all things — plants, animals, stones — are shaped by the *logos,* it is particularly in rational creatures — humans and gods — that the "divine fire" of the world soul burns brightest.

The goal, then, of a good person's life is to bring that life into ever greater conformity with this pervasive cosmic order; one is to live "according to nature." The good person is one who is in complete harmony with the rest of the universe, for he or she is guided by the same "life-giving word" which animates all the universe, humanity and nature alike.

As we would expect from this Stoic picture of the world as a vast organism (whose "soul" is God), every part within that organism has a purpose. This concept of the purposiveness of all things, which plays only a small role in Aristotle's thought, is very important in Stoicism. The air is a medium for birds, the sea for fish. Clouds bring water to the land, and rain is for plants and animals who need it for sustenance; plants and animals themselves are fitted to eat different foods and to inhabit different regions. To the Stoics, this order was clearly divine, and it was an ethical and religious duty for good persons to find their place in it.

However, humanity has a unique place in this beautifully ordered world: it is for humanity (and the gods) that the world exists at all. Cicero, in *On the Nature of the Gods,* puts it this way:

> Here somebody will ask, for whose sake was all this vast system contrived? For the sake of the trees and plants, for these, though without sensation, have their sustenance from nature? But this at any rate is absurd. Then for the sake of the animals? It is no more likely that the gods took all this trouble for the sake of dumb, irrational creatures. For whose sake then shall one pronounce the world to have been created? Doubtless for the sake of those living beings which have the use of reason. . . . Thus we are led to believe that the world and all the things that it contains were made for the sake of gods and men.[3]

In these words we see that the Stoic idea of humanity in harmony with nature does not exclude the idea of nature being for humanity. Note that nature is not *evil* or imperfect; it simply reaches its greatest perfection in humanity.

That nature is for humanity does not, for the Stoic, mean that one can do whatever one likes with nature. In the same work, Cicero writes:

> Think of all the various species of animals, both tame and wild! think of the flights and songs of birds! of the pastures filled with cattle, and the teeming life of the woodlands! Then why need I speak of the race of men? who are as it were the appointed tillers of the soil, and who suffer it not to become a savage haunt of monstrous beasts of prey nor a barren waste of thickets and brambles, and whose industry diversifies and adorns the lands and islands and coasts with houses and cities.[4]

Thus we see that, for the Stoic, though nature may be designed for human purposes, humans also have a purpose with respect to nature: they are to tend it, maintain its order, and beautify it with their industry.

Again, it is difficult to trace exactly the influence which Stoic thought has had on our own view of nature. One thing is certain, however: the generally negative attitude toward nature characteristic of Platonism was replaced in Stoicism by an understanding of nature as divine. Instead of imposing order on nature, the purpose of humankind was to live according to the divine order found in nature. Stoicism had a good deal

---

3. From Cicero, *On the Nature of the Gods,* cited in Clarence J. Glacken, *Traces on the Rhodian Shore* (Berkeley: University of California Press, 1967), p. 57.

4. Ibid., p. 59.

in common with Aristotelian notions of "a place for everything and everything in its place," but gave that doctrine much more moral force. Not only were humans to find their place, but they were to use their place in nature as a way of tending and embellishing its own order.

A number of Stoic conceptions were prominent in medieval thought, and at least one of these persists in our own time: the near-personification of the natural order, as when we speak of "Mother Nature" or "Nature's Way" or even (in a very Stoic phrase) the "laws of nature." Moreover, the Stoic doctrine of the indwelling *logos*, or order of things, contributes to and is clarified by the Christian doctrine of Christ as *logos*.

EPICUREAN VIEWS OF NATURE

It remains for us to speak briefly of yet one more Greek idea which has had a strong influence on Western views of nature: Epicureanism. However, since its greatest influence was exerted after the Middle Ages, when the unity of the Christian worldview was disintegrating, it has never had much influence on Christian thought. It is, nevertheless, an accurate prefiguring of some aspects of modern scientific views of nature, and thus we should be aware of it.

In the Epicurean view, all things are composed of atoms (an idea based on the theories of an earlier Greek philosopher, Democritus). Atoms are small, solid, indivisible, and indestructible, and they move about in empty space. They cannot be perceived by humans, but their motions result in collections of atoms, which are the bodies humans perceive. All things, including our thoughts and sensations, are the result of these atoms and their combinations. And although our senses are the only certain basis for knowledge of the world, the qualities we associate with the beauty of nature — color, taste, tone — are not a characteristic of that ultimate reality, the atom, but only an accident of the atoms' combinations.

Although the motions of atoms are regular and uniform, as is the behavior of the larger bodies which the congregated atoms form, this regularity is the result neither of divine direction nor of the internal form of the atoms themselves. There are no ends, purposes, or forms for nature, as Platonists, Aristotelians, and Stoics alike agreed there must be.

Since humans themselves are just one more part of nature, and since there is no divinity or order beyond it, they have no obligation with regard to nature, either to control it or to care for it. There is no purpose to a person's life — as there is no purpose to anything else in nature; the goal of human action, then, since there are no transcendent values motivating it, is to live as comfortably as possible.

As a giver of meaning to the individual's life, Epicureanism never had much following, and thus had little effect on the treatment of nature. But the basis of Epicureanism — a universe explicable only in physical terms, with no value other than what is available to the senses — also underlies modern scientific conceptions of nature. The potential effect of Epicureanism on our thoughts and treatment of nature is very great.

THE IMPORTANCE OF REVIEWING THE GREEK VIEWS OF NATURE BECOMES evident as we continue our study of historical attitudes. To summarize those Greek views we may begin by saying that nature is seen from two almost opposite viewpoints. In Platonism nature is presumed to be evil because of its mainly "chaotic" tendencies. Although there are signs of order in nature — there is some regularity in the change from day to night and in seasonal cycles, for instance — humans are the only beings in nature which can contribute, through their knowledge of the Forms, to that order. Epicureanism takes the idea of "chaos" even further, stressing that everything, including order, is the result of the random movements of atoms.

Nature is held in higher esteem, however, by the Aristotelians and Stoics. Again the focus is on the question of order, but unlike the Platonic and Epicurean view, this more positive attitude toward nature assumes that order is inherent in the universe. The goodness of humankind is thought to be rooted in the goodness of nature.

One thing that both the positive and negative views share is the idea that humankind is somehow the center of the universe. For Plato, this means that humankind is the source of order; for Aristotle (or his student) and the Stoics, this anthropocentrism is evident in the conviction that the purpose of nature rests in its relationship to humanity. We must not forget that Epicureanism is an exception to this rule — humans are just as much accidental as nature is — but, as we said earlier, Epicureanism had little effect on later attitudes toward nature, at least not until the scientific revolution.

When reading the following chapter on the medieval view of nature, it will be helpful to remember that Christendom was influenced by both the Platonic and the Aristotelian/Stoic viewpoints. At times nature appears to be evil; at other times it appears to be good. In either case, the belief in humanity as the center of the universe is rarely questioned.

In the past decade another aspect of ancient Greek thought has become important for those concerned with the earth: that is the thought of the pre-Socratic philosophers, especially as it is mediated through the twentieth-century thought of Martin Heidegger. The interest in the pre-Socratics is part of an important reaction against the main current of Western thought which — though it has been building for some time — has gained a great deal of strength in the decade since the first publication of *Earthkeeping*. We will deal with this postmodernist — and explicitly religious — reaction at greater length in chapter 9. But inasmuch as an authentic though neglected part of Greek philosophy is being recovered, we need to introduce it briefly here.

The work of the pre-Socratic philosophers survives only in enigmatic fragments which, despite their incompleteness, hint at quite a different way of being in the world. They have been particularly important in the thought of Martin Heidegger, who has increasingly been accepted as an important source of "ecological philosophy."[5] Four pre-Socratic fragments form the basis of a series of Heidegger's essays called *Early Greek Thinking* and serve as a good sampling of those parts of pre-Socratic thought which have been exerting their enigmatic appeal:

> But where beings have their origin there also their passing away occurs, according to necessity; for they pay recompense and penalty to each other for their injustice, according to the assessment of time. (Anaximander)

> Listening not to me but to the Logos, it is wise to say, in accordance with the Logos: all is one. (Heraclitus)

> Thinking and the thought "it is" are the same. For without the being in relation to which it is uttered, you cannot find thinking. For there neither is nor shall be anything outside of being. . . (Parmenides)

> How can one hide himself before that which never sets? (Heraclitus)[6]

---

5. See, for example, Bill DeVall and George Sessions, *Deep Ecology: Living as If Nature Mattered* (Salt Lake City: Peregrine Smith Books, 1985), pp. 98-100.

6. Cited in Martin Heidegger, *Early Greek Thinking*, trans. David Ferrell Krell and Frank A. Capuzzi (New York: Harper & Row, 1975), pp. 5-6.

These are difficult sayings which, because of their fragmentary character, probably cannot be completely understood (that sense of mystery and incompleteness is undoubtedly part of their appeal). Nevertheless, we can observe two important things about them.

First, they are concerned with wholeness, with totality, with the unity of things. Whereas most subsequent Western thought — starting with Socrates and Plato — has been analytical, seeking understanding of terms and relationships, the pre-Socratics were concerned with the fact of the whole — with Being itself, rather than beings or distinctions and relationships among beings. The appeal of such thought (however difficult it is) is easily understandable as we discover more and more about the damage done by looking at the parts alone.

Second, the pre-Socratics seem particularly concerned with a particular relationship of the self to being, with an attitude of receptivity, alertness, *presence.*

Admittedly it is difficult to distinguish genuine insights of the pre-Socratics from the interpretations which have been placed upon them, especially by Martin Heidegger and his followers. Yet there seem to be clear indications of another way of thought here, an alternative to the kind of manipulative thinking which has come from Platonic thought and has, through Christianity, exerted considerable influence on our treatment of all of creation. It has often been argued that Christianity has been unduly influenced by Greek thought, and that we need to reaffirm the wholism and earthiness, the sense of mystery, present in Hebrew thought. It is thus significant that the pre-Socratics thought in ways much closer to the Hebrew mind, and that interest in pre-Socratic thought is on the rise in our postmodernist, "New Age," ecologically sensitive generation.

CHAPTER 6

❧   ❧

The Medieval View of Nature

The human imagination has seldom had before it an object so sublimely ordered as the medieval cosmos.

— C. S. Lewis, *The Discarded Image*

Gradually against this grey background beauty begins to appear, as something really fresh and delicate and above all, surprising . . . the flowers and stars have recovered their first innocence. Fire and water are felt to be the brother and sister of a saint. The purge of paganism is complete at last. . . . Neither the universe nor the earth has now any longer the old sinister significance of the world. They await a new reconciliation with man, but they are already capable of being reconciled. Man has stripped from his soul the last rag of nature-worship, and can return to nature.

— G. K. Chesterton, *St. Francis of Assisi*

SINCE THE GREEK IDEAS OF NATURE WE HAVE BEEN CONSIDERING ARE at least twenty-two centuries old, it may seem irrelevant to spend so much time on them in a work prompted mainly by late twentieth-century problems. But the distance between our own thinking and that of the ancient Greeks is not, in time, as great as it appears. In addition to their influence (largely debilitating) on the Christian view of nature, these Greek ideas were an important part of those many centuries of intellectual stability we call "the Middle Ages." When in the sixteenth and seventeenth centuries the old ways of looking at nature began to be seriously challenged, it was a combination of Greek and Christian ideas which gave way. (Though it is worth pointing out that many of the ideas defended as Christian — the sun going around the earth, for example — were not really *taught* in Christian Scripture.)

On the popular level, many of these Greek views of nature (such as "Nature abhors a vacuum") are still a part of our understanding of the world. And, in the strata of fossil poetry which make up our language, we may discover innumerable imprints of those ancient understandings of how the earth worked. But more important than these figments of an old world picture is the shape of what has been rejected: modern views of nature took shape *against* old views, and so they are incurably affected by them.

In either case, Greek influence is mediated to us through the Middle Ages. It was not, for the most part, transmitted deliberately and carefully, as from teacher to pupil; rather, it was the unplanned product of a whole culture. The foundation was made up of the stones of Greek thought, held together by a common Christian mortar. (Sometimes, for example, medieval Christians thought of the universe after the Greek mode as "nature," almost a personal presence in itself; at other times they thought of it in the Christian way as "creation." In this chapter we follow that mixed usage.) The resulting edifice, erected over centuries and not yet entirely in ruins, is the great cathedral of the medieval picture of the universe. Those parts of the edifice which deal with the relationship between humanity and nature we can now consider briefly.

But it would be a mistake to stop with the outline of that structure. Cathedrals are for worship, and so was the intricate structure of the medieval worldview. It is a frequently repeated half-truth that medieval spirituality was otherworldly, looking on creation as a discardable backdrop for the drama of human salvation. There was, however, a much richer appreciation of God's immanence in creation than is widely realized, and in the past decade much of that medieval openness to God in creation has been recovered. But before considering the role of creation in medieval spirituality, we must look at the intellectual structure that underlay it.

THE MEDIEVAL PICTURE OF THE UNIVERSE

Above all, the medieval universe was ordered; not simple, by any means, but marvelously structured. There are many examples of this medieval intricacy. It may be glimpsed in the elaborate machinery of crystal spheres which carried the planets, one within the other, in a complex of movement explaining with near perfection the apparent motions of the skies at night. It may be glimpsed in another way in the *Summa Theologica* of Thomas Aquinas, which answers the basic questions about God, humanity, and the world with a calm sense of the accessibility of all information necessary to understanding the universe. It is evident in yet a different way in the *Divine Comedy* of Dante, which builds a marvelously symmetrical structure around Hell, Purgatory, and Heaven, ordering the circles of Hell, the plateaus of Purgatory, and the spheres of Heaven with an intricacy and confidence which admit little doubt as to the structure of the moral or physical universe.

The sense of order owes a good deal to Stoic and Aristotelian conceptions, but it is baptized by the Christian doctrine of a creating and purposing God. The most dramatic form of the idea is in the "great chain of being" or in the "principle of Plenitude." The idea is circuitously derived from Platonism; in its Christian form it consists of the assumption that since God wills to share his goodness with all things, everything which can be is; there is a niche for everything, and, in the divine chain of possibilities, no niche is left unfilled. The idea not only contains a great image of the order of the universe — beast, human, and angel alike — but it expresses clearly a principle of hierarchy. For the order of the universe is not arbitrary: the more noble things are placed above the lesser. A modern manifestation of this image of ascending order is the idea of evolution. But it is as characteristic of the medieval view of nature to see that hierarchy frozen in the universe like an infinitely decorated arch, as it is for the moderns to see the creatures of nature flowing and changing toward an unimaginable and yet-to-be-attained perfection. For, despite all the intricacy of the medieval model, it is changeless.

But if things are unmoving, they are unmoving not like stagnant water, but as a waterfall is unmoving — or, more accurately, as a dance is unmoving, though its members move continually in their appointed places. This ordered, dancelike quality of medieval motion is nowhere clearer than in its explanation of rest and motion. The doctrine is well summed up in lines of Chaucer:

> . . . every kyndely thyng that is
> Hath a kyndely stede ther he
> May best in hit conserved be;
> Unto which place every thyng,
> Through his kyndely enclyning,
> Moveth for to come to. . . .[1]

Everything has its "kyndely stede" or proper place. Thus, when stones fall to the earth or when fires rise, they do so not out of a blind submission to forces acting from without, but from something very much like desire — a "kyndely enclyning" to find one's proper place. The medieval world picture was therefore much more like a dance than a machine.

It was also something like an organism. Owen Barfield describes this ordered and organic universe with great vividness when he tries to re-create for us the "feel" of the universe to a medieval "man in the street":

> To begin with, we will look at the sky. We do not see it as empty space, for we know very well that a vacuum is something that nature does not allow, any more than she allows bodies to fall upwards. If it is daytime, we see the air filled with light proceeding from a living sun, rather as our own flesh is filled with blood proceeding from a living heart. If it is night-time, we do not merely see a plain, homogenous vault pricked with separate points of light, but a regional, qualitative sky, from which first of all the different sections of the great zodiacal belt, and secondly the planets and the moon . . . are raying down their complex influences upon the earth, its metals, its plants, its animals, and its men and women, including ourselves. . . . We know very well that growing things are specially beholden to the moon, that gold and silver draw their virtue from sun and moon respectively, copper from Venus, iron from Mars, lead from Saturn. And that our own health and temperament are joined by invisible threads to these heavenly bodies we are looking at. . . .
>
> We turn our eyes on the sea — and at once we are aware that we are looking at one of the four elements, of which all things on earth are composed, including our own bodies. . . . Earth, Water, Air and Fire are part of ourselves, and we of them. . . .

---

1. Geoffrey Chaucer, *Hous of Fame*, II, 730 sq., cited in C. S. Lewis, *The Discarded Image* (Cambridge: Cambridge University Press, 1964), p. 92.

A stone falls to the ground — we see it seeking the centre of the
earth, moved by something much more like desire than what we today
call gravity.[2]

Barfield here describes several important features of medieval nature. One
is the correspondence between the macrocosm and the microcosm — the
great world of nature, and the small world of the individual human. The
person was affected by the influences of that larger world, particularly by
the planets. Indeed, the word *influenza* is a forgotten fragment of that old
doctrine of human imbeddedness in the world of nature. Nor is it simply
the physical person which is affected by the macrocosm. One's very per-
sonality is made up of elements or "humors" which correspond to the four
elements in nature: phlegmatic, sanguine, choleric, and melancholic
temperaments, corresponding to water, fire, air, and earth, respectively.

We could go on characterizing that medieval model in great detail,
but we wish here only to convey a little of its "feel" or flavor. The reader
who wishes to explore it further may find a superb guide in C. S. Lewis's
The Discarded Image. But our purpose here is not contemplation of that
cathedral of ideas, however aesthetic an object of contemplation it may
be (and Lewis suggests that it is the greatest of medieval works of art). We
are interested rather in seeing how it affected the medieval treatment of
nature and how our own attitude toward nature is shaped by it.

(Another development of the last decade or two in our own culture
is a rekindled interest in the medieval model of the universe — in part as
a reaction against the excesses of modernity. Because the sense of order
and purpose resulting from the microcosm/macrocosm idea was so strong,
medieval ideas like astronomy, astrology, homeopathy, and various forms
of witchcraft and nature magic are seriously being pursued by meaning-
starved moderns tired of living in a world emptied of purpose. More of
this in chapter 9.)

From the very character of the medieval model of the universe, we
might accurately imagine what was, in fact, the primary feature of the
medieval attitude toward nature. Since nature was characterized by an
unchanging order, with everything in its place, and since people found
their place within that order, they had no impetus to rearrange nature or
to study it in order to determine its laws. The harmony of humankind

---

2. Owen Barfield, *Saving the Appearances* (London: Faber & Faber, 1957), pp.
76-77.

with nature was such that there was no great effort to stand apart from it and analyze it. The universe was experienced more as a dancer experiences the dance, not as a sociologist might observe it. And, since the conviction of the order, rationality, and fundamental changelessness of the universe was so great, there was little interest in observing nature for its own sake; one could as well determine how a body fell by *thinking* about its fall, as by measuring its fall. Thus medieval science was primarily deductive rather than inductive.

We are, however, oversimplifying. For within this picture of a harmonious but static universe, there did slowly emerge a greater emphasis on the human ability to order and change it. The emergence of this idea of human power over nature was slow, and it was confined to the world of the craftsman and the artisan. For the most part, it was kept separate from the philosopher's and theologian's ideas about what the universe ultimately was. Indeed, when the world of the craftsman and the world of the philosopher came together, the medieval age ended, and the scientific revolution — and not long after it, the industrial revolution — began. But before turning to a consideration of that great change, we should consider briefly the uses medieval people made of nature — some details of medieval technology.

MEDIEVAL USE OF CREATION

Since our own treatment of creation has as a backdrop those long centuries when the medieval view of the universe was taking shape, it will be helpful to consider what kind of actions resulted from that intricate medieval picture. We have sketched how medieval persons *saw* creation; it remains for us to consider what they *did* to creation. A danger for most modern people in considering those centuries which we call the "Middle Ages" is to assume that little of consequence went on in them. They are "middle," our language leads us to believe, because they are a transition (sometimes painfully slow) between the cultural vitality of the ancients and the progressive enlightenment of our own age. The less neutral phrase, "Dark Ages" (more strictly applied to the years between the fall of Rome and the year 1000, but often scornfully applied to all times before the modern), conveys even more vividly the idea that those centuries were (at least in Europe) a slow purgatory, a painful, continent-wide waiting for light.

It comes as a surprise then to learn that the Middle Ages were a time of considerable technological advance and a time of great impact on the natural environment. The great forests of Europe's plains were, in these centuries, largely reduced to fertile fields; marshes and estuaries were likewise drained and made habitable. All over Europe, rivers were harnessed in mills; by 1120, for example, there were over 5000 watermills in England. The popular image of a world sunk in savagery between the fall of Rome and the rise of science is certainly false, as contemplation of any one of the great medieval cathedrals will show. Human powers to build, to use, to alter, and to destroy creation were certainly alive in the Middle Ages.

There is, however, some basis for that impression of quiescence which we associate with medieval life. Despite the changes in agriculture, in milling, and in husbandry, there was still far more in common between the life of a fourth-century person and that of a fourteenth-century person than there is between the life of a fourteenth-century person and that of a twentieth-century person. Between the Middle Ages and our own time there occurred a great change in our way of viewing and using creation. The medieval world-picture was of a fixed, hierarchical order in which humans had a given place. The medieval concept of the relationship of humans to nature is summed up well by Clarence Glacken in his account of the thought of Gregory of Nyssa, a late Church Father on the threshold of the Middle Ages:

> Man is a master over nature which helps him on his way to God, nature itself being raised up and exalted in the process. God made an earth full of riches, including the gold, silver, stones, valued by man; he allowed men to appear on earth to witness these wonder works and to assume his role as master of them. Mastery over the lower beings was necessary to satisfy his needs: mastery over the horse because of the slowness and difficulty of human bodily movements; over the sheep because of our nakedness; over the oxen because humans are not grass eaters; over the dog because his jawbone is a living knife for men. His mastery of iron gives him the protection that horns and claws afford the animals.[3]

Gregory describes for humans a very high place with respect to the rest of

---

3. Gregory of Nyssa, cited in Clarence J. Glacken, *Traces on the Rhodian Shore* (Berkeley: University of California Press, 1967), p. 298.

nature, but there is no urge to move beyond that decreed place, which is furnished not only with deduced or inherited knowledge about the nature of plants, animals, and physical causes, but also with a kind of basic tool kit for using the world of nature. Though the medieval world was not a small one, it was enclosed. There was no "outside" — no concept of unlimited space, or even of undiscovered and, therefore, beckoning lands. That absence of a sense of the unknown, the very tidiness of the medieval view of nature, discouraged both the search for a more basic knowledge of nature and the search for more effective techniques of using nature. It is hard for us to comprehend, for example, that a simple, but workable, steam engine was built in ancient Greece — but neither then nor in the long centuries afterward did it occur to anyone to apply those energies to work.

Certainly one reason for the great slowness in the growth of these abilities to manipulate nature is the distinction between what the philosophers thought about nature and what the workers — the farmers, craftsmen, and artisans — did to (and with) it. Today we would call it a split between science and technology.

The reason for this split is, in large part, the Platonic view of the relationship between humans and nature. It will be remembered that a dominant theme in Platonism was that nature was an impediment to the soul. A consequence of this attitude was that the good person should be occupied not with things of the body, but with things of the mind. Those who worked with animals, or stone, or even fire were, by their very involvement with such physical stuff, limiting their soul's ability to achieve the ideal.

This otherworldly attitude dominated medieval science. Inasmuch as speculation went on about the movements and the appearances of the physical world, that speculation was directed toward understanding the changeless and eternal principles, not toward applying to practical work the knowledge thus gained. This general disdain of the learned person for involvement with the physical, together with the fact that the laborer was very likely unable to read and thus was without access to the physical theories of the scholars (either to confirm or to disprove them), produced a state of affairs in which the people who worked with nature had little knowledge of theories about nature, while the people who dealt with the theories did not apply them to working in the world. As the historian of science Reijer Hooykaas puts it, "In the Middle Ages, as in antiquity, reason led experience into captivity, art was judged incapable of successful competition with nature, and technology was separated from science. Head and hand were not encouraged to co-operate."[4]

The result was that, for most of the Middle Ages, the great wealth of human knowledge was not applied to human use of nature. The most significant technological inventions of the age — the horse-collar, the crossbow, the windmill — as well as the broadening application of older inventions like the waterwheel and the sail, were made not by the "scientists" — the people concerned with knowledge — but by the workers: the people concerned with getting the job done. Thus the treatment of nature in medieval Europe was not, on the whole, much accelerated by the philosophical or theological thinking; it proceeded slowly, out of the trial-and-error, day-to-day work of nameless craftsmen.

There were exceptions to this general separation of head and hand, and out of some of them grew the modern conception of the physical world. One of the most prominent and earliest exceptions came from the many Benedictine and Cistercian monasteries. These were often situated in remote places — in mountains or forests — far away from the run of ordinary life. But the monks felt a kind of obligation, in such a setting, to re-create a kind of earthly paradise. Jean Leclercq, a historian of monasticism, sums up this idea of the monastery as a kind of "Jerusalem in anticipation":

> The cloister is a "true paradise," and the surrounding countryside shares in its dignity. Nature "in the raw," unembellished by work or art, inspires the learned man with a sort of horror: the abysses and peaks which we like to gaze at, are to him an occasion of fear. A wild spot, not hallowed by prayer and asceticism and which is not the scene of any spiritual life is, as it were, in the state of original sin. But once it has become fertile and purposeful, it takes on the utmost significance.[5]

A necessary part of this siting of monasteries in remote places was the conviction that the work necessary to transform the wilderness into a fruitful Eden was itself a kind of spiritual activity. Work, far from being the exercise of their base and un-soulish nature, was to the monks a kind

---

4. Reijer Hooykaas, *Religion and the Rise of Modern Science* (Grand Rapids: Eerdmans, 1972), p. 88.

5. Jean Leclercq, *The Love of Learning and the Desire for God: A Study of Monastic Culture*, trans. Catherine Misrahi (New York: Fordham University Press, 1961), p. 130.

of prayer. And, most significantly for the history of the development of the West, it was in the Benedictine monasteries that complex machines were first used on a large scale for the processing of nature. Perhaps the most important of these was the monastery clock, which served the practical function of arranging the hours of prayer, but had the long-range consequence of rationalizing and segmenting time. In all sorts of other ways men in the monasteries used their hands and their heads to participate, with God, in the shaping of creation; and if their hands could be aided by river-powered mills, improved by clever heads, so much the better. Such large-scale physical work, coupled with the use and development of machines by men of the church, gave a kind of blessing to such machines and began the breakdown of the barrier between mind and hand which had impeded medieval use of nature.

A further impetus to the study and (ultimately) the manipulation of the sensible world came about in connection with the followers of St. Francis, whose joy in creation we will consider shortly. Suffice it to say here that the Franciscans kept alive the openness to the physical world; even when they did philosophy, they maintained little of that aloofness of the mind from nature which was largely a Greek heritage. Thus Bonaventure, the greatest of the Franciscan philosophers, wrote eloquently of the Book of Nature and the Book of Revelation (the Bible), and encouraged Christians to study nature in order to learn about God. It was within the Franciscan order that many of the greatest medieval scientists found a congenial home — men like Roger Bacon and Robert Grosseteste. Unlike the Greek and early medieval deductive science, this Franciscan science was based on *observation* of the world of nature; and that empiricism (which we now consider to be essential to science) was largely a result of Francis's openness to Sister Creation.

No immediate influential change in the treatment of nature came out of Franciscan science. But, just as the Benedictines broke down the barrier between hands and head, the Franciscans broke down the barrier between the senses and the head. The Benedictines encouraged technology, and the Franciscans encouraged an understanding of creation based on observation of creatures themselves, not on categories deduced from first principles and then imposed upon the world. This tendency culminated in the philosophy of a later Franciscan, William of Ockham, who maintained that "What can be done with fewer is done in vain with more." In other words, those explanations of creation are best which do not impose upon it a variety of hypotheses derived from reason but irrelevant to the facts. And, as the fourteenth-century followers of Ockham discovered, such explanations are the ones most likely to result in usable knowledge of creation. Indeed, it was largely through Franciscan thought that the more Christian notion of "creation" began to supplant the Greek notion of "nature," thus laying the foundation for science.

So, as the Middle Ages drew to a close, there were two tendencies at work in medieval thought which countered the generally otherworldly character of the medieval world picture and encouraged an increasing human involvement in understanding and manipulating creation. One was the accelerating control of the environment — through windmills, watermills, new kinds of harnesses, better ships, stronger metals, and so forth. These technological advances were still primarily the result of the work of common, uneducated people, though in the Benedictine monasteries there was a long tradition of learned, "spiritual" men, not ashamed of shaping nature with hand and tool.

The other tendency was a greater emphasis on the study of creation itself as the best source of knowledge about it. Franciscan scientists like Grosseteste and Roger Bacon founded their knowledge in the divinely given book of creation, and Franciscan philosophers like Bonaventure, Duns Scotus, and Ockham developed good reasons, theological and logical, for thus basing knowledge in the study of particular things. The old separation of mind from nature, encouraged by the prevailing Platonism of medieval philosophy, was ending. When mind, hand, and sense came together in the scientific and industrial revolutions, the view of nature drastically changed, and the human capability to alter creation began an acceleration which has continued into our own time.

CREATION IN MEDIEVAL SPIRITUALITY

Before turning to a consideration of that revolution in our knowledge of creation which we call science, and which ushers in modern times, it will be helpful to look briefly at a different sort of insight into the Creator and his works, a kind of insight which flourished diversely in the Middle Ages: the lived experience of God, sometimes called "spirituality." All the thinkers we are going to consider have been labelled mystics, and around some of them (given to colorful and paradoxical statement) hints of heresy have lingered.[6] But their chief offense seems to have been to celebrate the mystery and unfathomableness of the Creator's works — often in terms of his mysterious relationship to and presence in creation. When one turns to their work itself, it is clear that they speak out of a deep Christian orthodoxy. But they usually do so in ways quite different from the formulations of scholastic rationalism — a tradition of expressing Christian truth even more common in Protestant theology. The most common criticism levelled against them is that of pantheism. But they never lose sight of the distinctness of the Creator from the creation. Rather, they try to express (much as the Psalmist did, but with an added christological understanding) God's *closeness* to his work. It is unfortunate that we have pushed these thinkers to the margins of Christian truth, for they have much to teach us. We need to hear them not in opposition to theological clarity, but rather as a different expression of the very richness which it is the task of theology to clarify.

We cite examples from three sources in medieval Christianity: the Celtic church, Hildegard of Bingen, and St. Francis.

Celtic Christianity

Celtic Christianity is something of a puzzle for the Christian West. The dominant expansion of the Christian church came from a Roman center, and rose and fell with the fortunes of Rome. It first came to Britain — along with the legions, the laws, and the straight roads of the Empire — through the Roman presence, and it seems mainly to have been restricted to the ruling classes, the aristocracy. But when the Roman empire crumbled and various barbarians from the north overwhelmed Britain, Christianity essentially vanished. It returned in the eighth century with Augustine, an emissary of the pope (and hence Roman, Western Christianity), who began to rebuild Christianity in Britain along Roman lines.

But the history of Celtic Christianity is quite different. Although there is a great deal that we don't know about its early history, we know

---

6. The association of heresy with some of these writers has not been helped by the fact that their chief champion in the past decade has been Matthew Fox, a heterodox Catholic thinker who, in 1988, was censured by the Vatican for some of his own positions. In his "Creation Spirituality," Fox and his followers have indeed recovered important truths about ourselves and creation, but they have often been undiscerning in their acceptance of any mysticism or spirituality which challenges modernity.

that it flourished quite independently of the Roman presence, in those parts of the British Isles — Ireland and Scotland — where the Romans never established a foothold. It is likely that it had closer ties with the Eastern branch of the church, perhaps directly from the Mediterranean. (In any case, its attitude toward creation is much closer to that of Eastern Orthodoxy.) When Latin Christianity was reintroduced in the southeast of England, Celtic Christianity had long been a vital force in the north, evangelizing northern Britain — and much of Europe, as far as northern Italy — from the "Holy Islands" of Iona and Lindisfarne. Eventually Latin and Celtic Christianity merged, but at the expense of much of the genius of the Celtic church.

The Celtic Christians had a deep sense of the goodness of creation and the presence of God in it. The fountainhead of Celtic Christianity is St. Patrick, a fourth-century figure instrumental in the conversion of Ireland. Much of the tone of the Celtic attitude toward Creator and creation is captured in the hymn attributed to him under the strange title "St. Patrick's Breastplate." It is a long invocation of God's help beginning with these words:

> I bind unto myself today
> The strong name of the Trinity;
> By invocation of the same,
> The Three in One, the One in Three.

It continues, after calling on Christ and the angels, by invoking creation:

> I bind unto myself today
> The virtues of the starlit heaven,
> The glorious sun's life-giving ray,
> The whiteness of the moon at even,
> The flashing of the lightning free,
> The whirling wind's tempestuous shocks,
> The stable earth, the deep salt sea,
> Around the old eternal rocks.

Yet this openness to creation is not (as it has sometimes been called) nature magic, nor a lingering druidism. Creation, though splendid with its own vitality, is nevertheless always *creation,* perceived in relationship with the Creator. And this was not a distant, aloof Creator but Christ the Creator — and friend and comforter. The Celtic sense of God incarnate is evident in this splendid cadenza of invocation which interrupts the hymn:

Christ be with me, Christ within me,
Christ behind me, Christ before me,
Christ beside me, Christ to win me,
Christ to comfort and restore me,
Christ beneath me, Christ above me,
Christ in quiet, Christ in danger,
Christ in hearts of all that love me,
Christ in mouth of friend and stranger.[7]

In the words of Susan Power Bratton, "orthodox Christian theology frames the power of nature, and brings it into a Christian context."[8]

Celtic Christianity was highly monastic, transplanting the practices instituted by St. Anthony in Egypt in a remarkably short time to the rainy verdure of the British Isles. But it was a gentler, more creation-embracing monasticism. Whereas in the Christian monasticism of the desert a main impetus for withdrawal to the wilderness seems to have been avoidance of the city, the main impetus in Celtic monasticism seems to have been seeking a communion with God which was completely open to God's gifts in creation. The Celtic monks lived and meditated in rugged, wild places — such as the beehive-like stone structures of Skellig Michel, a rocky spire in the North Atlantic miles off the Irish coast. But even there creation was welcomed and loved, as is evident in this meditation of a monk on an island:

Delightful to me on an island hill, on the crest of a rock, that I
    might often watch the quiet sea;
That I might watch the heavy waves above the bright water, as
    they chant music to their Father everlastingly;
That I might watch its smooth, bright-bordered shore, no
    gloomy pastime, that I might hear the cry of strange birds, a
    pleasing sound;

and so on, through a rich and detailed description of the sea and its life: all of this in order

---

7. "Invocation of the Trinity (St. Patrick's Breastplate)," trans. Cecil Francis Alexander, *The Book of Common Praise Being the Hymn Book of the Anglican Church of Canada* (Oxford: Oxford University Press, 1938), p. 820.

8. Susan Power Bratton, *The Original Desert Solitaire: Wilderness and Christianity* (Scranton Press, 1991). This remarkable study contains a wealth of examples of and commentary on the place of creation in Celtic spirituality.

That I might bless the Lord who rules all things, heaven with its
   splendid host, earth, ebb and flood.

Nor is this a communion with the Creator which leaves human needs
aside. The monk's meditation continues:

. . . Now gathering seaweed from the rocks, now catching fish,
   now feeding the poor, now in my cell.[9]

Clearly, this is no otherworldly spirituality, but a spirituality eager to see
the bounty of God without turning away from the goodness of any of
God's creatures — including men and women.

Susan Bratton sums up the distinctives of the Celtic attitude toward
creation:

In regard to the person of God, the Celtic literature makes repeated
reference to God the Creator. This would be in contrast to naming
God savior, judge, help, deliverance, righteousness, etc. The [stories
of] saints' lives . . . call God "the Creator," "King of the elements,"
"dear Creator," "God, the Creator of things" and "King of the Stars."
The early Celtic church, at a distance from the violent theological
arguments engulfing the church fathers of the Mediterranean region,
may not have wrestled as strenuously with questions concerning the
persons of God and the means of Salvation, as the ecclesiastical bodies
of the dying Roman empire. The Celts emphasized the aspect of God
most interesting to them, the Lord as the wellspring of the universe.[10]

Hildegard of Bingen

Hildegard of Bingen was a remarkable German woman who lived from
1098 to 1179. The tenth child of her parents, she was given as a sort of
"tithe" to God at the age of eight. She became a nun, and ultimately an
abbess. She seems to have been a seer of some kind, having visions from
an early age. But not until the age of forty-three did she hear a voice telling
her to write them down. In the nearly forty years remaining to her she
produced (with the help of others) the *Scivias*, a series of visions setting
forth the divine scheme of creation, redemption, and sanctification; a

---

9. Cited in ibid.
10. Ibid., p. 33.

powerfully original set of songs, published collected (with music extant) as the *Symphonia;* many symbolically rich, icon-like paintings; and a kind of encyclopedia (for which she claimed no visionary inspiration) called *Nine Books on the Subtleties of Different Kinds of Creatures.*

Hildegard's work reflects a rich sense of the immediacy of God to creation. Sometimes she speaks of this presence as the Word:

> Without the Word of God no creature has meaning.
> God's Word is in all creation, visible and invisible.
> The Word is living, being, spirit, all verdant greening, all creativity.
> This Word manifests in every creature. Now this is how the spirit is
>   in the flesh — the Word is indivisible from God.[11]

Sometimes she speaks of this divine presence in terms of the Holy Spirit, as in this portion of a song from the *Symphonia:*

> Fiery Spirit,
> fount of courage,
> life within life
> of all that has being!
> . . . .
> O current of power permeating all
> in the heights upon the earth and
> in all deeps:
> you bind and gather
> all people together.
>
> Out of you clouds
> come streaming, winds
> take wing from you, dashing
> rain against stone;
> and ever-fresh springs
> well from you, washing
> the evergreen globe.[12]

---

11. *Meditations with Hildegard of Bingen*, ed. Gabriel Uhlein (Santa Fe, NM: Bear & Co., 1982), p. 49.

12. *Symphonia, A Critical Edition of the Symphonia armonie celestium revelationum* [Symphony of the Harmony of Celestial Revelations], ed. and trans. Barbara Newman (Ithaca: Cornell University Press, 1988), pp. 149-50.

Once again, but from a very different source, we hear in these words an openness to creation flowing from a devotion to the Creator.

St. Francis of Assisi

By far the best-known medieval figure is St. Francis of Assisi. Francis revolutionized medieval piety by living a life characterized by a joyous, self-giving poverty, and by a strong sense of kinship with the rest of creation. Though it is hard to distinguish fact from legend, it is clear that Francis possessed, for his time, a remarkable sensitivity to nature — indeed, to the whole material world. It was Francis, for example, who first placed animals in a churchyard at Christmas, saying, "Behold your God, a poor and helpless child, the ox and ass beside Him. Your God is of your flesh. . . ." His "Canticle of the Sun" (more familiar to English-speaking Christians as the hymn "All Creatures of Our God and King") sums up his spirit of joy toward creation and praise to the Creator:

> Most High, all-powerful, all good, Lord!
> All praise is yours, all glory, all honor
> And all blessing.
> . . . .
> All praise be yours, my Lord, through all that you have made,
> And first my lord Brother Sun,
> Who brings the day; and light you give to us through him
> . . . All praise be yours, my Lord, through Brothers Wind and
>   Air . . .
> All praise be yours, my Lord, through Sister Water . . .
> All praise be yours, my Lord, through Brother Fire . . .
> All praise be yours, my Lord, through Sister Earth, our mother . . .
> All praise be yours, my Lord, through Sister Death . . .[13]

The hymn is remarkable for several reasons. First, it is not the youthful exuberance of a young man, but was written by Francis in the last year of his life, as the distillation of a lifelong attitude. Second, it is very precise in its theology. Though accepting the various elements of creation as brother and sister creatures, and though appreciative of their splendor,

---

13. *The Writings of St. Francis of Assisi*, trans. B. Fahy and P. Hermann (Chicago: Franciscan Herald Press, 1964), pp. 127-31.

purity, gaiety, and strength, Francis nevertheless reserves praise for their Creator: there is nothing here of nature-worship. Finally, Francis shows an unusual grasp of the very fabric of creation when he speaks of death not as enemy, but as sister. Today we recognize the ecological necessity of death. But it was a rare insight in the Middle Ages.

As we have already indicated, the effect of the Franciscan fellowship with creation was incalculable. Within his lifetime Franciscan missionaries had spread over much of the Christian world, carrying with them an openness to look with thankfulness at the world of the commonplace, a perspective which nourished not only traditions of vernacular poetry in French, Italian, and English, but also — surprisingly — the whole scientific tradition. And as we have noted, the line of Franciscan philosophers passing from Francis through Bonaventure opened up the Christian mind to seeing creation as a kind of revelation, second only to Scripture, to be read with worshipful care.

Yet, as this brief anthology of medieval spirituality has shown, Francis's insights were not as unique as they are sometimes made out to be. Lynn White, in his influential 1967 essay linking Christianity with the "ecological crisis," suggests that Francis was an anomaly, an exception. We are now beginning to see more clearly that, although his influence was exceptional, his affirmation of creation was not new. It gathered up themes from Celtic and Germanic Christianity — themes more thoroughly stated in Eastern Orthodoxy — which (as we will see) are central to a biblical understanding. In fact, there is increasing evidence of influences on Francis of Celtic Christianity, on the one hand, and Eastern Orthodoxy, on the other. In any case we are now beginning to see in medieval Christianity an appreciation of the intrinsic worth of creation and the Creator's abiding closeness to it.

And although that sense of God's closeness to creation was essential to the scientific revolution, the scientific movement had, in a short time, reduced creation to a kind of clockwork, humanity to a kind of tyrant, and the Creator to a forgotten watch-maker God who had long since stepped out of the picture. To a consideration of that crucial movement in the history of the planet we now turn.

CHAPTER 7

❧ ❧

The Scientific Revolution

Then I felt like some watcher of the skies
When a new planet swims into his ken;
Or like stout Cortez when with eagle eyes
He star'd at the Pacific — and all his men
Look'd at each other with wild surmise —
Silent, upon a peak in Darien.

— John Keats, "On First Looking
into Chapman's Homer"

SCIENCE AND TECHNOLOGY COALESCED INTO A POWERFUL TOOL AT THE
same time as the discovery and initial exploitation of the New World.
The physical New World became a kind of symbol of the rapidly emerging
new world of human powers. The discovery of vast new lands across the
oceans and the growing tide of information brought back by the explorers
and exploiters washed at the foundations of that closed but splendid edifice
of the medieval understanding of creation. Several consequences of that
New World exploration need mentioning.

First, the discovery and the exploitation of the New World were far
more the work of practical men, with practical goals, than they were the work
of philosophers reasoning how the world should be. From the improved ships
that carried the explorers such vast distances, to the conquests and settle-

145

ments in the New World itself, these mind-expanding changes in the size of the world were being wrought by people who advanced knowledge not by reflecting on first principles, but by applying clever hands to axe, adze, tiller, and sword. The New World opened up possibilities for people of action which had been unavailable in the Middle Ages. The results, whether they were new lands or Inca gold, were immediate and satisfying.

A second consequence of the New World for the old view of nature was that its very existence strained many old categories of what nature had been understood to be. For example, voyages into the southern hemisphere proved false the honored notion of medieval science that people could not live in the Antipodes (since a supposed belt of fire would keep them from getting there). The discovery of a bewildering variety of new plants and animals, not to mention whole peoples of vastly different history, strained old conceptions of "a place for everything" to a disturbing — or exhilarating — breaking point.

A third consequence was more subtle, but it was perhaps the most important of all. The medieval world was self-contained. That physical "breaking out" of the bounds of previously known human endeavor became a symbol for a mental "breaking out" of old ways of thinking and old ways of action. The discovery of the New World was not only an effect, but also a cause, of a radically new attitude toward creation, the formulation of which we will attempt to trace briefly. For, with only slight changes, the understanding of the relationship between humanity and creation that emerged in the seventeenth century still shapes our treatment of the earth today.

THE THEOLOGIANS

Another "new world" that emerged in the sixteenth century was the Protestant Reformation. The new science was probably nourished as much by new (or newly recovered) ideas about God the Creator and Lord as it was by new knowledge of the creation. The exact nature of that influence of the Reformation on science continues to be debated. But it is clear that, though science certainly has deep roots in medieval Catholic Europe, it flourished most dramatically in the Protestant world.[1] Some of the reasons for this need to be mentioned.

---

1. Reijer Hooykaas argues this thesis persuasively in *Religion and the Rise of Modern Science* (Grand Rapids: Eerdmans, 1972).

In both Greek and medieval science, there was little incentive to examine creation itself for a knowledge of the Creator, because it was assumed that God — whether understood as the Ideal Goodness of Plato and Plotinus, or the First Cause and unmoved mover of Aristotle and the scholastics — was perfect and eternal, distinct from the flawed world of ordinary existence. Only by contemplating the eternal and the true could people arrive at truth, not by observation of the flawed physical world around them. The rationality inherent in creation was assumed to be discoverable more through reason than through observation and measurement.

But in the century following the Reformation a dramatic shift took place, from an emphasis on God's rationality to an emphasis on God's will, shown primarily in his love. Theologically, the origins of this change seem to lie in Franciscan philosophers such as Bonaventure, Duns Scotus, and William of Ockham (who appears to be the only scholastic Martin Luther admired). The Reformers felt that God's redemptive actions come not from rational necessity, but rather from God's overflowing — and, in human terms, his *unreasonable* — love.

This shift had profound consequences on the human attitude toward creation. In Greek philosophy and in the Middle Ages creation was unimportant as a source of knowledge about God. In the seventeenth century, however, it became supremely important. God is to be known only through his action: his self-revelation. The primary source for that revelation is Scripture, the Book of Revelation. But another important source is the physical world, the Book of Creation. Francis Bacon put succinctly this new attitude toward creation (and his rejection of the old):

> . . . we must entreat men again and again to discard, or at least set apart for a while, these volatile and preposterous philosophies, which have preferred theses to hypotheses, led experience captive, and triumphed over the works of God; and to approach with humility and veneration to unroll the volume of the Creation, to linger and meditate therein, and with minds washed clean from opinions to study it in purity and integrity.[2]

---

2. "The Natural and Experimental History for the Foundation of Philosophy: or Phenomena of the Universe: Which is the Third part of the Instauratio Magna," in *The Works of Francis Bacon*, ed. Spedding, Ellis, and Heath, vol. 5 (vol. 2 of the translations of *The Philosophical Works*), pp. 131-34, p. 132. Cited in Glacken, *Traces on the Rhodian Shore* (Berkeley: University of California Press, 1967), pp. 472-73.

And just as the meaning of Scripture did not require an authoritative interpreter in order to be understood, so also the meaning of creation lay open to anyone with eyes and will to see. Every believer was a priest, capable of interpreting both the book of Scripture and the book of nature.

One final Reformation idea was important both to the new science and to its vigorous application (especially in the New World): that is, the conviction that all callings are sacred, that to work with the stuff of the created world is not at all demeaning. Thus the ancient aristocratic prejudice against work — which had driven a wedge between science and technology since the ancient Greeks — was eliminated. The way was opened for a fateful union of science and technology.

THE ASTRONOMERS: COPERNICUS, KEPLER, GALILEO, NEWTON

The new world of science began to appear in the heavens. It had been accepted, throughout the Middle Ages, that the plain evidence of the senses was correct, and that the heavens moved around the earth. In order to account for these motions, ancient and medieval astronomers — and especially a first-century Greek, Ptolemy — had devised an elaborate hypothesis of moving crystal spheres within spheres (or epicycles upon deferents) which accounted reasonably well for all the observed motions of the heavenly bodies, and which did not violate the ideal of uniform circular motion around an earthly center. Such motion, the philosophers felt, was the only motion suitable to the heavens, since they were unaffected by the corruption, mutability, and general imperfection of the earth. Early in the sixteenth century a Polish canon, Nicholas Copernicus, developed a theory which explained the heavenly movements by placing the sun at the center of the system. Copernicus was timid, and he delayed publishing his theory for nearly thirty years. He need not have feared: revolutionary as the theory was, it was nearly a hundred years before it attracted much attention. But the most revolutionary part of the theory was not that it described the sun as the center of the planetary motions; it was that this explanation of the planetary motions was claimed to be not simply a convenient device for calculating the positions of the planets (as was the case with the old Ptolemaic astronomy), but a description of reality.

A word or two of explanation is needed here. It will be remembered that the Platonic conception of reality maintained that truth is to be encountered not by the senses, in nature, but by the mind, in contemplation of that which is beyond nature. Thus observation of the movements of the heavenly bodies, though it provided good training for the mind, would not in itself yield truth, which was beyond any appearance. The movements of the planets were, in fact, only an appearance of an ultimately trans-sensible (and transnatural) reality. The Ptolemaic theory was not, then, supposed to describe how the heavens were in fact actually composed and impelled. Rather, it was a way of "saving the appearances." When Copernicus (timidly, to be sure) proposed that "all that is beneath the moon, with the centre of the earth, describe among the planets a great orbit round the sun which is the centre of the world; and what appears to be a motion of the sun is in truth a motion of the earth,"[3] he signaled a radical change of the relationship of the mind to nature. He said, in effect, that the model which the mind makes of nature is a way of getting at the ultimate reality of a phenomenon, and that a hypothesis that saves all the appearances is not simply another hypothesis, but is equivalent with the truth.

It was nearly sixty years later that a fiery young Lutheran astronomer, Johannes Kepler, openly defended the neglected theory of Copernicus and said more strongly what Copernicus had said: a hypothesis which did not aim at final truth was an inadequate instrument for understanding God's universe. Thus Kepler, throughout most of his life, worked laboriously at developing principles which would describe the *real* motions of the planets. He based his calculations on a great wealth of data compiled over many years by Tycho Brahe, a Danish astronomer. And, unlike earlier astronomers, Kepler was absolutely loyal to what the data said. Once, a small discrepancy of eight minutes of arc forced him to abandon the ancient idea of the circularity of the motions of heavenly bodies. That decision to accept the authority of observed nature over the authority of traditions *about* nature had far-reaching consequences. As Hooykaas put it, "a lonely man submitted to facts and broke away from a tradition of two thousand years. With full justice he could declare: 'These eight minutes paved the way for the reformation of the whole of astronomy. . . .' "[4] They did more than

---

3. Copernicus, cited in Edward Grant, "Late Medieval Thought, Copernicus, and the Scientific Revolution," *Journal of the History of Ideas* 23 (1962): 213.
4. Hooykaas, *Religion and the Rise of Modern Science*, p. 36.

that: they paved the way for the triumphal march of that attitude toward creation which says that the way to certain knowledge and control of it is through precise measurement, which increasingly becomes the only basis for the truth.

A third figure whose speculations on the movements of heavenly bodies prepared the way for a new relationship between mind and creation is Galileo. Galileo is best known for being tried by the church for defending and teaching the Copernican system. It is important to note again, however, that the most significant issue was not the *idea* that the earth moved around the sun, but the conviction that this idea was equivalent with the truth. In any case, Galileo's greatest contributions to the changing view of creation are not in his defense of Copernicus, or even in his turning of the telescope onto the heavens and the revelations of the size and complexity of the universe that resulted; they are rather in his theories of the movements of bodies and in the method that underlies those theories. Galileo sought to answer ancient questions about why falling or projected bodies move in the way they do. However, unlike earlier (predominantly Aristotelian) attempts to answer those questions, Galileo attempted to explain such movements not by philosophy — what the bodies *should* do — but by observation, by seeing what the bodies actually *did* do. He accurately recorded these movements of falling bodies under different conditions. Based on these data, he arrived at principles of motion which, he asserted, encompassed the truth about such motions, even as he claimed that the Copernican theory got at the truth of the motions of the heavenly bodies. Much as Kepler did when he was forced, by the data of Tycho Brahe's observations (counter to all good philosophy about movements in the heavens), to declare that the orbit of Mars was not circular but elliptical, Galileo maintained that the precise measurement of falling bodies was the only way to knowledge about the laws that governed them. And his conviction that measurement and observation were the most certain way of knowing nature continues to our own times.

Another element of Galileo's thought is important for our modern view of nature. We have already encountered the distinction between "primary" and "secondary" qualities as part of the Epicurean explanation of the universe as the result of indestructible atoms moving forever in a void. Like Epicurus, Galileo maintained that such sensible qualities as color, smell, taste, and warmth were not a part of the fundamental particles, but "secondary," added by the mind. Said Galileo,

I think that tastes, odors, colors, and so on are no more than mere names so far as the object in which we place them is concerned, and that they reside only in the consciousness. Hence, if the living creature were removed, all these qualities would be wiped away and annihilated.[5]

The only thing that remains are the qualities which can be precisely measured and known, not by the senses, but by the abstract mind: size, shape, and weight.

Galileo's dismissal of the world of the senses as unimportant in arriving at genuine knowledge of nature is so basic to contemporary science that it may not strike us today as very important. We have no difficulty in understanding that the real world is not what our senses show us, but rather is what can be measured precisely and reduced to numerical data. But consider for a moment what this idea does to the old medieval view of humanity embedded in the world of nature. If Galileo is correct, then nature is not the colored, textured, fragrant complexity which the senses encounter, but is instead a sized, shaped, weighed abstraction about which the more spectacular sense information is irrelevant. Knowledge of such a nature is achieved, then, through the mind acting on data that have been reduced from sense knowledge to numerical certainties unavailable to the senses. That process of abstracting the mind from the world began with the Copernican theory, which presents the world not as we sense it, with sunrise and sunset, but as it would appear if we could be lifted out of the body, out of the planet, out of "nature" as we know it, and placed in a detached viewpoint far beyond the earth. (It is what some might call a "God's eye" view — but, as we shall see, that picture of God as merely distant is misleading if not balanced by a strong affirmation of God's closeness to his creation.) The process of abstraction continues with Galileo's views, which reduce nature to the measurable "primary" qualities — those which underlie and are basic to the world which our senses show us. Though knowledge is, for Galileo, rooted in observation of nature, there is no room in this observation for anything which cannot be reduced to number. Increasingly, then, the vital cosmos of the medieval view — in which stones fell because they desired their place, and the microcosm of

---

5. Galileo, "The Assayer," in *Discoveries and Opinions of Galileo,* trans. Stillman Drake (Garden City, NY: Doubleday, 1957), p. 274.

the person paralleled the macrocosm of the universe — is replaced by a kind of machine in which only the mind is alive.

It was left for Isaac Newton to make the final transition from the medieval to the modern view of nature. His laws of gravitation explained the movements of the heavenly bodies as the result of the same forces which affect the movements of things near us — apples, stones, ourselves. All motions could be accounted for, in Newton's theory, by the same simple mathematical explanations. His was an elegant simplification of that complex picture of the universe which had prevailed through the Middle Ages. But it was also a rather cold and mechanical model. The important things were matter and motion, not the colors, tastes, or textures of the world as we sense them. As a result of the burgeoning availability of new and effective knowledge about nature, intricate machines were being used and admired. And because Newton's universe seemed to work very much like a vast machine, nature, the heavens, and to some extent even humans came increasingly to be understood as a kind of elaborate clockwork.

Thus we see a profound paradox in the new science: it begins in awe at creation as a beckoning intelligibility, a work of the Creator, but it ends (at least in popular thought) with a creation demeaned to the status of a machine. Guided by the deep conviction that the universe was the creation of a faithful God, and that it thus contained patterns of order and regularity which could be discerned through careful observation and committed thought, scientists of this period derived laws which remarkably described the observable universe. Kepler's laws of planetary motion, Galileo's observations on acceleration, and Newton's laws of motion were the most important of these.

Together, these laws described a world so admirably constructed by its Creator that a common image for the universe came to be the clock. God was acknowledged as the cosmic clockmaker, who had done his work so well that there was no need for him to be involved in his universe. There was (in the words of Laplace's famous reply to Napoleon) no need of the hypothesis of God, whose transcendence had, throughout the first two centuries of the scientific revolution, become so exalted that he was irrelevant to the mechanism of the universe.

Thus from a Reformational assumption of the source of all things in God's will and God's faithfulness, science moved in two centuries through an assumption of God as transcendent craftsman to the conclusion that God's only relevance for creation was as an object of belief for human beings.

The old living world was dead; what had replaced it was a nature that could be explained in mechanical terms. The implications for the human use of creation, after such a transformation, are tremendous, as are the powers which became available to assist such use. But before considering those modern uses of nature, it will be helpful to consider two other seventeenth-century thinkers whose ideas about nature have shaped our own: René Descartes and Francis Bacon.

THE PHILOSOPHERS

Descartes' View of Nature

The Frenchman René Descartes was a younger contemporary of Galileo. He was a devout and brilliant mathematician, and as he viewed the increasing certainty available to the physicists when they acted on the assumption that the universe could be explained by mathematical principles, he longed for the same kind of certainty in philosophy and theology. Thus he determined to rethink human nature according to the insights available from the new physics.

Kepler, as we have seen, was determined to show of the motions of the heavens "how physical causes are to be given numerical and geometric expression." He said of the motions of the heavens, "What else can the human mind hold besides numbers and magnitudes? These alone we apprehend correctly, and if piety permits to say so, our comprehension is in this case of the same kind as God's."[6] Likewise Galileo declared of the "book of nature" that, "This book is written in the mathematical language, and the symbols are triangles, circles, and other geometrical figures, without whose help it is impossible to comprehend a single word of it."[7] Descartes wished to place philosophy and theology — and indeed all knowledge — on similarly certain foundations.

But we must point out here a kind of paradox that is evident in Galileo and Kepler, and indeed throughout the scientific revolution. We

6. Kepler, cited in Arthur Koestler, *The Sleepwalkers* (New York: Grosset & Dunlap, 1959), p. 524.
7. Galileo, cited in E. A. Burtt, *The Metaphysical Foundations of Modern Physical Science,* rev. ed. (Garden City, NY: Doubleday, 1932), p. 64.

have stressed that the great strength of the work of these men was due to their insistence upon accurate observation of the created world — on seeing, measuring, and recording nature itself, rather than determining by reason how nature *should* behave. And certainly neither Kepler's laws of planetary motion nor Galileo's ballistics would be possible without such data. But the wealth of observed data is not a wealth at all until it is somehow transformed into mental models — those which Kepler and Galileo understood to be mathematical. These models are then imposed as a form of intelligibility on that blossoming world of sense particulars from which they were derived. Ultimately, then, the basis for certainty is not the sense world, but the mental, mathematical categories to which the sense world is reduced. Descartes, while recognizing the importance of empirical data, stressed the supreme importance of this mental world.

Descartes concluded that there were two sorts of things in the world: "thinking things" and "extended things." The mind was a "thinking thing" and the only source of absolute certainty, for it was the one thing which could not be doubted. Inasmuch as the world apart from the mind, the world of "extended things," could be known with certainty, it could (and must) be reduced into measurable things, a conclusion much like Galileo's distinction between primary and secondary qualities. To the mind, the whole world is a vast machine. Any explanation of anything in nature (including one's own body) is to be given only in terms of that which can be measured, and hence is certain: extension, motion, and force.

The consequences of this view for the understanding of nature are far-reaching and extreme. One immediate consequence is a rigid distinction between body and soul (or mind). The body is a machine and the mind exists within it, but the mind is radically different. Sometimes the image of humans thus portrayed is characterized as "the ghost in the machine." Descartes had problems with this idea, for he could not determine clearly how the mind and the body affected each other. His half-hearted solution to the problem was to regard the pineal gland at the top of the brain (for which no other function was then known) as the organ of interaction between mind and body. But in this distinction of mind from body Descartes was only making explicit what was already implicit in physicists like Kepler and Galileo: knowledge is a function not of bodily participation in the world, but of the detached models which the mind builds out of that participation.

A further consequence of Descartes' view is that all of nature is a machine: it can be explained in terms of matter, extension, and motion, but not in terms of any purpose within it. That purpose is provided, rather, by the observing, thinking mind, which is detached from nature and is a different sort of substance altogether. Some of the destructive implications of this idea became immediately evident when Descartes said that, whereas a human was a machine with a mind conjoined, the body of an animal was simply a machine without a mind. There was no such thing as an "animal soul." Thus it was thought by Descartes (or at least, by Descartes' followers) to be impossible to be cruel to animals, since animals have no feelings. As one Cartesian put it, "An organ makes more noise when I play it than an animal when it cries out, yet we do not ascribe feelings to the organ." Nor was it long before some Cartesians began to apply this new view of nature. Lafontaine writes of Cartesian scientists of the seventeenth century who "administered beatings to dogs with perfect indifference and made fun of those who pitied the creatures as if they felt pain. . . . They nailed poor animals up on boards by their four paws to vivisect them and see the circulation of the blood which was a great subject of conversation."[8]

It is interesting to contrast this view of animals and humans with the Aristotelian view prevalent throughout the Middle Ages: that the human shared a "soul" with rocks, plants, and animals, but in addition had a "rational soul, which was his distinctive." In Descartes' view, the mind shares nothing with the body and hence with the rest of nature; it is completely and categorically separate from stone, tree, and beast alike. Its knowledge of those things is colored by no feeling of kinship with the nonhuman world, but is instead a reduction of that world to the certain mathematical qualities which only the "thinking thing" can know.

Subsequent thought has not taken very seriously Descartes' radical distinction between the mind and the body; in fact, the modern philosopher Gilbert Ryle goes so far as to say that we have no need of the category "mind"; we need only speak of actions, for the behavior of individuals does not require us to speak of their mind, any more than we are required to speak of "mind" or "soul" in animals. Contemporary behaviorist psychologists have effectively done the same thing, dispensing with concepts like purpose, value, and motivation, and approaching their study of humans and animals alike only in terms of measurable behavior.

Though such thinkers would disagree with Descartes' idea of the mind, they are following directly in the method he established: the attempt

---

8. Lafontaine, cited in Loren Eiseley, *The Firmament of Time* (New York: Atheneum Publishers, 1971), pp. 28-29.

to understand nature not according to any internal purpose or intrinsic quality, but by reducing it to only the measurable, mathematical qualities which the separated transcendent mind can comprehend. In the interests of putting knowledge on a secure footing, Descartes effectively eliminated (theoretically, at least) the meaningful participation of humankind in the world. This sort of draining of significance from things is described vividly by C. S. Lewis:

> At the outset the universe appears packed with will, intelligence, life and positive qualities; every tree is a nymph and every planet a god. Man himself is akin to the gods. The advance of knowledge gradually empties this rich and genial universe: first of its gods, then of its colours, smells, sounds and tastes, finally of solidity itself as solidity was originally imagined. As these items are taken from the world, they are transferred to the subjective side of the account: classified as our sensations, thoughts, images or emotions. The Subject becomes gorged, inflated, at the expense of the Object. But the matter does not rest there. The same method which has emptied the world now proceeds to empty ourselves. The masters of the method soon announce that we were just as mistaken (and mistaken in much the same way) when we attributed "souls", or "selves" or "minds" to human organisms, as when we attributed Dryads to the trees. . . . We, who have personified all other things, turn out to be ourselves mere personifications.[9]

This Cartesian process of reducing the world, the body, and ultimately, in twentieth-century thought, the mind to matter and motion is one consequence of the curious two-sidedness of the method that emerges in the seventeenth century: that is, the simultaneous importance of both mental models and empirical data in order to know nature. The first stresses the distinction between nature and humanity; the other stresses the unity between nature and humanity. And if Descartes stresses the separation of the mind from nature, there is another side to modern views of nature — a view which stresses the practical, empirical origin of knowledge. There the goal is not certain knowledge (which can be experienced only in the separated mind); more and more it is *power* over the nature which we daily encounter and which so often in human history, whether

---

9. C. S. Lewis, preface to D. E. Harding, *Hierarchy of Heaven and Earth* (London: Faber & Faber, 1952), p. 9.

in storm, disease, or earthquake, has disastrously encountered *us*. That use of knowledge of the world in order to have power over the world was the great theme of another seventeenth-century thinker, Francis Bacon.

Francis Bacon's View of Nature

"Nature, to be commanded, must be obeyed." These words occur near the beginning of Francis Bacon's most important work, the *Novum Organum*, and they summarize well not only Bacon's approach to nature and knowledge but also the underlying attitude that emerged from the new science of the seventeenth century. First of all, Bacon's aphorism leaves little doubt that nature is to be controlled; to do so is the rightful human place. But nature is also to be *obeyed*. What does Bacon mean by this paradox? Some of the background of his thinking will be helpful here.

Bacon grew up in Elizabethan England, the same era which produced Shakespeare. It was an exciting time. England, in defeating the Spanish Armada, had become a world power. Her ships were exploring the world, and there was a pervasive sense of a "brave new world" to be conquered and used. It was also an era of statecraft and intricate politics. Queen Elizabeth showed that she knew how to use power, as did her successor, King James. Francis Bacon was close to that power; his father had an important position in the court of Queen Elizabeth, and he himself held various offices in the court of King James, including that of Lord Chancellor, the highest political post in the kingdom. Thus Bacon was intimately involved with the use of political power.

But from his youth on, Bacon saw that ultimately power is derived from knowledge. And he was disturbed that human knowledge had, in the centuries of its accumulation, produced so little power over nature. Therefore he was bitterly critical of medieval science (which by then had been cast almost entirely in Aristotelian terms). Such knowledge had no offspring. And, declared Bacon, "knowledge that tendeth but to satisfaction is but as a courtesan which is for pleasure, and not for fruit or generation."[10]

Bacon's goal, then, was to establish a kind of knowledge which would bear fruit — or, to put it another way, a kind of knowledge which

---

10. Francis Bacon, cited in Max Horkheimer and Theodor W. Adorno, *Dialectic of Enlightenment* (New York: Seabury Press, 1972), p. 5.

would give power. Such a task sounds ominous to us who are aware of the misuses of power over nature. But it is important to recall the problems of life in the Elizabethan age: infant mortality was very high; plague was a frequent and awful possibility; transportation and communication were slow and difficult; and the distribution of wealth was such that the great majority of Europeans were ill-clothed and ill-fed. To Bacon, who believed in the biblical commandment that humankind is to have dominion over nature, this seemed like very poor dominion indeed. So he proposed a "great instauration": that is, a restoration to humankind of the power over nature which was given at creation but lost through the fall. He argued in the preface to *The Great Instauration*

> That the state of knowledge is not prosperous nor greatly advancing; and that a way must be opened for the human understanding entirely different from any hitherto known, and other helps provided, in order that the mind may exercise over the nature of things the authority which properly belongs to it.[11]

The old kind of knowledge, which "was not prosperous nor greatly advancing," Bacon compared to the work of a spider, who from his own innards spun forth webs: this was the deductive, rationalistic knowledge, which reasoned from first principles and had little room in it for learning directly from nature. The kind of knowledge which Bacon proposed would be, instead, of the sort produced by bees who went from flower to flower and penetrated deeply into them. Thus they produced sweetness (honey) and light (the wax from which candles could be made). In other words, what Bacon proposed was a knowledge which would provide power over nature and which would proceed not by deduction from rationally derived first principles, but by the observation of nature. This is what Bacon meant when he said, "nature, to be commanded, must be obeyed": obedience to nature is becoming like a child before its facts, the information brought through the senses. That sense data, meticulously observed, would then issue in knowledge and power. This method was far preferable to the infertile, ancient method of proceeding from first principles, a method which Bacon felt all the ancients — with the possible exception of

---

11. Bacon, in the preface to *The Great Instauration*, in *The Works of Francis Bacon*, ed. Spedding, Ellis, and Heath, popular edition (New York: Hurd & Houghton, 1878), vol. 1, part 2, p. 25.

Democritus — were guilty of. Bacon himself summed up the relative benefits of this untried "inductive method":

> There are and can be only two ways of searching into and discovering truth. The one flies from the senses and particulars to the most general axioms, and from these principles, the truth of which it takes for settled and immoveable, proceeds to judgment and to the discovery of middle axioms. And this way is now in fashion. The other derives axioms from the senses and particulars, rising by a gradual and unbroken ascent, so that it arrives at the most general axioms last of all. This is the true way, but as yet untried.[12]

Thus Bacon proposed a "new organ" of knowledge, which would proceed with unfailing progression from nature to knowledge and from knowledge to power over nature, applied for the good of humankind, who had too long been subject to nature's power.

Such an achievement would depend neither on genius nor on great discoveries, but rather on the systematic work of ordinary people applying the method to the study of nature. Thus Bacon anticipated the basic form of modern scientific research.

Equally important, Bacon recognized the time, money, and manpower which such an enterprise would require; indeed, in his dedication to the *Novum Organum*, Bacon asked King James to take it upon himself to furnish the means for carrying out such a plan. It was perhaps the first request for a government grant to fund research. "I have provided the machine," Francis concluded, "but the stuff must be gathered from nature."[13] And for such gathering, large resources of time, money, and personnel were needed — then, as they are now.

Francis himself was no scientist, but he saw clearly what science could be used for, and how it could proceed; thus he articulated more than anyone else the place of nature in modern science. Three things about his method that are important for our view of nature stand out very clearly. First, the goal of human knowledge is to have power over nature. Second, the way to attain that knowledge is by studying nature itself — not for nature's sake, but for humankind's. Third, knowledge is to be built up out of particulars; there is no overarching meaning to the knowledge thus

---

12. Bacon, Book II, Aphorism XIX, *Novum Organum,* in *The Works of Francis Bacon,* p. 71.

13. Bacon, "Letter to King James I," in *The Works of Francis Bacon,* p. 24.

inductively arrived at. It need have no coherence, so long as it yields *usable* knowledge.

Whether he prophetically described the course science was to take regardless of himself, or whether he actually shaped that course, Bacon nevertheless succeeded in setting forth with boldness and clarity the way in which twentieth-century knowledge and use of nature proceeds. The ancient and medieval goals of a harmonious world-picture, which included human values and physical facts in the same framework, as well as Descartes' rationally, mathematically coherent universe, are eclipsed by the simple admission that the real value of what we know of nature is in the power it gives. And the way to that knowledge is not by looking at the meaning of larger and larger wholes, but rather by examining behavior of smaller and smaller parts.

We would be foolish not to acknowledge our debt to the method of gaining knowledge which Bacon pioneered. We have learned profoundly from the created world: this book and the ecological understanding which lies behind it represent some of the fruits which have resulted from making ourselves students of nature. But there is a darker side to Bacon's approach. Perhaps, in recent years, it has been exaggerated, but it cannot be ignored. Carolyn Merchant, for example, in her book *The Death of Nature*, makes a convincing case that an underlying suspicion toward women, which in Bacon's day surfaced horribly in witch trials, colors Bacon's attitude toward nature, which was conventionally understood as a woman. She quotes Bacon's famous words about experiment:

> For like as a man's disposition is never well known or proved till he be crossed, nor Proteus ever changed shapes till he was straitened and held fast, so nature exhibits herself more clearly under the trials and vexations of art than when left to herself.[14]

This picture of nature as a passive (and female) figure to be tortured for human benefit is not a pleasant one. But it is an unfortunate accompaniment of that restored human dominion which Bacon sought.

Nowhere have the ambivalent fruits of such an approach to nature been more obvious than in the New World. Indeed, the New World may be seen as a kind of proving ground, a giant laboratory, for the testing of the emerging view of knowledge as power. The cover of the first edition

---

14. Francis Bacon, cited in Carolyn Merchant, *The Death of Nature: Women, Ecology, and the Scientific Revolution* (San Francisco: Harper & Row, 1980), p. 169.

of Bacon's *Novum Organum* suggests this, for it pictures two ships sailing westward into open sea, past two pillars which (Bacon tells us) are the pillars of Hercules — the ancient limits to the known. The ships of human endeavor are heading for a western frontier to prove themselves. It is one of the more significant coincidences of history that the date of publication of *Novum Organum* is 1620, the date of the first permanent settlement in North America. It is appropriate, then, that we consider the way in which our attitude toward nature has been shaped by the European presence on this vast, fertile American continent.

CHAPTER 8

🍂   🍂

The North American Experience

We primeval forests felling,
We the rivers stemming, vexing we and piercing deep the mines within,
We the surface broad surveying, we the virgin soil upheaving,
Pioneers! O pioneers!

— Walt Whitman, "Pioneers! O Pioneers!"

. . . as the moon rose higher the inessential houses began to melt away
until gradually I became aware of the old island here that flowered
once for Dutch sailors' eyes — a fresh, green breast of the new world. . . .
For a transitory enchanted moment man must have held his breath in
the presence of this continent, compelled into an aesthetic contemplation
he neither understood nor desired, face to face for the last time in history
with something commensurate to his capacity for wonder.

— F. Scott Fitzgerald, *The Great Gatsby*

POWER OVER NATURE IN THE NEW WORLD

WE HAVE ALREADY REFERRED TO THE WAY IN WHICH THE OLD
World's discovery of the New World helped to change European
understanding of how the earth should be known and used. What we are

to consider now in more detail is the way the actual experience of living in the New World began to shape attitudes toward creation that are still with us.

In the previous chapter, we outlined Francis Bacon's conviction that knowledge should give power over nature. Bacon was not a Puritan, but he was a Christian and was quite sympathetic to Puritan attitudes. His attitude toward creation is not at all unlike that of the first Puritan settlers in New England. In a very practical sense they were using knowledge to bring creation under human control. Since the creation they found in North America had an extent and vitality that had not been encountered in Europe for more than a thousand years, the New World became a great proving ground for that ideal of knowledge as power which Bacon had so eloquently outlined.

Like Bacon, the first American Puritans saw the recalcitrance of nonhuman creation as a consequence of sin; indeed, the whole New World, with its tangled forests and untamed beasts, became a kind of metaphor for the human heart which, since the fall, was desperately wicked. To attempt to build a place to live, a commonwealth, in such an environment was a fearsome task for the first settlers. William Bradford, in his account of the Plymouth Colony, described their situation in these words:

> Neither could they, as it were, go up to the top of Pisgah to view from this wilderness a more goodly country to feed their hopes; for which way soever they turned their eyes (save upward to the heavens) they could have little solace or content in respect of any outward objects. For summer being done, all things stand upon them with a weather-beaten face; and the whole country, full of woods and thickets, represented a wild and savage hue. If they looked behind them, there was the mighty ocean which they had passed, and was now as a main bar and gulf to separate them from all the civil parts of the world.[1]

Nor did the people encountered by the Puritans in this rugged world (Bradford described it as full of "wild beasts and wild men") give them at first any reason to consider that wild creation in the New World as anything other than an enemy.

Though it was not long before the first settlers had established

---

1. William Bradford, *Bradford's History of Plymouth Plantation: 1606-1646*, ed. William T. Davis (New York: Charles Scribner's Sons, 1908), p. 96. Spelling modernized.

comfortable farms and villages, the great western forest and its sometimes hostile inhabitants continually impressed upon them that the rest of creation was to be brought under their dominion. And that conquest was often understood in religious terms. Not only was the state of nature itself seen as a metaphor for the fallen condition, but the settlements were understood to be the first victories in a promised land. Indeed, place names such as "Salem" (Jerusalem), Massachusetts, testify to the religious zeal with which the New World was transformed (as Bacon would have approved) into prosperous human communities where nonhuman creation was tamed to serve humanity, God's viceroy. Though the idea of "the Promised Land" was indeed present, the Puritans understood the promise to refer not to the land in its natural state, but to the land which, through human enterprise and divine blessing, it could become. To cut down the trees, to build cities and farms, was to bring order into chaos and to advance the kingdom of God.

Though the religious zeal and rigor of the early colonies did not last long, the practical Baconianism of that Puritan attitude toward nonhuman creation has survived, in modified forms, even into the present. The 3000-mile breadth of the continent provided nearly three centuries to perfect the skills needed to develop human power over the earth. And the great wealth of the earth in the New World — whether it was the lumber of the forests, the fertility of the plains, the coal of the hills, or the fish and game of the wilderness — confirmed Bacon's idea that knowledge equaled power. One of the fruits of that determination to apply knowledge to the task of making the earth serve humankind was what has come to be known as "Yankee ingenuity": the ability to take a hard problem and solve it, whether in building a bridge, a reaper, or a cotton gin. On the frontier, at least, nature was an enemy to be turned into a servant. There is little recorded to prove that the early settlers ever saw it as much more than that; they were merely trying to find a place to live and a source of food and pasture. The result was a great deal of practical knowledge about how to use the land, but not much interest in the land for its own sake. The attitude is captured excellently in Alexis de Tocqueville's description of the pioneer — in contrast to the European — attitude toward nature.

> In Europe people talk a great deal of the wilds of America, but the Americans themselves never think about them: they are insensible to the wonders of inanimate Nature, and they may be said not to perceive the mighty forests which surround them till they fall beneath the

hatchet. Their eyes are fixed upon another sight: the . . . march across these wilds — drying swamps, turning the course of rivers, peopling solitudes, and subduing Nature.[2]

This understanding of nature as primarily something to be conquered is a main subject of that most American of poets, Walt Whitman, who wrote many poems in celebration of "the New arriving, assuming, taking possession, a swarming and busy race settling and organizing everywhere." In "Song of the Broad-Axe," Whitman summed up this prevailing theme in the American treatment of the land:

> The axe leaps!
> The solid forest gives fluid utterances,
> They tumble forth, they rise and form,
> Hut, tent, landing, survey,
> Flail, plough, pick, crowbar, spade,
> Shingle, rail, prop, wainscot, jamb, lath, panel, gable,
> . . . .
> Hoe, rake, pitchfork, pencil, wagon, staff, saw, jack-plane, mallet,
>   wedge, rounce,
> Chair, tub, hoop, table, wicket, vane, sash, floor . . .

These, Whitman says, are the utterances of the forest — yet they are all human products, as though the only purpose of the forest is to be raw material for human inventions.

This Baconian (and Puritan) attitude toward nature as something to be used resulted in great prosperity. But it also resulted in the slaughter of billions of passenger pigeons, the near-extinction of the bison, the destruction of whole forest ecosystems (such as the white pine in Michigan), and the near-eradication of both tall- and short-grass prairies. The list of such tragedies for creation in North America (and throughout the earth) is long. One of the greatest tragedies we are just coming to acknowledge: the humiliation, enslavement, and murder of the human beings who lived here, and whose remnants still preserve for us some wisdom about how people and place can live in harmony. Yet few in North America have seriously questioned the beneficence of reducing the continent to human

---

2. Alexis de Tocqueville, *Democracy in America,* trans. Henry Reeve (1835, 1840; reprint, London: Oxford University Press, 1952), pp. 343-44.

use. Many today still share that basic Puritan idea that uncontrolled nature is a failure to fulfill the divine commandment to have dominion.

PROTESTANTISM AND THE LAND

The link between Calvinist Protestantism and the domination of the North American continent has been made very explicit by some scholars. Max Weber, early in the twentieth century, published a book called *The Protestant Ethic and the Spirit of Capitalism* that continues to influence discussion of our use of creation. Weber's argument, briefly, is that the Calvinist doctrine of divine election, though giving no guarantees about eternal salvation, is nevertheless accompanied by a promise that God will materially bless those he has chosen. This promise places a sort of pressure on earnest Christians to regard every occupation as a sacred calling, requiring them to work hard, be frugal, and make the most of those bits of creation given into their stewardship — not primarily for the creation's sake, but as a confirmation of their salvation. Accompanying this single-minded pursuit of wealth for spiritual reasons is a reductive rationality which encourages those Baconian and Cartesian tendencies to simplify the diversity of creation into machine-like components that could be easily understood and controlled. Weber puts this Protestant legacy in the New World in these words:

> The Puritan wanted to work in a calling; we are forced to do so. For when asceticism was carried out of monastic cells into everyday life, and began to dominate worldly morality, it did its part in building the tremendous cosmos of the modern economic order. This order is now bound to the technical and economic conditions of machine produc-tion which today determine the lives of all the individuals who are born into this mechanism, not only those directly concerned with economic acquisition, with irresistible force. Perhaps it will so deter-mine them until the last ton of fossilized coal is burnt. In Baxter's view [Richard Baxter was a Puritan theologian] the care for external goods should only lie on the shoulders of the saint like a light cloak, which can be thrown aside at any moment. But fate decreed that the cloak should become an iron cage.[3]

---

3. Max Weber, *The Protestant Ethic and the Spirit of Capitalism* (New York: Scribner's Sons, 1976), p. 181.

Weber caricatures Calvinism, to be sure, and his explanations of the *reasons* for what he calls characteristic Calvinist attitudes are not always convincing. But despite his oversimplification of a rich and nourishing theological system, there is a great deal of validity in the connection he draws between Calvinism and the "iron cage" of the modern attitude toward creation. Consider, for example, these lines from a poem written by Stanley Wiersma (under the name Sietze Buning), who grew up in mid-century in a community in northwest Iowa which was shaped by a Dutch Calvinist interpretation of our place in creation. Wiersma describes the theological precision with which "our Calvinist fathers" planted their corn:

> A field-length wire with a metal knot,
> every three feet ran through the planter and clicked off three kernels
> at each knot. Planted in rows east-west, the rows also ran north-
> south for cross-cultivating. Each field was a checkerboard even to
> the diagonals. No Calvinist followed the land's contours.
>
> Contour farmers in surrounding counties
> improvised their rows against the slope
> of the land. There was no right way.
> Before our fathers planted a field,
> they knew where each hill of corn
> would be . . .
> . . . .
>
> Contour fields resulted
> from free will, nary a cornstalk pre-
> determined. The God contour farmers
> trusted, if any, was as capricious
> as their cornfields. Calvinists knew
> the distance between God and people was
> even greater than the distance between people
> and corn kernels. If we were corn kernels in God's
> corn planter, would we want him to plant us at random?
> Contour farmers were frivolous about the doctrine of election
> simply by being contour farmers.
> . . . .
>
> We youngsters pointed out that the tops
> of our rises were turning clay-brown, that bushels of black dirt

washed into creeks and ditches each time it rained, and that
in the non-Calvinist counties the tops of the rises were
black. We were told we were arguing by results, not
by principles. Why, God could replenish the black
dirt overnight. The tops of the rises were God's business.
Our business was to farm on Biblical principles.
Like, Let everything be done decently and in good order . . .[4]

Wiersma is sympathetic here to the Calvinism he gently chides. But he confirms the general accuracy of Weber's analysis: something in the rigidity of the way God's relationship to his creatures was understood (though such an understanding was probably never Calvin's intention) seems to have entered the Protestant understanding of work — and hence, to have shaped our treatment of the earth. As Wiersma's poem suggests, an assumption about the nature of dominion (God's dominion over us, our dominion over the earth) has contributed to a harsh treatment of the earth, particularly in North America.[5]

AMERICA AS PROMISED LAND: THE AGRARIAN IDEAL

Alongside the prevailing view of nature as raw material to be subdued and used, there arose very early a gentler conception of nature, especially in the United States, which was implicit in the Puritan metaphors of the New World as the Promised Land. This is sometimes referred to as the pastoral or agrarian ideal, and it achieved its most eloquent description in the words of Thomas Jefferson. People and place should be in harmony,

---

4. Sietze Buning, "Calvinist Farming," in *Purpaleanie and Other Permutations* (Orange City, IA: Middleburg Press, 1978), p. 61.

5. But while regarding the North American continent as raw material to be subdued was certainly the prevailing attitude of the first settlers, and is perhaps the prevailing attitude today, it has by no means been the only way of understanding nature. The Canadian attitude (though perhaps no gentler in result) is subtly different from the American. In Canada, where the haunting proximity of the vast and hostile North has been a continual pressure on both success and imagination, the idea of subduing nature has never predominated. Thus the triumphant image of a receding frontier has not shaped the national attitude quite so much as in the U.S. As Canadian novelist Margaret Atwood has argued, "surviving" is the root metaphor for the Canadian experience, just as "the frontier" is for the American.

according to this attitude, and that harmony is most realized in the husbandry of agriculture, which has no need of cities for its support. Jefferson's ideal for America was a nation of independent farmers. He wrote:

> . . . we have an immensity of land courting the industry of the husbandman. Is it best then that all our citizens should be employed in its improvement, or that one half should be called off from that to exercise manufactures and handicraft arts for the other? Those who labour in the earth are the chosen people of God, if ever he had a chosen people. . . . Corruption of morals in the mass of cultivators is a phenomenon of which no age nor nation has furnished an example. . . . Let our work-shops remain in Europe. . . . The mobs of great cities add just so much to the support of pure government, as sores do to the strength of the human body.[6]

Underlying Jefferson's remarkably strong defense of an agricultural way of life is an attitude toward the land significantly different from the ideal of subjection which seems to characterize Bacon and the Puritans. While nature is not personified or deified, by Jefferson's time there nevertheless had crept into American thought the possibility of the land as a source of strength: "Those who labour in the earth are the chosen people of God."

One source of this softening attitude toward the land is undoubtedly a sort of nostalgia. As the frontier moved further and further westward, those left in the comfortable (and increasingly crowded) East remembered with a kind of longing the nature which had given way for the cities, and the rewarding human endeavor which had made it give way. Indeed, a persuasive and influential theory of the American character, sometimes called the "frontier thesis," was developed near the turn of this century (shortly after the official disappearance of the American frontier in the census of 1890) by Frederick Jackson Turner. He maintained that the frontier had been a kind of safety valve for social discontent; the continual possibility for people to prove themselves by shaping nature to their ends had given rise to a kind of democratic greatness. Whether or not we accept Turner's thesis, it is clear that by the nineteenth century, people regarded American nature — especially if it was safely in the West,

---

6. Thomas Jefferson, *Notes on the State of Virginia*, ed. William Peden (Chapel Hill, NC: University of North Carolina Press, 1955), pp. 164-65.

or encountered under conditions which could be easily controlled — with a kind of fondness.

Americans also viewed nature with a kind of pride, as they cast about for ways of defending their young nation in the presence of the older and often snobbish European nations. The one thing that America had in greater abundance than the Europeans was undisturbed nature. Thus, in the nineteenth century, a kind of national pride in the American wilderness helped to shape a kindlier attitude toward unhumanized nature — and probably gave considerable impetus to the uniquely American "National Parks" movement.[7]

But by far the largest influence on this change of the American attitude from animosity to awe and affection is an amorphous and hard-to-define change in sensibility usually called by the unhelpful name of "Romanticism." And in order to understand Romanticism, it will be necessary to return to the Old World.

THE ROMANTIC VIEW OF NATURE

In many ways, Romanticism (which emerged as a force in European thought at about the same time as the American and French Revolutions, and which was not entirely unconnected with those revolutions) may be seen, at least in its attitude toward nature, as a reaction. It was a reaction against the mechanization of nature — which came about as a consequence of the scientific revolution — and against the pervasive image of the universe as a machine. Toward the end of the eighteenth century, a few German and English poets began to believe that seeing the earth, animals, or their own selves as an elaborate machine and thinking mathematically in a way that excluded sights, smells, colors, and odors from importance was more than inaccurate: it was false and evil. Thus William Blake sang the praises of a "fourfold" vision of nature, and prayed, "May God us keep/From a Single vision & Newton's sleep!"[8] Accompanying this

---

7. This story of growing American pride in wilderness is well told by Roderick Nash in *Wilderness and the American Mind*, 3rd ed. (New Haven: Yale University Press, 1982), esp. chapter 4, "The *American* Wilderness."

8. William Blake, "To Thomas Butts," in *The Letters of William Blake*, ed. Geoffrey Keynes (London: Rupert Hart-Davis, 1968), p. 62.

disgust at mechanistic portrayals of both people and nature was a stress on the beauty and vitality of creation, strengthened by a kind of wonder and awe which some critics have mistaken for pantheism.

But it is quite misleading to see this changed Romantic attitude toward nature as merely a reaction against the new mechanistic ways of thinking and an attempt to go back to some sort of primitive nature worship. (It is, however, a mistake which is often made by both contemporary Romantics and critics of Romanticism alike.) Rather, the Romantics were vividly and painfully aware of that exclusion of humanity from the earth which was a consequence of the new science. In every case, whether we speak of Kepler, Galileo, Descartes, or Bacon, the early theorists of science maintained that the aesthetic aspects of sense knowledge — the things delightful to the eye, the ear, the touch — were irrelevant or even misleading in getting at the real truth. There was no room for the feelings in such an attitude. Yet the Romantics agreed with the idea underlying this mechanistic distinction between primary and secondary qualities; that is, they too saw the primacy of the mind over nature and the dependence of nature on the mind for any beauty, meaning, or significance which it seems to have. Samuel Taylor Coleridge (the deepest thinker of the English Romantics) expressed this in a poem:

> I may not hope from outward forms to win
> The passion and the life, whose fountains are within.
> O Lady! we receive but what we give,
> And in our life alone does Nature live.[9]

The philosopher who most systematically articulated the ideas underlying the Romantic view of the relation between mind and nature was Immanuel Kant. He maintained that the mind could know the world only through the categories which it imposed upon the world; thus the very act of knowing structured the world, so far as the perceiver was concerned. And there was no way of getting outside these mentally constructed categories to the experience of nature itself.

Though the pioneers of the scientific revolution, whose thought we have briefly summarized, stressed the detachment of the mind from nature, the goal of their detachment was measurable knowledge, resulting

---

9. Samuel Taylor Coleridge, "Dejection: An Ode," in *The Complete Poetical Works of Samuel Taylor Coleridge*, ed. Ernest Hartley Coleridge (Oxford: Clarendon Press, 1912), vol. 1, p. 365.

in accuracy of prediction, consistency of hypothesis, or efficiency in manipulation. Not so with the Romantics. For them, the proper use of the mind's distinctness from nature was the creative revitalization of the natural world. Coleridge's line, "in our life alone does Nature live," should not be read "without us nature is dead," but "with us nature *lives*." For the Romantics, the great agent of this revitalization of nature was the imagination. Coleridge called it "the repetition in the finite mind of the infinite I AM," and thus linked human imaginative power over nature with the divine creative power itself.

Thus an unexpected consequence of the mind's detachment from nature was an ability to experience nature with a great intensity of feeling. Indeed, many of the contemporary appreciative attitudes toward nature which we now take for granted — the motives for mountain climbing, bird watching, wilderness camping — have their origins in what we could call the "Romantic Revolution." The imaginative synthesis of the mind with nature brought both intense personal pleasure and an appreciation of the things in nature which, in the light of the human imagination, now stood forth in a kind of radiant worth never before noticed.

TRANSCENDENTALISM AND WILDERNESS

When this Romantic attitude toward nature crossed the Atlantic and began to influence American thought, it combined with those other tendencies toward an appreciative view of nature which we spoke of earlier, and began to be a potent force in what Americans did with and to their land. The most identifiable form of Romanticism in America is sometimes known as "Transcendentalism," and its two main prophets were Ralph Waldo Emerson and Henry David Thoreau. Both men exercised — and continue to exercise — a tremendous influence on American thought in general and on American attitudes toward nature in particular.

The label "Transcendentalist" is somewhat paradoxical, if we consider that the ideas of Transcendentalism led Thoreau to immerse himself in the woods by Walden Pond for two years and John Muir (an ardent disciple of Thoreau) to spend weeks at a time alone in the wilderness of the western mountains. "Immanentalist" would at first glance seem a more accurate label. But the word "transcendental" reveals that the origin of the new view of nature is in the separateness of the mind from nature and in the consequent access of the mind to a reality beyond nature. Said Emerson, "Nature is the symbol of spirit. . . . The world is emblematic."[10] And Thoreau echoed this statement in his version of empiricism: "let us not underrate the value of a fact; it will one day flower in a truth."[11]

The philosophy behind Thoreau's thought may have stressed the transcendence of the mind. But in practice that awareness of the transcendent mind impelled Thoreau to a deep appreciation of the natural world and a fundamental critique of the manipulative attitude toward nature which seemed to motivate the "lives of quiet desperation" he observed in his contemporaries.

"In wildness is the preservation of the world," said Thoreau, and his words sum up the change in attitude toward nature that took place in nineteenth-century America, and which continues unabated in our own time. Thoreau's was still a very lonely voice in his time, but by the last quarter of the nineteenth century he had come to be regarded by some as a prophet. Toward the close of that century the first official recognition of the new view of nature took place in the establishment of the Adirondack forest preserve, "forever wild" in upstate New York, and in the creation of Yellowstone, the world's first national park.

A key figure in this growing American enthusiasm for wilderness was John Muir, founder of the Sierra Club. Muir's father was a Scottish Calvinist who immigrated, with his family, to Wisconsin in the nineteenth century. The young Muir, eventually repudiating both his father's faith and his father's harsh pioneering spirit, ended up in California, where he became a lifelong spokesman for preserving the wildness of the Sierra Nevada. (In the process, he seems to have reaffirmed at least his faith in the Creator.)[12] Muir argued eloquently that mountains and forests are God's temples, and that we need them for our own spiritual health. Muir was not only instrumental in the establishment of Yosemite (first as a

---

10. Ralph Waldo Emerson, "Nature," in *Nature, Addresses and Lectures: The Works of Ralph Waldo Emerson* (Boston: Standard Library, 1883), vol. 1, pp. 28, 35.

11. Henry David Thoreau, cited in Roderick Nash, *Wilderness and the American Mind,* rev. ed. (New Haven/London: Yale University Press, 1973), p. 85.

12. Richard Cartwright Austin, in a book on John Muir called *Baptized into Wilderness* (Atlanta: John Knox Press, 1987), has gone so far as to argue that wild creation became for Muir a kind of mediator to God, taking the place of the Christ his father's severity had made hard to accept. Austin's attempt to baptize Muir into orthodox Christian faith is not convincing, but his portrayal of Muir as an authentically prophetic voice for the creation which Christians have often neglected or misused is powerful.

California park), but he was also influential on the conservation strategies of Theodore Roosevelt.

But these token preserves of unutilized nature and even the growing enthusiasm for the wild which swept America in the early twentieth century (resulting, for example, in such oddities as Roosevelt's "Boone and Crockett Club" and in the establishment of the Boy Scouts) failed to slow significantly the rate at which America was subduing creation for human use. But the interest in "wilderness" reveals a peculiarly modern response to the relationship between people and nature. Instead of establishing a kind of harmony (as is evident in some European countries, and as is clearly called for in Jefferson's agrarian ideal), the American solution is to use most of the land intensively and even destructively, but to leave large tracts of land untouched as "wilderness areas." Such an attitude did not become official policy until the Wilderness Act of 1963, but it was already implicit in the nineteenth century. It shows a recognition, forced perhaps by the uniqueness of the North American experience, of both the priority of human use of the land and an equal priority to preserve and care for it.

CONSERVATION: THE BIRTH OF THE "ENVIRONMENTAL MOVEMENT"

Out of this deep tension between our need to use the land and our need to care for it emerged what today is commonly called the "environmental movement." In its first form it was primarily a concern for "conservation." In the last half of the nineteenth century and in the early years of the twentieth there was, as we noted, a growing interest in preserving bits and pieces of scenic beauty and wild nature (as places for experiencing aesthetic pleasure or for practicing the pioneer arts of hunting and pathfinding). But North American use of the land was still controlled by a frontier attitude: land was there to be used, to be transformed into human profit. In these days free-market capitalism was the unquestioned economic system, and guidance by the government was minimal. It was a day, too, of rapid technological change — the beginning, in fact, of a period of technological acceleration which continues into our own time. But there was little suggestion then that some technologies might be "inappropriate." Conquests and tamings of nature were everywhere evident and exciting: the crossing of the continent by railroads and highways; the decrease of distance by the automobile and the airplane; the application of machine technology to agriculture, resulting in intensive farming and increased yields — these were all seen as unqualified blessings, despite their growing dependence on a massive use of natural resources. By the beginning of this century, the deforestation of Michigan had nearly ended, and a similar large-scale logging of Oregon and Washington was just getting underway. The plow was breaking the Plains states at an increasingly rapid rate, and the virgin soil was still producing rich crops. Settlers were spreading into the western states, and there was still room for them; immigrants were still streaming into the port cities of the East Coast, in search of the opportunities of the last frontier.

There was little to change that frontier model eighty years ago — except the disappearance of the frontier itself. That disappearance took place officially in the national census of 1890, and it signaled the beginning of that slow recognition of limitations on resources which, in the last third of this century, has brought a model based on limits — the spaceship-earth model — into public consciousness.

These limits were first recognized by the artists, the writers, and the historians — not by the loggers, miners, and farmers. We have already referred to Turner's "frontier thesis," which explained the distinctiveness of the American character in terms of the frontier and speculated on what the disappearance of that frontier would do to the American psyche. Toward the end of the first quarter of the century a disillusioned group of writers and artists emerged, many of whom, in reaction to a kind of loss and bewilderment which they felt in America, lived abroad. "The Lost Generation" was a label applied to these writers, and the most famous of them, Ernest Hemingway, set forth clearly his perception of what had gone wrong with America. In *The Green Hills of Africa* he wrote:

A continent ages quickly once we come. The natives live in harmony with it. But the foreigner destroys, cuts down the trees, drains the water, so that the water supply is altered and in a short time the soil, once the sod is turned under, is cropped out and, next, it starts to blow away as it has blown away in every old country and as I had seen it start to blow in Canada. The earth gets tired of being exploited. A country wears out quickly unless man puts back in it all his residue and that of all his beasts. When he quits using beasts and uses machines, the earth defeats him quickly. The machine can't reproduce, nor does it fertilize the soil, and it eats what he cannot raise. A country was made to be as we found it.[13]

This is a remarkably contemporary-sounding insight for 1935. But drought, the Dust Bowl, and the Depression had struck America, and its people were learning, on a number of fronts, the consequences of the frontier model. The remarkable thing about the Hemingway passage is neither the accuracy of its insights into the health of a landscape nor his recognition of the dangers of a frontier mentality; rather, it is his continued longing for a frontier, and his reluctance to give up the idea. For he follows this eloquent passage with these words:

> Our people went to America because that was the place to go then. It had been a good country and we had made a bloody mess of it and I would go, now, somewhere else as we had always had the right to go somewhere else and as we had always gone. You could always come back. Let the others come to America who did not know that they had come too late. Our people had seen it at its best and fought for it when it was well worth fighting for. Now I would go somewhere else. We always went in the old days and there were still good places to go.[14]

Hemingway clearly recognized, in 1935, the dangers of the old frontier attitude. But his solution was to search for another frontier, not to recognize the limits of the earth. The full lesson of the twentieth century, the lesson made so vivid by space flight and the photographs of the earth it has given us, is that we can no longer say, with Hemingway, that we will "go, now, somewhere else as we had always had the right to go somewhere else and as we had always gone." For, unlike Hemingway, we now realize that there are no more "good places to go."

The Dust Bowl years and the years of the Great Depression were times for North Americans to take stock of the nation. And, out of the necessity for survival, they caused some of the earlier Romantic and Transcendentalist notions to come together with a scientific and utilitarian concern for the land itself. "Conservation" became a common word in the thirties, referring mainly to the conservation of soil, which, to the

---

13. Ernest Hemingway, *The Green Hills of Africa* (New York: Charles Scribner's Sons, 1953), p. 284.
14. Ibid., p. 285.

horror of farmers and of a whole nation, blew away in the dry years following several decades of farming for quick profit. The American people, heretofore optimistic pioneers, were forced by the limitations of the land and of the planet to reflect on the consequences of pioneering when the frontier disappeared. Though the change toward a conservation ideal proceeded slowly, it drew considerable force from these years of agonized introspection. In some people it took the form of a kind of detached despair about humanity's ability ever to live wholly on the land. The poet Robinson Jeffers wrote:

> . . . however ugly the parts appear the whole remains beautiful. A
> severed hand
> Is an ugly thing, and man dissevered from the earth and stars and
> his history . . . for contemplation or in fact . . .
> Often appears atrociously ugly. Integrity is wholeness, the greatest
> beauty is
> Organic wholeness, the wholeness of life and things, the divine
> beauty of the universe. Love that, not man
> Apart from that, or else you will share man's pitiful confusions, or
> drown in despair when his days darken.[15]

Nevertheless, there were some in those times who did not despair at the painful lesson of limitations, but worked toward enabling Americans to adopt a different understanding of the earth and their use of it. The most important of those persons was Aldo Leopold. Trained as a forester, and with a deep appreciation for both the beauty and the complexity of what he called "healthy land," he did more than anyone to bring the precise knowledge of the scientist together with the aesthetic sensibility of a Thoreau or a Muir. As a forester in the Southwest, as a teacher at the University of Wisconsin, and especially as the author of many powerful essays and articles (brought together and published posthumously in *A Sand County Almanac*), Leopold was primarily responsible for replacing the frontier model with that of spaceship earth. That insight is expressed clearly in the following passage:

> We know now what was unknown to all the preceding caravan of
> generations: that men are only fellow-voyagers with other creatures in

---

15. Robinson Jeffers, "The Answer," in *The Selected Poetry of Robinson Jeffers* (1927; New York: Random House, 1933), p. 594.

the odyssey of evolution. This new knowledge should have given us, by this time, a sense of kinship with fellow-creatures; a wish to live and let live; a sense of wonder over the magnitude and duration of the biotic enterprise. . . .

These things, I say, should have come to us. I fear they have not come to many.[16]

Based on his understanding of the interrelationships of creatures, Leopold proposed the necessity of a "land ethic." Humanity, wrote Leopold, once felt it proper for slaveholders to treat slaves without concern for ethical principles. Hanging slaves at the mere suspicion of misbehavior was not regarded as wrong; it was simply what one did with property. Today we have extended our concept of right and wrong to include all of humanity. No civilized person is likely to defend the idea that other persons are to be treated as property; but land is a different story. Writes Leopold:

There is as yet no ethic dealing with man's relation to land and to the animals and plants which grow upon it. Land, like Odysseus' slave-girls, is still property. The land-relation is still strictly economic, entailing privileges but not obligations.[17]

So, based on his recognition that humanity is not "conqueror of the land community," but "plain member and citizen of it," Leopold observes that

The extension of ethics to this third element in human environment [the land and its nonhuman life] is, if I read the evidence correctly, an evolutionary possibility and an ecological necessity. It is the third step in a sequence. The first two [affirming relationships to individual and to society] have already been taken. Individual thinkers since the days of Ezekiel and Isaiah have asserted that the despoliation of land is not only inexpedient but wrong. Society, however, has not yet affirmed their belief. I regard the present conservation movement as the embryo of such an affirmation.[18]

---

16. Aldo Leopold, *A Sand County Almanac* (New York: Oxford University Press, 1949), pp. 109-10.

17. Ibid., p. 203.

18. Ibid.

That embryonic conservation movement has since reached a kind of maturity (or at least a late adolescence) in America, due in large part to Leopold's influence. Leopold's understanding of the earth as the biosphere, a great network of living and nonliving things, has made us much more deeply aware of the land as not just "resources" but as our "environment." Thus the "environmental movement" was born.

The influence of that broad "environmental" movement began to be exerted in the early fifties, contemporaneous with that postwar enthusiasm for convenience, development, and rapid growth whose technological consequences for the earth we noted earlier. It is hard to say how much the movement on the part of many people toward something like a "land ethic" is a reaction against the negative aspects of that growth (from smog to shopping centers on farmland) or the result of the ideas put forth by Leopold and others. Certainly many factors contributed to the growth of the idea of the earth as a fragile, limited ecosphere, a "spaceship." One factor was the threat of worldwide destruction that came from the development of atomic weapons. Another was the dramatic increase in certain

From *The New Yorker*, September 25, 1989. Drawing by Dedini; © 1989 The New Yorker Magazine, Inc. Used by permission.

kinds of pollution, chronicled most dramatically in Rachel Carson's *Silent Spring*. The space flights themselves have tremendously increased our appreciation for the finitude and beauty of the planet. In America, the incident of the Arab oil embargo, the Iraqi invasion of Kuwait, and the subsequent war in the Middle East have taught us our dependence on limited supplies of fuel — and so on.

Whatever the combination of reasons, we find in North America today a strongly developed awareness that we cannot live our lives as though human beings were the only things important on earth. The last decade in particular (since the first edition of *Earthkeeping*) has seen that movement become almost religious in its strength. So we now turn to a consideration of that recent development (mainly in the decade of the eighties) of the environmental movement into a call for something like a new religion for our times.

CHAPTER 9

❧   ❧

The Environmental Movement: Searching for a New Religion

The wind blows to the south and turns to the north; round and round
it goes, ever returning on its course. All streams flow into the sea, yet
the sea is never full. To the place the streams come from, there they
return again. . . . Is there anything of which one can say, "Look! This
is something new"? It was here already, long ago; it was here before our
time. . . . I have seen the burden God has laid on men. He has made
everything beautiful in its time. He has also set eternity in the hearts
of men; yet they cannot fathom what God has done from beginning to
end.

— Ecclesiastes 1:6-7, 10; 3:10-11, NIV

SOMETIME IN THE LATE SIXTIES — AT LEAST BY "EARTH DAY" IN 1970 —
the "environmental movement" was born. Both words — "environment" and "movement" — are significant. "The Environment" (often
capitalized) has come to be the accepted term for speaking of what used
to be called "nature" or "creation." It came originally from a verb meaning
"to surround," and thus has long been used to speak of "surroundings."
In its current usage as a synonym for the whole biosphere it suggests
the relatively new ecological insight that nothing on earth can fully be
understood in isolation, apart from its environment. But it nevertheless

raises the question, "environment" (or surroundings) of *what,* or *whom?* Either the word means something like "everything on the planet considered as a mutual environment for everything else" (a very confused understanding) or it means something much more anthropocentric: *our* environment — that which supports human beings and their culture. In either case "environment" is an oddly arid word, more sterile than words which it has replaced, like "nature," "creation," or "earth." All three of these older terms are rooted in a religious understanding. And by its very poverty, "environment" invites a religious framework to give it meaning. Hence, much of our concern in this chapter is to show how that religious vacuum implied by the abstraction "environment" has come, in the last decade, to be filled by a variety of religious options.

The word "movement" is suggestive as well. In the United States, the sixties were a decade of "movements": the civil rights movement, the anti-war movement, and the women's liberation movement, to name the most prominent ones. To some, the atmosphere of all-encompassing change was so great that all of the various ferments were lumped together and referred to simply as "The Movement." The word "movement" suggests a force, larger than the personal or individual, in which individuals are caught up (sometimes against their will). The roots of that transpersonal understanding of "movement" are at least twofold, and both are important for understanding the current force of the environmental "movement."

The first and most recent root is a popularizing of the biological theory of evolution. Charles Darwin and Alfred Russel Wallace, in the middle of the nineteenth century, provided good empirical evidence of organic change through time — a general "movement" from the simple to the complex. More important, they suggested a rough theory — "natural selection" — to explain that movement. A more sophisticated form of natural selection theory, which includes an understanding of how living things are adapted to their environment, is an indispensable tool of twentieth-century biology and ecology.

But right from the beginning that biological theory of evolution — which, strictly speaking, can only describe *change* — was confused with much grander notions of *progress.* These older ideas of progress form the second root of the potent modern understanding of "movement." Marx's understanding of an inevitable evolution of economic forms has exerted tremendous influence on political thought in the twentieth century, and much of the force of the word "movement" comes from that source. (Significantly, Marx wanted to dedicate *Das Kapital* to Charles Darwin.)

But Marx's ideas (and the evolution-as-progress popularization of Darwin's) have older sources. The philosopher Hegel — who postulated a grand dialectic of Absolute idea coming to realize itself in time — is the most important of these. But even Hegel's ambitious picture of the emergence of the Absolute idea is rooted in more obscure Romantic notions of human thought as the emerging consciousness of nature. Recall (from the previous chapter) Coleridge's line, "in our life alone does Nature live." Ultimately, it is probably the case that the whole idea of progress — of Evolution with a purpose, of Movement toward a conclusion — is a secularization of the biblical idea of history. We will return to that biblical view in a later chapter. For now it is enough to note that the "movement" in "environmental movement" has behind it a great political, ideological, and religious weight: it can suggest (and does, to many people) an inevitable sweeping of cosmic history toward a utopian end: a "New Age" is coming, and we must speed up its arrival.

It is no surprise then that the "environmental movement" has acquired, in the past decade, a philosophical and religious complexity. It is an ethic in search of a religion, so in an era increasingly suspicious of religion, concern for the earth has become something of a religion in itself.

"DEEP ECOLOGY"

This concern to move beyond "shallow environmentalism" into religious significance is most evident in the "Deep Ecology" movement. The main features of that approach are outlined in a book called *Deep Ecology: Living as If Nature Mattered*, written by two philosophers, Bill DeVall and George Sessions, and published in 1985. The book is a kind of compendium of both "deep" and "shallow" responses to environmental problems, and it works out a thesis first stated by the Norwegian philosopher Arne Naess in a 1973 essay, "The Shallow and the Deep, Long-Range Ecology Movements." Naess criticizes as shallow those approaches to environmental problems which see them as short-term technical problems requiring only technological fixes: installing better "scrubbers" in our industrial smokestacks, for example, or developing some inexhaustible source of nonpolluting energy. In contrast (as DeVall and Sessions restate the idea),

deep ecology goes beyond the so-called factual scientific level to the
level of self and Earth wisdom. . . . [It] goes beyond a limited
piecemeal shallow approach to environmental problems and attempts
to articulate a comprehensive religious and philosophical worldview.
The foundations of deep ecology are the basic intuitions and experiencing of ourselves and Nature which comprise ecological consciousness. . . . Many of these questions are perennial philosophical and
religious questions faced by humans in all cultures over the ages.[1]

The authors of *Deep Ecology* go on to acknowledge that people in "many
different spiritual traditions — Christianity, Taoism, Buddhism, and Native American Rituals" — have asked fundamental ecological questions.
In fact, the authors imply, ecological wisdom may be the main thing that
diverse religions have in common. So the authors go on to list a variety
of sources of "Deep Ecology." Some of these are classical ancient or more
tentative forms of the "perennial philosophy," monism: the "new" physics;
Christianity; Feminism; Martin Heidegger; and the Eastern spiritual tradition (especially Taoism). Others are an attempt to go further back in time
and recapture prehistoric human attitudes toward the earth. The authors
of *Deep Ecology* make a convincing case that Western culture is in a kind
of eclectic religious revival motivated mainly by ecological concerns. In
the following pages we discuss some of the main features of that attempt
to find a religion with which to support an environmental ethic.

Monism

"Monism" is a philosophical term describing the belief that despite the
appearance of diversity, at their core all things are one. The monist premise
appears occasionally in Western thought (in some of the pre-Socratics, for
example, and in the philosophy of Spinoza), but it is central to Oriental
thought. According to the monist, all distinctions — between one self and
another, between humanity and nature, between God and the world —
break down. All is one and all is God (thus pantheism is a kind of monism).

It is not surprising that some form of monism is attractive to those
who have discovered the nature of ecological connectedness. "When you
try to pick anything out by itself," said John Muir, "you find it hitched

---

1. Bill DeVall and George Sessions, *Deep Ecology: Living as If Nature Mattered*
(Salt Lake City: Peregrine Smith Books, 1985), p. 65.

to everything else in the universe." From the fact that most of the elements in our bodies were forged in the heart of long-dead stars, to the fact that the oxygen we breathe was transpired by green plants, to the fact that the aerosols we use today might widen the hole in the ozone layer over the poles in the spring — in the past few decades we have discovered wonderful and alarming instances of being "hitched to everything else in the universe." One must, of course, make a series of metaphysical leaps to move from these instances of interconnectedness to the belief that God, self, and nature are one. But several features of the modern experience have encouraged such a conclusion, erroneous though it may be.

Perhaps the most important is a general disillusionment with the consequences of the opposite view: that I am distinct from, over against, everything in the universe. In chapter 7 we saw such an attitude emerging, in the seventeenth century, out of the complex, fruitful, but dangerous conjunction of Baconian science, Cartesian philosophy, and some aspects of Protestant theology. It is widely perceived to be the case (whether or not it is true) that Christian thought encourages (1) a belief in the otherness of God from creation (a kind of dualism inescapable in the very notion of creation); (2) a corresponding otherness of man from nature (especially "man" — women, it is said, have been regarded as suspiciously embedded in nature); and (3) a consequent feeling of lordship and dominion over nature, which is perceived to be other than ourselves.

The monism invoked in support of the environmental movement is itself supported by a number of sources, some old, some new. We will consider them in turn, from the most recent to the oldest.

The Gaia Hypothesis

Gaia is the Greek word for the goddess of the earth. (It is hidden in words like *geology, geography,* and *geometry.*) In recent years the word has increasingly come to be applied to the earth considered as a live being. More and more *Gaia* has come to have a religious meaning as an old name for "Nature": mother, source, earth goddess. The religious conclusion drawn by contemporary Gaia-worshipers is the wrong one, but the evidence prompting it deserves to be taken seriously.

This return to an ancient religious use of the name "Gaia" has its origin in a serious and important scientific theory: that is, "The Gaia Hypothesis," first proposed in a book by that title published by British scientist James Lovelock in 1979. (American biologist Lewis Thomas had proposed something similar to Lovelock's idea, but with less detail, a few years earlier.) Lovelock designed several of the experiments carried by space probes attempting to find evidence of life on Mars. Through a comparison of the atmospheric chemistry of other planets with that of the earth, and through projections of what earth's air and oceans *ought* to be like if their various chemical processes proceeded to equilibrium apart from life, he came to a startling conclusion: living things on the planet precisely regulate their own environment. In Lovelock's own words (in a 1975 *New Scientist* article):

> It appeared to us that the Earth's biosphere is able to control at least the temperature of the Earth's surface and the composition of the atmosphere. Prima facie, the atmosphere looked like a contrivance put together cooperatively by the totality of living systems to carry out certain necessary control functions. This led to the formulation of the proposition that living matter, the air, the oceans, the land surface, were parts of a giant system which was able to control temperature, the composition of the air and sea, the pH of the soil and so on as to be optimal for survival of the biosphere. The system seemed to exhibit the behaviour of a single organism, even a living creature.[2]

Lovelock put the matter more colorfully in his book:

> Disequilibria on this scale suggest that the atmosphere is not merely a biological product, but more probably a biological construction: not living, but like a cat's fur, a bird's feathers, or the paper of a wasp's nest, an extension of a living system designed to maintain a chosen environment.[3]

Though not beyond dispute, the Gaia hypothesis has a wide following in the scientific community. It is not surprising that it has become an important component in the eclectic mix of "new age" religions, for it strongly suggests that there is a purpose reflected in the very nature of life on earth. The self-regulation of the earth suggests intelligence, and not our own. It is no wonder that on learning of it many are moved to worship. But worship of the earth is misplaced, as would be worship of any other organism (cats, birds, wasps) whose bodies provide a wonderful physical environment for themselves. The proper object of worship is hinted at in

---

2. James Lovelock, *The New Scientist* 65 (1975): 304.
3. James Lovelock, *The Gaia Hypothesis* (1979).

Lovelock's words: "the system seemed to exhibit the behaviour of . . . a living creature." To call earth a creature implies a Creator. That the earth may be the greatest of all creatures, and that we are physically a part of it, is important for us. But such knowledge does not at all point to the monist conclusion that the earth is divine. Rather, it points to the question (as do all God's creatures), "Who made it? And why?"

The "New" Physics

Another area of recent science which has been fertile soil for modern monism is the "new" physics. Speculations on the philosophical and religious meanings of the strange new picture of the universe emerging from Einsteinian relativity and quantum theory have challenged the mechanism of the Newtonian world-picture which has reigned for three centuries. None of the physics involved is really new: most of the ideas we now find filtering into popular culture were proposed early in the twentieth century. But in the last decade or two many popular books seeking to draw religious or metaphysical conclusions from these ideas have been published. Two of the earliest and most influential are *The Tao of Physics* by Fritjof Capra (Berkeley: Shambhala, 1975) and *The Dancing Wu Li Masters* by Gary Zukav (New York: William Morrow, 1979). As the titles suggest, both attempt to make sense out of the new physics through reference to some form of Eastern monism. Two ideas recur regularly in such popularizations.

The first is the impossibility of attaining an absolute, detached, or preferred vantage point on the universe. Einstein proposed the idea first in his theory of relativity, which implied that parameters of space and time vary depending on one's vantage point and velocity: space shrinks, time slows down, objects change their mass. Most of the implications of Einstein's theory have since been verified, and they have destroyed the picture — derived from Descartes and Newton — of the universe as a vast, invariant machine in which human consciousness is a sort of homeless ghost. A similar point about the role of the observer was developed by Werner Heisenberg in his principle of indeterminancy. He showed that certain paired variables, such as position and velocity, or energy and time, cannot both be precisely determined simultaneously. For example, the mere act of measuring the position of a particle, by virtue of the measurement process, renders precise determination of its velocity impossible. The more precisely one determines one variable, the more indeterminant the value of the other member of the pair will be. Thus we can never have an absolute picture of the particle: the properties we observe the particle to have depend upon the observations made to determine the properties. And even the intrinsic nature of the "particle" is in question; at the most fundamental level, "particles" exhibit wave properties and waves exhibit particle properties. Both relativity and indeterminancy, despite the abstraction and distance from ordinary experience of what they describe, nevertheless seem to be re-establishing in the modern mind a feeling that we are not detached from the rest of the universe: rather than being "out there," the nature of things depends upon our relationship to them. Thus, though such an idea need not point in the direction of a full-blown monism, many have nevertheless drawn monistic conclusions from relativity and indeterminancy.

The second idea regularly recurring in popular discussions of modern physics which has nudged many towards monism is the hypothesis of some sort of underlying, instantaneous connection between apparently separate objects. Paired polarities whose qualities depend upon their opposite were first theorized — then, in the last decade, observed — to instantly assume a definite state only when the opposite member of the pair was investigated. Such oddities have led physicist David Bohm to suggest that there is an "implicate order" in the universe. The word *implicate* means "enfolded"; thus Bohm's conclusion is that

> everything is enfolded into everything. This contrasts with the *explicate order* now dominant in physics in which things are *unfolded* in the sense that each thing lies only in its own particular region of space (and time) and outside the regions belonging to other things.[4]

None of these findings carries a metaphysical or religious explanation with it, and most physicists are cautious about drawing metaphysical or religious conclusions. Certainly, however, they point to the inadequacy of mechanistic notions of the universe as a collection of separate particles. As physicist John Polkinghorne said (in a work which argues not for philosophical monism but for a view of creation in which the transcendent Creator God is intimately interacting with creation), "the EPR experiment indicates an astonishing togetherness in separation, even for elementary

---

4. David Bohm, *Wholeness and the Implicate Order* (London: Routledge & Kegan Paul, 1980), p. 172.

particles. . . . At the very root of reductionist physics we find holism reasserting itself. Even electrons are not self-contained solitaries."[5]

But the overwhelming tendency in religious reflection on modern physics has been to assume that these indications of holism in the universe point to a holism between creation and Creator. Thus Fritjof Capra, a physicist attracted to the monist complementarity of Taoism, concludes:

> Relativity theory has made the cosmic web come alive, so to speak, by revealing its essentially dynamic character; by showing that its activity is the very essence of its being. In modern physics, the image of the universe as a machine has been transcended by a view of it as one indivisible dynamic whole whose parts are essentially interrelated and can be understood only as patterns of a cosmic process. At the sub-atomic level the interrelations and interactions between the parts of the whole are more fundamental than the parts themselves. There is motion but there are, ultimately, no moving objects; there is activity but there are no actors; there are no dancers, there is only the dance.[6]

The exclusion of the Creator from the dance of creation is unwarranted, as is the paradoxical assumption that our thoughts about the universe must be only "patterns of a cosmic process." The monism which merges mind and universe is as unacceptable as the monism which merges Creator and creation. Though the oddities of modern physics certainly do point away from Newtonian mechanism and are more in keeping with what we are discovering from ecology about interconnectedness, they are not made more intelligible by explanation in Taoist, Buddhist, or Hindu terms. The best explanation lies in the Trinitarian understanding of creation, which we will take up in the next chapter. For now we will attempt to point out the strong appeal of the monism of the Oriental religions.

Oriental Religions

As Western culture has moved further from its Christian roots, the interest shown by many in Oriental religions has increased. This growing openness — in our increasingly secular culture — to aspects of traditional Hindu,

---

5. John Polkinghorne, *One World: The Interaction of Science and Theology* (Princeton: Princeton University Press, 1986), p. 90.

6. Fritjof Capra, *The Turning Point: Science, Society and the Rising Culture* (New York: Bantam Books, 1982), pp. 91-92.

Buddhist, and Taoist thought is (from a Christian perspective) not entirely negative, for it reflects the awareness that we are spiritual beings whose purpose, meaning, and destiny are not explicable within the mechanistic framework of Western scientific materialism. But it is negative in that it contains an implicit rejection of what Christianity has been perceived to be. Rightly or wrongly, some features of Christianity have been linked with the aggressively consumerist technocracy of the West, and many people have felt that an entirely new religious base is needed for dealing with new ecological insights and problems. We need to distinguish carefully the heart of the Christian message from its various cultural accretions, and to let the revelation of God in Jesus Christ provide the basis for judging our various cultural worlds, whether they are called Christian or Buddhist. But for now it is enough to point out that at least part of the environmentalist interest in non-Christian Oriental religions is a reaction against, and rejection of, what Christianity is *perceived* to be.

Several East Asian religions have exerted an influence on recent Western culture. Hinduism has probably made its largest impact through Yoga, a discipline intended, through careful control of thoughts, body, and breathing, to discover one's true nature, a reflection of *Brahman*. For central to all Hindu thought is the premise that *Atman* (the individual soul or self) is *Brahman*, the eternal reality of which the phenomenal universe is but an appearance. Taoism has as its main goal the harmony of the individual with the inner way of the universe. The key premise of Taoism is the complementary relationship of all things — thus the famous Taoist symbol: two comma-shaped forms nested within each other and forming a circle.

But of all the Oriental religions, by far the most influential on contemporary Western attitudes toward the earth is Buddhism. Here again, the great appeal of Buddhism seems to be that its central tenet (regardless of the various schools and traditions) seems like a welcome change from attitudes which have proved destructive in the West. Whereas Western thought has focused on the uniqueness and separateness of the individual, Buddhism seeks, through a variety of means, to undo the illusion of separate, self-conscious identity. When one perceives that one is not a separate self, striving to meet that self's needs ceases, and one can live at peace and unity with the rest of nature. One of the most tireless apologists for a Buddhist approach to nature is West Coast poet and wilderness advocate Gary Snyder. Snyder is a younger, enduring member of that literary/cultural movement known as the "beat generation," which formed

in the fifties in the San Francisco community of artists. They were disturbed by an America which they saw settling into an earth-denying orgy
of postwar consumerism. The Christian church seemed to exert little
influence, so they looked elsewhere for spiritual resources — mainly to
Zen Buddhism. Snyder spent time in a Zen monastery, and he still draws
heavily on Buddhist themes. In an essay written in 1984 and published
as an appendix to *Deep Ecology* he defends the Buddhist outlook in these
words:

> Buddhism holds that the universe and all creatures in it are intrinsically
> in a state of complete wisdom, love and compassion, acting in natural
> response and mutual interdependence. The personal realization of this
> from-the-beginning state cannot be had for and by one"self" — be-
> cause it is not fully realized unless one has given the self up and away.[7]

Here is clearly stated a crucial Buddhist theme: that before we can live
rightly, we must rid ourselves of the illusion of selfhood. Such a shrinking
of the center of personal desire enables one to live benevolently, com-
passionately, richly — not through increasing what we consume, but by
decreasing what we desire. Implicit here is a second crucial Buddhist
theme: that of interconnectedness, interrelationship, unity with all that
is. *Satori* (enlightenment) in the Zen tradition amounts to a snuffing of
that persistent candle of self-consciousness and a realization of our unself-
conscious identification with the universe. Hence the emphasis on proper
breathing. Through the give-and-take of breath we exchange being with
the universe, and through right-mindfulness we can experience our oneness
with it.

ALTHOUGH BELIEFS AND PRACTICES DIFFER, THE APPEAL OF ASIAN RELIGIONS
in the environmentalist movement is that they promise the possibility of
stepping right out of our voraciously excessive self-consciousness. Such a
self-consciousness is linked (so the accusation goes) with Christian notions
of individual salvation, and with the corresponding treatment of creation
as merely a backdrop and fuel supply for the human drama. Whether
through Zen *satori,* Taoist "inner laws of the universe," or Hindu disciplines, Western followers of Eastern religions are trying to align themselves

---

7. Gary Snyder, "Buddhism and the Possibilities of a Planetary Culture," in DeVall
and Sessions, *Deep Ecology,* p. 251.

harmoniously with the universe. The motive is a good one, and it would be foolish to deny the discipline and dedication of many of the followers of Oriental thought. Yet there are several problems with these views. The most glaring is that denial of self and assertion of oneness with the universe makes stewardship — indeed, makes thought and action — impossible. All monist ethical systems, since they merge god, self, and universe, leave no room for action, since by "aligning oneself with the universe" one simply chooses to accept what is happening regardless of one's ability to change it. They exclude or deny not only the reality of evil, but also the possibility of acting to bring about the good.

Yet, as has often been the case in the history of Christianity, responding to error might help us see more clearly what is true. And it may be that these various modern attempts to reject the Christian picture of creation, fall, and redemption by a personal and loving Creator, in favor of the impersonal and timeless cycles of Oriental religion, may yet help us see with greater clarity what we are created and redeemed to be: fully personal and self-conscious servant-stewards, in responsible relationship to a personal Creator of us and our fellow-creatures.

Going Further Back: Searching for Old Ways

The environmentalist interest in Oriental religion represents one strand of recent monist attempts to find ecologically attractive alternatives to a Judeo-Christian worldview. These alternatives draw on living — though ancient — religious traditions with well-formed scriptures, priesthoods, and disciplines.

But there is another sort of attempt to find an environmentally suitable religion. It seeks to go back beyond history entirely, to the unwritten, dimly remembered legends, traditions, rites, and beliefs of prehistoric, neolithic peoples who seemed to have lived in harmony with their place for thousands — perhaps tens of thousands — of years. One such dipping into the well of the past we will discuss under the name of "ecofeminism," the other under the heading of "bioregionalism." For the most part, ecofeminism draws on prehistoric European sources — bioregionalism, on North American prehistory.

Ecofeminism

Ecofeminism (the term was coined in 1974 by the French writer François d'Eaubonne) argues that the exploitation of nature which has led to the environmental crisis is parallel to — in fact, is a part of — a male, patriarchal domination of women. Such domination is ancient, but it is not, ecofeminists argue, basic to the human condition. We can glimpse examples of an alternative arrangement which values women's insight and experience in early religious traditions (long branded pagan) and in some remnants of contemporary "primitive" societies.

The outlines of the ecofeminist argument can be seen by reflecting on our language. "Nature" is universally spoken of as feminine, as in "Mother Nature" and in the reemerging Gaia tradition. At the same time, we commonly use phrases like "*man* against *nature*." A "virgin" forest is one which "man" has not yet submitted to his uses. Hurricanes — epitomes of the destructive and uncontrollable in nature — have traditionally been called by women's names. In general, our language suggests that nature is to culture as woman is to man: mysterious, beautiful, bountiful, and dangerous, and thus in need of control, taming, submission to the clarity of reason — reason which is best exemplified in the male.

Carolyn Merchant, in her 1980 study entitled *The Death of Nature*, argues persuasively that most of this destructive imagery of nature as a mistress to be mastered originates rather suddenly in the scientific revolution. She points out, for example, that Francis Bacon, in describing a new technique for studying nature, uses phrases such as "putting nature to the test" and "wresting her secrets from her" — language which seems to be taken from contemporary witch trials.[8]

In fact, ecofeminists argue, the Western (and Christian) attitude toward witches is a good example of the destructive attitude toward women and the fear of both nature and the feminine. Properly understood, a witch is not one who consorts with the devil, but rather one who seeks to "bend" (the meaning behind the term *wicca*) the powers of nature to her end, as a basket-weaver plies her softened reeds. Masculine, patriarchal culture has feared such dark and intuitive powers — powers which seem to operate from an inner identification between the shaper and the shaped — and has preferred instead a rational, mechanistic understanding which comes from the outside.

---

8. Carolyn Merchant, *The Death of Nature* (San Francisco: Harper & Row, 1980).

The ecofeminist position proposes a profound critique of the Judeo-Christian tradition. They believe it to be so warped by patriarchy that it must be either discarded altogether or deeply altered if it is to regain validity. This warping patriarchy is pervasive: a God portrayed as male and a male savior are proclaimed exclusively (till recently) by male priests and clergy. Within that patriarchal framework women's insights have been marginalized and their roles have been restricted. Traditionally the mysteries of the female body have been regarded as a temptation, a hindrance, or even as being unclean, a curse. These suspicions of the feminine parallel suspicions of nature.

Ecofeminists urge the rediscovery of an ancient alternative, which they believe to have preceded patriarchal theism: that is, a worship of the goddess, which did not exalt warfare and domination, but instead led to a nurturing culture in which men and women lived together in equal and complementary partnership.

The ecofeminist argument should not be ignored. We will attempt a fuller (though largely indirect) response to it through an unfolding of the outlines of Christian thought in chapter 14. Many of the ecofeminist criticisms are accurate. But they are accurate because Christians have often misunderstood the nature of God. As we shall see, we have stressed God's transcendence, his dominion and rule, and have seen "man" as likewise master and ruler over nature (and over woman). We have missed the dramatic story of biblical history: that the God who created (a creation sometimes spoken of in feminine terms) is also the God who, as Augustine put it, is "nearer to us than we are to ourselves," the God in whom "we live and move and have our being" (Acts 17:28), the God who (like a woman in childbirth) allowed himself to be stretched in pain for the creation he loved. Thus ecofeminist thought can help us rediscover much about our relationship to creation and Creator. We must sympathize with the anger and hurt resulting from the millennia of denied feminine gifts (in both women and men) caused by a long misunderstanding of masculine and feminine in God and people. But we should not let a reaction against those injustices, and a rediscovery of the nurturing immanence of God, obscure the reality of his Lordship.

Bioregionalism: Re-inhabiting Home-Place

Bioregionalism is an awkward word for a widespread and largely positive phenomenon: the conscious and respectful "re-inhabiting" of places where we have dwelt carelessly. Not surprisingly, the movement is strongest in North America and in New Zealand and Australia, where European (and at least superficially Christian) people and traditions engulfed a complex, ancient, and delicate ecology and culture. And (again not surprisingly) in North America bioregionalism is strongest in the West, where our sense of being new arrivals on an ancient scene is (or ought to be) strongest.

Bioregionalism (whether or not it is called by that name) is based on the premise that "biology," "ecology," and "culture" are abstractions which can only be learnt in a particular place which itself is the result of a unique geological, biological, and cultural history. The earth is full of an almost infinite number of such places, though we can identify large "bioregions" fairly easily. Usually, bioregions transcend political boundaries, which have been imposed for other reasons. Watersheds, for example (all the land drained by a river system between two ridges or mountain ranges), are "bioregions," known and respected by ancient inhabitants, but usually overlooked by our political boundaries.

The bioregional insight has two implications for us. One is simply learning all we can about the created life of an area: the native plants and animals, the soil, the growing conditions, the weather. In urban areas almost everything but the weather has been obscured by human constructions, but even the largest city has not completely obscured the created world on which it depends, and pockets of original wildness can still be found. It is particularly crucial, in the bioregional vision, that city dwellers come to appreciate that they do indeed depend on the land, and that they come to know where their water comes from, where their food is grown, where their garbage and sewage go.

The other implication of bioregionalism is that the people who have lived in a place know better how to relate respectfully to it. Most of us, however, are aliens to our place in a double sense. First of all, we are alienated from the wisdom of our own agriculture. As farms grow in size and dwindle in numbers, an agricultural tradition many centuries old, often embodying ancient principles of husbandry brought from the Old World but sensitively adapted to the New, is being pushed off the land in the name of a bland efficiency. Thus we need to listen to farmers who farm by traditional methods. But there is, say the bioregionalists, an even more radical way in which we (including all our agriculture) are newcomers. The native peoples have lived here for thousands of years; their very language, culture, religion, and mythology are inseparable from the place. Thus the native people have an immense store of wisdom about how to relate to the unique life of a place. We latecomers have brought with us our own plants and animals, and stories to go with them. This cultural thrust of bioregionalism suggests that we should forsake the arrogance by which we have imposed our culture on a region where it may not fit, and learn instead from the people who have been shaped by the place.

This is where the religious element of bioregionalism comes in. Some have argued that Christianity is foreign to North America (if not to most of the world). It has its roots in the patriarchal nomadism of the Middle East, it spread in the Hellenic and largely urban dualism of the Mediterranean, and it was nurtured in feudal Europe — so how can it fit here, in the vast and varied places and cultures of the New World? Since there are many sad instances of inappropriate European imposing of Western culture and agriculture on native peoples (sometimes with disastrous cultural and ecological consequences), it is assumed that Christian faith is always such an imposition.

Christians believe that the revelation of God in Jesus Christ is for all peoples and times and is the fulfillment and correction of all human religions. Their best response to other religions, in telling the story of the gospel, is to use the words Paul spoke in Athens to a people embedded in their own bioregionalism: "Now what you worship as something unknown I am going to proclaim to you" (Acts 17:23, NIV). Jehovah is not a local God, a God of place: he is Lord of the universe. Yet he did reveal himself to a particular people at home in a particular place, and (as many of the psalms make clear) he is the nourisher and sustainer of all place. There is indeed a God associated with each place, however fragile, unique, and precious, but it is the same God — the one God, who is God of all people and places.

We have a good example of such an approach in Paul's response to a group of pagans in Asia Minor who, sensing the truth and power in his message, wanted to convert it into the terms of their own bioregional religion, the worship of Zeus and Hermes. Paul's response does not turn aside their recognition of a divine blessing on their own local place — its crops, fields, and creatures. Instead he builds on it, by reference to the Creator:

> We are bringing you good news, telling you to turn from these worthless things to the living God, who made heaven and earth and sea and everything in them. In the past, he let all nations go their own way. Yet he has not left himself without testimony: He has shown kindness

by giving you rain from heaven and crops in their seasons; he provides you with plenty of food and fills your hearts with joy. (Acts 14:15-17, NIV)

On such a foundation we can perhaps begin to respond, not only to those who seek a "bioregional" religion, but to all those we have considered in this chapter who, in the past decade or two, through a vivid glimpse of the Creator in creation, have sought a fuller knowledge of him.

IN THESE PAST FIVE CHAPTERS WE HAVE ATTEMPTED TO TRACE THE MAIN influences, apart from Christianity, on Western use of nature. It will be helpful at this point to sum up what those influences have been.

The Greeks were ambivalent in their attitude toward the natural world, and we in the West have inherited much of that ambivalence. One pole of Greek thought distrusted all that is natural — and hence, mutable and imperfect. The only thing worthy of our attention, in this view, was the eternal realm of ideal Forms. This tradition was embodied in Platonism. The other pole of Greek thought, however, affirmed the idea of nature as a vast organism, with the human mind as its rationality. Human reason was not in tension with the natural world (as in Plato), but was a self-conscious embodiment of its essence. The good person, then, was in tune with "nature" — and was nature's highest form. This tradition was expressed in the thought of Aristotle and, more religiously, in Stoicism.

During the Middle Ages, both of these Greek views combined with Christianity. The Platonic distrust of nature appeared in the Middle Ages as an attitude of contempt for the world, resulting in attempts to deny the value of the physical. But the affirmation of nature as organism is embodied in most of medieval cosmology, from the idea of the "great chain of being" to the macrocosm-microcosm correspondence which is the foundation of both alchemy and astrology.

The scientific revolution is an outgrowth of both the positive and the negative attitudes toward nature. It is rooted in an empiricism which comes from the more positive pole of medieval thought: from the Franciscan scientists onward, the investigation of phenomena, not prior ideas about the phenomena, was seen as an important pathway to truth. At the same time, however, the Platonic separation of the mind from nature increasingly worked its way into the investigative method, so that both Descartes and Galileo could affirm, in different ways, that a mathematical expression of the world was a higher form of truth than any sense experience of it. This increasing conflict between a mathematically consistent explanation and a sensuously experienced one was very evident in the Copernican controversy. The new science maintained that the fundamental truth was not the truth which a person embodied on solid earth perceived, but the truth perceived from a point in space which a person could experience only mentally.

Accompanying this detachment from nature was an increasing awareness that knowledge of nature could bring power over nature. This was the motivating force of Bacon's work and the practical attitude that formed the basis for the exploration and settlement of the New World.

The Puritan settlers operated on the Baconian assumption that it was their Christian duty to subdue a wild and heathen nature, and this model of dominance became the prevailing American attitude until quite recent times. By the beginning of the twentieth century, the North American continent had already been, for nearly three centuries, a kind of laboratory for working out ideas about the relationship between humankind and nature which had been developing for millennia in the Old World.

In America, although the prevailing idea was that the land was to be subjected to human purpose, there grew up a more preserving attitude. This concern was nurtured by the Romantic ideal of imaginatively reviving a world drained of its meaning. But it was also aided in America by a recognition of the beneficial role contact with wilderness had played in the nation's development. The result has been a uniquely modern polarity between wilderness preserves on the one hand and a completely humanized landscape on the other.

The twentieth century, with its spectacular increase in the power available to us, its rapidly expanding technology, its explosion of human population, and its spread of Western ideas about nature, has seen the blossoming of these historical roots into flowers both horrible (pollution and the atomic bomb) and beautiful (the control or elimination of many diseases, rapid communication, and human flight).

One such "flower" is the environmental movement itself, which in the short space of two decades has made an awareness of human responsibility for the health of the earth a worldwide phenomenon. And though the scientific understanding and impulse toward stewardship which inform that movement have roots in Jewish Christian tradition, many people have seen the way in which a misapplication of Christian principles has contributed to the problem. At the same time there has been a turn toward "Deep Ecology": a recognition that ultimately many environmental problems are spiritual, not technical. Thus, many have looked to religious frameworks (ranging from Buddhism to paganism) as being more suitable for nourishing human life on the earth.

Clearly, we need to consider in some depth what the Bible does imply about our relationship to the earth. But before doing so, we must first consider, and evaluate, the means through which we most clearly impose our values and beliefs on the creation: that is, the economic system through which we turn "earth" into the "world" of commerce.

Part B

❧   ❧

Our Mind Today

CHAPTER 10

⁂ ⁂

Models: What's Behind Our Mind Today?

No Model is a catalogue of ultimate realities, and none is a mere fantasy. Each is a serious attempt to get in all the phenomena known at a given period, and each succeeds in getting in a great many. But also, no less surely, each reflects the prevalent psychology of an age almost as much as it reflects the state of that age's knowledge.

— C. S. Lewis, *The Discarded Image*

. . . try to escape
From the darkness outside and within
By dreaming of systems so perfect
that no one will need to be good.

— T. S. Eliot

ONE WAY OF SUMMING UP MUCH OF THE MATERIAL IN THIS LONG discussion of the sources of our modern mind is through the concept of *models*. People have treated the earth differently in different periods, in part because they have used different models to help them understand it. Sometimes these have been conscious and deliberate models, especially in recent times. More often, they have not been consciously developed by anyone, but stand, like folklore or mythology, as a sort of backdrop to all thought about the world and human action in it. These various world models have in turn shaped models of the person, and thus have provided different motives for acting toward the earth and its creatures. Before we look at the more influential of these models of the earth, however, we should consider briefly what a model is, and how it affects our thinking.

Currently, we use the word *model* to mean many things. It can mean a miniature replica, as in "model airplane." It can mean a kind of design, as in a "1980 model car." It can refer to an ideal, as in "model home." "Mathematical models" represent a system or a process by means of formulae and relationships. Finally, ideas that have been used since the scientific revolution have come, in recent times, to be spoken of as "theoretical models."

The purpose of such models is to sum up or represent a complex reality, including the main features of the system one is seeking to explain, but omitting details which will not contribute to the basic idea. The model of the solar system, with the sun at the center circled by tiny planets (a model which most of us carry unconsciously in our head) neglects the relative size of the sun and the planets, the mass distribution of the individual planets, the rotation of the sun around the center of the system, and so forth.

The danger of such models is that they can be mistaken for reality. This is particularly the case in the utilitarian marriage of science and technology discussed earlier in this section. As long as we understand knowledge to be power, we are likely to take very seriously those models of the universe which give us power over it. Thus our era — particularly those who do not make the models, but experience the beneficial consequences of manipulations based on them — is particularly prone to forget that its models are only abstractions. The relationship of models to reality is not, however, as C. S. Lewis puts it, a matter of saying,

> "The medievals thought the universe to be like that, but we now know it to be like this." Part of what we know is that we cannot, in the old sense, "know what the universe is like" and that no model we can build will be, in that old sense, "like" it.[1]

In any case, whether we are dealing with a tenth-century-B.C. Egyptian or a modern scientist's model of the universe, the following principles about models and their effect on our motives hold true:

1. Our behavior is strongly affected by internal models; they de-

---

1. C. S. Lewis, *The Discarded Image* (Cambridge: Cambridge University Press, 1964), p. 218.

velop a type of hidden mind which helps us structure the world in our thought and directs the specific use we make of it.

2. The predominant models of a given period (and of preceding eras) have a strong effect on the private and internal models constructed by an individual. To quote Lewis again, "in every age the human mind is deeply influenced by the accepted Model of the universe."[2]

3. We are often careless in recognizing the tentative nature of the models we deal with, and that carelessness is likely to lead to unwise actions toward the natural world. This has been particularly crucial in recent times, when the very utility of the model urges its acceptance as reality.

4. World models can, and perhaps *should*, be changed. That change can come about when we learn that the accuracy, scope, or simplicity of another model makes it more valid. And one of the ways in which we learn that our old model needs changing is through the problems which result when we try to apply that model to action in the world.

So much for models in general. What then are some of the models that have shaped — or continue to shape — our treatment of the world?

The ancient model of the earth seems to have been that of the earth as a god. This was not a model which any one person developed, but it was present in the origins of nearly all mythologies. The American Indian attitude toward nature often included much of this kind of reverence for the divinity of the earth and its creatures. Such an attitude was also in the background of Greek thought, but it was largely replaced by another model by the time of those Greek philosophers who have most influenced Western attitudes. But so appealing is the attitude of reverence which this model of the earth as god encourages, that more than a few people in our own age have attempted — unsuccessfully — to revive it.

The model of the earth that emerged in Aristotelian and Stoic thought, and which was very influential in medieval times, was that of the earth as an *organism* — a vast animal whose behavior could be understood by analogy with the human body. Earth, air, fire, and water were like the "humors" of human bodies. Objects fell to the earth or rose in the air out of a longing to seek their proper place. This view also suggested harmony, but not reverence, since the consciousness of the organism was in humankind, the master of the whole.

---

2. Ibid., p. 222. On the role of and changes in models, or paradigms, see also Thomas Kuhn, *The Structure of Scientific Revolutions* (Chicago: University of Chicago Press, 1962).

Both the organic and the divine models of the world had as a kind of backdrop a similar model of space and time. Space was limited (though very large); it was something one could come to the end of. Though the limits of the earth were not yet clearly known, there was no picture of an infinite universe or earth to encourage wasteful use. It was a limited world, where everything had its place and proper use.

Time, in both views, was cyclic: all things would grow old and be renewed after the manner of the cycles of the moon, day and night, and the progression of the seasons. An appropriate figure to illustrate this view of time would be the circle.

With the scientific revolution, a very different model of the universe entered human thought, accompanied by different ways of picturing space and time. Although parts of the new model had been implicit in Judeo-Christian beliefs, this new model did not begin to have much effect on popular views of the world until the sixteenth or seventeenth century. The universe came to be understood as a mechanical artifact — a created object, constructed by the great artificer, God. Its laws could, with diligence and skill, be learned, controlled, and applied to other machines. Space came to be viewed as infinite. And time came increasingly to be modeled by the arrow of progress: it was going somewhere, and humankind was going somewhere with it, eager to hasten the journey.

There were several consequences of this model for the way in which people used the earth. Seeing nature as a machine, rather than as a god or an organism, drew forth neither reverence nor respect; the world was instead something to be changed and used. The view of space as infinite (an idea which was supported by the practically unlimited resources being discovered in the New World) encouraged the accelerated use of nature, as did the triumph of linear time, which gave humankind a justification for regarding things as means to a beckoning — but always elusive — end.

In many ways, our current use of the earth has been shaped primarily by this model of the earth — or the universe — as a machine. Without the restrictions on its use imposed by the models of deity or organism, we have been able to use creation more thoroughly and efficiently. This thorough use was supported by the idea of progress suggested by linear time, and by the idea of limitless resources suggested by infinite space (and made concrete by the New World).

A particular form of this model of the universe, especially related to the use of resources in North America, can be called the "frontier" model. Nature, in this model, is there for human use. When it is used up,

"Then we're all agreed. As it has always done with its difficulties in the past, America will somehow find a way to solve its energy problems."

From *The New Yorker,* June 18, 1979. Drawing by Dana Fradon;
© 1979 The New Yorker Magazine, Inc. Used by permission.

we can move on, for there is always — further on — a *West* to move into. This attitude was exemplified by the American doctrine of "Manifest Destiny." Obviously, the vastness and the fertility of the North American landscape encouraged this model, one which was in force for at least three centuries. It still affects many of our policies today — in land use, in mining, in logging, and so forth.

Thinking of resources by means of the model provided by one's own finances is another way of understanding the frontier model. A person is likely to have two sources of wealth: income — from wages or a salary — and capital — as in a savings account. It is a truism of personal economics that one must live within one's income. But the frontier model of resources, which implies that there is always *more* — land, timber, game, iron, oil — encourages one to regard *capital* — all finite and limited resources — as *income*. As we saw in an earlier chapter, solar energy is the only real income the earth has on which to operate. Yet we have ignored that fact in North America, drawing on the "capital" of fossil fuels and mineral deposits as though they could be used forever. Only very recently have we made minor attempts to "live within our income." The growing use of words like *sustainable* suggest the emergence of a new model of resource use.

This recent rise of the "sustainability picture" has been influenced by a vivid new model of the earth — that is, the earth as a spaceship. Such a model was not even possible until we had at least some imaginative experience of what it would be like to be out in empty space in a limited, but life-supporting, environment. Shortly after that possibility entered our imagination, it became a reality in early space flight. Thus phrases like "life-support system" entered our vocabulary, pointing to our basic need for food, air, and water. More dramatically, those early space flights gave us images of the earth which immediately began forcing us to restructure the old models — especially the model of the earth as a machine and the frontier model of resources as infinite. For, as those photographs continue to remind us, the earth is clearly somewhat like a spaceship: finite and vulnerable, with a cargo of life.

On our trip through space we have limited resources, both of energy and of material, just as do those who travel to the moon in contemporary spaceships. Astronauts going to the moon, however, have the advantage of knowing how long the trip will last, and thus they know at what rate they must use their resources. On "spaceship earth" we have no knowledge of the length of the trip. Therefore, the only way to be fair to future generations is to assume that the journey will go on a long time — effectively, forever. Thus the spaceship-earth model indicates that we must recycle our material resources (our "capital") and live within our income resources of energy.

Some have objected to the spaceship model of the earth, for it still pictures the earth as a machine. Real spaceships are machines designed to re-create an environment for human organisms. As the pictures of earth from space suggest, the earth is far more like a vast living organism than a machine. To use the model of the spaceship to speak of the earth neglects the fact that the real machines — individual spaceships — are very imperfect attempts to reproduce the stability of the earth itself, which has far more complexity, stability — and intrinsic worth and beauty — than any machine.

So, by informing the insights gained by the "spaceship" model with the insights provided by ecological knowledge, some have suggested that we ought to think of the earth once again — as in medieval times — as an organism. This is the basic insight behind Lovelock's Gaia hypothesis. But now our understanding of how that organism lives is much more precise and thorough. As we have learned more about ecosystems, about energy flow in a food chain, and about the ways in which living things are adapted to each other and to their nonliving environment, it has been possible to see the earth as an "ecosphere." Or, as one modern biologist has suggested, it is like a living cell: separate parts working in symbiotic relationship, surrounded by an information- and energy-exchanging membrane, the atmosphere.

The advantage of seeing the earth as a living thing, rather than as a spaceship, is that it does not encourage us to manipulate the earth as though it were entirely different from ourselves. But whether one views the earth as a living organism — a vast "cell" in space — or as a spaceship, the pattern suggested for use of nature is much different from that suggested by the frontier model. Ultimately, as in a living cell, the goal should be to live on incoming energy, using that flow to use and re-use the materials which cannot be replaced. There is no room in either the spaceship model or the cell model for seeing the earth as an infinite source of raw materials for human use, the waste of which can be poured indiscriminately back into the earth; in such a model the earth becomes an infinite storehouse and an infinite garbage pail. The contrast between the two views — the frontier model and the spaceship model — is shown accurately in Figure 10.1.

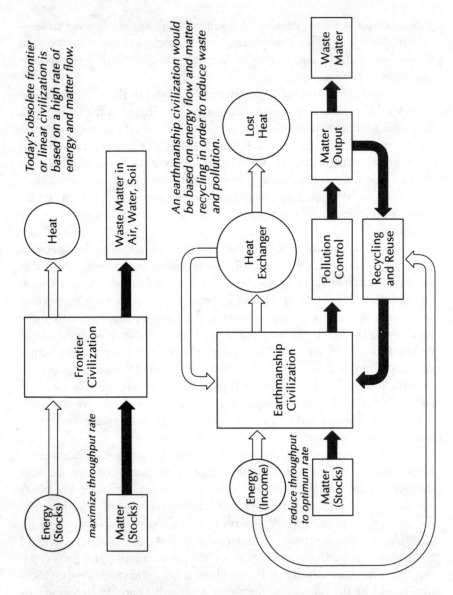

Figure 10.1. The frontier model of our world assumes an infinite supply of resources and a pass-through process of resource utilization. The spaceship-earth model assumes limited stocks of resources and an income of energy, along with recycling of material resources. Adapted from *Living in the Environment: Concepts, Problems, and Alternatives* by G. Tyler Miller, Jr. © 1975 by Wadsworth Publishing Company, Inc. Reprinted by permission of Wadsworth, Inc.

Whatever the combination of reasons, we find in North America today two strongly developed models by which we understand our relationship to natural resources: the model of the frontier, which would encourage us to go on using resources indiscriminately, and the model of the spaceship, which encourages restraint, recycling, and sustainability. The frontier model is certainly giving way; but there are long traditions of thought which make it an attractive model. Before going on to consider two areas of human activity — economics and technology — in which the model has had a profound effect on our use of creation, we need to take one more look at the history of thought — at ideas about human nature which have been incorporated into the frontier model.

Philosophies tend to draw together the prevailing mood and underlying values of an age in precise and easily identifiable form. Thus, like a barometer, a philosophy registers the shifting weather of its time. At the same time, the very precision and perceptiveness of some philosophies have meant that they themselves have exerted a considerable pressure on the intellectual currents of a period. The most important philosophies thus partake of the characteristics of both barometers and weather fronts: that is, they both reflect human values and change them. But whether we look at a barometer or watch the line of advancing clouds, it is helpful to know something about a hurricane before we deal with its consequences.

One ethical idea in particular has blown with gale force through the institutions and attitudes which control our treatment of nature — and indeed, of each other — since the eighteenth century. We will refer to it, with some violence to established usage, as "Utilitarianism." More than anything else, a Utilitarian attitude has shaped the frontier model which has been so powerful in North America.

We do not have to look far to find the origins of the Utilitarian ethic in Western thought. It first appears in Epicurus; then, after a nearly total absence through most of the Christian era (at least as an explicit philosophy), it reappears in force in the philosophy underlying the scientific revolution.

Epicurus maintained that the universe had no purpose, but was only the consequence of random combinations of atoms moving endlessly in a void. As far as personal ethics were concerned, all that mattered was pleasure and pain — the subjective effect of all those purposeless atomic swervings.

Galileo, who was the first to revive Epicurus's view in modern times, adapted it, saying that what mattered was not the "inner" or Aristotelian cause of a particular action, but its outward, observable *consequences*. For the Epicurean, since there was no intrinsic right and wrong by which to judge action, the only valid standard of action was the more immediate one of avoidance of pain. Likewise, Galileo dismissed as unfounded those ideas of intrinsic purpose and desire which had informed Aristotelian physics — such as a stone falling to the ground because it "desired" the ground, accelerating out of inner jubilation at approaching the object of desire. He maintained that it was futile to speculate on the inner *causes* or "motives" of such action; true knowledge, and the only kind of any value, was knowledge of outer *effects*. Galileo, and others of his time, revolutionized physics by observing and measuring what things actually *did*. The irreducible truth about a thing, they believed, could be gained by obtaining an ever more precise record of what happened, not by reflecting on the Aristotelian cause. *How* things worked came to be more important than *why* they worked (an attitude encouraged by the tendency to study creation as though it were a great machine). Truth was in the measurable effects, not in the working out of some intrinsic principle or purpose. Any "law" of nature which resulted from this method was thus rooted not in speculations about intrinsic reality, but in the observation of particular consequences.

Utilitarianism is an application to ethics of the same attitude — the divorce of values from anything intrinsic to the action, and a focus on the consequences of actions. It thus partakes of that general increase in the detachment of mind from nature whose development we have traced sketchily from Christian beginnings to the present. For in this viewpoint, only humans experience "intrinsic" qualities; to see such qualities outside of humankind is to postulate a false animism. In thus denying intrinsic meanings or values to everything but the human, these thinkers furthered that image of the mind as a detached presence in a lifeless, mechanical world.

In the following chapters, we will concentrate on the manifestations of Utilitarianism in economic thought and in our presuppositions about technology. We will also discuss various modern reactions against narrowly utilitarian attitudes toward resource use. But before turning to those considerations, we will discuss briefly the main outlines of Utilitarian thought. Briefly stated, Utilitarianism is that doctrine which states that "the rightness or wrongness of actions is determined by the goodness and badness of their consequences."[3] Such an ethic is in sharp contrast to any ethical

---

3. *The Encyclopedia of Philosophy*, vol. 8 (New York: Macmillan, 1967), p. 206.

theory which maintains that the goodness or badness of an action is in the act itself. This had been the predominant ethic throughout the Middle Ages. Just as color, scent, and taste were seen to be qualities in a thing, rather than varying responses to it, so the moral quality of an action was, in earlier times, thought to inhere in the act itself.

In the Utilitarian view, not only is the moral value of an action independent of the act itself; it is also independent of the motive. Thus greed is wrong not in itself, but only because it tends to produce actions with bad consequences. It is even conceivable that greed could produce actions with good consequences. This was, in effect, the argument of some defenders of capitalism who argued that the greatest good for society could be achieved by each person acting out of self-interest which is regarded as a virtue; an "invisible hand" would, in the long run, cause self-interest to produce the greatest good for everyone in society.

Value, for the classical Utilitarian, is determined by wants and desires. The satisfaction of desires is, by definition, good; the frustration of desires, evil. Ultimately, all desires are reduced to the avoidance of pain or the fulfillment of pleasure. Thus pleasure is the only good, and pain the only evil. The satisfaction of a desire is happiness; the frustration of a desire (and thus the consequent pain) is unhappiness.

It is important to note that we are speaking not only of basic *needs* such as food, clothing, and shelter (though they too may be desired). If a chocolate bar is desired more than an apple, then the chocolate bar has more value for the person, despite the fact that it could be shown on nutritional grounds that the eater has much more *need* of an apple. But Utilitarianism is not based on objective needs; it is based on subjective *wants*.

It is important to understand that the amount of satisfaction is the *total* satisfaction over a period of time. It is possible, for example, that our hypothetical eater would be more immediately happy with a chocolate bar than with an apple; but if he or she calculates the unhappiness which is likely to follow from the two, he or she may not choose the chocolate bar, for it will result in pimples, fat, and a bad conscience, the unpleasantness of which outweighs the immediate pleasure of the candy. Thus a person who carefully calculates the full results of pleasures and displeasures is likely to choose the apple. Jeremy Bentham, the eighteenth-century philosopher usually considered the founder of Utilitarian philosophy, developed a complex "hedonic calculus" for weighing happiness and unhappiness and coming up with guides for action.

It is obvious that Utilitarianism is subjective: one decides one wants a car because of the happiness it will bring, not because having cars is good in itself, or good for society. It is also individualistic, in that the basis for the rightness or wrongness of an action is always in the individual, not in the consideration of the health and well-being of a community. The basis of value is still the satisfaction of *individual* wants and desires. A community is not an organic whole for which value is to be determined apart from the individual; rather, it is a collection of individuals. Effects of one's actions on a specific human community, on other species, or on the whole household of life are not the starting point; rather, the happiness of the individual is always primary.

The fact that the basis for value is the satisfaction of the individual's wants does not mean, however, that the welfare of the broader community is irrelevant. At least one form of Utilitarianism maintains that the goal is "the greatest good for the greatest number." And even if one stays with the more "egoistic" form of Utilitarianism, in which the individual's happiness is the only consideration, one may recognize that an immediate satisfaction of a desire (stealing a chocolate bar in a store, for example) will ultimately result in more unhappiness — such as a jail sentence for shoplifting. Thus a concern for individual happiness may work out for the total welfare of the whole society and even for the greatest good for the greatest number. Moreover, it is conceivable that a sufficiently enlightened awareness of the interrelationships of the ecosphere could, motivated purely by individual human satisfaction, lead to a wise use of resources. That has, in fact, been the implicit assumption in the past. But such deteriorations of the environment as have been outlined in earlier sections argue against such an optimistic outcome of egoistic Utilitarianism.

Before we turn to some specific workings out of this aspect of the modern mind in economics and technology, it will be helpful to point out a basic assumption behind Utilitarianism: freedom is its underlying ideal, for only personal freedom allows one to experience pleasure and avoid pain. The freedom that the Utilitarian has in mind, however, is freedom from impediments to the satisfaction of individual desire. This is a far cry from the sort of freedom the Scriptures hold as ideal when, for example, they claim that Christ brings freedom from sin. The Christian ideal of freedom is freedom from impediments — and sin is an impediment — to being what God intended us to be. So the Utilitarian approves freedom from what stands in the way of satisfying our desires (however sinful), whereas the Scriptures approve freedom from what stands in the path of being what we are meant to be.

The consequences of these ideas for our use of resources may not be immediately obvious. However, they will become clearer when we consider the working out of the Utilitarian ideal in two main areas of modern action: economics and technology. So crucial are these areas to our treatment of nature that both of them — usually in some combination — are frequently blamed, almost as though they were vast demons, for current misuses of creation. We are not arguing, however, that economics and technology are the demons of our age; rather, we are concerned to point out how both economic and technological activity have been thoroughly formed by the Utilitarian ethic. Therefore, until that Utilitarian center is transformed, it is unlikely that economics or technology will be likely to provide much positive direction for stewardship of the earth.

The Utilitarian presuppositions appear in different ways in economics and technology. As will become clear in the next chapter, contemporary economic thought is based very firmly on the premise that what drives economic activity is individual happiness, or utility. Indeed, a favorite idea of economic theory is that people are "rational utility maximizers."

In modern attitudes toward technique, on the other hand, the emphasis is not so much on the importance of individual happiness as it is on the fact that the consequences of an act, rather than the act itself, are important. This emphasis on ends (consequences) rather than means (acts) can produce a way of thinking in which there is no room for any thing, process, or person which fails to achieve the best end in the most efficient way. In different ways, then, the theory and practice of both economics and technology are permeated by the ethical individualism of Utilitarianism. Regarding creation in a strictly Utilitarian way has made us see the whole continent as a source of raw material for our industry, or a dump for our waste. This Utilitarian, frontier model is always in the background when we think about economics and technology in the modern world.

CHAPTER 11

❧   ❧

Economics: Managing Our Household

Wes would not agree. "An energy economy still wouldn't be compre-
hensive enough."
"Well," I said, "then what kind of economy would be comprehensive
enough?"
He hesitated a moment, and then, grinning, said, "The Kingdom of
God."

— Wendell Berry, "Two Economies," in *Home Economics*

THE WORD "ECONOMICS" COMES FROM TWO GREEK WORDS: *OIKOS*, house, and *nomos*, order (or law). *Oikonomos*, then, is the ordering of a household, the principles by which it is managed. By a significant linguistic coincidence, the word "ecology" has a very similar origin: it comes from *oikos* and *logos*. The word *logos* in this usage means "under-standing" or "study of." *Oikonomos* is an ancient word (it occurs many times in the New Testament), but *oikologos*, "ecology," is a recent word, invented by a nineteenth-century biologist. "Economics," in its original sense, meant the management of one's own household, and thus was quite limited in scope. (Its meaning, as we shall see, has since broadened con-siderably.) But "ecology" has, from the first, denoted a recognition of humanity's extended household — the worldwide community of living things in all the intricacies of their coherence and exchange.

216

"Economics" could be roughly translated as "managing the household," and "ecology" as "understanding the household." And the differences between "managing" and "understanding" suggest why it is important to consider "ecology" and "economics" together. For, in order to manage the narrow household of human enterprise, we have increasingly managed — and thus interfered with — that broader household of the earth's life. Usually our management has run far ahead of our understanding. When that happens in any household — domestic or planetary — the consequences are grave.

The most common translation of the word *oikonomos* in the New Testament is "steward," and *oikonomia* is "stewardship." The concerns of ecology suggest that we broaden our stewardship to include not only monetary wealth and income, but also the great, living wealth of the planet. This involves "economics," for, as the word suggests, in one sense stewardship *is* economics.

Which brings us back to that more literal translation of *oikonomia* — economics. One thing this brief reflection on the word has shown is that we all are "economists," since we all have some responsibility for managing the affairs, financial and otherwise, of our household. Inasmuch as a million — or a billion — household managers determine that they require the use of an automobile, electrical appliances, and the convenience of disposability, then those "economists" require also some degradation of the creation on which those conveniences depend. For most of human history we have overlooked the impact of our household management on creation — the effect of our "economy" on the biosphere. But in the past decade or so ecology has begun to catch up with economy: we no longer suppose that we can indefinitely manage creation without understanding and caring for it. The growing impact of our housekeeping has begun to make earthkeeping a necessity.

But a word means more than its origins, and although "economist" is a translation of a word that means "steward," and thus applies to all of us, it has also come to have a meaning which is both more specialized and much more widely known. In the more modern sense of the word, an "economist" is one who seeks to understand principles of economics not only for the purpose of understanding in itself, but also for the purposes of prediction, management, and control. Nevertheless, the basis of economics — the thing the economist studies — remains the behavior of individual "managers-of-the- house." Thus we should take great care before blaming economists or economics for environmental problems. To blame

"Oh, for Pete's sake, let's just get some ozone and send it back up there!"

From *American Scientist Magazine.*
© 1976 by Sidney Harris. Used by permission.

the descriptive discipline of economics for our environmental dilemmas would be somewhat like the legendary despot who killed the messenger bringing bad news. A better approach would be to learn from the economist the principles, held consciously or not, by which we manage the various levels of our private and collective household. When we understand those principles and the patterns that clarify them, we may be in a better position to change and direct our management of both the small household and the great.

In the rest of this chapter we outline something of the history of "economics" as it has influenced our earthkeeping; in the next chapter we look more closely at the nature, premises, and environmental implications of contemporary economic understanding — all in an attempt to broaden economics into earthkeeping.

The questions raised by earthkeeping — that is, by our stewardship of creation — are at the very heart of economics. How much materials and energy should we use? For what should we use them? With what processes and techniques of production do we turn them from "raw" materials into human goods? Who gets the benefits? These questions about materials raise in turn other questions about human actions and attitudes: what motivates people to be "productive"? How do we measure "productivity" — given our growing knowledge about the environmental impacts of human action? What kind of social and economic organization will provide for human needs and at the same time preserve and enhance the creation which sustains us?

These questions are basic to the human enterprise of turning God's earth into cultural worlds, and in previous cultural worlds these questions have legitimately been answered in different ways. But increasingly (especially since the 1989 collapse of the Communist bloc's experiment with centrally planned economies) we live in one economic world: that of Western, free-market capitalism. The fact that capitalism now has no real rival makes it even more essential, therefore, that we examine the free-market pattern of economic activity. For free-market capitalism is unavoidably one of the main means by which we "keep" the earth.

Is it, however, the *best* means of earthkeeping? The answer is not so clear. Despite obvious gains in material well-being, our modern approach to production has introduced social, psychological, and environmental stress. Sometimes these stresses are referred to as a crisis in values — or a religious crisis. This is why the "Deep Ecology" movement calls not only for new kinds of economic relationships, but, quite deliberately, for a whole new religion.

But before we can begin to evaluate the adequacy of contemporary economic activity, we need to look briefly at other, earlier economic arrangements which have tended to assign value through means other than the market system.

HISTORICAL VIEWS OF "ECONOMIC REALITY"

Economics in Plato and Aristotle

For Plato, the production of goods was not the result of any longing for wealth or propensity for trade. It was, rather, based on inherent differences among individuals: some were sculptors, some carpenters, some teachers. The purpose of society was to give each of them a field in which to work out his own nature. If the city needed to grow, it was only because more room was needed for another sculptor to fulfill his character as a sculptor. In Plato's economy, then, "division of labor" is dictated by the essence of the individual. The driving force is not the production of goods or the accumulation of wealth; it is the full development of the individual person.

Aristotle's economic theory is similar. In his thought, property and goods have no value in themselves apart from the way a person uses them to attain happiness or well-being. Values are not determined by scarcity or demand, but by whether or not they enable a person to achieve true humanity. "It is impossible," said Aristotle, "or not easy, to do noble acts without the proper equipment."[1]

However, included in this concept of "proper equipment" is the idea of "too much," for an excess of goods might well be as detrimental to noble action as a deficiency. Thus, says Aristotle,

> external goods have a limit, like any other instrument, and all things useful are of such a nature that where there is too much of them they must either do harm, or at any rate be of no use, to their possessors.[2]

Aristotle holds an instrumental view of wealth:

> The life of money-making is one undertaken under compulsion, and wealth is evidently not the good we are seeking; for it is merely useful and for the sake of something else.[3]

Moreover, in its instrumental role, it is limited:

---

1. Aristotle, *Politics* 1323a-b, trans. Benjamin Jowett (Oxford: Oxford University Press, 1905).
2. *Politics* 1323b.
3. *Nicomachean Ethics* 1096a.

for the amount of property which is needed for a good life is not unlimited, although Solon in one of his poems says that, "No bound to riches has been fixed for man." But there is a boundary fixed, just as there is in the arts; for the instruments of any art are never unlimited, either in number or size.[4]

Its limit is not, however, always observed. In Aristotle's words again:

some persons are led to believe that making money is the object of household management, and the whole idea of their lives is that they ought either to increase their money without limit, or at any rate not to lose it. The origin of this disposition in men is that they are intent upon living only, and not upon living well; and, as their desires are unlimited, they also desire that the means of gratifying them should be without limit.[5]

Clearly, for both Plato and Aristotle, economic activity is not an end in itself or even an important part of the human makeup. Instead, another ideal — the achievement of full human selfhood or the doing of noble acts — is the controlling value. In both cases, the resource-devouring spiral of economic growth for its own sake is avoided.

In setting forth an economics motivated by values of fulfillment and nobility, Plato and Aristotle are undeniably reflecting something of the Greek culture of their day. But the very fact that Aristotle, at least, speaks of the possibility of *too much* wealth indicates that the attitude of wealth-for-its-own-sake was already a problem. That some avariciousness was prevalent in the ancient world is evident in an anecdote related by Augustine, who told of the theater performer who promised he would reveal what was in the mind of each person in the audience. He made good on his promise by telling them that each of them wanted to "buy cheap and sell dear."

Medieval Christian Economics

Such an attitude would ultimately produce a "growth" economy. That it failed to do so during the Middle Ages is probably the consequence of

---

4. *Politics* 1256b.
5. *Politics* 1258a.

a vigorous Christian doctrine of sin and an accompanying emphasis on the need for salvation. Throughout the Middle Ages, economic interests were subordinated to the real business of life, which was understood to be the salvation of one's soul. Economic activity was simply one element of personal conduct, over which the rules of morality were totally binding. Unlike our own time (at least in theory) a business transaction was much more likely to be called off because it was immoral than because it was uneconomic. Typical of such an early Christian understanding of economic activity are these words from Evagrios the Solitary, a fourth-century monastic:

> When buying or selling you can hardly avoid sin. So, in either case, be sure you lose a little in the transaction. Do not haggle about the price from love of gain, and so indulge in actions harmful to the soul. . . . If possible it is best to place such business in the hands of someone you can trust, so that, being thus relieved of the worry, you can pursue your calling with joy and hope.[6]

Despite such discouragements of gain in the name of sanctity, there certainly were, in the Middle Ages, accumulations of wealth. Material wealth was even viewed as necessary — if not for everyone, then at least for feudal lords. But whereas material wealth was considered to be necessary, economic motivation — in which an action was undertaken only to gain wealth — was (as the warning from Evagrios makes plain) morally suspicious. As another medieval commentator put it, "To engage in economic activity is to have a wolf by the ears."

Toward the end of the Middle Ages, Thomas Aquinas combined the philosophical system of Aristotle with Christian theology, and worked out, as part of his monumental synthesis, a Christian economic theory. Like Aristotle's, it was pragmatic with regard to economics. Economic activity, and wealth itself, had a place, but only if they led to improvement of the soul. So underlying its pragmatism was a Christian foundation: the state of the soul was understood not in Greek terms of balance, order, and individual fulfillment, but in Christian terms of salvation and righteousness.

Aquinas maintained that the acquisition and administration of

---

6. *The Philokalia,* compiled by St. Nikodimos of the Holy Mountain and St. Makarios of Corinth, trans. and ed. G. E. H. Palmer, Philip Sherrard, and Kallistos Ware (London: Faber & Faber, 1979), vol. 1, p. 35.

wealth and property were legitimate private rights, which could result in greater care, order, and satisfaction within a society than if they were held in common. Use of resources, however, was understood, as it was with Aristotle, to be common: things were to be shared with the needy in accordance with their purpose, as created by God. Implicit in this idea — private acquisition and administration, but public use — is a strong concept of stewardship. It is clear that in Aquinas's economics, the welfare of the whole community (which today we would extend to include the whole *oikos* or household of life) is to receive the benefit of a person's wealth. Aquinas strengthens this idea by citing Ambrose: "Let no one call his own that which is common," and again, "He who spends too much is a robber."

The Economics of the Reformers

Some hold that the Reformation led to an explosion of individualism, self-interest, worldly activity for gain, and, of course, capitalism. With the institutionalized moral yoke of the church thrown off (so the argument goes) the individual was left to please God in ways governed only by his own conscience. But this view, to the extent that it is historically defensible at all, clearly does not represent what the Reformers actually said about economic activity. (Of course, what the intellectual descendants of the Reformers did with the economic seeds which they planted is a very different matter.)

Take Luther's view of his economic environment, for example:

> I have wished to give a bit of warning and instruction to everyone about this great, nasty, widespread business of merchandising. If we were to accept the principle that everyone may sell his wares as dear as he can, and were to approve the custom of borrowing and forced lending and standing surety, and yet try to advise men how they could act the part of Christians and keep their consciences good and safe, — that would be the same as trying to teach men how wrong could be right and bad good, and how one could at the same time live and act according to the divine Scriptures and against the divine Scriptures. For these three errors, — that everyone may sell what is his own as dear as he will, borrowing, and becoming surety, — these, I say, are the three sources from which the stream of abomination, injustice, treachery and guile flows far and wide: to try to stem the flood and not stop up the springs, is trouble and labor lost.

But though he may have been angry with private economic activity, Luther was no friend either of economic activity conducted by the state. After a long list of examples of private abuses, Luther concludes:

> Kings and princes ought to look into these things and forbid them by strict laws, but I hear that they have an interest in them, and the saying of Isaiah is fulfilled, "Thy princes have become companions of thieves." They hang thieves who have stolen a gulden or half a gulden and trade with those who rob the whole world and steal more than all the rest, so that the proverb may hold true: Big thieves hang the little ones, and as the Roman senator Cato said: Simple thieves lie in prisons and in stocks; public thieves walk abroad in gold and silk. But what will God say to this at last? He will do as He says by Ezekiel; princes and merchants, one thief with another, He will melt them together like lead and brass, as when a city burns, so that there shall be neither princes nor merchants any more.

With the Reformation came a new emphasis on the salvation of the individual, and it was accompanied by a theology which ultimately gave greater validity to individual wealth. A strong element in John Calvin's teaching, for instance, was the appropriateness of material things as instruments of God's grace. And money was the symbol of these material things. As André Biéler, an interpreter of Calvin, puts it:

> Money is the means which God uses in granting to man what is necessary to the support of the existence of man and his companions. God puts wealth at the disposal of man so that he may organize his life and the life of society for which he is solidarily responsible as well.[7]

From this affirmation of money as a symbol of God's providence, Calvin derives two important ideas. By far the most influential (perhaps unfortunately) is the idea of money as a sign of the favor of God. Again, we quote Biéler's summary of Calvin:

> Further, by dispensing all material goods and particularly money to his creature, the Creator makes himself known as a life-giving Father. Money therefore does not have a merely utilitarian function. It has

---

7. André Biéler, *The Social Humanism of Calvin*, trans. Paul T. Fuhrmann (Richmond, VA: John Knox Press, 1964), pp. 30-31.

really a spiritual mission. It is a sign of the grace of God who makes his children live. Moreover, money is a sign of the Kingdom of God.[8]

The fact that money can be a sign of the grace of God does not necessarily mean, however, that the more wealthy are the more blessed. Indeed, says Calvin, money can also be "a sign of condemnation of him who gets the goods of his living without discerning that they are a gift of God." For money is always, by both its absence and its presence, a way of testing both our trust in God and our readiness to love and obey him.

This brings us to the second, and more neglected, of Calvin's important economic concepts: through their wealth or poverty, both rich and poor have a spiritual mission to fulfill. The inequality of wealth is not arbitrary. It exists instead to provoke "a continuous distribution of goods." The poor person has a mission: to be the neighbor to whom the rich person can give. The rich person, obviously, has a complementary mission: to be the poor person's benefactor. The goal of this redistribution, however, is not the perpetuation of inequality, but a state of equality. In Calvin's words:

> Thus the Lord recommends to us a proportion of this nature, that we may, in so far as every one's resources admit, afford help to the needy, so that there may not be some in affluence, and others in need.[9]

The motive for this redistribution is love. Indeed, says Calvin, economic exchange is one of the ways God ordained in which we demonstrate love or fellowship. Such fellowship is clearly evident in marital love and in the family. But it is also evident in the exchanges of work and of the marketplace. For the division of labor separates us from each other, but mutual exchange reunites: it is a concrete sign of fellowship, of the solidarity of human existence. Sin has ruined this harmonious picture; and restoration comes from Christ. To be born again is to be born into the body of Christ, and "the saints . . . are gathered into the society of Christ on the condition that they mutually exchange among themselves the gifts conferred to them by God."[10]

Ultimately, then, for Calvin the goal of economic activity is a

---

8. Ibid., p. 31.

9. From John Calvin, *Commentary on II Corinthians,* cited in W. Fred Graham, *The Constructive Revolutionary* (Richmond, VA: John Knox Press, 1971), p. 70.

10. Biéler, *The Social Humanism of Calvin,* p. 22.

harmonious society, bound together by love. Calvin declares this clearly in a sermon on Ephesians:

> It is not enough when one can say, "Oh, I work, I have my trade, I set the pace." This is not enough; for one must be concerned whether it is good and profitable to the community and if it is able to serve our neighbors. . . . And this is why we are compared to members of a body. But now, if one's hand be employed to give some sport to another member and that even to his damage, the whole body will by this means fall into ruin. . . . It is certain that no occupation will be approved by him which is not useful and that does not serve the common good and that also redounds to the profit of everyone.[11]

We have, in this summary of some important economic ideas preceding current free-market capitalism, dealt at somewhat greater length with Calvin's thought. The reason for this emphasis is that interpreters of Calvin, both from within and without the Calvinist tradition, have seen a basis for the industriousness and the exploitativeness of the capitalist countries in his teaching of money as a sign of God's blessing. The "Protestant work ethic," as it has sometimes been called, is seen by some as underlying and justifying the acquisition of private wealth. But whatever the connections might be between Calvin's teaching and the current market system, it is plain that Calvin saw economic activity as secondary to the goals of fellowship among people and profit to the whole community.

Max Weber's thesis on the relationship between Calvinism and the spirit of capitalism is perhaps the most famous of the views of the role of religion in the emergence of capitalism. Weber emphasized two aspects of Calvinism: the doctrines of predestination, election, and calling; and the attitudes and habits of mind that went with rigorous theological reflection on the part of the laity. Thus religious responsibility and economic performance were wed. Economic activity did not have to be sanctified by the church or shunned as perilous to the soul. As R. H. Tawney puts it in his foreword to Weber's book *The Protestant Ethic and the Spirit of Capitalism*:

> So far from there being an inevitable conflict between money-making and piety, they are natural allies, for the virtues incumbent on the elect

---

11. From Calvin, "Sermon XXXI on the Epistle to the Ephesians," cited in Graham, *The Constructive Revolutionary*, pp. 80-81.

— diligence, thrift, sobriety, prudence — are the most reliable passport to commercial prosperity.[12]

Weber does indeed show that some kinds of Calvinism contain certain elements which nurture capitalism. But only very tangentially is it connected with Calvin's purpose. Weber himself makes this clear, for Weber qualified his thesis far more than virtually all of his critics and respondents. He limited his analysis, for example, to only "ascetic" forms of Calvinism found after 1600. Weber goes out of his way to say that Calvin's own views are different from those of his followers. It is when interpreters of Calvin saw the pursuit of gain as a morally approvable act in itself that capitalism and Christendom began to be closely associated. Thus it was in the Christian West that our current economic system, dominated by the idea of "scarcity," originated. And it is primarily through that system that we make our major impact on creation today.

For today we are as likely to encounter creation in the marketplace of economic activity as we are in its natural state. We use lumber, not trees; steel, not rock; meat, not animals. In each case, some economic transaction has taken place. Objects in creation have become "property" or "goods" to be sold, bought, and used. Such a way of valuing creation represents a profound shift in human thought about the created world; less obviously, it also reflects a profound shift in our thought about ourselves. Before we could come to regard objects in creation as things to be bought and sold, we had to come to regard ourselves as individuals, standing apart from "nature" (the modern use of the word "nature" itself reflects the process of individuation) and from each other. Modern economic activity depends upon a decline in awareness of community (both with other human beings and with nonhuman creatures) and a corresponding rise in our sense of being isolated individuals.

A highly developed individualism is a basic premise of free-market capitalism from Adam Smith onward. But before such individualism could be accepted as the basis for economic valuing it had to overcome deep religious and moral reservations. These reservations were rooted in the Aristotelian/Thomistic heritage we discussed above, and they persisted well into the early industrial revolution. In the seventeenth century the European mind was struggling to absorb rapid changes in society, religion,

---

12. Max Weber, *The Protestant Ethic and the Spirit of Capitalism* (New York: Charles Scribner's Sons, 1958), p. 3.

science, and knowledge of the physical earth. In this social ferment immediately prior to the industrial revolution and the modern capitalist era,
two English thinkers — Thomas Hobbes and John Locke — played key
roles in overcoming those reservations about individualism which survived
from medieval Christianity. It is temptingly easy to defend the idea that
the community-based economics of the Middle Ages is "Christian," and
that the economic individualism of modern times goes squarely against
the Christian vision. But it is not that simple, for there is in the Christian
message that which encourages the inwardness, subjectivity, and individualism we see represented — however imperfectly — in modern times.[13]

Thomas Hobbes

In the middle of the seventeenth century Thomas Hobbes articulated two
notions about human behavior which became central to economic liberalism. The first is that all behavior is disguised self-interest. Hobbes wrote
that in life we "must suppose to have no other good, nor other garland,
but being foremost." The second is that all striving is for relative position,
and hence is competitive. Said Hobbes: "in the first place, I put for a
general inclination of all mankind, a perpetual and restless striving of
power after power, that ceaseth only in death."[14] The objects of desire
therefore depend on what others have and their position relative to our
own. Striving for superiority is universal and lifelong; the result is perpetual
competition with no end in sight. So long as this striving also requires
material goods, no end to growing consumption is in sight either. So long
as position depends on relative, not absolute, level of possessions, all one
can do from cradle to grave is continually to strive for more, but perhaps
succeeding only in maintaining one's position. In such a picture of steadily
accelerating consumption, it is clear that the earth, at least, will be the
loser.

---

13. For a detailed discussion of the Christian roots of the modern notion of
individual selfhood, see Charles Taylor, *Sources of the Self: The Making of the Modern Identity*
(Cambridge: Harvard University Press, 1989).

14. Thomas Hobbes, quoted in *The Encyclopedia of Philosophy*, vol. 4 (New York:
Macmillan, 1967), pp. 39, 41.

John Locke

But Hobbes's form of liberalism was perceived by many to be too radical, too cut off from grounding in traditional communitarian values. John Locke, late in the seventeenth century, seemed able to provide for individualism some of the legitimacy which Hobbes had failed to give it. Locke sought to explain how things legitimately came to be possessed by *individuals* even though, as he held, the earth and all it yields were given to humankind *in common*. Locke describes the problem this way:

> But this [that the earth was given to humankind in common] being supposed, it seems to some a very great difficulty, how any one should ever come to have a *Property* in any thing. . . . I shall endeavour to shew, how Men might come to have a *property* in several parts of that which God gave to Mankind in common, and that without any express Compact of all the Commoners.[15]

Locke's solution was based on the assumption that to begin with, everyone "owns" his own person; hence whatever his personal labor produces from nature (in Locke's words, whatever "he has mixed his labor with") is his to keep. Modern libertarian economists are fond of quoting Locke on this point as a basis for saying that eventually all of creation is there for the taking of ambitious human beings.[16] However, Locke set forth two high-level principles that would seem to radically limit private property. The first is that this principle of private appropriation holds only "where there is enough, and as good left in common for others."[17] This limitation is almost always overlooked, both in practice and in defense of capitalism. If it had been taken seriously and applied continuously, policies governing access to the resources of the earth, as well as the effects of our production on the earth's biosphere, might have been radically different. For this limit which Locke places on the acquisition of private property is both a strong principle of justice and a strong principle of sustainability.

Locke's second provision would likewise function as a stringent limit to individual appropriation. We might call it the "manna" provision:

---

15. John Locke, *Two Treatises of Government, Second Treatise*, section 25, ed. Peter Laslett (Cambridge: Cambridge University Press, 1963).

16. See, for example, Walter Block, *Environment and Economics: A Reconciliation* (1989).

17. *Second Treatise*, sect. 27.

As much as any one can make use of to any advantage of life before it spoils; so much he may by his labour fix a Property in. Whatever is beyond this, is more than his share, and belongs to others. Nothing was made by God for Man to spoil or destroy.[18]

And this in a day lacking refrigeration or canning techniques!

Both principles would seem to apply to a strict state of nature, but a crucial convention radically changes their application. This convention is the invention of and the consent to use money and accept the consequences of such use.

Locke's early reasoning seemed to assume the frontier mentality which considered (for example) the vast lands in the New World as "unused." He implied that the presence of such land negated concern over whether there would indeed be "enough, and as good left for others." By the third edition of his *Treatises,* however, Locke had shifted the argument in a way very significant for ways of thinking about "wealth." He argued:

To which let me add, that he who appropriates land to himself by his labour, does not lessen but increase the common stock of mankind. For the provisions serving to the support of humane life, produced by one acre of inclosed and cultivated land, are . . . ten times more, than those, which are yeilded by an acre of Land, of an equal richnesse, lyeing wast in common.[19]

In other words, since land brought under human control was ten times more productive than when it was left in its natural state, the wealth created would more than pay for the lack of commons available for others to appropriate. Locke did not seem concerned that property, wealth, income, work, and the very opportunity to act as a steward of the earth would likely be distributed differently under this new arrangement. Here he stands firmly in the liberal tradition of greater concern for the quantity of wealth created than for other effects, including the quality of justice. And significantly, he sees creation apart from human activity as simply "lyeing wast."

The spoilage limitation was likewise modified by the convention of money — for money, of course, does not spoil, and may be accumulated without limit. Locke seems to see money as valuable more for the forma-

---

18. Ibid., sect. 31.
19. Ibid., sect. 37.

tion of capital than for mere hoarding; nevertheless, the imperishable quality of money seems to eliminate an earlier constraint on accumulation.

Thus Hobbes and Locke lay the foundation (or at least describe a foundation already implicit in their time) for several principles of our economic system: the right to private property, the absence of limits to such rights, inequality in ownership justified by wealth creation, and a labor basis for value. We have built a rich human world on these foundations — but in doing so we have done great harm to the earth.

Bernard Mandeville

Even in their day the Hobbesian/Lockean world was not a very pretty one, despite the arguments that it was grounded in nature and that it led to the creation of wealth. A latent moral anxiety — if not indignity — over this new economics was expressed well by Bernard Mandeville in his anthropocentric *Fable of the Bees*. Mandeville saw a double standard. The enlargement of economic activity and the arguments of the philosophers created tension between traditional moral and religious standards (which, as we have seen, were opposed to greed and covetousness) and the desire to get in on the action and get rich. Mandeville's hive tried virtue and found it wanting: its reward was poverty. Given a choice, the hive prefers the vice of greed. For though vice-ridden individuals intend no good to the hive through their pursuit of gain, the hive is nevertheless benefited through the resulting increase in commercial activity. The clincher is: "the very poor lived better than the rich before; and nothing could be added more." Thus Mandeville justifies avaricious accumulation and declares it a closed system:

> After this I flatter myself to have demonstrated that neither the friendly qualities and kind affections that are natural to man, nor the real virtues he is capable of acquiring by reason and self-denial, are the foundation of society: but that what we call evil in the world, moral as well as natural, is the grand principle that makes us sociable creatures, the solid basis, the life and support of all trades and employments without exception: that there we must look for the true origin of all arts and sciences, and that the moment evil ceases the society must be spoiled, if not totally dissolved.

Adam Smith

This bold claim stirred no less a respondent than Adam Smith. Smith was furious with Mandeville — but not because of his defense of the morality of unintended consequences, nor for his argument on behalf of the pursuit of self-interest. What Mandeville had been guilty of was miscategorization: self-love, said Smith, was a virtue, not a vice.

Working within the framework of Scottish moral philosophy, Smith explored the roles of prudence (consideration of self) and sympathy (concern for others) in his early work, *Theory of Moral Sentiments* (1759). The principle of sympathy finds little explicit application in his later, more famous work on economic organization (*An Inquiry Into the Nature and Causes of the Wealth of Nations*, 1776). But the earlier work established some important viewpoints. For one, it explored the difference between those conditions necessary for the survival of society and those that make for a happy society. Observance of justice — and for Smith, justice meant mainly not interfering in the pursuits of others — was seen as an instance of the former. Genuine concern for the well-being of others was an instance of the latter. In addition, the principle of the invisible hand, so important to the ideology of a market system, was first articulated in *The Theory of Moral Sentiments*, though with a different tone. In that early work Smith seems to share with Locke a notion of natural limits as a fundamental principle of distribution. But rather than spoilage, it is the limited size of the stomachs of the rich which insures that enough will be left over for others. A long passage from *The Theory of Moral Sentiments* makes this clear, and it also makes clear a number of implications of the market system for our use of creation — what we have called *earthkeeping*.

> The pleasures of wealth and greatness . . . which first prompted them to cultivate the ground, to build houses, to found cities and commonwealths, and to invent and improve all the sciences and arts, which ennoble and embellish human life; which have entirely changed the whole face of the globe, have turned the rude forests of nature into agreeable and fertile plains, and made the trackless and barren ocean a new fund of subsistence, and the great high road of communication to the different nations of the earth. The earth, by these labours of mankind, has been obliged to redouble her natural fertility, and to maintain a greater multitude of inhabitants. It is to no purpose that the proud and unfeeling landlord views his extensive fields, and without a thought for the wants of his brethren,

in imagination consumes himself the whole harvest that grows upon them. The homely and vulgar proverb, that the eye is larger than the belly, never was more fully verified than with regard to him. The capacity of his stomach bears no proportion to the immensity of his desires, and will receive no more than that of the meanest peasant. The rest he is obliged to distribute among those who prepare, in the nicest manner, that little which he himself makes use of, among those who fit up the palace in which this little is to be consumed, among those who provide and keep in order all the different baubles and trinkets which are employed in the economy of greatness; all of whom thus derive from his luxury and caprice that share of the necessaries of life which they would in vain have expected from his humanity or his justice. The produce of the soil maintains at all times nearly that number of inhabitants which it is capable of maintaining. The rich only select from the heap what is most precious and agreeable. They consume little more than the poor; and in spite of their natural selfishness and rapacity, though they mean only their own conveniency, though the sole end which they propose from the labours of all the thousands whom they employ be the gratification of their own vain and insatiable desires, they divide with the poor the produce of all their improvements. They are led by an invisible hand to make nearly the same distribution of the necessaries of life which would have been made had the earth been divided into equal portions among all its inhabitants; and thus, without intending it, without knowing it, advance the interest of the society, and afford means to the multiplication of the species.[20]

Smith's work of more limited focus, *The Wealth of Nations,* is by far the more well-known and remembered work. Here self-love steps boldly forward, elbowing benevolence away from the dinner table:

But man has almost constant occasion for the help of his brethren, and it is in vain for him to expect it from their benevolence only. He will be more likely to prevail if he can interest their self-love in his favour, and shew them that it is for their own advantage to do for him what he requires of them. . . . It is not from the benevolence of the butcher, the brewer, or the baker, that we expect our dinner, but from their regard to their own interest. We address ourselves, not to their

---

20. Adam Smith, *The Theory of Moral Sentiments* (New York: A. M. Kelly, 1966), pp. 263-65.

humanity but to their self-love, and never talk to them of our own necessities but of their advantages.[21]

So interdependent society, made all the more so by the principle of division of labor, confronted with individualism, is reintegrated through commercial activity and the unintended consequences of self-absorbed action:

> As every individual, therefore, endeavours as much as he can both to employ his capital in the support of domestic industry, and so to direct that industry that its produce may be of the greatest value; every individual necessarily labours to render the annual revenue of the society as great as he can. He generally, indeed, neither intends to promote the public interest, nor knows how much he is promoting it . . . he intends only his own gain, and he is in this, as in many other cases, led by an invisible hand to promote an end which was no part of his intention.

At least the integration is accomplished if maximum "national produce" (we would say "gross national product") is really what we all want, what harmonizes the various interests of individuals thrown together into a society. What Hobbes, Locke, and Mandeville took to be the chief end of humankind, materialistic wealth, is likewise appropriated by Smith for the moral justification of economic activity and the glue that holds society together. And such ideas of material betterment have long been the golden thread of continuity in mainstream Western economic thought.

RECENT DEFENSES OF THE MARKET

If we are to understand the stress which economic activity places on the earth, we must first understand how central to economic thought is this assumption that for our well-being we must wrest the bounty away from a reluctant nature. The words of more recent economists make this clear.

In 1930, grimly anticipating another century of economic progress, John Maynard Keynes observed:

---

21. Adam Smith, *The Wealth of Nations* (Modern Library, 1937), p. 14.

I see us free, therefore, to return to some of the most sure and certain principles of religion and traditional virtue — that avarice is a vice, that the exaction of usury is a misdemeanour, and the love of money is detestable, that those walk most truly in the paths of virtue and sane wisdom who take least thought for the morrow. We shall once more value ends above means and prefer the good to the useful. We shall honour those who can teach us how to pluck the hour and the day virtuously and well, the delightful people who are capable of taking direct enjoyment in things, the lilies of the field who toil not, neither do they spin.

But beware! The time for all this is not yet. For at least another hundred years we must pretend to ourselves and to every one that fair is foul and foul is fair; for foul is useful and fair is not. Avarice and usury and precaution must be our gods for a little longer still. For only they can lead us out of the tunnel of economic necessity into daylight.[22]

More recently, Charles Schultze, a past chairman of the (U.S.) President's Council of Economic Advisors, two hundred years after the publication of *The Wealth of Nations,* revives and reframes Smith's thought about the efficacy of self-love and the pursuit of gain:

Marketlike arrangements not only minimize the need for coercion as a means of social organization, they also reduce the need for compassion, patriotism, brotherly love, and cultural solidarity as motivating forces behind social improvement.

Learning how to harness the "base" motive of material self-interest to promote the common good was perhaps *the* most important social invention mankind has yet made. Turning silk into a silk purse is no great shakes, but converting a sow's ear into a silk purse does indeed partake of the miraculous. . . . There is indeed a role for "preaching" as a means of creating a political and cultural situation in which consensus can be reached on social intervention. Cleaning up the environment will only be achieved as environmental quality takes a higher place in the value system of most citizens. But when it comes to the specifics of getting the job done, preaching, indignation, and villain identification get in the way of results.[23]

---

22. John Maynard Keynes, *Essays in Persuasion* (New York: W. W. Norton, 1963), pp. 371-72.

23. Charles Schultze, "The Public Use of Private Interest," *Harper's,* May 1977, pp. 45-46.

Thus far in this survey of economic history we have neglected a crucially important development. What is this wealth that humankind is so anxious to have? How do we know it when we see it? What measures its value? How can the value of what is being pursued through commercial activity be compared to the value of other things, things found outside of markets? How and why do we value creation? "Earthkeeping" suggests one kind of valuation; the day-to-day "housekeeping" of economics suggests another. So we turn in the next chapter to a more detailed consideration of how the economic system of free enterprise puts values on creation.

CHAPTER 12

ใช้   ใช้

Valuing Creation

There's no such thing as a free lunch.

— Economist's maxim

Ho, every one who thirsts, come to the waters;
And he who has no money, come, buy and eat!
Come, buy wine and milk
Without money and without price.

— Isaiah 55:1

CREATION IS GOOD: IT IS VALUABLE. WE KNOW THIS BECAUSE GOD proclaimed it so. Sin has twisted creation, but has not cancelled its fundamental goodness. The story told thus far in this book describes and celebrates this creational goodness; it also describes the long human relationship to this good earth. In that relationship creation has sometimes been appreciated and has sometimes been degraded. Much (though not all) of the story of human valuing of creation has occurred under the heading of "economics," and in the last chapter we surveyed the history of that economic valuing. But before we look explicitly at the way that process of valuing works in economic practice today, let us consider some general characteristics of valuing.

THE BASIS FOR VALUE

First, we have no reason to doubt the basic goodness of creation and the "goods" we make from it. We stand outside of any nature/grace duality or worldly asceticism which would question the value of matter. But knowing *how good* goods are is not so simple. Are they absolutely good in themselves? Instrumentally good for human purposes? Good in principle because God called them so? Doxologically good because they honor and glorify their Creator? They may be all of these things. But when they are good in more than one way, how do we weigh these different values?

What do we mean when we say that something is valuable? How do we arrive at the value of a sunset, a tree, a wetland, or a seam of coal? The answers have changed throughout history. A common contemporary answer is that things have *emotive* value only. This definition of emotive valuing was put most powerfully by its early spokesman, Swedish philosopher Axel Hagerstrom. Hagerstrom (and many others) have maintained that in truth content, the statements "That is bad" and "Ugh!" are equally valid: "bad" means only "I don't like it." Conversely, the meaning of "good" is nothing more than "I like it." Such a theory of values implies two things: (1) human beings are the sole source of valuations, not merely instrumentally, but morally as well; and (2) the grounds for valuations are subjective, nothing more than personal likes or dislikes.

Although this way of thinking about value is common, most people resist it (for good reasons). The very concept of value seems to point outside of ourselves. Usually we try to support our feelings of value by referring to transcendent norms, or at least by appealing to common opinion. To say that the Mona Lisa is good art only because I like it is not convincing, even to ourselves. But if we can say that it is beautiful, that it is important, that it has merit, or at least that a lot of other people like it as well, we seem to be on safer ground. Another common way of grounding valuations is to refer to things as being useful. In these terms, a tree need not be deemed *good,* only *good for,* as in "good for making paper." Both of these attempts to find solid ground for valuations reflect our uneasiness with the idea that purely emotive and subjective grounds for value are adequate. However (as we will see), in modern economic theory, purely subjective valuation is understood to be the only appropriate grounds for calling something "good."

Recently, however, we have seen signs of a return to notions of intrinsic value — to the idea that things are good because of what they are, not merely because they please us or are "good for" something. This line of thought seems most powerful among non-Christians, who base it increasingly on some idea of the intrinsic goodness of the earth, Gaia, or the cosmos. But it is increasingly present in Christian thinkers as well, who are recovering the full biblical notion of the goodness of creation. Accompanying the Christian idea of intrinsic value is the concept of *stewardship*. Valuing, as with naming, is a job given to men and women — servant-stewards, who stand in a unique relationship of responsibility to the Creator. Those whose notion of goodness is based not on the Creator but on Gaia, the cosmos, have sometimes criticized the Christian notion of stewardship as arrogant, for it seems to set human beings over nature, not as caretakers, but as landlords.

Though much harm has been done when "dominion" is taken to mean "autonomy," the stewardship task cannot be denied. To say that humans are God's stewards is not to say that humans are God. Put another way, though the value of things must comport with God's principles for correct valuing, humans are still the Creator's agents for this task.

So the Christian view sees that God values creation and that he placed men and women within that creation with a special role: that of steward. A part of the task of stewards is to make decisions about the various possible uses of the goods entrusted to them. Valuing is an inevitable part of this task. However, this identifies only the agent involved in valuing, not the principles for valuation. The candidates for such principles put forward by the world around us — purely subjective valuations, usefulness for human purposes, and intrinsic value — are all deficient by Christian standards. The missing element is transcendence: valuing of the creation ought to be grounded in the Creator's norms. Such valuing, based on real norms, raises critical concerns about the emotive theory of valuing found in economics.

ECONOMIC VALUE

Much of the intellectual history of economics is the search for a way to value things. Closer to home, much of our practice of economics reflects the same search. When we are deciding what to buy and how much to pay, we are participating in economic valuation — usually without reflection. So let us reflect a little on our economic valuation, keeping in mind that economic valuation is not the only way to value things.

How does economics deal with values which are central to this book — ecological integrity, sustainability, the well-being of future generations, and the planet itself? Is the economic system in tune with its environment, both social and natural? Can ecologists talk with economists, or is their language (and their system of values) incommensurable? The ecologist says: "It's worth any cost to preserve (or clean up) X." But the economist says: "But if we spend everything on X, there will be nothing left for other goods." We are familiar with such dilemmas. We have often heard it said of a new safety device or medical technology that "if it saves just one life, it will be worth it." The argument is irrefutable — especially if the life it will save is, say, my own, or my child's. But as a general principle, it is unworkable.

As technology allows us to do more and more (at higher and higher cost) to try to intervene in what were once thought of as natural processes or acts of God, this problem of incommensurable values gets more burdensome. When one discipline (such as ecological ethics) speaks in terms of absolutes and the other (such as resource economics) speaks in terms of trade-offs, conflict is inevitable. So we need more open and honest and less defensive dialogue. We need a richer language of public discourse in order to recover the values essential to human and ecological communities. We should drop the language of "hard" economic values and "soft" ecological ones. We should resist the translating of all decisions into cost-benefit terms, and of all cost-benefit terms into dollars. Yet (as the disastrous failure of the Communist attempt to eliminate markets makes clear) we must enact ecological values in the presence of a market system. Given the necessity of a market system, how can we keep such a system from encouraging the degradation of creation? In regard to this question, let us think about the way economic systems work.

Economic thought has traditionally been grounded in the fact of scarcity: no scarcity, no economics. Is this true? Our struggle with household management seems to be that of confronting the eminent constraint of scarcity: too much of the month left after the paycheck is gone. And nationally, we are caught up in the same struggle: if only we had more resources we could clean up the environment, feed the poor, develop alternative energy sources to end our dependence on the Middle East. So scarcity is a fact, but to regard it as the foundation of economics is dangerous. Where did economic activity come from; at what moment did it enter human history? When were humans first confronted with the necessity of making wise choices about the use of creation? (Though once again we must remember that not all choices about the use of creation are economic choices.) To understand these questions of origin is to clarify some of the basis for economic activity, both when scarcity is present and when it is not.

We believe that human economic activity began not with scarcity, but with creation itself — with the first time men and women reflected on their unique stewardly role in it. The wise and fruitful disposition of the good things that God made was mandated of human beings from the very beginning. To be sure, not all wisdom with regard to creation is economic wisdom. But stewardship is at the heart of our use of creation, whether the created goods we deal with are scarce or not. The fact of stewardship is prior to the fact of scarcity.

We need not speculate on such questions as whether there was scarcity in Eden, or whether in the wealthy West much of our sense of scarcity is contrived. We can make the point with experiences far closer to home.

The contrast between the scarcity foundation and that which we will call the "entrustedness" foundation (for stewardly activity emerges from our having been *entrusted* with the care and use of the creation) can be illustrated with homely examples. Take a common experience: going through a cafeteria line. Imagine that two means of payment are possible: meal ticket and à la carte. In the first, we pay no more for extra food; in the second, each helping costs us more. Do we behave differently under these circumstances? Usually, we do. Taking more than we need and wasting (or waisting) the excess is common in the first method, whereas careful choice and "economical" eating is part of the second. Why? It is quite likely that in very real and concrete ways we have adopted the scarcity mentality: no scarcity, no economizing.

Contrast this to the entrustedness view of the same choice: if it is God's creation — here in the form of food — shouldn't wise and frugal use of it, as a response to the Creator, follow regardless of how we are paying? These cases are multiplied many times over in our experience. How (and whether) we care for common property, the property of others, and the possibilities of future generations all depend to some extent on whether we have adopted a notion of economizing under conditions of scarcity and individual property rights, or, alternatively, whether we are acting out of responsibility for creation regardless of conditions of scarcity.

Our choice between the two foundations affects our treatment of anything not actually "ours": rental cars, motel rooms, parks, or any shared-use entity. We will "economize" differently if we start from the premise of stewardship.

THE MARKET SYSTEM

Economic activity as most of us know it goes on in the institutional context of a market system. In the previous chapter we outlined the history of the market system as it emerged in Western thought as the primary means (adequate or not) of our stewardship of creation. We have now to consider in some detail how the market system works, especially how it deals with questions of the valuing, use, and preservation of the creation.

Initially, a market system can be described as a *private-property price* system. Each term describes crucial institutional characteristics. *Private property* describes our basis for participation in the system: the conditions under which we may take part in it at all. Property creates boundaries within which the administration, use, and exchange of goods goes on. Full property rights include the right to destroy, to transfer, and to enjoy the benefits of the goods in question. Typically these goods are subject only to respect for the property of others. As such, private property rights grant to their holders tremendous power and freedom from interference. In the traditional liberal view (which goes back to John Locke and his foundational values of "life, liberty, and the pursuit of property"), owners need consult no one — neither state, church, nor neighbor — in order to exercise the privileges of property.

Prices in a market system are the symbols which signal value and conditions of exchange. As exchange ratios, prices can signal only relative, never absolute, value. Nevertheless, within this limitation they have an objective status that is open to the world to see. A price is, in effect, a declaration of willingness to buy or sell without further qualification. It states the public conditions under which the owner of the property is willing to release the property from his own stewardship. Thus a wage, for example, represents the terms by which an employer is willing to accept work from someone, or the terms by which a worker is willing to let go of the right to his or her own labor. The only qualifications that one needs in order to participate in the market are (1) property or labor to offer in exchange and (2) willingness to accept the terms of exchange. The demand for qualification beyond this would be seen as discriminatory: application of an irrelevant condition.

Seen in this light, property is a moral boundary as well as an economic, legal, and political one. Within the boundaries of one's own decisions about property, no one from the outside may kibitz. In a market system, price is the only basis for relationship with the outside world: it is the boundary condition. And if, in turn, we take the qualification for exchange to be the freedom to take part in transactions freely agreed to "between consenting adults," then *freedom* (in the sense of absence of coercion) becomes the only characteristic beyond the sanctity of property (and perhaps of contract) that need be socially guaranteed.

The market system cannot answer several crucial questions, the most important being how one comes to hold legitimate title to property to begin with. Another obvious shortcoming of the market view of reality is that it leaves no room for questions of *public* good, let alone such imponderables as the good for creation itself. All such questions are concealed behind the veil of individual freedom over the use of private property. Individuals should do what they want to do, so the market view says, for there is no authority other than the free self. What they do in relation to others is a matter of autonomy as well, for anyone is free to refuse an exchange that he or she thinks unacceptable, no questions asked. The stark details of this liberal (and libertarian) argument outline clearly the way in which free markets allocate creation to various uses.

Obviously, only limited claims can be made for such a system. We can claim freedom, for example, so long as we define freedom in a very limited way. We can claim that such a system is just only if we constrict the meaning of "justice" to something like absence of interference. Claims for good beyond these limits are strained. Thus to call a society "good" only because it is a market society is hollow, for if we relate only by means of the market, we hardly have a society at all. The market system is simple, but that simplicity does not in itself make it attractive, primarily because of doubt about its claims to legitimacy or goodness.

The highest claim that can be made for a market system is that it is efficient. And that is a remarkable claim, for it suggests that without values, plans, or motivation (other than self-interest) all resources in a market system end up in their highest-valued uses. What then can the claim of "efficiency" mean?

In *Counting the Cost: The Economics of Christian Stewardship*, Robin

Klay, a Christian economist who addresses many of the same questions about land stewardship that concern us in this book, attempts to explain the way in which free markets make our stewardship efficient. Speaking of the use of land, she says:

> the price that people are willing and able to pay for a certain good or service indicates the relative value they attach to it. Thus, when people are willing to spend more on land for housing than on land for agriculture . . . land is converted from agricultural to residential use. . . . the market allocates land among alternate uses — recreational, agricultural, residential, and commercial — in such a way that the total value of output on the land is maximized.[1]

Klay refers to this value as "social value." That this value is and should be measured by price continues the argument in her previous chapter that prices and not regulations should be used to deal with air and water resources: "putting a price on air and water use is not the moral issue; deciding *what* price to charge is, however, heavily laden with values."[2] So the argument seems to be this: the market allocates resources to their highest socially valued uses (i.e., what people are willing and able to pay). This value is measured by price, so that when there is no market to place prices on such things as air, water, and wildlife, prices should be placed on them by government. Klay shares this opinion with many other neo-classical economists, Christian and non-Christian alike, who assume that efficiency and pricing raise no moral questions.

But profoundly important moral questions *are* raised when we let price and ability to pay be the sole criteria on which our treatment of creation depends. Let us look more closely at the moral implications of these criteria.

First of all, willingness to pay is a matter of preference. But mere preference is a remarkably thin basis for choice, not much different from the emotive criteria we considered before; it is based only on individual will, not on any larger value. Second, value is not determined by all humans, but only by those with current purchasing power. This fact invites a serious criticism: those who have too little purchasing power, and those who cannot be represented — such as all future generations — have no

---

1. Robin Kendrick Klay, *Counting the Cost: The Economics of Christian Stewardship* (Grand Rapids: Eerdmans, 1986), pp. 102-3.

2. Ibid., p. 96.

voice in a market system and cannot even begin to influence the value of anything.

But there is another fundamental criticism of basing economic valuing on preferences. Many of the utilitarian views of economic welfare argue that the objective of economic activity is the maximum satisfaction of individual preferences. But why, asks Mark Sagoff, is this good? Is satisfaction of preferences always an intrinsic good? His answer:

> It cannot be argued that the satisfaction of preferences is a good thing in itself, for many preferences are sadistic, envious, racist, or unjust. Preferences may be coerced or adapted to coercive circumstances. . . . Many preferences . . . like the urge for a cigarette — are despised by the very people that have them.[3]

Sagoff argues that it is good that people should be free to pursue some of their preferences, but that it is not necessarily good that they succeed in satisfying all of them. On the other hand, argues Sagoff, "It may be good in itself that certain preferences be satisfied, namely, preferences that are good in themselves." Such an argument clearly has left the "hedonic calculus" of Utilitarianism behind and has returned to the assumption that some actions are good in themselves. Aristotle embodies such notions of intrinsic value, and Aristotle's outlook has been given new strength by several recent studies (most notably Alasdair MacIntyre's *After Virtue*). It suggests that progress is not to be found in satisfying more preferences, but rather in *better* preferences.

Making ability to pay central to the determining of value raises another set of questions. In a market system, such ability dictates not only who benefits from creation's goods but also much more — namely, what is produced. Most people believe a market system to be driven by consumer demand (though in real-life economic systems other factors, such as advertising, make such an assumption questionable). If so, then the products that really are produced and the resources used to produce them will be strongly influenced by the willingness and ability to pay. All goods are on the auction block and the benefits go to the highest bidder. In a market, money talks and it announces whether your views are to be taken seriously or not. A group which is convinced that (for example) a marsh is worth

---

3. Mark Sagoff, *The Economy of the Earth* (Cambridge: Cambridge University Press, 1988).

preserving may be willing to pay, but unless the willingness is accompanied by ability, its voice is mute.

Thus the claim that the market is (through pricing) the best way to determine which resources are to be used can never be taken seriously if it is not accompanied by a correct distribution of the *ability* to pay. Otherwise, to any claim that one use is better than another (forest or treefarm, wetland or subdivision) we would have the right to say: "Who says so?" If the only answer is "Those with money," we could ask who gave them the right.

Likewise, the claim for the market's efficiency is not in itself convincing. The efficient achievement of a bad is not good. As Kenneth Arrow (a distinguished market economist) puts it: "The price system . . . does not provide within itself any defensible income distribution."[4] The same could be said for wealth, or for ability to pay in general. Justification for a given distribution must come from outside of the price system.

PRICE AND VALUE

What is the relationship between price and value? When we want to say, "This is valuable," is appeal to its price the only legitimate reference? Price sends a clear signal. But perhaps it is too clear. For example, when we try to determine the value of a wetland, we should consider many things: ecological niches, species preservation, retention of open spaces, maintenance of water table, beauty, etc. All of these count; all are valuable. But as soon as price enters into the picture ("This wetland is worth $100 an acre; $200 an acre if drained") all other aspects become invisible. And if we ask whether the wetland should be preserved for future generations, someone is sure to suggest that all assets (like the wetland) must pay a return at least equal to the current interest rate. This means that the higher the interest rate and the further into the future the asset is to be preserved, the more the future benefit will be discounted. So it is no wonder that economic wisdom sees little reason to preserve assets in their natural state: it's better to get a return now — say, by draining the wetland (it helps if we call it a swamp) and building a mall.

---

4. Kenneth Arrow, *Limits of Organization,* p. 22.

Should we therefore let such goods as wetlands be subject to bidding? In market theory, such a process would objectively determine the highest-valued use. To answer the question, we must consider another aspect of the relationship between price and value.

In terms of human symbols, which of the earth's goods are signaled to be the most valuable and which the least? A plausible answer for both is *those with no price:* silence, happiness, integrity, life itself. Why should pricelessness be a characteristic both of highly valued goods and of those not valued at all? What is the effect of this lack of price?

Most economists have a deadly fear of non-priced goods. Their fear is that such goods will be abused; they will not be "economized." Examples supporting this view are easy to come by: air, water, land, lakes, oceans — all have suffered abuse attributable to their status as common property resources. Garrett Hardin labeled such abuse "the tragedy of the commons." A "free" good is typically overexploited — used beyond its carrying capacity, or just plain used up. Such poor use leads many economists and policy makers to believe that the price system should be more extensive, that what we have is not market failure, but failure to use markets. Their remedy for most existing abuses of the environment is to establish prices for *everything* (clean air, clean rivers, sea otters, virgin timber, spotted owls, and so on). When these resources are in the hands of private individuals, the owners will surely not part with them without exacting a price. The sale of pollution licenses is a good (and moderately successful) example of an attempt to extend price to previously non-priced goods. Once goods enter the price system, some economists are fairly confident that they will be well cared for — that is, allocated to their highest-valued use. There is some merit to this approach. But it reckons with only one aspect of non-priced goods: undervaluation of "free" goods. What of the other aspect, where lack of price signals high value?

To place a price on sexual relationships, family heirlooms, babies, memories, etc., is repellent to us. It is repellent because we assume that some things should remain outside of market activity, and thus should never be sold or bargained for. We feel that pricing these things would diminish them and cheapen both buyer and seller. Thus we feel that some things are, quite precisely, priceless: beyond price. What do we do then with a good which is highly valued but which has no price? The lack of price does not indicate absence of care. Such goods are frequently precious either to individuals or, in many cases, to whole communities or cultures. In general, the reason they have no price is not that no one thought to give them one. It is rather that to price them would reduce their value. Some would put it more strongly: they feel intuitively that to price such goods would be wrong.

Two crucial observations: first, such goods are *above* price, not merely high-priced. The way we value such things is through means other than price, and this valuing — perhaps *cherishing* is a better word — is incommensurable with price. To be sure, such a high view of non-priceable value is subject to erosion, for there is always the temptation, if the price is high enough, to compromise. We have all heard of the scoundrel who sells the family treasures, or the traitor who sells his country's honor. The point is made grimly in the familiar and unfunny story of the man who asks a woman if she will go to bed with him for a million dollars. When she says yes, he asks if she will go to bed with him for five dollars. "What do you think I am?" she replies indignantly. "We have established what you are," he responds; "we are just haggling over the price." Such an episode degrades both parties, of course. But the point of all such stories is that we readily acknowledge that some good things do not lie within the price system. Much of creation is such a good and (as native peoples have long argued) should never be bought or sold.

Another erosion of the idea of non-priceable value is to define any good that someone refuses to sell as having infinite price. This should be avoided. To claim infinite price is to claim that price is always the relevant means of valuing. Everything is included, but some prices are higher than others. It is assumed therefore that we need no value language other than price. But this is a category mistake that excludes the very possibility of valuing by any other means. And it might further imply that things are still open to negotiation — if we wait long enough or if conditions change or if we bargain hard enough, the price might come down from infinity.

A second observation about priceless goods is this: to say that some things cannot be priced is to fly cheerfully in the face of the efficiency criterion. For when we accept alternative ways of valuing and allocating goods we agree that no efficiency claim need be made for the outcome. Efficiency — sometimes important as a characterization of means — does not pay for all. In fact, it is clear that efficiency must have a moral qualification if it is ever to be acceptable: efficient killing of children, for example, is not laudable, nor are we likely to discuss seriously an efficiency-equity tradeoff. If it is wrong to kill children, it should not be done, not even efficiently.

The point of all this is to emphasize that with regard to many goods

— things that we hold to be valuable — we do not need, in fact we do not want, to use the price system. If this is true for obvious examples, what of other things? If (for example) human beings are such that their offspring should not be marketed, are there other entities that should be extended the same exemption? Are there other parts of the creation that should not be priced, traded, or disposed of in markets? If so, we should be answering many policy questions differently than we are.

But in economics, business, and government today, the dominant policy regarding the use of creation is to "privatize": to establish a more extensive use of private property rights and prices. Those who argue for greater privatization as a means for better stewardship of creation say that the price system is not deficient so much as it is underemployed. They are likely to recommend more extensive use of prices and the rejection of alternatives such as restrictions, injunctions, zoning laws, or any form of "interference" with the price system. As we have tried to show, however, our attitude toward and stewardship of creation should resist such one-dimensional valuing.

Money

We cannot leave this discussion of prices and value without speaking briefly of money. What money can buy — and what it can't — is largely culturally determined. Consider (for example) human beings, criminal justice, and political office. What stands in the way of simply buying such things? Primarily, it is the notion of rights: the right to be treated as something other than a commodity for sale. In this light, the debate over the rights of nature takes on weight. We accept such rights for human beings. Should we accept them for other creatures? Should everything in creation (in principle) be for sale, right down to the last animal species? If not, then we must reject the idea that the only solution to the problem of common property resources is a more extensive system of common property rights. For if some creatures are not to become the objects of monetary exchange, it may be best that society steward them in ways other than through the price system and cost-benefit analysis.

What then can (or should) money buy? Perhaps the answer must be, "whatever anyone will sell." But as to what it will legitimately buy, we once again obviously have a cultural — and ultimately a moral and religious — answer. Sociologist Lee Rainwater answers: "Money buys membership in industrial society." He means that people's identity in such a society has increasingly become a matter of the economic commodities they command. He argues further that "when people are not protected from this inexorable dynamic of money economies by some local cultural enclave, they cannot fail to define themselves most basically in terms of their access to all that money can buy." Thus money, it seems, is a two-edged sword, creating the possibility of dominating both the self and other creatures. We do not propose to reject a money economy, but we need to resist its extensive power. We saw in the previous chapter that John Locke proposed spoilage to be a limit to individual accumulation, and that Adam Smith saw a similar limitation in the capacities of the bellies of the rich. But money renders both limits meaningless. The fluidity of money allows us — at our peril — to ignore the limits imposed by the earth.

Goods

A brief look at the nature of goods and the character of people's inter-action with them will help to explain how people have valued creation. First, let us challenge three underpinnings of the conventional economic view: that goods are properly defined by individuals, that these individu-als are self-centered, and that individual preferences drive the economic valuing system. There is truth in each of these assertions, but there is also crucial error. The emphasis on *individual* valuing misses the *social* character of goods. Though speaking of a broader category of goods than economic goods, Michael Walzer puts it this way: "[Goods] are not and cannot be idiosyncratically valued. . . . Goods in the world have shared meanings because conception and creation are social processes."[5] Thus goods can have different meanings — and different values — in different societies.

Another aspect of the social character of economic goods is the fact that many of them are "positional." Considerable psychological research shows that it is not the absolute level of income or wealth that makes people content or discontent; it is the relative level. So both in definition and in valuation, goods are thoroughly social. What counts as a good is largely a matter of shared conceptions. This also helps to explain why

---

5. Michael Walzer, *Spheres of Justice* (New York: Basic Books, 1983), p. 7.

goods are important far beyond their role in subsistence. Walzer calls them "the crucial medium of social relations."[6] If this is so, the valuing of goods is not in the final analysis a purely individual matter; it is more often and more fundamentally a cultural matter exercised, in a market system, through the effective demand (desire backed by purchasing power) of individuals and groups. In other words, what is primarily cultural in origin is filtered through those that have the franchise. The franchise is largely distributed in accordance with "dollar votes" — raising interesting questions for a society founded on democratic principles. But it also raises questions about cultural valuing in relationship to what is expressed with money.

A market system is a social subsystem. As such, its compatibility with society and culture needs to be evaluated. What are the purposes of this subsystem? How do its characteristic values and practices fit with the rest of life (culture, ecology, etc.)? Are its institutions in harmony or in tension with the values of the society? Are the size, influence, and interaction of this subsystem appropriate to the health and well-being of the rest of society and culture? Is there synergy, compatibility, and commensurability between this subsystem and the rest? Even granting considerable autonomy to the sphere of economics will not dismiss these sorts of questions.

The price system does aid us in the practical task of valuing creation. At times its very independence from other valuational systems can be a virtue, as when people might wrongfully discriminate against someone because of race or color, but still be willing to take that person's money in exchange for goods. But creation has values that neither price nor money nor the concept of "goods" can touch. The price system can never, by itself, be adequate to the stewardly task of earthkeeping.

STEWARDLY INADEQUACIES OF "ECONOMIC MAN"

Thus far we have stressed the inadequacy of the price system for valuing creation. But it is also inadequate to express the complexity of our human nature and the richness of our stewardly task. Let us then, in conclusion,

---

6. Ibid.

touch on some of these inadequacies in the view of human nature presented by the price system.

The role that people are presumed to play in a price system is actually a very limited one. The very abstract assumptions about human behavior common to modern economics make this abundantly clear. "Economic man" is so one-dimensional and uninteresting a human being that we could hardly expect valuations arising from such assumptions to be adequate to the richness and value of God's creation.

In the price system there are two primary roles for human beings: consumer and producer. The system assumes that people in these roles are guided by two very restricted motivations: maximization of satisfaction and maximization of profit. But when we look at people without such narrow blinders we see that they are much more than "maximizing" consumers and producers. They occupy other relevant roles as well: for example, that of citizen. In such roles, the objectives and the valuational systems are far more complex than they are in the limited roles of the price system. As a citizen, I am interested in more than just what is good for me; I am also interested in a good society. As a citizen of the planet, I am also interested in a healthy biosphere. These larger values cannot be achieved through individual maximization of profit or satisfaction; indeed, they often conflict with such self-serving maximization. And we are used to such conflict. Mark Sagoff, in a recent study entitled *The Economy of the Earth,* makes this case eloquently. In his words:

> As a *citizen,* I am concerned with the public interest, rather than my own interest; with the good of the community, rather than simply the well-being of my family. . . .
> In my role as a consumer . . . I concern myself with personal or self-regarding wants and interests; I pursue the goals I have as an individual. I put aside the community-regarding values I take seriously as a citizen, and I look out for Number One instead.[7]

When acting as a citizen, the vision of what is good and what needs to be done to achieve it changes and this change will frequently transcend the price system as an optimal mechanism. (And if one is expected to lay aside self-interest as a citizen of the state, how much more should Christians expect to do so as citizens of the kingdom of heaven?)

---

7. Sagoff, *The Economy of the Earth,* p. 8.

Some might argue that this view of a role outside of individual concern may once have held some sway, but that it doesn't any longer. Such books as *Habits of the Heart* by Robert Bellah and his colleagues and *The Naked Public Square* by Richard John Neuhaus make a good case for such a shift away from community values to an all-consuming individualism. It may indeed be the case that the United States, for example, affected from early times by a strong streak of individualism, has proceeded furthest in that direction. There are many reasons for this; but one, we suggest, is the individualistic economic views that we have chosen to espouse in the classroom and from political podiums. The message, in both theoretical and practical terms, is that the good life does not require concern for neighbor, that the neighbor will be taken care of by the unintended consequences of self-love. And the economic institution that best reflects this individualistic view is the autonomous price system.

Another weakness in the conventional view of economic men and women is that dividing economic responsibility into that of consumer and producer leaves out a key task: keeper. It clearly embodies the assumption that the earth is there for the taking, that the only needs that ultimately count are human needs, and, of course, that the only effective expression of human need is individualistic and therefore contemporary. The keeper task requires a different view. Keepers are concerned for their responsibility to others. Christians, mindful of their stewardship task, would put God first on the list of those to whom they are responsible, and this list would also include the neighbor and future generations. Keepers are not idle, as was the unfaithful steward in the parable of the talents. Their task is fruitful preservation and enlargement of the endowment they were given to work with. But the definition of fruitful use and preservation will be different from that construed on the conventional basis of consumption and production. We attempt to explore these implications further in our "Guideposts" chapter.

Another shortcoming in the economists' view of human nature is that it reduces motives to financial self-interest. It does so in the name of effectiveness, if nothing more. That is to say, the morality of such motivation is usually defended only half-heartedly; efficacy is the prime justification. But if motivations — the desires of the heart — matter (and we think they do), then can we be so cavalier about employing, rewarding, and enlarging self-interest motivation? In the end, financial self-interest tends to overcome prudence and become greed. And a system whose stewardship of creation is founded on greed, efficient or not, is a deficient system.

The lesson of this chapter, then, is that valuing creation is complex; that such complexity arises out of the very nature of created reality; and that we therefore need to resist the capture of the valuation process by any limited viewpoint — we need to resist economic and any other form of imperialism. We need to give attention to the best decision-making possible economically and in every other way. Good stewardship is an active task, leading us to search for better ways. But where we search and what conclusions we draw need special reflection in this age of specialization. Universal claims are being made, explicitly or implicitly, from partial perspectives. Perhaps worse, we seem to be losing the language and habits of public discourse that allow us to transcend the partial viewpoints of disciplines or interest groups. In some ways, the economic assumptions of subjective individualism are coming true, like a prophetic nightmare — not only for economic activity, but for all of society and culture. This too is reductionism and must be resisted, not in favor of some new reductionism (to go from "all is material" to "all is mystical" is not progress), but in favor of a rich and multidimensional view of reality. The human mind, especially the analytical part of it, is not used to functioning this way. But that only prescribes retraining, not capitulation. The heart, so frequently at the root of human action even when the head is blamed, must be the starting point of the valuation process. The wise heart is used to weighing complex matters without paralysis. The Christian heart (in individuals and in communities), though not unaffected by sin, should lead the way, for only it can be tuned to God, Creator and Redeemer.

CHAPTER 13

❧   ❧

The Appropriateness of Technology

> *And lastly, since all Heaven was not enough*
> *To share that triumph, He made His Masterpiece,*
> *Man, that like God can call beauty from dust,*
> *Order from chaos, and create new worlds*
> *To praise their maker. Oh, but in making man*
> *God over-reached Himself and gave away*
> *His Godhead. He must now depend on man*
> *For what man's brain, creative and divine,*
> *Can give Him. Man stands equal with Him now,*
> *Partner and rival. . . .*

> — architect's speech in Dorothy Sayers,
> *The Zeal of Thy House*

SOMETIMES WE SPEAK OF "TECHNOLOGY" AND "ECONOMICS" AS THOUGH they were vast movements and processes beyond our control. Some Christian thinkers have even seen in the apparent autonomy and irresistibility of these forces a good indication that they are demonic — inherently destructive, anti-human, and anti-creational in their thrust. So it is often easy to blame technology or economics for environmental (and other) problems. We have seen in the preceding two chapters, however, that economics is a broad name for one aspect of our stewardship, and it seems to be inseparable from our human creatureliness, sinful or not.

The same is true for "technology":[1] it is a label for the variety of ways in which we carry out our tasks in creation. Just as we are all "economists" (in that we carry on the orderings and exchanges which nourish our households), so we are all "technologists" (in that we apply the skills and ingenuity our Creator has given us for the use, care, and enjoyment of creation). The word *techne* means craft, skill, or art (indeed, it is the basic Greek word for art). It describes the general human ability to shape the world to our ends. *Techne* is "know-how": knowledge of how to do things with creation. Thus all humans are "technicians," whether they are interested in shaping a flint, cooking an egg, or building a power plant. Technology is not inherently either "good" or "bad." But neither is it "neutral," any more than human beings are. Our techniques are a way of being human, God's stewards in creation, and must always be evaluated in the light of the *shalom* to which God is drawing the cosmos. Because we have often limited our understanding of salvation to a transaction between individual humans and God, we have sometimes failed to regard the *means* by which we work in the earth as ultimately important. But if stewardship of creation is our basic task, then we cannot divorce our means — our techniques — from our life in Christ.

Much has been written in recent years about the relationship between technology and the Christian life, so we will not attempt a general discussion of it here.[2] But because the means by which we carry out our stewardship are almost inseparable from the stewardship itself, we would like to indicate some of the ways in which our ever-expanding ensemble of techniques enhance, illuminate, and threaten our stewardship of creation, and then to suggest some guidelines for our use of those techniques.

---

1. A better word for what we commonly call "technology" is "technique." "Technology" really means the study of techniques (just as "economics" really means the study of economies). In spite of this, we will follow common usage, using the word "technology" to refer to the various means by which we do things in and to creation.

2. One of the most helpful works is *Responsible Technology*, edited by Stephen Monsma (Grand Rapids: Eerdmans, 1986), a work which (like *Earthkeeping*) was produced by an interdisciplinary team working together for a year at the Calvin Center for Christian Scholarship. The book not only surveys the main works and opinions about technology, but it also lays down guidelines for evaluating techniques in various areas of creation, guidelines suggested by the work of Herman Dooyeweerd.

Technology is important for our stewardship of creation in five major ways, each of which requires some discussion.

- First, technology gives us ever-increasing *power* to accomplish whatever we do, for better or worse, to the earth. Our fires have always polluted the atmosphere, but today new techniques and fuels enable us to pollute it in discernible, planet-wide ways.
- Second, technology introduces new substances (plastics and pesticides, for example) into the fabric of creation, and ecological processes often cannot cope with them.
- Third, the sheer scale, complexity, and inter-relatedness of our technical civilization make it easy to act as though technology were autonomous, outside our ability to choose or control. Such an attitude can foster either complacency or despair.
- Fourth, technology enables us to have a much deeper knowledge and appreciation of the intricacy and beauty of creation.
- Fifth, technology enables us to heal the damage caused by destructive techniques and to develop stewardly, appropriate ways of working with creation.

Let us consider in turn each of these implications of technology for our stewardship of creation.

TECHNOLOGY INCREASES OUR POWER

We have already pointed out in chapter 4 the way energy (particularly from fossil and nuclear fuels) enhances our power: men and women in the industrialized world enjoy the equivalent, in sheer energy units, of the labors of at least 100 slaves. And we have discussed some of the obvious consequences of this recent increase of available energy. The most obvious consequences are benefits, such as the speed and ease with which we transport ourselves and our goods. Less obvious, but of growing concern, is the steady degradation of creation: the valleys we flood for kilowatts, the fields we cover with highways and parking lots, the forests which wither in the acid rain caused by our power plants. The power and comfort which our technologies bring exact a price from creation.

But technology does far more than simply increase the energy

"Remember — it's better to light just one little thermonuclear
power station than to curse the darkness."

From *American Scientist Magazine.*
© 1974 by Sidney Harris. Used by permission.

available to us. Technological power changes the very nature of our relationship to the earth: creation is no longer an awesome mystery and a
reminder of our finitude; it becomes a problem to be solved. We noted
earlier that near the beginning of the technological revolution Francis
Bacon (and others) pointed out that the human condition was not pros-
pering, that we had lost our original dominion over creation. Bacon's
solution was to develop a "New Organ" for the restoration of human

dominion. We call it the inductive method. Through observation of nature's operations we are able to command it; we know how it "works" and thus can make it work for us. As our knowledge of the mechanisms of creation increases, the whole created world (actually or potentially) becomes an extension of our machines. Theodore Roszak, in a work published in 1973, sketches the consequences of that technological vision of creation:

> Already in the western world and Japan millions of city-dwellers and suburbanites have grown accustomed to an almost hermetically sealed and sanitized pattern of living in which very little of their experience ever impinges on non-human phenomena. For those of us born to such an existence, it is all but impossible to believe that anything is any longer beyond human adjustment, domination, and improvement. That is the lesson in vanity the city teaches us every moment of every day. For on all sides we see, hear, and smell the evidence of human supremacy over nature — right down to the noise and odor and irritants that foul the air around us. Like Narcissus, modern men and women take pride in seeing themselves — their product, their planning — reflected in all they behold. The more artifice, the more progress; the more progress, the more security.[3]

The subtle price of an increase of technological power is thus that it encourages us to surround ourselves with a world completely in our control. The apex of such an artificial environment is, of course, a city: it is well run precisely to the extent that it excludes the wild and the unpredictable. And we have it in our power to banish wildness and unpredictability from the whole earth. In the long run, therefore, the unintended side effects of our technologies (serious as they are) are probably less troubling than the things that we intend. For technologies enable us to bring steadily more and more of creation into human control. But there is no indication that a creation entirely in our control, managed entirely according to human notions of rationality and efficiency, would be good stewardship of the creation that God showed to Job: a self-sustaining complexity which transcends our attempts to manage or rearrange it rationally.

---

3. Theodore Roszak, *Where the Wasteland Ends* (Garden City, NY: Doubleday, 1973), p. 10.

TECHNOLOGY AND NEW MATERIALS

One of the means by which we have increased our power over creation is through the recombination of naturally occurring materials into a vast range of new substances. Look around the room where you are reading this; it's likely that most of what you see is composed, covered, or colored with substances which did not even exist fifty years ago. The finish on the walls, the tile or fibre on the floor, the fabrics that you wear, the pen you're writing with — all are likely to be "artificial" materials. In one way, this distinction between "natural" and "artificial" is a difficult one to maintain. All human societies, without exception, surround themselves with an "artificial environment," be it so little as a grass shelter, a bark loincloth, and a blowgun and darts. (And we should not too quickly dismiss such technologies as "primitive": they grow out of a knowledge of and skill with natural materials which most of us have lost.) We humans have always lived (far more than any other creature) in worlds of our own construction, be they simple or complex. But we ourselves are, after all, "natural" creatures doing things with and to a natural world. Why then are our constructions "artificial," whereas a wasp's nest, a spider's web, and a beaver's dam are "natural"? Even the most complex synthetic materials and industrial chemicals are (like ourselves) made of simple, abundant elements: carbon, hydrogen, nitrogen, oxygen (and often scarcer elements like phosphorus or flourine) combined into new forms. It is difficult to argue (as some have) that it is presumptuous to develop thus the latent capacities of the elements into new forms and substances. We *are* a part of "nature" — a creature like carbon, oxygen, or hydrogen. So in that sense what we do is "natural." But we are also (like it or not) different from the rest of nature: we are creatures given special abilities to relate to both creation and Creator — and we are called into a special responsibility to the Creator. To tinker thus with the stuff of creation is not inappropriate: it is clearly one of the things we are called to do.

Yet it is not nearly so simple as that. In a kind of mimicry or parody of our Creator, we have the ability to make new things. There is nothing in God's creation like the chlorinated fluorocarbons which break down ozone in the stratosphere — or like dichloro-diphenyl-trichloro-ethane, better known as DDT. It is not wrong for us to make such things, but we should make and use them only in an awareness of their effect on the whole of creation. Technology does indeed give us a kind of god-like power to make new things. But when their newness threatens the integrity of the creation which we are to serve, we need to question very severely the way in which we use our ingenuity. There are now tens of thousands of substances in the web of life which are alien to it and which the metabolic processes of plant and animal cannot deal with. Some of these are released intentionally into the environment; others are there only accidentally, or as waste products. But they make up one of the most severe threats of technology to the integrity of creation. And it is a relatively recent threat. Barry Commoner, in a book called *The Closing Circle,* points out the disproportionately rapid growth since World War II of such artificial materials. First he points out that the greatest increase in damage to the natural environment has come in the years since World War II. Whereas population in the United States increased only a modest 42 percent between 1945 and 1970, the increase in most kinds of pollution was many times greater. Also greater were the increases in production of a number of manufactured goods:

> The winner of this economic sweepstakes, with the highest postwar growth rate, is the production of non-returnable soda bottles, which has increased about 53,000 percent in that time. . . . In second place is the production of synthetic fibers, up 5,980 percent; third is mercury used for chlorine production, up 3,930 percent; succeeding places are held as follows: mercury used in mildew resistant paint, up 3,120 percent; air conditioner compressor units, up 2,850 percent; plastics up 1,960 percent; fertilizer nitrogen, up 1,050 percent; electric housewares (such as can-openers and corn-poppers) up 1,040 percent. . . .[4]

And so on. From such statistics, Commoner concludes that the primary change, the change which has brought about such damage, is not increase in population. Instead, says Commoner,

> The over-all evidence seems clear. The chief reason for the environmental crisis that has engulfed the United States is the sweeping transformation of productive technology since World War II. The economy has grown enough to give the United States population about the same amount of basic goods, per capita, as it did in 1946. However, productive technologies with intense impacts on the environment have replaced less destructive ones. The environmental crisis is the inevitable result of this counterecological pattern of growth.[5]

---

4. Barry Commoner, *The Closing Circle* (New York: Bantam Books, 1972), pp. 140-41.

5. Ibid., p. 175.

Commoner calls this rapid growth of productive technology "counter-ecological" — and it is counter to ecological cycles primarily because it releases into the fabric of creation man-made materials which created cycles cannot cope with. This fundamental incompatibility between many of the substances which we make and the earth which our Creator sustains is one of the gravest problems arising from our technical abilities.

THE AUTONOMY OF TECHNOLOGY

When we are aware that some of the new things which we make (and discard) are damaging to the fabric of creation, why do we persist? There is no easy answer, but one which has been seriously suggested is that our commitment to rationality and efficiency is such that we cannot say no to new technologies. This argument for the irresistible autonomy of technique has been advanced by many, but no one has made such a consistent, eloquent case as Jacques Ellul. Ellul, a French social critic, has been analyzing the effect of technique on modern society since the days after World War II. Much of his work (for example, *The Meaning of the City*) is explicitly biblical, for he argues that the biblical picture of humanity in rebellion against God makes intelligible the shape of modern experience with technique. He maintains that our complex technological society — of which the city is the best example — is an elaborate way of trying to elude our Creator's claim on us. But much of his work — including the book for which he is best known — *The Technological Society* — is written for (and read by) many who are not aware of the biblical shape of his argument. His argument in *The Technological Society* for the autonomy of technique is worth considering in some detail.

First of all, Ellul distinguishes between "technical operation" and "technical phenomenon." "Technical operation" simply consists of the ordinary choices made by a person in getting a job done.

> Every operation obviously entails a certain technique, even the gathering of fruit among primitive peoples — climbing the tree, picking the fruit as quickly and with as little effort as possible, distinguishing between the ripe and the unripe fruit, and so on.[6]

---

6. Jacques Ellul, *The Technological Society*, trans. John Wilkinson (New York: Alfred A. Knopf, 1964), pp. 19-20.

Thus all humans, in all times, in doing any task, have used technique. The "technical phenomenon," on the other hand, begins when "consciousness and judgment" enter in. This intervention "takes what was previously tentative, unconscious, and spontaneous and brings it into the realm of clear, voluntary, and reasoned concepts."[7] The result, says Ellul, is "a rapid and far-flung expansion of technique"[8] — it is indeed that technology whose environmental consequences we have been discussing. But why should the use of reason and judgment have such profound consequences when applied to technique? Because, says Ellul,

> The twofold intervention of reason and consciousness in the technical world, which produces the technical phenomenon, can be described as the quest of the one best means in every field. And this "one best means" is, in fact, the technical means. It is the aggregate of these means that produces technical civilization.[9]

The fact that reason and judgment point to "the one best means" ultimately eliminates the individual's freedom of choice, for

> The choice is less and less a subjective one among several means which are potentially applicable. It is really a question of finding the best means in the absolute sense, on the basis of numerical calculation.[10]

The consequence of this narrowing of choice to the one absolute best way is not only the effective elimination of freedom of choice, says Ellul; it is "the creation of a science of means." All things — including friendship, swimming, war, industrial organization, and economic activity — are henceforth done according to the best means. "Today," says Ellul, "no human activity escapes this technical imperative."[11]

The society which is thus governed irresistibly by the choice of the best means is a technocracy. And it is very difficult — if not impossible — to resist it. As Ellul puts it:

> If a desired result is stipulated, there is no choice possible between technical means and nontechnical means based on imagination, in-

---

7. Ibid., p. 20.
8. Ibid., p. 21.
9. Ibid.
10. Ibid.
11. Ibid.

dividual qualities, or tradition. Nothing can compete with the technical means. The choice is made *a priori*. It is not in the power of the individual or of the group to decide to follow some method other than the technical.[12]

Nor is there, in this autonomy of technique, any room for hesitation or resistance on moral grounds — "a principal characteristic of technique . . . is its refusal to tolerate moral judgments. It is absolutely independent of them and eliminates them from its domain."[13] Since decisions to exercise stewardly care are in fact attempts to limit "the one best means" on moral grounds, we can see the profound consequences for our use of creation if Ellul is correct.

Ellul's argument for an overarching tyranny of means (though it may be overstated) certainly helps us understand much in modern life. Ellul's analysis appears most powerfully correct when it is combined with an economic argument. A simple example illustrates the general accuracy of his analysis. When the Alaska pipeline was built, there was a good deal of fear in the Pacific Northwest (based on disastrous oil spills elsewhere) that supertanker transport from the Alaska pipeline terminus in Valdez to refineries in the fertile and sheltered waters of Puget Sound would result, sooner or later, in a major oil spill. Since maneuverability for large ships in the restricted waters at both ends of the route was a particular worry, a representative of a large refinery depending on the tankers was asked why smaller ships did not bring the oil. "Oh, there's a formula for that," he answered, and he proceeded to explain that for a completely efficient operation, oil transport distances of a certain length must be covered by tankers of a certain size — that was the efficient means, and no other factor could seriously counter it. For a decade and more the formula seemed to work — until Good Friday morning of 1988, and the disastrous grounding of the ESSO Valdez in Prince William Sound.[14] The same sort of thinking has dictated the placement of shopping centers, the design of buildings, the siting of power plants, and the safety of cars. Given the desired end, one means emerges, and there seems to be little one can do to counter the decision.

---

12. Ibid., p. 84.
13. Ibid., p. 97.
14. This Valdez-based example of the danger of oil-tanker traffic off the West Coast appeared in the 1980 edition of *Earthkeeping;* it gives us no pleasure now to point out how what was then hypothetical has since become a sad reality.

Ellul's is perhaps the grimmest analysis of technology, and we must take it very seriously — both because of its explanatory power and because it is rooted in profound truths of human pride, sinfulness, and rebellion. Yet overarching even the fact of human sin is the continuing goodness of creation and our continuing responsibility to be obedient to the Creator through a stewardship which is careful of creation. Thus there remains the possibility of a redemptive technology.

TECHNOLOGY DEEPENS OUR KNOWLEDGE OF AND WONDER AT CREATION

When God finally answered Job's long complaint, he did so not by careful theological reasoning but by broadening Job's knowledge of creation. The human world of his troubles was expanded by the grandeur, beauty, and mystery of creation, and in recognizing his creatureliness Job learned humility: "Surely I spoke of things I did not understand, things too wonderful for me to know" (Job 42:3, NIV). Today, technological extensions of our senses give us something like God's answer to Job. The best-known form of that answer is the mute eloquence of the planet itself as seen from space — not just the famous photos of the whole earth, but the inexhaustibly detailed "Landsat" pictures of every part of the globe now available to us.

Such technology has unquestionably increased our knowledge. Many of the questions with which God challenged Job we now can answer. Remote sensing devices enable us to observe and monitor the mountain goat; they give us access to "the springs of the sea" and "the recesses of the deep"; we now know something of the father of the rain, the womb of the ice. And therein lies the danger of technology: it encourages us to think that we have a "God's-eye" view, that by means of our technological towers we can lift ourselves to a heaven of our own making.

But there is a healthier hope in technology. It is only the shallow and arrogant scientist who feels that he or she has understood all there is to know about whatever aspect of creation he or she chooses to investigate. The further we penetrate into creation — the more we come to know — the greater the complexity which we discover. Even in the (relatively) straightforward quest for the smallest particles of matter we have come to recognize an awesome and increasing complexity: the further in we go, the more puzzling matter itself appears to be. The same sort of aston-ishment has come to those who investigate the vastly more complex structures of living things. We have come to know a great deal about the structure and function of organs, tissues, cells, and genes; we are slowly mapping the genetic code of simple organisms. But even DNA — which we are fond of representing as though it were a great mechanical puzzle — is not nearly so predictable or mechanical as the models suggest. And haunting the whole investigation of molecular genetics is the uncanny sense that we are dealing not with random processes, but with information — a possibility which calls into question the reductive materialism of the popular understanding of science. The same sort of eerie mystery appears when we turn our techniques (for example) to a study of the biosphere. We have already spoken of the strange way in which the living and non-living systems of the planet interact to keep its environment stable — a way which unavoidably suggests *telos:* purpose. And at the cosmo-logical level a whole series of coincidences about the nature of matter and cosmic process have combined with infinite improbability to create the only sort of universe where we could exist to carry on the investigation. A name has been given to the whole tangle of coincidences: the anthropic principle. But the name only masks the mystery.

All of these findings are the result of enormous technological ad-vances. But rather than implying that we are god-like for being so clever, they suggest that something is going on here that we don't understand. Not surprisingly, therefore, modern science, which is carried forward by many of the same technologies which threaten creation, is for many an avenue into wonder at creation and faith in the Creator.

A final obvious significance of technological advances for creation: not only do they teach us humility, but they also begin to give us the knowledge we need to understand the impact of our own activity. One of the great ironies of the environmental movement is that although it cat-alogs the evils which technology is responsible for, it does so only through using the same high level of technology which has brought about the damage.

And that brings us to the final aspect of the relationship of technology to our stewardship of creation: not only does technology give us at least a partial understanding of how creation works, but it also provides us with hints and clues about how we can use our skills as makers, our technical skills, to heal the very damage our making has wrought.

TECHNOLOGY CAN BE A MEANS OF STEWARDSHIP

Technology helps us to heal the damage we have done to creation and minimize the damage we might do through future human activity. But here we face an agonizing fact: there is no way in which our technology, however wisely applied, actually increases the health and vitality of the biosphere. Creation is very good without our tinkering; the best we can do is remedial. Here and there we might free a bird caught in the bushes, or turn back the advance of a forest fire. But even those well-intentioned interferences might in the long run do more harm than good. Sometimes foresters use phrases like "over-mature trees" to justify logging an old-growth forest, implying that the forest desperately needs human management. But one only has to compare the health and extent of North America's forests 500 years ago to what they are now to see how false is the notion that somehow the trees *need* our care. The same sort of argument could be used for water, soil, animals, and birds: they don't seem to need our stewardship until after we start disrupting the created order. The conservation movement inspired by the dust-bowl years was a very good thing, and the ensuing stewardship of the prairies has kept much of the prairie soil from blowing or washing away. But the erosion which our conservation techniques stop is an erosion which we started. Before we broke the thick prairie sod, there was no need to conserve it.

Some have concluded from this fact that humanity is a sort of mistake, whether it is blamed on God or evolution. We disagree. Humans do have a function in creation: to know creation, to name it, to love it, to give it a voice — and thus to offer it back to the Creator. In the next chapter we look in some detail at that human place in creation.

Here we acknowledge that the best thing our technologies can do is to heal the damage we have done — and enable us to live more gently on the earth, in such a way as to inflict less damage. Technological ingenuity keeps devising ways of minimizing our impact on creation: special coatings on glass (for example) make it as opaque to heat as an insulated wall, thus saving fuel; steadily improving solar-cell technology holds out the possibility that we can decentralize our energy generating systems; computers enable us to move enormous amounts of information without the wasteful use of paper; light-weight materials reduce the consumption of oil products — and so on. Though we may not actually improve on creation, technology can be "appropriate" in its minimizing of damage to creation.

Much has been written in the past two decades about such "appropriate" or "intermediate" or "soft" technologies. One of the most influential of such works is *Small Is Beautiful* by E. F. Schumacher. In it, Schumacher repeats Gandhi's distinction between "mass production" and "production by the masses" and argues eloquently for the latter, what he calls "technology with a human face, which, instead of making human hands and brains redundant, helps them to become far more productive than they have ever been before."[15] Schumacher's description of such a technology is worth quoting at some length:

> The system of *production by the masses* mobilises the priceless resources which are possessed by all human beings, their clever brains and skilful hands, *and supports them with first-class tools.* The technology of *mass production* is inherently violent, ecologically damaging, self-defeating in terms of non-renewable resources, and stultifying for the human person. The technology of *production by the masses,* making use of the best of modern knowledge and experience, is conducive to decentralisation, compatible with the laws of ecology, gentle in its use of scarce resources, and designed to serve the human person instead of making him the servant of machines. I have named it *intermediate technology* to signify that it is vastly superior to the primitive technology of bygone ages but at the same time much simpler, cheaper, and freer than the super-technology of the rich . . . a technology to which everybody can gain admittance and which is not reserved to those already rich and powerful.[16]

We are only groping toward what such a technology might be. But we may say that it certainly does not involve a curtailment of human ingenuity or invention. Indeed, it requires this more than ever, as anyone who has tried to repair a factory-produced machine can witness. In Schumacher's words, "Any third-rate engineer or researcher can increase complexity; but it takes a certain flair of real insight to make things simple again."[17] Such a technology might include a much greater involvement of individuals in producing their own food, in private or communal gardens; it might involve small-scale use of the sun for home and water heating.

---

15. E. F. Schumacher, *Small Is Beautiful* (New York: Harper & Row, 1973), p. 145.

16. Ibid., pp. 145-46.

17. Ibid., p. 146.

What is certain, however, is that it would place people more in touch with the physical sustenance of their life in the bounty of the earth and the sun. To do so would increase not only our need as individuals to become capable and ingenious stewards of the earth but also our awareness of being masters of the earth and fellow creatures with it.

Thus it cannot be said that technology itself is a force requiring us to do various dehumanizing and destructive things. Such things are indeed done, but it is the whole person who does them, not technology. Daniel Callahan makes this point very clearly:

> At the very outset we have to do away with a false and misleading dualism, one which abstracts man on the one hand and technology on the other, as if the two were quite separate kinds of realities. I believe that there is no dualism inherent here. Man is by nature a technological animal; to be human is to be technological. If I am correct in that judgment, then there is no room for a dualism at all. Instead, we should recognize that when we speak of technology, this is another way of speaking about man himself in one of his manifes-tations.[18]

It is through this idea, that "to be human is to be technological," that we must disagree in one important way with the critics of technology. We do not disagree with their analysis of the deplorable things which have been done to the earth and its inhabitants. But it is we ourselves who have done these things, not technology. It is not technology, for example, which forces us to invent the automobile and then (because of increased mobility) to spread out from our cities into suburbs and shopping centers which cover good farmland. It is rather that we humans like to be mobile. And we like to live outside the city, on a plot of ground big enough to have grass and trees around us; the mobility makes that goal possible. And having chosen to live outside the city, we prefer also to have our shopping areas and even our places of work close by. We could choose otherwise, but we usually do not. The mobility of the automobile makes it possible for us to make such choices, but they are still our choices, not those of technology.

The same sort of response could be made for any of the things which "technology" has supposedly done. The tides of oil that increasingly

---

18. Daniel Callahan, cited in Samuel C. Florman, *The Existential Pleasures of Engineering* (New York: St. Martin's Press, 1976), pp. 58-59.

wash up on miles of beaches near shipping lanes are not the product of technology; they are the result of a complex of decisions which begins with an individual's desire for cars, fuel, and plastics and which ends with an oil company's decision to ship the oil in the cheapest way possible. Cars, furnaces, oil wells, and supertankers are tools which we choose to make or use in certain ways. We often choose wrongly or unwisely, but it is we who choose, and not technology.

However, this recognition of the flaw in the arguments of those who blame technology for our social and environmental problems should not diminish our concern for the problems. The increasing power available to us through technology means that the consequences of our choices continually become greater. Neither should we overlook the subtle ways in which a concern for efficiency and the end product is likely to affect our very thinking. It is important, then, that we consider the truth in Ellul's (and others') contention that technology becomes a force in itself, taking away our freedom of choice. As we have pointed out, it is dangerously misleading to blame technology; the problem lies rather in individual choices. But our choice can be so warped or obscured that technology effectively does become an independent force.

For we might succumb to that tendency to separate mind from nature and proceed to reduce nature, humankind — indeed, the whole of reality — to numerical values only. We saw the emergence of that tendency to disembody the mind in our survey of the scientific revolution. If, indeed, our thoughts become thoroughly guided by the Cartesian view of the transcendent mind manipulating a nature which is quite alien to itself, then we are likely to be persuaded by the inexorable logic of a way of thinking which rationally establishes the "best means" for every task. But to do so would be to forsake a part of our humanity — we are not only minds. To rigidly distinguish the mind from the body, and both from nature, is to abandon a part of one's humanity. For whole people, technology is a tool. But for people who have given in to the illusion that their mind is totally apart from nature, technology is indeed likely to become a master. A person genuinely sensitive to the task and joy of growing crops in rich but fragile soil is not likely to give in to the logic which determines that the fertile soil of a flood plain is the best place for a shopping center. The person who maintains a barefoot, wet-skinned wonder at the life of the tidal pools is not so likely to let efficiency convince him or her to risk those starfish, crabs, and urchins for Alaskan (or Kuwaiti) crude oil. As long as people remember that the mind that makes technical decisions is part of the much more complex whole of a flesh and blood person embedded in the natural world, they need not fear an autonomous technology. But the claims of an unquestioned technology always need to be challenged from the standpoint of our stewardship of creation. And to a more careful consideration of that stewardship we now turn.

SECTION III

❧   ❧

THE EARTH IS THE LORD'S

CHAPTER 14

❧   ❧

Dominion as Stewardship:
Biblical Principles of Earthkeeping

He, therefore, who is not illumined by such great splendor of created things is blind; he who is not awakened by such great clamour is deaf; he who does not praise God because of all these effects is dumb; he who does not note the first principle from such great signs is foolish. Open your eyes, therefore, prick up your spiritual ears, open your lips and apply your heart, that you may see our God in all creatures.

— St. Bonaventure, *The Mind's Road to God*

It was the divinely appointed function of the first man . . . to unite in himself the whole of created being; and at the same time to reach his perfect union with God and thus grant the state of deification to the whole creation. . . . Since this task was not fulfilled by Adam, it is in the work of Christ, the second Adam, that we can see what it was meant to be.

— Vladimir Lossky, *The Mystical Theology of the Eastern Church*

THE CENTRAL CHRISTIAN CLAIM IS THAT JESUS CHRIST, THE CREATING Word in whom all things hold together, "became flesh and dwelt

*"But pastor, why can't the church stick to its own business instead of
meddling into people's beliefs?"*

From *Christianity Today*, May 24, 1974.
© 1974 by John Lawing. Used by permission.

among us" (John 1:14). Through his life, death, and resurrection the
alienation between ourselves and God has been broken down, and we are
invited, through the power of God's Spirit, to take part in the healing and
reconciliation which our Creator and Redeemer is bringing about. What
do these truths mean for our treatment of creation? Or perhaps we should
ask a more fundamental question: What *should* they mean? For (unfortunately) answers to the two questions are often not the same. Christians
— and Christendom — have often failed to live according to the truths
they have affirmed. When it comes to our treatment of creation, that
failure has attracted a great deal of recent criticism. For, it is often said,
Christianity actively encourages treating everything else as a backdrop for
the human drama of salvation.

The idea that Christianity is the main source of environmental
problems has become something of an axiom in the environmental movement. It was first proposed clearly by Lynn White in his 1967 essay, "The
Historic Roots of Our Ecologic Crisis." His famous and often-repeated

conclusion in that essay is that "Christianity is the most anthropocentric religion the world has ever seen."[1]

Much of the environmentalist search for a new religion which we considered in chapter 9 is in part an attempt to correct what is perceived to be the human-centered excesses of Christianity. Often the criticism is simply assumed; just as often it is made explicitly, as in these words of the landscape planner Ian McHarg, whose book *Design with Nature* has been enormously helpful in setting forth principles for how we place the structures of the human world on the contours of the created earth. In the opening of that book, McHarg says that the biblical story,

> in its insistence upon dominion and subjugation of nature, encourages the most exploitative and destructive instincts in man rather than those that are deferential and creative. Indeed, if one seeks license for those who would increase radioactivity, create canals and harbors with atomic bombs, employ poisons without constraint, or give consent to the bulldozer mentality, there could be no better injunction than this text. Here can be found the sanction and injunction to conquer nature — the enemy, the threat to Jehovah.[2]

Based on the Bible and on the whole weight of Christian understanding, we disagree profoundly with the assumption that God's purpose for men and women is the kind of "bulldozer mentality" which McHarg describes. Though individual Christians may have held such a view, the whole weight of biblical teaching and Christian thought is against it. To a consideration of that biblical teaching, and of the theological thought which has come from it, we now turn. We begin with the subject which has been central throughout this whole book: creation.

CREATION

In chapter 9 we sampled the strong currents in the recent environmental movement impelling people to a kind of monist or pantheist under-

---

1. Lynn White, "The Historic Roots of Our Ecologic Crisis," *Science* 155 (1967).
2. Ian L. McHarg, *Design with Nature* (Garden City, NY: Natural History Press, 1969), p. 26.

standing. In such an understanding we are a part of nature, and "Nature" (or Gaia, or "Evolution") is all the god there is. This is by no means a recent development. It is an all but universal characteristic of human religion. In such religions, ranging from the early Greek belief in the Olympic pantheon to the various earthy animisms of the American Indians, there is always some degree of identity between nature and the god or gods.

Christians have always disassociated themselves from all such confusions of God and creation, and they always should. For if there is one thing about biblical religion which is abundantly clear, it is that God is the maker of all things; thus he is not to be confused with those things. He does not depend on creation, but creation depends utterly and completely on him. This profound *otherness* of Creator from creation does not, however, mean that God is distant or uninvolved with creation. Rather (as Paul told the Athenians, using words from their own poets), "in him we live and move and have our being" (Acts 17:28). God is lovingly involved with creation *because* God is other than his creation (Christians have often called that involvement "providence," for it is characterized by God's gracious *providing*). This willed, deliberate, and costly giving of the Creator for creation is in sharp contrast to Hinduism and other monist systems. In them creation is ultimately an illusion, an accident, an epiphenomenon — a sort of inevitable and unwilled dream. In such systems "God" (or "Brahman" or "Gaia" or "The Absolute") is no more responsible for creation than human beings are for the circulation of their blood or the growth of their hair. In the biblical view, God is indeed intimate with and immanent in creation, but that immanence depends upon his otherness. Indeed, all creation depends upon God's transcendent otherness.

The inescapable otherness of the Creator, and the adamant Jewish and Christian refusal to call nature God — or Goddess — sheds light on another aspect of that biblical understanding of the Creator which has, in recent years, become objectionable to some: that is, the predominantly masculine language for God in the Bible. Ecofeminists in particular have argued that Western patriarchy, informed by worship of a God portrayed as masculine, is responsible for much of the environmental problem. There is undoubtedly truth in this criticism. But — while granting that both masculine and feminine language for God is analogical — we should not be too hasty to abandon the largely masculine imagery of the Bible, particularly with regard to creation. For "mother" is the most natural thing in the world to call the earth: as a mother brings forth children from the womb, so the earth also "brings forth" living things (the womblike imagery of the earth "bringing forth" is from Genesis 1). Speaking of God as "mother" does reinforce important and biblical notions of God's self-giving care. But it also makes it easier for us to make the dangerous mistake of equating God with the earth, creation with Creator — and the Creator's immanence is not of that sort. We do not achieve a proper view of God's immanence by denying his transcendence; rather, we open the way to another error, just as serious. The Canadian writer Rudy Wiebe has said some excellent things on this subject in his novel *My Lovely Enemy:*

> All words are image, speaking is the only way human beings can handle large reality. But the difference between the image and the reality has to be clear, and when man speaks of "God as Mother" her acts usually become so closely identified with nature — the physical world every-where — that he forgets the image-ness and begins to think the words as physical actuality. For a person to say: "All is brought forth from the womb of God" is so close to what actually happens every minute in animal nature that he starts acting out copulation and birthing and begins to think he's God while he's doing it. . . . But God subsumes and is far beyond both Nature and Image. So it is better to contemplate the concept of GOD THE FATHER because no natural father ever brings forth any life by himself. You are then forced to contemplate the creation of the world not as an act of physical birth out of God's womb, but rather as the act of being spoken into existence by Words coming out of God's mouth. This is an image so strange, so profoundly human, that no one can ever mistake it for what happens in nature.[3]

This dependence of the earth on God is the clearest teaching of the creation account in Genesis. "In the beginning, God created the heavens and the earth" (Gen. 1:1). Creation is his, and he is not to be confused with it. The confusion of creation with Creator is a sin against which the Hebrews are repeatedly warned and which they repeatedly commit. In those days (as now) it appears to have been a very easy sin to commit — almost an inevitable one. To "kiss one's hand to the sun" (a gesture of reverence for creation which Job declares himself to be innocent of; see Job 31:26-27) or to build a temple in a grove on a hilltop and there

---

3. Rudy Wiebe, *My Lovely Enemy* (Toronto: McClelland & Stewart, 1983), pp. 140-41.

to merge ecstatically with the divine forces of nature — that was what came naturally. Such nature-worshiping paganism, even if we sought it, is probably not possible today although (as we saw earlier) its appeal is strong, and growing. Nevertheless, it is clear that this confusion of creation and Creator is as much a sin for the contemporary Christian as it was for the Hebrew in biblical times.

Genesis teaches that God is completely distinct from creation. But the Creator's otherness does not imply a lack of care: quite the contrary. A composer is *other* than the symphony he composes, but he is not therefore disinterested in the way the symphony is performed. The musical analogy is a good one: God is the composer and conductor (and the instrument-maker) of the symphony of creation. We humans are the musicians, wooed by his baton into performance of the score. There's plenty of room for cadenza and variation (indeed, the music of creation seems to be a lot closer to jazz than to the classical symphonies — wonderful though they are — that have descended to us from the deist era of clockwork invariability). The Creator/composer/conductor winces at our destructive ignorance and our willed cacophonies, but he continues to conduct the performance with care and concern. In the Genesis account, this divine concern for creation is abundantly evident, not only in the intricate ordering of the created world, but also in the repeated statement of its goodness.

There are two ways of reading the phrase "and God saw that it was good," which appears six times in Genesis 1. The first is that the goodness of creation is a reflection of the goodness of God — a way of saying "I am good." This meaning is evident in such declarations of the Psalmist as "the heavens are telling the glory of God" (Ps. 19:1). Unquestionably, then, one purpose of creation is to give God glory.

The other dimension to the phrase does not contradict the first, but it is often overlooked. The statement is not only a reflection of the goodness of God. It is often misquoted as "God *said* that it was good," implying that the goodness of creation is the result of divine fiat. But in the wording "God *saw*," there is a recognition of the separateness of creation — and of the goodness in the separateness. Most profoundly and mysteriously, it points to the price the Creator was willing to pay for the independence of his creation.

Thus God does not simply "say" or "declare" the goodness of what he has made: he *sees* its goodness, as a free response to his own calling. Though its origin is clearly from God, the very fact of creation gives creatures an independence, a goodness, and a freedom of their own. "God *saw* that it was good" is thus not so much a declaration as it is a *response* to creation.

Also implicit here is not only the possible independence and way-wardness of a creature separated from the Creator, but also God's ultimate response to a wayward creation: the crucifixion of Christ, the suffering of God, "the Lamb that was slain from the creation of the world" (Rev. 13:8, NIV). The cost of a free creation, for all the good it brings, is pain — or at least the possibility of pain — to the Creator.

If there were nothing but God, there would be no possibility of evil. (Thus there is no room for stewardship, good or bad, in the various kinds of monism being explored today by environmentalists in search of a religion.) The first instant of creation implies a breaking of that unity: before, there was only God; afterward, there was God and something not-God, something potentially free to turn to God — or away from him. That very logical necessity which has impelled Christian theologians to go beyond Scripture and declare that God created *ex nihilo,* out of nothing, implies this breaking at the heart of God's making. For God to make "out of nothing" he must first allow "nothing" to be — which is to withdraw himself from part of creation. Jürgen Moltmann has put it well:

> . . . when God permitted creation, this was the first act in the divine self-humiliation which reached its profoundest point in the cross of Christ.
>
> God makes room for his creation by withdrawing his presence. What comes into being is a *nihil.* . . . God 'withdraws himself from himself' in order to make creation possible. His creative activity out-wards is preceded by this humble divine self-restriction. In this sense God's self-humiliation does not begin merely with creation, inasmuch as God commits himself to this world: it begins beforehand, and is the presupposition that makes creation possible. God emptied himself and as creator took upon himself the form of a servant.[4]

It is clear, then, that in creation God creates something other than himself; he upholds it, but is not present in it. It is clear also that he gives that creation both goodness and freedom. Creatures are not God's slaves, as his delight in their goodness makes plain.

---

4. Jürgen Moltmann, *God in Creation* (London: SCM Press, 1985), pp. 87-88.

We have yet to consider the creation of humans and their relationship to the rest of creation. But these hints of the sacrifice which is fundamental to God's *response* to creation — in which God allows freedom for the individual creature to be — already counter the claim of those who maintain that the doctrine of creation gives men and women who see themselves as being in God's image license to exploit. These verses in Genesis 1 make clear that the goodness of creation is a goodness in the things themselves, not in their usefulness to humans, who are not even mentioned until the end of the chapter. To say that the goodness of creation is only a goodness of utility, because it can be used by the one creature made in God's image, is not only (as we shall see) to misunderstand seriously what "the image of God" means; it is also to miss most of the force of the boisterous and blossoming complexity of life which Genesis 1 suggests.

A number of other passages in Scripture make clear that creation is good for its own sake, not just because it can be used by humans. One of the most striking of such passages is Psalm 104. Although in this remarkable hymn some of the bounties of creation are clearly described as being for people's use ("plants for man to cultivate," "wine to gladden the heart of man," "bread to strengthen man's heart"), all of them are things good in themselves, which humans may adapt to their use. In the same psalm the more specific descriptions are of a detailed, lovingly perceived world where humanity does not figure in at all — yet God cares for it just as much as he does for humanity:

> The trees of the LORD are watered abundantly,
>   the cedars of Lebanon which he planted.
> In them the birds build their nests;
>   the stork has her home in the fir trees.
> The high mountains are for the wild goats;
>   the rocks are a refuge for the badgers.
>
> (Ps. 104:16-18)

There is no suggestion that cedars, storks, goats, or badgers are there for the sake of humans; yet, the Psalmist says, God cares for them and exults in their individuality.

This is not an isolated passage; there are many like it throughout the Old Testament. But perhaps the most striking is in the book of Job, where God answers Job's complaint by referring to various works of creation. And the point of the answer is precisely that these things in creation are outside human understanding and control. Humans have neither use for nor understanding of them, yet they are God's and they are good. God's answer to Job spans several chapters, but a brief sampling makes the point: creation is not just for human benefit. It is good in the very strength of its strangeness and diversity.

> Then the LORD answered Job out of the whirlwind:
> "Who is this that darkens counsel by words without knowledge? . . .
> Where were you when I laid the foundation of the earth? . . .
> when the morning stars sang together,
>   and all the sons of God shouted for joy? . . .
> Have you entered into the springs of the sea,
>   or walked in the recesses of the deep? . . .
> Have you entered the storehouses of the snow,
>   or have you seen the storehouses of the hail . . .
> Do you know when the mountain goats give forth?
>   Do you observe the calving of the hinds? . . .
> Is the wild ox willing to serve you?
>   Will he spend the night at your crib? . . .
> Is it by your wisdom that the hawk soars,
>   and spreads his wings toward the south?
> Is it at your command that the eagle mounts up
>   and makes his nest on high?"
>
>   (Job 38–39, passim)

The message is clear: stars do not shine simply to provide light for humans; snowflakes do not fall only for human appreciation; there are oxen we should not tame, deer whose freedom is to be preserved, hawks and eagles which fly far above us.

As we will see, humans do have a unique place in creation and a unique responsibility to all of it. But such passages as these make plain that the goodness of creation does not depend on people. Its purpose is not merely to fuel the engines of human progress; it is also to provide water for the thirsty trees, crags for the goats, and open sky for the south-flying hawks.

HUMANITY AND DOMINION

We may now consider the explicit — but inexhaustibly rich — biblical insights of the opening chapters of Genesis about the relationship of humanity to the rest of Creation. As a preliminary, it is helpful to point out what many biblical scholars have speculated on with varying degrees of insight: the Genesis record of the origin of humanity is divided into two accounts, or at least into two perspectives on the same event. One common explanation for this division is that we find here two revelations, of different age and source, patched together with the seams still showing. Whether or not this is the case is unimportant for our purposes, for it is as *one* story that the account has shaped Christian thought. So, in the discussion which follows, we will ignore the break which most commentators agree occurs at Genesis 2:4, and discuss the account as though it were a single story.

When we consider what is said or implied in Genesis 1 and 2 about what humans are, two sorts of images emerge. First of all, we see that humans, like stars, seas, whales, fish, and birds, are simply a part of creation. They are made on the sixth day and are (short of the Sabbath) the final act of creation. But they share a day of creation with other animals, and they are clearly made in the same way the animals are. Thus they are embedded in creation. This image of human relatedness to all other created things is made even more vivid when they are described as being made "from the dust of the earth." The Hebrew word used here for "earth" is *adamah,* and the Hebrew word for man is *Adam.* What the words and the whole account suggest, then, is what contemporary biologists and ecologists have been trying hard to tell us: whatever else we are, humans are also *earth;* we share our nature with its soil, its plants, its animals.

Yet this earthiness of humanity — its commonality with the rest of creation — is only half of the Genesis picture. (It is, however, a half that needs more recognition, especially by Christians.) It is balanced by another aspect of humanity, and it is this aspect that writers like Ian McHarg and Lynn White are speaking against when they speak of human separation from nature. For humans are also described as being very special in creation; that uniqueness is described as their being made "in the image of God."

The meaning of the phrase "image of God" has been endlessly speculated over. But the premise underlying much of that speculation has only perpetuated a serious misunderstanding of our place in creation.

Douglas John Hall, in an excellent recent study called *Imaging God: Dominion as Stewardship*, has not only summed up the debate, but has pointed out the danger of our understanding the "image of God" as one particular trait or characteristic, whether it be rationality, language, creativity, or something else which only humans *possess*. The image of God is rather, says Hall, something which we do. Because we have understood God's image to be some substantial way in which we *possess* a likeness to God, we have tended to justify any sort of action toward creation by analogy with our supposedly God-like superiority over it.

The "image of God" is not substantial, but relational: it describes our unique calling to be in responsible relationship with God, with each other, and with the rest of creation. It is a kind of relationship which takes its substance from the example, in Christ, of God's relationship with us. It affects our human notion of what "God-like" relationship is, and it has

"Eve, this place is so vast we couldn't pollute it if we tried."

From *Christianity Today,* February 27, 1970.
© 1970 by John Lawing. Used by permission.

profound implications for our relationship to the rest of creation. Such a relational understanding of "the image of God," says Hall,

> points to an image of the human that presupposes and conjures up an entirely different arrangement of things. It introduces us to a view of the universe and of the human place in it that contains, in fact, a radical critique of every hierarchical ordering of earthly life, every elevation of one species at the expense of others, and every attempt to divinize or demonize the human creature.[5]

Men and women have been called to a unique place in creation: they have been given the task of *modelling* the gracious and self-giving nature of their Creator to each other and to the rest of creation. The "Garden of Eden" (which has been understood variously as either a specific and limited place or as a now-flawed harmonious relationship to the whole earth) is planted for human use. Thus Genesis pictures humanity as being both *in* the rest of creation and *over* it. Christians and critics alike, fixing on a domineering notion of God, have stressed human transcendence over creation at the expense of human immanence in it. One of the ways we can understand the uniquely relational character of the image of God is to reflect on what human beings are told to *do*.

The first instance of humans being told to do something is contained in Genesis 1:28. It is a notorious verse, for, more than any other passage of Scripture, it has been understood as giving humans license, even a command, to exploit the earth.

> And God blessed them; and God said to them, "Be fruitful and multiply, and fill the earth, and subdue it; and rule over the fish of the sea and over the birds of the sky and over every living thing that moves on the earth." (NASB)

"Be fruitful" and "multiply" are commands given to other creatures. But in this divine command to humanity are two commands which are given to no other creatures: "subdue" and "rule." Any softening of these forceful words would not be an adequate translation; in fact, this translation of the Hebrew words *(kābaš* and *rādāh)* is already considerably milder than the Hebrew terms themselves. *Kābaš* is drawn

---

5. Douglas John Hall, *Imaging God: Dominion as Stewardship* (Grand Rapids: Eerdmans, 1986), p. 112.

from a Hebrew word meaning "to tread down" or "to bring into bondage"; it conveys the image of a conqueror placing his foot on the neck of the conquered. In one passage the word even means "rape." The other verb, *rādāh,* comes from a word meaning "to trample" or "to press." Thus there is no doubt at all that men and women are placed *over* the rest of creation. These verses express that superiority in the strongest possible terms.

Certainly if these commands were the only directive given to humanity, it would be correct to see the Hebrew-Christian tradition as a source of Western exploitative attitudes toward nature. But the image of forceful dominion which this verse conveys is balanced (and, in some sense, reversed) by the rest of Scripture. That balance first appears in the next chapter, where Adam is given tasks which seem quite different from the kind of dominion decreed earlier: "The LORD God took the man and put him in the garden of Eden to till it and keep it" (Gen. 2:15). Again, human responsibility is described by two verbs, *'ābad* and *šāmar,* here translated "till" and "keep." The first of these verbs, *'ābad,* is often translated "till," but it is sometimes translated "work" or "serve." And in fact, *'ābad* is the basic Hebrew word for "serve" or even "be a slave to." The other word, *šāmar,* is translated variously "keep," "watch," or "preserve." The significant thing about both words is that they describe actions undertaken not primarily for the sake of the doer but for the sake of the object of the action. The kind of tilling which is to be done is a *service* of the earth. The keeping of the garden is not just for human comfort but is a kind of *preservation.* Both verbs severely restrict the way the other two verbs — "subdue" and "rule" — are to be applied. Human ruling, then, should be exercised in such a way as to *serve* and *preserve* the beasts, the trees, and the earth itself — all of which is being ruled. It is in such a relationship that we demonstrate the image of God — again, not as something which we are, but by carrying out a pattern of self-giving service demonstrated by the Creator.

The original command to subdue and rule is not contradicted, but the *type* of ruling is explicitly directed. There is never any doubt that humans are masters; but the concept of mastery itself here begins to be clarified and reversed in a process which will culminate only in the cruci-fixion of Christ.

Some further direction to this uniquely human "subduing-which-is-service" is indicated in yet another, more specific task which God gives Adam.

> So out of the ground the LORD God formed every beast of the field
> and every bird of the air, and brought them to the man to see what
> he would call them; and whatever the man called every living creature,
> that was its name. (Gen. 2:19)

We can understand this task in the superficial modern sense of naming,
in which the mystery of a thing is reduced to a label and applied to the
object named. In modern thought, however, naming tends to become one
more way of imposing on a nameless world the categories of our mind.
In terms of that Cartesian caricature we referred to in an earlier chapter,
it is the human-ghost's way of running the great machine nature. And
when we "name" fellow creatures in such a way it is out of an abstract
sense that we have a characteristic of God which places us above other
things. But in doing this, we are not *imaging* God. For naming in the
biblical sense is not "labeling," but is a recognition of the innermost being
of a thing. When Abram makes a covenant with God and acknowledges
God's full purpose for him, that change is expressed by his new name,
"Abraham." A similar use of naming occurs in the change from "Jacob"
to "Israel." Ideally, names are not imposed labels, but recognitions of what
a creature is. True naming thus involves a deep knowledge of the creature
and a sympathetic relationship with it.

Further, this naming ability links Adam (which means humanity,
male and female) the namer with God the maker, clarifying human uniqueness from the rest of Creation, but doing so in terms of our relationship
— our action. This human potential to share in the creative act is suggested
by the curious wording of the verse: God brings the creatures to Adam
"to see what he would call them." The clear impression is that God *waits*
for Adam's perception and for the creative (and responsive) act of his
naming, as though it is in humanity that God's creation is made complete.
We noted a similar wording in God's blessing of creation. God does not
simply declare that things are good; he *sees* that they are good. Likewise,
God waits to see what Adam will see in the creature — and as a result of
that seeing, what he will utter.

It has become commonplace to associate the exploitative aspect of
the human relationship to creation with Genesis 1, in which those harsh
verbs are used to describe the human task, and the more careful human
relationship with creation with Genesis 2, where the gentler verbs are used.
But, as we have seen, a consideration of what humans *are* shows that in
the first chapter they are most closely linked with the rest of creation, and

in the second chapter they are most clearly placed above creation, all of Eden being made for them. Certainly, then, one way to harmonize this apparent paradox is to recognize that it is only by virtue of human separation from nature that they can serve, and that it is the ability to be consciously a part of nature which enables them to be its legitimate master. The great surprise (especially if we tend to think that the "image of God" in us is some sort of privileged trait) is that in all that we do we are to be servants: dominion is to be understood as stewardship — that is how we "image" God.

That, at least, is the pattern suggested by Genesis, particularly when we regard this account as one coherent story and not as a kind of patchwork. But that pattern has not been used as a basis for human action; both biblical history and our own observation of the past show that we departed very early from the ability to use superiority as a basis for service.

The Long Lesson: Dominion in the Old Testament

The whole of biblical history, and even of church history, can be helpfully understood as a long lesson in how humans are to use their ability to manipulate, dominate, and rule. We are accustomed to considering that story mainly in connection with our relationship to God and to other people, but a third dimension of that relationship concerns our attitude toward "nature" — nonhuman creation.

The lesson begins with human sin. In the biblical story, the tempter's appeal is to the human desire for illegitimate authority — their desire to eat of the tree of knowledge and thus become, in human terms and time, like God. It is the first time in history that humans have longed for the power of gods, but it is certainly not the last. The consequence of their action is just the reverse of the imaging of God we discussed in the preceding pages, in which power is exercised as service, as reconciliation. Human sin results in alienation between God and humans, between man and woman, and between humanity and nature. But the verses describing the "curse on nature" need a closer look, for they have often been appealed to as a justification of the harsh measures people must take toward their natural environment:

> cursed is the ground because of you;
> in toil you shall eat of it all the days of your life;

thorns and thistles it shall bring forth to you;
    and you shall eat the plants of the field.
In the sweat of your face
    you shall eat bread
till you return to the ground,
    for out of it you were taken;
you are dust,
    and to dust you shall return.

(Gen. 3:17-19)

This passage is usually read in such a way as to suggest that "thorns and thistles" — that is, weeds in general, all plants which "get in the way" — are not a part of the created order, but are a consequence of human sin. In the Middle Ages this doctrine was expanded from biology into geology, and the very ruggedness of the earth, so often a burden to humans trying to move about on it, was seen as a result of the fall. But, as our own time has shown us painfully, there are very few plants which we are not capable of regarding as weeds, and the same is true for animals, hills, valleys — indeed, most things in creation. The ground is cursed because we are set against it. Significantly, the word here translated "ground" is *adamah,* which suggests that the curse pronounced on *Adam* is in fact describing a division within himself. That division is his own inability to be at harmony with the earth — his tendency to regard his difference from nature as enmity with nature. In short, the curse describes not a quality in the earth itself, but human misuse of dominion. An accurate reading of the Hebrew would be: "cursed is the ground *to you.*"

Because of this attitude of enmity between people and nature, humanity has lost its ability to be the "preserver" of the garden in which it was placed. This loss is poignantly implied in the statement that God "placed the cherubim, and a flaming sword which turned every way, to guard the way to the tree of life" (Gen. 3:24). The word "guard" translates the same word, *shamar,* used to describe humanity's failed task in the garden. Their misunderstanding of dominion, a dominion that issues in enmity, makes humans unable to "guard" or "preserve" the life of the garden. It is an inability we still see manifested today.

An early indication of this human failure to understand dominion is Cain's murder of Abel. Not only is the killing a clear misuse of divinely given strength, but when Cain defends himself against God's questioning, he does so by asking, "Am I my brother's keeper?" (Gen. 4:9). The verb again is *šāmar*, the same used to define human care for nature. Here Cain reveals the human reluctance to use strength for service, whether it be toward people or toward nature.

Such misuse of human dominion occurs throughout the Bible. It climaxes early in an earth filled with violence, which God determines to wipe clean by a flood. Yet in this climax of evil in which the misused strength of humans is nearly responsible for the destruction of life on earth, there is also a divinely given indication of how humans can use their dominion for the sake of the rest of creation. The story of Noah still stands, for Christians, as a kind of metaphor for how humanity should use its capacities for dominion; the beneficial result of human tool-wielding is the ark, a means of salvation for the earth's creatures, many of which humans consider useless.

Another misuse of dominion is the tower of Babel — an early manifestation of the human dream to be like God. If Noah's ark is a primeval example of *appropriate* technology, used to preserve life in a flood, Babel is an excellent emblem of *inappropriate* technology, for its only purpose is to lift its builders up for their own glory. The ark symbolizes a use of human creativity to identify with and preserve nature; the tower of Babel symbolizes a use of those same powers to lift humans out of nature.

From Abraham (who is asked to sacrifice his son, his one link with dominion) on through the prophets (who continually proclaim to the people God's message that their strength is not in their chariots, but rather in their giving up of their strength to God), the Old Testament is a record of this painful lesson which God must teach his people: whether we speak of humanity or nature, dominion does not mean simply imposing one's will on the weaker.

A passage in Ezekiel will serve to show clearly the typical sorts of reminders, given to the Hebrews, of the legitimate uses of dominion. Ezekiel is told to say to the "shepherds," the spiritual and political leaders of Israel:

> Ho, shepherds of Israel who have been feeding yourselves! Should not shepherds feed the sheep? You eat the fat, you clothe yourselves with the wool, you slaughter the fatlings; but you do not feed the sheep. The weak you have not strengthened, the sick you have not healed, the crippled you have not bound up, the strayed you have not brought back, the lost you have not sought, and with force and harshness you have ruled them. (Ezek. 34:2-4)

The passage is directed against the "shepherds of Israel," and it is clear that the shepherd/sheep relationship is a metaphor used to speak of the leaders' treatment of their people; it is a parable about the use of dominion, not primarily a tract on livestock management. But what Ezekiel is saying about the leaders of Israel will only be meaningful if the principles from which he draws are valid guides for shepherding sheep. Since shepherding is a particularly good example of the exercise of human dominion over the natural world, we are justified in treating the passage also on its literal level of meaning — that is, as telling us something about the way in which dominion may be properly exercised over any of the creatures which, as the Psalmist says, have been put "under our feet" (Ps. 8:6).

It is immediately obvious that the primary duty of the shepherd is to maintain the welfare of the flock. Though the ultimate purpose of the flock is to provide wool and food for human use, the fact that the shepherds are chastised for taking these things without "feeding the flock" suggests strongly that maintaining the welfare of the sheep *for the sheep's own sake* is an important use which the shepherd is to make of his position of superiority. This is made very clear when the writer accuses, "With force and with severity you have dominated them" (NASB). The word "dominated" is from *kābaš*, the same word used in Genesis 1 to describe the general human stance toward nature. The lesson about dominion is clear: unless such dominion is used for the benefit of the dominated, it is misused. Dominion exercised for power alone is wrong: for men and women, the exercise of dominion ought to be the exercise of stewardship.

Isaiah 53, one of the most powerful passages in the Old Testament, also teaches that the divine model for dominion is a radical kind of servitude. Christians have understood this portrait of the "suffering servant" to speak of the supreme demonstration of the character of dominion manifest in Jesus. But whatever prophetic or messianic content is present in this description of one "despised and rejected by men" (v. 3), the increasingly familiar pattern is evident: dominion is servitude. That such a use of authority is counter to human expectation — which normally equates dominion with *lording*, not serving — is evident in the question at the opening of the chapter: "Who has believed what we have heard? And to whom has the arm of the LORD been revealed?" That the *arm* of the Lord — his strength, his authority, in short, his dominion — could be revealed in meekness and servitude is so contrary to the warped human expectation for the uses of dominion that the implicit answer to the question is, "No one will believe this." Yet the whole chapter — indeed,

"This will surely be disappointing to many meek people. The legacy
has been successfully contested, and it is now the arrogant who
are to inherit the earth."

one might say the whole of biblical history — is a demonstration of this link between dominion and vulnerability.

We have only sampled briefly the abundant Old Testament teaching that the dominion which humans are to exercise is not a kind of exploitation, but a kind of service. Though most of the passages we have considered do not speak exclusively of the human relationship to creation, they nevertheless outline the *concept* of dominion. And they point to the same thing we noticed in the Genesis account: though the words describing human authority are very strong, that authority over nature is to be applied in the ways indicated by such other-directed verbs as "serve" and "guard." Such use of strength goes counter to most of what seems to come naturally to us as humans — so much so that many would say it is simply not possible. But Christians say such a transformation of dominion is possible because of the sacrifice of Christ, which is both a pattern for action and a power enabling us to carry it out. The whole long lesson of Old Testament history points to this supreme example of God's use of dominion, which henceforth must be the model for all who would, in the name and service of God, exercise stewardship over his creation.

Christ and Dominion

It is, perhaps, an indication of our fallen condition that we humans have not only seized the Genesis commandment to rule as a permit to use nature only for *human* comfort, but have also interpreted the sacrificial death of Christ as being only for *human* salvation. Thus the most compelling argument in favor of any degradation of the environment, whether it be strip-mining a hill, clear-cutting a mountain, or butchering a whale, is always the contribution such an action will make to *human* survival — if not the actual survival of individuals, at least the survival of a certain kind of comfort or security.

The unique message of the Christian gospel, however, is not only the proclamation of the infinite worth of human life (for God, in Christ, died to redeem it); it is also the importance of being willing to give up that life — or at least to forgo one's comfort and material security — for the sake of another. We have tended to interpret that sacrificial Christian *caritas* as directed only toward other humans. Yet our record — particularly in North America — of forgoing some wealth and comfort even for other suffering people is a dismal one. Despite the remarkably explicit teaching of Christ on sharing one's wealth, we still find it very difficult to do anything other than multiply our own comforts and securities. It is not that wealth or the creation of wealth is bad; it is rather that we are to share the creatively augmented wealth of creation for the benefit of fellow creatures.

Biblical teaching leaves no room for the kind of self-centered dominion condemned (for example) in Ezekiel's criticism of "the shepherds of Israel." The abuses of wealth and power criticized in such passages are clearly a misuse of our power over other humans, to be continually judged by the gospel of Christ. But the principle goes further (and this is a new idea for many Christians). If the pattern for our use of power is established in Christ, then it is a pattern for our treatment of all of creation, not only of humanity.

This is not to say that one should treat human and nonhuman creatures as though they had equal value. But to acknowledge a greater worth to the human creature than to the nonhuman does not mean that the human is of infinite value and all other creatures are of no value. Since it is clear from Scripture that God values all of creation, and that we are placed in it to care for it, we cannot lightly treat other creatures as mere raw material to be used to enhance our well-being. We must make the difficult choices between the good of human and nonhuman creatures with care, wisdom, and a willingness to feel the pain we inflict on fellow creatures. For such a stewardly dominion, all of creation "waits with eager longing" (Rom. 8:19). All of our actions should be guided by the example of the use of dominion provided by Christ.

The central description of that divine use of power is in Philippians 2. There Christians are told to have the "mind of Christ." And the following verses leave little doubt as to the sort of actions the mind of Christ should impel us to. For Christ,

> though he was in the form of God, did not count equality with God
> a thing to be grasped, but emptied himself, taking the form of a servant,
> being born in the likeness of men. And being found in human form
> he humbled himself and became obedient unto death, even death on
> a cross. (Phil. 2:6-8)

In the view of Ian McHarg, with whose bitter criticisms of Christianity we began this chapter, the misuse of creation is attributed to the damaging consequences of the idea of humans as divine: "Show me a man-oriented society in which it is believed . . . that the cosmos is a structure erected to support man on its pinnacle, that man exclusively is divine and given dominion over all things, . . . and I will predict the nature of its cities and their landscapes."[6] Yet Christians place at the center of their faith the example of one who, "in the form of God" and thus on the "pinnacle of the cosmos," gave up the dominion which was a consequence of that position, not regarding it as "a thing to be grasped," and became a servant. But that McHarg (and others) should make such accurate criticisms of what a Christian civilization has done to creation suggests that we have almost totally ignored the application of "the mind of Christ" to our treatment of the natural world.

Christians have not only neglected to apply "the mind of Christ" to their use of creation, but they have also rarely reflected enough on the involvement of Christ in creation. It is easy to neglect care for creation if we see it only as a backdrop for the drama of human salvation. But the Bible is quite clear in affirming that Christ's involvement with creation is not an involvement with humans only.

It is true, as Christians and their critics alike have affirmed, that God the Creator is utterly other than what he has made. Thus it is idolatrous to worship nature as divine — whatever the environmental benefits of such nature worship may be thought to be. But it is equally true that Scripture teaches a continual, creative, and sustaining presence of God with his creation. And that creative and sustaining presence is understood as the second person of the Trinity, Christ Jesus of Nazareth, who is the Word without which nothing was made. In choosing to speak of Jesus as the Word, the Logos, the Gospel of John brilliantly clarifies those half-understood gropings of the Stoics to comprehend the ordering presence of God in nature.

Another source for this idea of the presence of the Word of God in nature is the Jewish Wisdom literature, in which a passage from Proverbs is the most striking. There the personified figure of Wisdom speaks:

> The LORD created me at the beginning of his work,
>   the first of his acts of old.
> Ages ago I was set up,
>   at the first, before the beginning of the earth.
>   . . . then I was beside him, like a master workman;

---

6. McHarg, *Design with Nature*, p. 24.

and I was daily his delight,
   rejoicing before him always,
rejoicing in his inhabited world
   and delighting in the sons of men.

(Prov. 8:22-23, 30-31)

Christians have usually seen this figure of God's master workman, "rejoicing in his inhabited world," as a prefiguring of Christ. And there is abundant Scripture in the New Testament which, in a similar way, describes the involvement of Christ with nature. It will be enough simply to enumerate these passages, emphasizing the lines which speak of Christ's involvement with nature. The author of Hebrews writes that God

> has spoken to us by a Son, whom he appointed the heir of all things, *through whom also he created the world.* He reflects the glory of God and bears the very stamp of his nature, *upholding the universe by his word of power.* (Heb. 1:2-3; italics added)

Paul writes in 1 Corinthians:

> yet for us there is one God, the Father, from whom are all things and for whom we exist, and one Lord, Jesus Christ, *through whom are all things* and through whom we exist. (1 Cor. 8:6; italics added)

Likewise Paul declares in Colossians:

> He is the image of the invisible God, the first-born of all creation; *for in him all things were created,* in heaven and on earth, visible and invisible, whether thrones or dominions or principalities or authorities — *all things were created through him and for him.* He is before all things, and *in him all things hold together.* (Col. 1:15-17; italics added)

The best known of these many passages that speak of Christ's involvement with nature is the Prologue to the Gospel of John:

> In the beginning was the Word, and the Word was with God, and the Word was God. He was in the beginning with God; *all things were made through him, and without him was not anything made that was made.* (John 1:1-3; italics added)

In the face of these clear statements of God's involvement in the created order, it is necessary to balance the way we understand God's transcendence with a recognition of God's immanence. Though God, the Creator, is indeed beyond creation, he is also in it. The historical Incarnation is the center, the exemplification in time, of God's willingness in Christ to create, sustain, delight in, and suffer for creation. It is because God stands apart from his creation that he creates and sustains it. Likewise, it is because of the specific, historic entrance of Christ into creation that we are able to understand the continual involvement of Christ, the upholding and redeeming Word, in all of creation.

If we grant that Scripture teaches an involvement of Christ in creation, what does this imply for *human* involvement in creation? Without yet considering the pertinent Scripture, we can notice a kind of symmetry between God's relationship to creation and our relationship to creation. We noticed it first in Genesis, but when we come to the gospel of the Incarnation, its significance for contemporary Christians becomes much more practical. God is transcendent over nature. That is a fact of Christian faith, but it has been scorned, in recent years, because of the supposed indifference to nature which that divine transcendence produces in people. For we have also seen, in the doctrine of the "image of God" and the accompanying task to have dominion over creation, that Scripture speaks of a kind of *human* transcendence.

A consideration of the Incarnation shows, however, that in Christ, both as Creator and as Redeemer, God is immanent in creation. The "equality with God" enables the creating Word to share the flesh of his creation in an immanence which does not grasp at either glory or survival, but which leads ultimately to death. Likewise, though Christians transcend the world, they are also directed to become a redemptive part of what they transcend. Humans are to become saviors of nature, as Christ is the savior of humanity (and hence, through humans, of those parts of creation placed under their care).

This idea of men and women being, along with Christ, the saviors of nature is not simply theological speculation. It is implied in all of those many Scripture passages which speak of redeemed humans as "fellow heirs" with Christ. As Christ is Ruler, Creator, and Sustainer of the world, so also are we to be. Being heirs with Christ involves (as Paul saw) being crucified with Christ; it also involves sharing in Christ's sustaining, suffering activity in creation.

Most specifically, this startling — but orthodox — idea of humans sharing in the redemption of creation is taught in several verses in Romans 8. After a passage which speaks of Christians as fellow heirs with Christ, there follow these words:

For the creation waits with eager longing for the revealing of the sons of God; for the creation was subjected to futility, not of its own will but by the will of him who subjected it in hope; because the creation itself will be set free from its bondage to decay and obtain the glorious liberty of the children of God. We know that the whole creation has been groaning in travail together until now. (Rom. 8:19-22)

In this suggestively cryptic passage, it is clear that the fate of creation is bound up with the fate of humanity and that whatever glory comes to humans as a result of their participation in divine redemption will come also to creation. Is this a promise in reference only to some far future millennial kingdom, or are we *now* to be redemptively involved in that groaning and suffering creation? Scripture does not generally put tasks off into some eschatological future, a fact which would point to the present as the occasion for our work with creation. So also does the wording of the final sentence: the "until now" suggests that the childbirth is over and that humans, who have been shown the pattern of their dominion as stewards of the earth, can begin to exercise it wisely, according to the mind of Christ. It remains for us to see how Christians have understood and acted on that stewardship in the centuries since the Incarnation.

The Long Lesson Continued: Dominion in Church History

In Western thought, the biblical theme of a redemptive human involvement in creation has been countered, and often cancelled, by a misleading interpretation of another biblical theme: the notion of human dominion, based on an understanding of human uniqueness in creation — the "image of God." We have seen how that image of God ought to be understood: not as a forceful "lording," but as a relationship of active service.

Unfortunately, the idea of human transcendence became joined, in the early years of the church, with the prevailing Platonic idea of physical nature as a source of ignorance and evil and as a snare to the soul. The result was a theology which laid most stress on the salvation of the *soul,* and which tended to dismiss as insignificant the body and the creation of which it was a part.

Yet there was from the very beginning a strain of Christian thought which did not make this unbiblical distinction between the physical and the spiritual, and which did not encourage an understanding of salvation which turned men and women away from creation. We find such a creation-affirming theology in the earliest systematic discussion of the atonement, by Irenaeus in the second century. Irenaeus emphasized the New Testament doctrine of Christ as the "Second Adam." But he did not forget, as did so many subsequent theologians, that Adam was given responsibility for nature. Christ succeeds, said Irenaeus, in doing what Adam was to do. And that success amounts not only to a victory over Satan, but to a redemption of nature as well. In Christ, nature has the kind of human master God intended for it. And through both his example and our adoption into him, we share in that redemption of nature. Said Irenaeus, "It is right, therefore, for this created order to be restored to its pristine state."[7]

> For the Creator of the world is truly the Word of God: and this is our Lord, who in the last times was made man, existing in this world, and who in an invisible manner contains all things created, and is inherent in the entire creation, since the Word of God governs and arranges all things; and therefore He came to His own in a visible manner, and was made flesh, and hung upon the tree, that He might sum up all things in Himself.[8]

This clear early understanding that there is no tension between redemption and creation is even more explicit in one of the greatest of the church father — Athanasius. In his work *On the Incarnation*, Athanasius declared:

> We will begin, then, with the creation of the world and with God its Maker, for the first fact that you must grasp is this: the renewal of creation has been wrought by the Self-same Word Who made it in the beginning. There is thus no inconsistency between creation and salvation; for the One Father has employed the same Agent for both works, effecting the salvation of the world through the same Word Who made it at the first.[9]

This early understanding of a redemption which is not just the saving of human beings out of a doomed creation, but which involves the healing of all of creation by the Word who made and redeemed it, was

---

7. Irenaeus, in *Against Heresies: Early Christian Fathers*, ed. and trans. Edward Rocie Hardy (Philadelphia: Westminster Press, 1955), vol. 1, p. 385.

8. Irenaeus, *Against Heresies*, V.xviii.3, pp. 546-47.

9. Athanasius, *On the Incarnation*, p. 26.

diminished, however, in Western Christendom. It is as though the larger our understanding of the world has become, the smaller our understanding of what the new life in Christ can mean. As one Christian thinker puts it:

> the smaller the dimensions of man's world, the more wide-ranging is likely to be his systematic account of reconciliation. As his world expands, so his system seems to contract. When the limits of his universe have vanished into far-off distances, his concentration of concern tends to be focussed upon the small-scale world of the isolated inner self. Such a sequence can certainly be seen in the history of theories of the Atonement.[10]

Perhaps the most influential of those who taught that Christians should turn away from the world and devote their attention solely to the spiritual and the eternal was St. Augustine. Augustine arrived at Christianity after a long pilgrimage through the religions of the day, including Neoplatonism, which held a strong doctrine of the evil of matter. Augustine never quite ceased to be influenced by this idea; his Platonic attitude is clearly evident in these words from his *Soliloquies:* "These things of the senses are to be utterly shunned and the utmost care must be used lest while we bear this body our wings be impeded by their snare."[11]

Augustine was also an important source of a related idea which we traced in some detail through Western thought: the superiority of the mind over nature. Augustine was acutely aware of his own consciousness, and this emphasis on self-consciousness grew in the West — slowly, to be sure — until it appeared in a powerful form in those ideas of the detached mind (as in Descartes, or Bacon, or Galileo) which were so important in the scientific revolution. Notice how, in this passage from the *Confessions* (a remarkably mind-centered book for its day), the emphasis is on the importance of the separateness of the mind from nature:

> Men go forth to marvel at the heights of mountains and the huge waves of the sea, the broad flow of the rivers, the vastness of the ocean, the orbits of the stars, and yet they neglect to marvel at themselves.

---

10. F. W. Dillistone, *The Christian Understanding of Atonement* (Welwyn: James Nisbet, 1968), p. 406.

11. Augustine, *Soliloquies,* I, xiv, 24, in Erich Przywara, *An Augustine Synthesis* (New York: Sheed & Ward, 1945), p. 1.

Nor do they wonder how it is that, when I spoke of all these things,
I was not looking at them with my eyes.[12]

Thus both in his ethics — his understanding of what is good — and in
his epistemology — his understanding of what and how we know —
Augustine tends to stress the transcendent human mind, or soul, above
nature. Nature, for all its beauty (which Augustine readily responds to),
is counted of no worth on the soul's journey to God. With some exceptions, this has been typical of the Western approach to nature. Humans
— their minds, their souls, their eternal destinies — are placed as the
central object for salvation. There is little concern for — or even awareness
of — creation itself. The *contemptus mundi* tradition, with a few exceptions, keeps Christendom from recognizing an essential part of Christianity
— that is, to the same extent that humans' mind, soul, creativity, and
destiny elevate them over nature, they are to use those gifts for the lifting,
the nourishing, the *husbanding* of the creation for whose care they are
responsible.

Unfortunately, with the Platonically inclined influence of
Augustine on Western Christian thought, the idea of human involvement
in the redemption of nature has played very little part. But it does appear
sporadically. For example, we saw it in the tradition of the Benedictine
and Cistercian monasteries discussed in chapter 6, in which work becomes
a kind of prayer, and human presence is directed toward transforming
nature into a kind of New Eden or "Jerusalem in waiting." We saw it in
the tradition of the Celtic Christians, who had a deep sense of the goodness
of creation and the presence of God in it. We also saw it in St. Francis
and his followers, who demonstrated a remarkable sense of kinship with
and love for the rest of creation. Yet even this insight of Francis, though
it begins to direct people's attention to close observation of nature, does
not succeed in substantially altering Christendom's view of nature. Its
greatest influence (somewhat ironically) is on the empiricism at the roots
of modern science. The nature-centered attitudes of St. Francis are,
through time and the Western milieu, mutated into a mind-centered, and
ultimately manipulative, *observation* of nature.

Thus in the West — with such important exceptions as the Franciscans and the Benedictines — Christian theology and action have

---

12. From Augustine, *Confessions,* in *Augustine: Confessions and Enchiridion,* trans.
Albert Outler (Philadelphia: Westminster Press, 1955), p. 210.

stressed not human involvement with the rest of creation but human separation from creation, and particularly the individual, conscious separation of the mind from nature. And as we saw in our discussion of Genesis, that distinctness of humanity from creation is an important part of the created order — including the *power* over creation which goes with it. Unmodified, however, the sheer human difference from nature, that naked human power over nature, is a horrible thing. Some of the degradations resulting from that unredeemed human transcendence have been spoken of in previous chapters, and in itself it is clearly not a reflection of the mind of Christ, however much it validly affirms human distinctiveness.

But Christendom has not been without a consistent, coherent, and ancient tradition of the involvement of humanity in the redemption of creation. That idea has been maintained as an important part of Eastern Orthodox theology.

Because Eastern Orthodoxy has not stressed the very thing which has been at the center of Western theology — that is, the experience of personal, individual salvation — it has tended to appear stagnant to critics from Western Christendom. Long beards, black robes, and a vague impression of Byzantine complexity is all that has filtered through to most Western Christians. This sense that Eastern Orthodoxy is a kind of theological and cultural dead end has until recently been the prevailing attitude among Western historians of the church, who have contrasted the otherworldliness of Eastern Orthodoxy with the activism of its Western counterpart. This dynamic activism appeared not just in theology, but also in the working out of culture. It was in the West, not in the Byzantine East, that the great changes in outlook and technology took place which shaped the scientific revolution. Lynn White, whose opinions on Christendom we have already referred to, records the astonishment of a visitor from Greece to Italy in the fifteenth century who "is amazed by the superiority of Western ships, arms, textiles, glass. But above all he is astonished by the spectacle of waterwheels sawing timbers and pumping the bellows of the blast furnaces. Clearly, he had seen nothing of the sort in the Near East."[13] But the very fact that it is this technological dynamism which has produced so many of our environmental problems, combined with the fact that its theological basis is the thoroughgoing separation in Western thought between mind and body or humanity and nature, makes it essen-

13. Lynn White, "The Historic Roots of Our Ecologic Crisis," p. 1204.

tial to consider Eastern Orthodoxy's embodiment of the truth of the gospel.

When we turn to a consideration of the theology of the East, we discover that its strength is precisely in the area where Western thought is weakest: in its inclusion of the whole of creation, and not humans only, in redemption. Instead of that general suspicion of creation which dominates Western Christianity, there is a strong affirmation of the goodness of matter, its redeemability, and its dependence upon humans for its access to that divine redemption. In such a view humans are not so much pilgrims, leaving the world behind, as they are priests, lifting it all, through their priestly actions, into a kind of divine life. A contemporary Eastern Orthodox theologian puts it this way:

> The first, the basic definition of man is that he is *the priest*. He stands in the center of the world and unifies it in his act of blessing God, of both receiving the world from God and offering it to God — and by filling the world with this eucharist, he transforms his life, the one that he receives from the world, into life in God, into communion with Him. The world was created as the "matter," the material of one all-embracing eucharist, and man was created as the priest of this cosmic sacrament.[14]

Thus in Eastern thought humans are the agent for the "deification" of nature and the lifting of all of creation up into Godhead. This does not imply consciousless union; rather, it is a development of that idea of humans as "heirs" with Christ, the second Adam of the fully redeemed creation.

Vladimir Lossky, another contemporary Orthodox theologian, confirms this idea of humans as the priests of nature: "In his way to union with God, man in no way leaves creatures aside, but gathers together in his love the whole cosmos disordered by sin, that it may at last be transfigured by grace."[15]

One of the results of this idea — or perhaps one of its causes — is a healthier view of matter than has prevailed throughout much of Western

---

14. Alexander Schmemann, *For the Life of the World* (Crestwood, NY: St. Vladimir Seminary Press, 1973), p. 15.

15. Vladimir Lossky, *The Mystical Theology of the Eastern Church*, trans. members of the Fellowship of St. Alban and St. Sergius (London: James Clarke & Company, 1957), p. 111.

Christendom. Instead of considering matter (and nature in general) a snare to drag down the soul, for example, John of Damascus states its value by linking it with the Incarnation: "I do not venerate matter, but I venerate the creator of matter, who became matter for my sake, who assumed life in the flesh, and who, through matter, accomplished my salvation."[16]

Out of this high view of matter, and out of the idea of humans as the agents for extending redemption to all of creation, there comes an attitude toward creatures much different from that which has often prevailed in the West. St. Isaac the Syrian declares, for example:

> What is a charitable heart? . . . It is a heart which is burning with charity for the whole of creation, for men, for the birds, for the beasts . . . for all creatures. . . . This is why such a man never ceases to pray also for the animals. . . . He will pray even for the reptiles, moved by the infinite pity which reigns in the hearts of those who are becoming united to God.[17]

The purpose of this brief consideration of Eastern Orthodox attitudes toward creation is not to imply that Western Christianity is completely wrong and Eastern Christianity is completely correct. But it does suggest that in Eastern Christianity there has been a fuller development of those scriptural teachings which speak of human responsibility to the rest of creation, and even (in the case of the passage in Romans about the eager longing of creation) of the human role as a kind of mediator for creation, which waits to find its proper head in men and women who are restored to God in Christ.

And yet it is in the West, and especially since the Reformation, that human individuality has reached its fullest development. That individuality is one gift of the gospel, a basis for true personhood, for it is fundamentally as individuals that we stand before our Creator. But as we have seen, that same Western individualism can be terribly destructive of both person and planet when we let our individual identity sever us from our connections with the rest of creation — and with the Creator. It is likely that the dramatic and (from a creational viewpoint) ambivalent development of Western technology is an accompanying feature of this

---

16. John of Damascus, cited in John Meyendorff, *Byzantine Theology: Historical Trends and Doctrinal Themes* (New York: Fordham University Press, 1974), p. 46.

17. St. Isaac the Syrian, cited in Lossky, *The Mystical Theology of the Eastern Church*, p. 111.

individualism — as is the idea that the rest of creation is raw material to be manipulated.

These considerations indicate that in the unfolding of the meaning for creation of the gospel of Incarnation, the church needs both Eastern and Western theology. We need the rich Eastern Orthodox development of the biblical concept of the redemption of all creation through men and women, as they are redeemed through Christ. And we need the Western church's development of radical, but responsible, individuality — an individuality for the purposes of sacrifice and service, for the tending of creation, not its domination. As we have seen in our consideration of Scripture, each of these insights is based in biblical revelation, and each complements the other. Perhaps a fuller understanding of the Incarnation and the cross, in which the Creator shows his Lordship in the form of a servant, points to the way in which the manipulative subjectivity of the West might be directed by the meditative, sacramental, and other-directed *caritas* of the East. At any rate, some such union seems necessary if Christendom is to apply with power the teaching of the gospel on the threefold reconciliation of persons with their Creator, with each other, and with creation itself.

CHAPTER 15

❧   ❧

Stewardship

. . . the rule of no realm is mine, neither of Gondor nor any other, great or small. But all worthy things that are in peril as the world now stands, those are my care. And for my part, I shall not wholly fail of my task, though Gondor should perish, if anything passes through this night that can still grow fair or bear fruit and flower again in days to come. For I also am a steward.

— Gandalf in J. R. R. Tolkien, *The Lord of the Rings*

. . . these same critics of an imperialist Christendom, when they cast about for any good that might have come out of Nazareth, point with uncanny unanimity to the concept of stewardship. Here, they say, is an image of humanity that, if it were pursued with some imagination, could offset the bad effects of a religion that made too much of humankind's superiority to the natural world.

— Douglas John Hall, *The Steward:*
A Biblical Symbol Come of Age

WE HAVE CONCLUDED, BASED ON SCRIPTURE, THAT HUMANS HAVE been given dominion over nature and that they are to use that dominion to serve nature and humanity. Such service is the will of him

307

who charged us with dominion; its purpose is to preserve, enhance, and glorify the creation, and in so doing, to glorify the Creator. In short, we are *stewards* of God, managers of this particular part of his household (to recall the *oikonomos* root of the word "steward").

If stewardship is indeed dominion as service — as the whole Christian gospel suggests — then stewardship (used or misused) is an inescapable condition of human existence. All humans exercise dominion over things and over people. Most often, that dominion is used only to increase their own glory and does not seem like "stewardly" behavior. But the basic question is not *whether* we are stewards; the fact of dominion, and the possibility of using it for service, decides that. The question is *how* we are to exercise our stewardship.

In claiming that humans are stewards appointed by God, we suggest answers to some of the basic questions about what being human means. Some of those questions are these:

- What is the essential nature of the human?
- What is the composition of humans? Are they mind (or soul) and body? Mind only? Body only? Or none of these?
- What tasks (if any) should humans perform?
- Are we responsible for those tasks as individuals, or as part of a community?
- What, finally, is the destiny of humanity?

To call stewardship the exercise of delegated dominion in the service of creation is to say something about human nature and the human task. It is also to imply a good deal about our composition — about what we humans are. But to clarify these implications of calling people stewards, it will be necessary to look in some greater detail at traditional ways of answering such questions about human nature. The result will be a more thorough understanding of what sort of creature God has charged with the care of his creation.

THE NATURE OF THE HUMAN

The question concerning the essential nature of humanity needs to be clarified. It expresses our concern to know what is distinctively human:

what is it that distinguishes humans from all other creatures in the universe? The question also attempts to get at the important distinguishing marks of humanity. To say that humans are furless and featherless bipeds may distinguish them from everything else, but the distinction is trivial and unimportant. We are concerned with the *important* distinctive of humanity.

Perhaps the question can be framed more precisely this way: what characteristic (or characteristics) do *all* humans possess, *only* humans possess, and humans possess *necessarily?* If there are any such characteristics, they would constitute the essential nature of the species. All three parts of the question are important. The first part requires that the characteristic be possessed by everyone. The second requires that the characteristic be possessed by nothing else than humans. The third requires that possession of these characteristics be necessary for being human — that is, when one lacks such a characteristic, one is not human.

Furthermore, all parts of the question are important in conjunction. It may be true that all humans are featherless, furless, and bipedal, to the exclusion of everything else. But our humanity does not depend upon that fact. Had God given us feathers and four feet, while leaving the rest of our makeup the same, we would still be human. To be an *essentially* human trait, the characteristic must meet all the criteria: all humans, and only humans, must have it, and they must have it necessarily.

In discussing the origins of human attitudes about nature, we have already encountered several answers to this question about what makes the human distinct. For Plato and Aristotle, the ability to reason constitutes the human essence; for Descartes, it is sheer consciousness; for Francis Bacon, it is the ability to manipulate the world for human ends. And there are many other theories of human uniqueness we have not considered. Some say humans are symbol-making animals; others, that they are the only creatures able to step outside the deterministic cause-and-effect chain; still others, that they are the only organisms capable of love. Mark Twain said that humans are the only animals that can blush — or that need to. And so on.

Within the last century or so, all of the traditional ideas of human uniqueness have come under attack. Tool-making was once thought to be a uniquely human trait, but chimpanzees make sponges of leaves in order to drink water trapped in inaccessible cracks, and finches have been observed to use a twig to extricate ants from holes. So our uniqueness is not in the ability to use tools. Humans were long thought to be the only beings capable of reason, but many of the great apes, as well as dolphins and killer whales, have solved problems by a process that cannot be distinguished from "rationality." For a while there was excitement over the fact that chimps had been taught not only to recognize words, but to combine them in order to "say" new words. Most of that work has since been called into question: language still seems a distinctive human characteristic. But on the whole, there seems to be little left to distinguish humans from the rest of creation; indeed, recent studies in human psychology have led many to question whether people are significantly free from the push and pull of cause and effect, and to conclude that we are "beyond freedom and dignity."

Because of this rapid erosion at the pedestal of human uniqueness, many today have answered the question "What is the essential nature of the human?" with a simple reply: nothing. The differences between humans and animals, according to this modern view, either are trivial or are differences in degree, not kind. Humans can undoubtedly use tools, symbols, or intelligence *better* than the animals. But they seem to have no capacity that is not shared by at least some animals. Humans have no essential uniqueness.

At this point we should recall from our discussion in chapter 14 Douglas John Hall's recent work *Imaging God*, in which he argues that the "image of God" is not something which men and women *have*, but rather, something which they *do:* that is, to demonstrate the character of God through the exercise of dominion as service. We should also recall the significant paradox arising out of our rapidly growing recognition of how deeply and thoroughly we human beings are embedded in creation. Though we are organisms, connected in complex ways with mineral, vegetable, and animal (indeed, with the whole cosmos), it seems to be *we* who are concerned about the creation, not the creation about us. Though our activity does indeed threaten much of the earth's created diversity, we are the only creature with the knowledge and the ability to be concerned about it. Like it or not, we seem to be the only creature who can exercise stewardship of creation.

To call humans "stewards of God" is to claim implicitly that humans are accountable — that is, *responsible* to God. In giving men and women dominion over the earth, God has made them answerable for the way in which they use that dominion. And, as far as we know, such accountability is unique to humanity.

Being held accountable in this way is no trivial characteristic. For to be accountable to the very Creator of heaven and earth is to be endowed with dignity and honor. The Psalmist expresses this wonder at the high place God has given humans when he exclaims, "Thou hast made him [the human] a little lower than God, and dost crown him with glory and majesty" (Ps. 8:5, NASB). And in the same psalm, that place of honor is explicitly linked with human dominion over nature:

> Thou hast given him dominion over the works of thy hands;
>   thou hast put all things under his feet,
> all sheep and oxen,
>   and also the beasts of the field,
> the birds of the air, and the fish of the sea,
>   whatever passes along the paths of the sea.
>
> (Ps. 8:6-8)

But (as we discussed in the previous chapter) the Christian's exemplar of this dominion is Christ. Though God has given him "the name which is above every name" (Phil. 2:9), his greatest glory is in "taking the form of a servant" (v. 7); Christ's Lordship is most clearly exemplified in his stewardship. And in addition to our receiving a similar kind of dignity and honor, it is a similar kind of lordship and stewardship for which we are accountable to the Lord of the universe. This accountability is the distinctive of our dominion — and our humanity.

We are accountable, of course, not only for the way in which we exercise our dominion, but also for a variety of other tasks: to love and cherish others, to seek justice, to develop our own abilities, and so on. Accountability permeates our existence.

To be declared accountable by the Creator implies, furthermore, that God has given humanity what it needs for actually *being* accountable. We need rationality for the planning, imagining, and knowing necessary to exercise dominion, love, and justice. Likewise we need the ability to manipulate the natural world, and we also need to be able to act freely and independently of causes working upon us, for one cannot be held accountable for that which one does not do freely. Finally, we need the human symbol-making capacity — and the language, the mathematics, and the art which come from it — if we are to know, name, and celebrate creation successfully. Thus, much of what seems to be distinctly human is actually God-given capability for being accountable — for stewardship.

THE COMPOSITION OF THE HUMAN

Thus far we have been dealing with the essential nature of humanity — what it *is*. And we have determined that, as far as stewardship is concerned, the human distinctive is *accountability* to the Creator. We have now to consider what sort of creature it is who is thus accountable to the Creator. For, as we shall see, different theories about how we are composed can produce very different theories about how we are to act toward creation. Is there, then, a clearly Christian teaching on the composition of the human?

It is difficult to discuss human "composition" with much precision. For the very language of the question, "What is the composition of the human?" betrays traces of a time-honored, but troubling, premise of the question, namely, that humans are composed of parts, or aspects. In different discussions and times the two main parts have had different names. But most often the division has been made in this way: on the one hand is that part of humans which is clearly like the rest of nature — the material component, body, flesh; on the other hand is that part which seems unlike anything in nature — the mind, or soul, or spirit. And, without exception and whatever terms are used, it is the spiritual, mental, "un-natural" part which is considered to be of primary importance, while the material, bodily, "natural" part is considered to be of secondary and derivative value.

Perhaps we can better see the importance of the question by returning to the views of Plato and Aristotle, whose contrasting visions of what it means to be human continue to exert an enormous influence on our way of regarding ourselves and the world. As we have noted before, Plato believed that the essential nature of the human was rationality. This rationality, however, is not a characteristic of anything in the shifting, mutable, and imperfect world of nature. Rather, says Plato, it resides in a unique sort of entity, the soul. Essentially, humans are souls. To be sure, for an unfortunate part of their existence humans are embodied (or *en-natured*) souls: that is, their souls are joined, in an uneasy union, with something within nature — a human body. It is to the soul that the body owes its life; it is the body which keeps the soul from fully realizing its rationality. For rationality is a characteristic only of the soul, not of the body.

This Platonic view of human composition has, of course, been profoundly influential in the history of Western thought. In some Christian circles it has even been accepted as the straightforward teaching of

Scripture. Descartes' view of the human as "the ghost in the machine" is only one example of this.

Aristotle's understanding of the relation of soul to body was quite different, and his ideas will help us understand better the composition of human beings. As we have seen, Aristotle thought of humans not as separate from nature, but as a part of it. He agreed with Plato that rationality was the essential part of human nature. But, in contrast to Plato (who believed that rationality was imposed from a transcendent realm onto a recalcitrant physical body), Aristotle understood rationality to be the distinguishing and "natural" characteristic of one sort of thing within nature — namely, the human. Humans are things within nature with a special capacity, not things from outside of nature saddled with an alien body. Rationality is uniquely human, but the rationality is rooted within nature, not imposed from without.

One way to bring the difference between Plato and Aristotle into sharp relief is to ask this question: "Can one exist apart from one's body?" For Plato, the answer is a relieved "yes." For Aristotle, the answer is flatly "no." For Plato, humans are not a part of nature, and hence are not fundamentally joined to their bodies. For Aristotle, humans are a part of nature, and hence are inseparable from their bodies.

And how does the Christian answer this question? What do the Scriptures say about the composition of humans, these creatures who have been given dominion, yet are accountable before their Lord? The Scriptures speak of humans in a multitude of ways, implying a variety of ideas about their makeup. Consider just a few:

> You shall love the Lord your God with all your heart, and with all your soul, and with all your mind. (Matt. 22:37)

> For the word of God is living and active, sharper than any two-edged sword, piercing to the division of soul and spirit, of joints and marrow, and discerning the thoughts and intentions of the heart. (Heb. 4:12)

> . . . do not be anxious about your life, what you shall eat, nor about your body, what you shall put on. (Luke 12:22)

Here, in three passages, are found six names for humans or aspects of them: "heart," "soul," "mind," "spirit," "body," and "life." Other passages use yet other terms to speak of humans: "flesh," "conscience," "innermost part," and "reins."

One approach to this plethora of components is the Platonic and Cartesian approach — understanding these names as descriptions of distinct parts of humans, then choosing one of them as the "truly" human, and determining the relationship between this "truly" human part and the other parts. Thus Descartes decided that the "truly" human part is the mind, and he speculated on its relationship with the body through the pineal gland. But as G. C. Berkouwer has convincingly argued in *Man: The Image of God*, the biblical writers did not use these terms to designate distinct parts of humans, nor did they intend any sort of Platonic mind-body dualism. Rather, the writers focused on *the whole person*, calling attention through these terms to a variety of characteristics possessed by that wholeness.[1]

Of course, the fact that the biblical writers did not, for example, use the term "soul" *(psyche)* to designate the "true" human does not necessarily mean that humans cannot exist apart from their bodies. The biblical writers had no intention of presenting a philosophical anthropology — an abstract, technical discussion of human composition. They were concerned with more important things, and they speak the language of everyday life. Says Berkouwer:

> The general judgment of theologians has been that the Bible gives us no scientific teaching on man, no anthropology, which should or could concur with scientific anthropological research on man in the many aspects of his existence or with philosophic anthropology.[2]

The Bible is not a handbook of either science or philosophy.

In distinction from this Platonic attempt to choose one part of humans and subordinate the rest to it, there is another approach to the multitude of biblical terms for the composition of humans — one which agrees better with the biblical writers' emphasis on the whole person, thus paralleling Aristotle's approach. In this view, one's "body," one's "mind," and one's "soul" all designate only one whole person, but they all call attention to different functions and characteristics of that person. Thus to speak of the "body" of a person is to speak about humans insofar as they have physical, chemical, and biotic characteristics. To speak about the

---

1. G. C. Berkouwer, *Man: The Image of God,* trans. Dirk W. Jellema (Grand Rapids: Eerdmans, 1962), chap. 6.

2. Ibid., p. 194. On the human relationship to God and the human task, see also Edwin D. Roels, *God's Mission* (Grand Rapids: Eerdmans, 1962).

"mind" of a person is to speak of humans in their psychical, rational, language-using capacities. And to speak of the "soul" of a person is to refer to human aesthetic, moral, and religious capacities.

We may also think of these characteristics of the human as together forming a unity. In order for a person to have aesthetic, moral, and religious capacities, the person must also have psychical, rational, and language-using capacities, and having these qualities of "mind" depends upon possession of physical, chemical, and biological characteristics. Put another way, being a soul depends upon being a mind, and being a mind depends upon being a body. The person *is* body, mind, and soul. But this is not to say (as a Platonist would) that the human is a collection of separate entities, only one of which is the "truly" human. Rather, the human is a unity displaying a remarkable variety of interdependent characteristics.

The implications of such a view for the human relationship to the rest of the created world are profound. For, if it is correct, we see that the human is embedded in the life of the earth, and shares characteristics with stones, trees, fish, and dogs. But humans also transcend earth: they have capacities which everything else lacks. Humans are fully dust, and fully soul; they are soulish dust.

The Christian, however, must raise one powerful objection to the integrity and unity of humans which this view attempts to capture: such an understanding implies that persons cannot exist apart from their bodies. Yet it seems to be the clear teaching of the New Testament that those who have died, and whose bodies decay, nevertheless continue to exist until the day of resurrection, when they will be clothed with "spiritual bodies." Thus this portrayal of mind and soul as dependent upon the body would seem to be incorrect.

Yet something of the basic unity of body, mind, and soul must be preserved. Scripture is also clear that humans were *meant* to have a body, meant to be a part of the physical world of creation. To allow some sort of interim existence apart from the body (and thus apart from "nature") does not eliminate the idea that there is an intimate connection between humanity and nature. Nor does it suggest, as the Platonists did, any devaluation of the human body or of nature in general. The Christian's hope, therefore, is not for disembodied existence, but for bodily existence on the day of resurrection and in the unimaginable hereafter. We *are* bodies: we were made for the earth.

We were made for "heaven" too. We don't know much about heaven. But while our difficulty in giving a meaning to the word should not mean that we abandon it as a piece of outworn mythology (as the secularizing pressures of our day prompt even Christians to do), neither should our ignorance of heaven make us think that it involves a repudiation of our bodily, earthly existence. Somehow we need to learn to live on earth and in the hope of heaven without either making heaven just another name for earth or assuming that all of physical existence (whether we speak of the biosphere or of our body) is unimportant. In the words of Gerard Manley Hopkins, "Man's spirit will be flesh-bound when found at best."[3]

The rest of creation is not something alien to us: we bear a most intimate relationship to it, and it is good. It is the same creation which God made, sustains, and is making new in Christ. It is the creation which waits in eager anticipation of our proper stewardship of it.

THE HUMAN TASK

Accountability to God and embeddedness in nature make the human perfectly constituted to carry out the task of stewardship. In the course of talking about the sort of creature who is called to be a steward, we have already implied a good deal about the *task* of stewardship. Let us now consider that task explicitly.

First of all, the task of stewardship is a *general* task. It is ours simply because of our humanity, and it overarches our entire life. Unlike our more specific tasks and obligations, it does not arise from any particular circumstance in which we find ourselves. The specific task of providing for children, for example, normally arises from the particular circumstances of being a parent. Those who are not parents do not normally have that task. This is not the case with stewardship: we are called to that task whatever our life situation might be.

Stewardship is a general task in another sense as well: it is *contextual* — that is, it forms the context within which more specific obligations are understood and the horizon within which they are performed and given meaning. The general task of stewardship, for example, gives rise to the more specific obligation not to mistreat animals or let cropland erode. Thus stewardship is, in a sense, a general axiom from which more specific

---

3. Gerard Manley Hopkins, "The Caged Skylark," in *A Hopkins Reader*, ed. John Pick (New York/London: Oxford University Press, 1953), p. 15.

principles, relating to the situations we encounter in day-to-day life, can be drawn. (We will consider some of these more specific principles in Section IV of this book.)

Our concentration on stewardship may have given the impression that it is our *only* general task. This is not the case. Clearly, we also have the task of love, *agape*. We are to love our Creator and our fellow creatures. In addition, we have the task of doing and seeking justice. These tasks are also general tasks; they too are a part of our humanity. They overarch our lives and form the context within which more specific tasks are carried out. Sometimes we are tempted to set these tasks against each other, as when the need for love and justice to fellow humans seems to require doing irreparable harm to the earth in order to provide them food, clothing, and general well-being. But we need to resist such false tensions among our human tasks. For over even these general tasks is the primary task which defines our nature: we are here to image God. True stewardship does not violate our need to live out God's love and God's justice.

Before we attempt to clarify the meaning of the task of stewardship, let us recall three points already discussed. First, our authority over the earth is derived from its Creator and Sustainer: *our dominion is a delegated dominion.* Second, our use and keeping of the earth must be of service to God, to our fellow humans, and to the earth itself: *the steward is a servant.* Third, as stewards we are responsible to God for the way in which we treat the earth and for the ends we choose in using it: *the steward is accountable.*

Another feature of stewardship, closely related to the fact that our dominion is a delegated dominion, is that God is *owner of all.* As stewards, we are not the owners of that over which we have authority. Thus our authority is more characteristic of a trustee than an owner: the use and care of nature is entrusted to us, but the Creator retains ownership. This is the clear and repeated testimony of the Scriptures. Over and over again the Old Testament writers record divine declarations of ownership: "all the earth is mine" (Exod. 19:5) or "the land is mine" (Lev. 25:23). A psalm of David declares, "The earth is the Lord's and all it contains, the world and those who dwell in it" (Ps. 24:1, NASB). And a prayer of David makes it plain that any dominion humans have is a delegated dominion:

> Thine, O Lord, is the greatness and the power and the glory and the victory and the majesty, indeed, everything that is in the heavens and the earth; Thine is the dominion, O Lord, and Thou dost exalt Thyself as head over all. (1 Chron. 29:11, NASB)

Nor are such affirmations of God's ownership of all things limited to the Old Testament; in the New, all wealth, gifts, and even our own bodies are understood as gifts from God, the owner of all things. In 1 Corinthians, Paul declares, "Do you not know that your body is a temple of the Holy Spirit within you, which you have from God? You are not your own" (1 Cor. 6:19). And in John's Revelation, all dominion is declared to belong to Christ, whose sacrifice provides our own great example of dominion:

> Worthy is the Lamb that was slain to receive power and riches and wisdom and might and honor and glory and blessing. . . . To Him who sits on the throne, and to the Lamb, be blessing and honor and glory and dominion forever and ever. (Rev. 5:12-13, NASB)

This repeated biblical reminder that the earth is the Lord's is the reason why we must be very cautious in our approval of any economic system which regards human property — and freedom to use it in any way the owner sees fit — as absolute. The fact of our stewardship does mean that individuals and communities may appropriately exercise tremendous power over parts of nonhuman creation. But ultimately it is God who says "mine" of all things, not us: not any human person, corporation, or government. Our use of creation should never overlook the ultimacy of God's ownership. And our stewardly task to *keep* the earth will often curtail what we might do if, indeed, our ownership were absolute.

If God is owner of all and human dominion is clearly delegated, then it is also clear that the steward is both a servant and a *manager*. The Greek term for steward, as we discussed earlier, is *oikonomos,* manager of the household. Thus God's steward over nature is to be a manager of the earth's household: rock, water, air, tree, bird, and beast, in the infinite complexity of their interrelationships. This human management or stewardship must be directed to benefit the household of the earth and the creatures who depend on it for life, health, and fulfillment. Thus the manager of the earth, even in the most ideal conditions, is often called upon to balance conflicting needs. For the richness of nature is given, in part, to provide for the human necessities of food, clothing, shelter, health, delight, work, and joy. But that richness is also there to fulfill similar needs for nonhuman creatures: food, shelter, health, procreation, delight — and perhaps other needs we have not yet learned about. The stewards of nature must balance these needs, establish priorities, smooth out conflict. In short, they must *manage* for the welfare of the creation and the glory of God.

The earth's managers must also balance present needs with future ones — the needs of present humans and nonhumans with the needs of future humans and nonhumans. Since we don't know much about the shape of the future, this obligation to future creatures implies a cautious and conservative use of our powers. We dare not interfere irrevocably with the well-being of the biosphere — or even individual ecosystems — in the hope that we will come up with something better in the future. It is appropriate that we shape creation into cultural worlds. But the goal of such worldmaking should be earthkeeping. So the steward should use creation sparingly, sharingly, and caringly.

In order to manage correctly — with all the intricate decisions required by such managing — the stewards must have "ecological knowledge." As we noted earlier, the same Greek word which has given us "steward" and "economic" has also given us "ecology." A century ago the German biologist Ernst Haeckel defined *ecology* as:

> the knowledge of the sum of the relations of organisms to the surrounding outer world, to organic and inorganic conditions of existence; the so-called "economy of nature," the correlations between all organisms living together in one and the same locality, their adaptation to their surroundings, their modification in the struggle for existence, especially the circumstances of parasitism, etc.[4]

As stewards, we should have such a rudimentary knowledge of ecology. We cannot adequately "manage the household" without knowing something about that great household of life which we are to manage. In order to manage and to balance (or maintain a balance), we must become acquainted with at least the general features of the interrelationships of God's living creatures and of their relationship with the inorganic. Otherwise, we shall be ignorant of the effects on creation of our own use of it, and we will not be able to act responsibly in the sustaining, renewing, and preserving of the rich diversity of that creation.

Finally, as stewards we are not hedged in on every side by exact rules concerning the proper use of nature. God has not given us a hand-

---

4. Ernst Haeckel, cited in John Black, *The Dominion of Man* (Edinburgh: University Press, 1970), p. 2.

book for deciding precisely how we are to manage, how to balance, how to set priorities; rather, he has set general guidelines, and within those guidelines he holds us responsible for our decisions. Stewards have a *range of freedom* in their managing. Different stewards might make different decisions, but, as long as the goal is the care of the whole household, both decisions might be correct. The freedom given us as stewards of creation is suggested in the description of Adam's naming the animals: not only does such naming require deep knowledge, but God "waits to see" what the naming will be. It is like this with our managing. As long as we draw our principles for management from the Creator and his creation, we are given the freedom to be co-creators with God, sons and daughters of him in whom all things consist.

SHARED STEWARDSHIP

We have spoken thus far as though stewardship were only an individual matter. But it is not the case, of course, that each person is delegated to be responsible for *all* of creation. It is often to humanity corporately that God has given stewardly responsibility. We have divided among ourselves that responsibility, and thus we have limited the scope of any one person's actual exercise of stewardship.

To divide our stewardly responsibility in this way is, in many cases, right and proper. Just as, for example, some portions of nature were given to Abraham and others to Lot, so too some responsibility is given to us and some to others. Of course, the actual divisions that have taken place historically may not have expressed the will of God; some people may have received too much, others too little, still others the wrong sorts of things. But there is nothing intrinsically wrong in dividing stewardship possibilities.

The Scriptures certainly condone private property — and private property implies a division of stewardship. In forbidding stealing and coveting, for example, the eighth and tenth commandments imply rights of ownership. Even in the early Jerusalem church, which Luke characterizes as possessing "everything in common," Christians apparently held some private property. As Ron Sider points out, the fact that Christians are described in Acts 2 and 4 as periodically selling their possessions in order to help each other suggests that they did divide stewardship possibilities among them.[5] Clearly, then, division of stewardship among people is not wrong according to the Bible.

And yet, since our stewardship possibilities are given by God, clear directives in Scripture show that private ownership is to be exercised for the benefit of the whole community. In the formation of the nation of Israel, limitations on acquisition and use of the land were embodied in divine legislation. The Law of Jubilee required that after a certain length of time the land be redistributed among families. The laws of the Sabbath, the tithe, and gleaning required that a portion of the harvest be left for the poor, the sojourner, the fatherless, and the widow.

These divine directives concerning the acquisition and use of private property in early Israel show God's concern that our stewardship profit not only ourselves, but our neighbor and the land itself as well. Of course, such directives were issued to an agrarian people and are not always applicable to our industrialized societies. The fact is, though, that we are quite accustomed to having ordinances limit what property we may acquire and how we are to use it; the exercise of our stewardship is restricted by government. Cities, townships, counties, and other governmental units severely limit what we may do on and with our houses and the land they occupy, our farms and the fields they contain. We are used to submitting to such limitations on our ownership. And we ought to let all our understanding of ownership — by individuals or groups — be guided as well by the fact that the real owner is God and that we are stewards.

We said at the outset that opportunities for stewardship are divided among *people*. Left unqualified, that is misleading. To be sure, one important type of division is that which occurs among individuals (or families). The division into things which are "mine" and "yours" is only one sort of division, however. We must consider other sorts of division and the challenges of stewardship which they entail.

Often stewardship is exercised by entities other than individual persons or families. Consider just a few: governments are stewards of roadways, parks, forest lands, waterways, wilderness areas, buildings, and so forth; corporations, businesses, and banks exercise stewardship over lands of various sorts, raw materials, manufacturing plants, distribution centers, and the like; institutions such as churches and denominations, private schools, and service clubs are stewards of lands and buildings. All

---

5. Ronald Sider, *Rich Christians in an Age of Hunger* (Downers Grove, IL: Inter-Varsity Press, 1977), pp. 98-103.

of these are in a position to exercise stewardship over nature, and the portion of nature over which they are stewards is vast.

But individuals are not unrelated to these entities. We are citizens of political units in which governments act, and in most nations we are (theoretically) the authority behind those governments. We are often stockholders in corporations or partners in a business. We are members of churches and denominations, of associations which control private schools, or of service clubs. And some of us are in direct positions of authority: besides being citizens, some hold political office; besides being members of a church, some are ruling elders. Individuals are related to these stewardship-exercising entities in a variety of ways, and some of us are more directly connected with these entities than others.

The fact is, however, that in many of the entities mentioned above, no one individual (or even small group of individuals) exercises stewardship — no one person is directly responsible for the actions of the entity. Take, for example, the actions of governments such as those of North America. Decisions are made by a *body* of people — the legislature. But no individual is directly responsible for the decisions; the body as a whole — and, to a more limited degree, the citizens who, as a body, elect that legislating body — are responsible.

In instances when entities other than individuals exercise stewardship over nature — and our influence as individuals on the decision-making bodies of these entities can vary from being quite strong to very weak — our stewardship is always less than fully direct and is shared with others.

But what is our individual duty toward these entities and their decision-making bodies? Given that we are called to be stewards, our task of stewardship with respect to the actions of these entities involves at least the following: if we are part of a group — whether a church, a business, or a government — which allows us a degree of influence upon its decisions (perhaps we should seek influence if we do not yet have it), we must use that influence in order to make the entities' decisions and actions conform to the norms of stewardship. Clearly, the politician bears greater responsibility for the actions of government than the private citizen; the member of the board of trustees more than the association member; the chairman of the board more than the stockholder. But all have some degree of responsibility.

So far we have discussed the division of humankind's shared stewardship over creation. With respect to some parts of creation, however, we have not seen fit to make a division. Consider the air we breathe, the oceans — their fish and their mineral deposits — the navigable rivers, and the like. In an important sense, these have remained "ours together." They do not belong to any individual; neither do they belong to a government or any other human institution. They are a common heritage. They are, as we discussed earlier, the "commons."

The trouble is that these "commons" — at least a large number of them — face despoiling, if they are not already spoiled. Perhaps, therefore, the call to stewardship of the "commons" translates into a call to establish appropriate governing bodies, capable of restricting the use of the commons in ways which nevertheless respect everyone's right to them. If so, the efforts at various levels of government to establish and enforce reasonable pollution levels should be encouraged. And likewise, we should support international efforts to establish and enforce standards for proper use of the ocean, as well as just standards for the exploitation of its common resources, such as fish and minerals. This kind of encouragement and approval, manifested in our political lives, may be what stewardship demands of the individual today. Or perhaps the days of the commons should be over. To remove areas from the commons is not to strike out in totally unexplored areas; we have models for change. The national, state, and county parks and forests are "ours together," but the use of them is severely restricted.

In this discussion we have not aimed at solving the complicated problems surrounding shared stewardship — divided or not. Rather, we have attempted to promote an awareness both of the complexities which divisions of stewardship introduce and of the varying degrees and types of stewardship responsibilities which these divisions create. Translation of the overarching task of stewardship into concrete tasks must take into account these realities of *shared* stewardship. For it is clear that we exercise stewardship over nature not only as individuals but also as members of various groups to which are entrusted the care of vast quantities of the earth's resources.

THE DESTINY OF NATURE AND HUMANITY

The Old Testament writers spoke repeatedly of a time when peace, *shalom*, would reign again as in Eden. Once and for all, the awful alienation between God and humanity, between fellow human beings, and between humanity and the rest of creation would be healed; no longer would dominion be understood as tyranny. In the place of hostility would come harmony; in the place of enmity, tranquility.

The Old Testament writers saw, however dimly, that the Lord would usher in the reign of *shalom* through the Anointed One, the Christ, the Prince of Peace:

> For to us a child is born,
>   to us a son is given;
> and the government will be upon his shoulder,
>   and his name will be called
> "Wonderful Counselor, Mighty God,
>   Everlasting Father, Prince of Peace."
> Of the increase of his government and of peace
>   there will be no end,
> upon the throne of David, and over his kingdom,
>   to establish it, and to uphold it
> with justice and with righteousness
>   from this time forth and for evermore.
> The zeal of the LORD of hosts will do this.
>
> (Isa. 9:6-7)

The zeal of the Lord will bring *shalom* — and not only to humanity, but to humanity living in nature:

> The wolf shall dwell with the lamb,
>   and the leopard shall lie down with the kid,
> and the calf and the lion and the fatling together,
>   and a little child shall lead them.
> The cow and the bear shall feed;
>   their young shall lie down together;
>   and the lion shall eat straw like the ox.
> The sucking child shall play over the hole of the asp,
>   and the weaned child shall put his hand on the adder's den.
> They shall not hurt or destroy
>   in all my holy mountain;
> for the earth shall be full of the knowledge of the LORD
>   as the waters cover the sea.
>
> (Isa. 11:6-9)

The prophet's vision is one of harmony between humanity and the rest of creation, not of enmity between them, nor of a creation forced cruelly into doing human tasks. It is important to note that these apocalyptic visions do not diminish the diversity of creation, nor do they speak of it as something to be destroyed. The evil is not in the cobra, the viper, or the lion; rather, it is in the alienation between those things and human beings — and between those things and other nonhuman creatures. In fact, this glimpse of a future peace for the earth is nothing less than a restoration of the peace of the Sabbath, that tremendous vision of the harmony of a creation resting with and in its Creator.

The New Testament writers proclaim Jesus of Nazareth as the Prince of that once and future Peace. Jesus does so himself in the Nazareth synagogue when he reads from Isaiah 61 about the good news, freedom, and healing which would come in "the year of the Lord's favor," concluding: "Today this Scripture is fulfilled in your hearing" (Luke 4:16-21, NIV). It is he who is calling the world to himself, redeeming it to himself. And it is he who calls us to partnership in his glorious work: "The creation waits with eager longing for the revealing of the sons of God" (Rom. 8:19).

His kingdom of peace shall come. The king has already come and is reigning. In Galilee he has already shown his power over water, wind, plant, beast — and over death itself. He reigns, and his peace shall reign with him: "The zeal of the LORD of hosts will do this."

Throughout the Scriptures, the visions of the kingdom of God are visions of men and women in harmony with creation — men and women as stewards. We need to recover this central biblical concept. As Douglas John Hall puts it:

> It is no wonder that an increasing number of ecologists and others, many of whom have no personal relation to the Christian faith, find in this Judaeo-Christian symbol one of the most profound metaphors of what is best in the Western world. . . . Our first responsibility as Christian stewards today may be to become better stewards of the stewardship idea itself![6]

---

6. Douglas John Hall, *The Steward: A Biblical Symbol Come of Age* (New York: Friendship Press, 1982).

CHAPTER 16

❧   ❧

Inheriting the Land:
Creation and Justice

You shall not pervert justice. . . . Justice, and only justice, you shall follow, that you may live and inherit the land which the LORD *your God gives you.*

— Deuteronomy 16:19-20

The earth is one but the world is not.

— *Our Common Future*

You are the salt of the earth. . . . You are the light of the world.

— Matthew 5:13-14

THE CREATOR HAS MADE US STEWARDS OF AN EARTH IN WHICH LIFE proceeds through the use of things. A tree "uses" light, air, soil, and water; a fox "uses" rabbits; a person "uses" food for her dinner or fuel for her car; a nation "uses" the minerals that lie beneath its soil. Such use proceeds in the nonhuman earth, and we call it neither just nor unjust. But in the human world, our use of creation raises questions of justice. We are not just users of the earth; we are stewards, called to use creation

326

responsibly for each other, for the Creator, and for creation itself. Thus we cannot speak of stewardship without speaking of justice.

Doing justice in and for creation is no simple matter. For unlike the animals, we are sinners — hence we use far more than we need. And we have the power (at least some of us do) to meet endlessly not just our needs but also our wants. Thus we set up patterns of using creation which deny stewardship of it to other people and which steadily diminish the diversity and richness of creation itself.

We are concerned in this chapter with the fair sharing of the creation entrusted to us. Who should use how much of what? Who "owns" what? How, in short, may the goods of creation be justly used?

Consider some of the places where our stewardship of creation raises questions of justice.

- A growing population in regions of Africa — with its cattle, goats, and need for firewood — has deforested and then turned to desert a larger and larger area. Climate shifts and political unrest further erode the base by which people subsist, and a drought pushes the whole country over the edge into starvation: millions are dying. The voice of justice and compassion dictates the sending of food. But another voice says: "No. It's a biological fact that populations overrun their carrying capacity and starve. Stern justice dictates that we only give aid to people who are controlling their population." "No," says another voice. "With our resources we support not just food, but a high-meat diet, cars, weapons, and luxury. It is just to forgo that to keep people alive."

- In a community in the Northwest where logging is the main employment, environmentalists make a case that the one remaining valley of virgin forest should be left in its wild state. "Future generations have a right to see something of the original forests," they argue. "And the valley itself (Douglas fir, spotted owls, even the soil) has a right to remain in its undegraded state. It is a matter of justice."

  "Spotted owls!" reply the loggers. "What about people? What about our jobs, our families, our community? We have a right to employment, and people have a right to use wood in their houses. It is unjust *not* to use the forests, to let usable timber rot into the soil."

"It's great! You just tell him how much pollution your
company is responsible for and he tells you how many
trees you have to plant to atone for it."

- In a community in the Southwest where urban population has grown far beyond the meager water supply, planners and developers face the melancholy fact that though many people want to move to the area, all wells and rivers have been used up. Hundreds of miles to the north, cold rivers flow into the sea in unused abundance. So the south says: "You're not using the water; it's going to waste. If we can figure out a way to get it down here it's only just that you sell your water to us." And the north replies: "Just! The water belongs here; to transport it might do great environmental damage. It's a matter of justice that you learn to live within your limits."

- In a community in Central America a large company grows bananas on fertile flatlands. Many local people work on the land for wages with which they buy food at the company store; others are forced to grow their food on steep, unproductive land that deteriorates rapidly when they farm it. So a group of landless families gets weapons together and takes a part of the farmland. "It's unjust for a few rich absentee owners to make money from the land while we who live here starve," they say. "But we own it!" the landowners say. "It's unjust for you to steal it from us."

- A South American country is crippled by interest payments to richer nations who have loaned it money for development. To pay its bills it logs its rain forest and brings new lands into cultivation. "It's unjust — to the future, to the forest itself — to destroy the rain forest," say the richer nations. "Pay your debts some other way."

  "No!" says the debtor nation. "You got rich by using your resources. It's only just to allow us at least to survive by using ours."

  "Then stop destroying the rain forest and we'll cancel some of the debt."

  "No!" says a neighboring nation with just as much debt, but no rain forest to hold hostage. "Our people are being destroyed by the debt. Aren't they as valuable as trees and birds? It's only just that you cancel our debt too."

None of these is a hypothetical example, and the list could go on and on. Our use of creation raises enormous questions of justice.

Some of these are ancient questions. Is it just for the propertied rich to prosper while the landless poor languish and starve? But even this old problem is given new force by the complexity of our economic and technological interrelationships. Is my comfort related (however distantly) to the discomfort of someone half a world away? If so (given the complexity of the systems by which we use and transfer the goods of creation), what do I do about it?

Old problems are also given new force by modern communications media. We can no longer distance ourselves from evidence of suffering and injustice. Human starvation is nothing new. But pictures of starving children brought into our homes while we're eating dinner give us a discomforting new perspective on starvation.

Other questions about the justice of our use of creation are new not merely in perspective but in kind, giving rise to a new word: "ecojustice." Many of these are gathered under the term "sustainability." As the opening chapters of this book make clear, we are gaining today a vivid sense of the planet's limits, of the natural and biological systems which sustain its life, and of the ways in which human activities degrade those systems. Thus we are beginning to ask questions such as: "Is it just to use resources now (oil is a good example) so that future generations will have none? Is it just to farm or log in such a way that good returns today mean a degraded and unproductive land in the future?"

So far these have all been human-centered questions. However, our growing sense of connectedness to the other creatures in creation has given rise to a new type of justice question which challenges that human center. When we use animals for food, or destroy forest ecosystems for wood — all for solely human use — are we not guilty of "speciesism"? "Speciesism" (another new word) says that human beings are merely one more part of the web of life, with no greater rights than bears, trees, or rocks. When we make slaves of other living things (chickens, cows, redwood trees) and force their life to serve our purpose, we are (so this argument goes) as guilty of "speciesism" as other people have been guilty of racism by making fellow humans slaves. Ecojustice demands that we right such wrongs. An influential "animal rights" movement is the most vocal evidence of this dimension of the new ecojustice.

How should Christians respond to these issues? Obviously we cannot answer every difficult question in advance. But we can set forth some biblically informed principles. And here a biblical perspective makes our task more complicated, for the biblical understanding of justice is much richer and harder to categorize than modern, more specialized concepts of justice. We prefer to speak today of segments of justice: *commercial* justice (which involves faithfulness to agreements), or *retributive* justice (which deals with the punishment of those who have violated laws), or *procedural* justice (which deals with the fair application of rules, principles, or policies). In this specialized way of thinking it is only *distributive* justice which touches on questions of stewardship. Such an approach to justice descends to us from Greek and Roman legal thought and is concerned with precise distinctions, rights, and requirements. Our understanding of "property rights," for example, in which owners have complete jurisdiction over what they "own," is informed by this Latin legal tradition. Likewise we have tended to shrink the biblical doctrine of "justification" to something which can be fully explained in legal categories. (As we mentioned in chapter 14, an understanding of justification which includes restoration, making whole, is more biblical and provides a better basis for speaking of salvation for all of creation.)

The biblical view of justice is much more spacious than this merely legal understanding. Its concern is not so much with precisely defined rights and obligations as it is with an overall picture of righteousness and peace. Our tendency has been to simplify the two main Hebrew words for justice, *tzedek* and *mishpat,* making *tzedek* mean "righteousness" (in a private, individual sense) and *mishpat* mean "judgment" in a legal sense. But such a distinction is misleading: justice and righteousness both refer to an inner goodness *and* to outer behavior; further, both include a sense of total health and rightness extending beyond the individual, beyond society, and into creation as a whole. They are "wholistic" terms. This word has become trendy, but nevertheless "wholistic" (or simply "whole") is the right word, for in its roots it is related to both "health" and "holiness." Thus the biblical concept of justice already approaches "eco-justice," for it is concerned with overall health, not mere defining of rights. We will return to this inclusive Hebrew understanding of justice shortly. But first we need to consider how the narrower concept of distributive justice has been applied to our stewardship of creation.

PRINCIPLES OF DISTRIBUTIVE JUSTICE

"To each his [or her] due" is perhaps the oldest simple formulation (at least in Western history) of the principle of distributive justice. It expresses a fundamental ideal of fairness. Aristotle articulated it this way: parties which are alike ought to be treated alike, and those which are different

ought to be treated differently, and in proportion to their relevant differences. This is helpful in principle, but it is such a high-level generalization
that it has always been necessary to spell it out in particular cultural
situations. Two fundamental problems recur: (1) what do we include in
the term "each" — that is, which things are "considerable"? and (2) how
will we determine what is "due" to morally considerable entities — what
is a just distribution?

What Things Are "Considerable"?

"Moral considerability" has become a major technical term in the new
discipline of environmental ethics. Not that the issue is completely new.
For example, there have been many times and places where some men and
women — slaves — would have been excluded from the "each" referred
to. In today's world this deliberate exclusion of some of humanity from
moral considerability is less likely, but there is still plenty of discrimination
in the actual outworking of distributions. We have all witnessed the sad
fact that some "eaches" are not as equal as others.

Another problem in "considerability" deals with future human
generations. Do they count in a distribution, such that it is unjust to fail
to render them their due (perhaps by consuming less now, or reserving
some parts of creation for their exclusive use)? This is a particularly crucial
problem when we consider current use of "non-renewable" resources. Until
we became (in the last generation or two) clearly aware of absolute limits
to many things which now seem essential to us (minerals and fuels are
prime examples), this was not much of an issue. It has been focused by
the unprecedented (and unsustainable) use of creation's goods in this
century. It has been focused as well by the deterioration which we have
brought about during this century in the planet's life-support systems: soil,
water, air, and the diversity of living things. It seems likely that our
great-grandchildren will suffer from such a degraded creation, and there
is growing concensus that our current practices are not just with regard
to the future.

But a third problem in "considerability" has to do with nonhuman
creation. Do nonhuman entities figure in the justice of a distribution? Are
animals due anything? How about plants or the Rocky Mountains or the
Pacific Ocean? Are these morally considerable entities?

A great deal of thought has gone into this question in the past couple of decades. In 1972 Christopher Stone, a California law professor, published an essay called "Do Trees Have Standing?" It had the significant subtitle "Toward Legal Rights for Natural Objects," and it made a substantial case for the "moral considerability" (and the right to be represented in court) of "trees, mountains, rivers and lakes." In his preface to the 1974 book form of that essay, Garrett Hardin stressed the need for a broadening of ethics, citing Aldo Leopold's observation at the beginning of his seminal essay "The Land Ethic":

> When god-like Odysseus returned from the wars in Troy, he hanged all on one rope a dozen slave girls of his household whom he suspected of misbehaviour during his absence. The girls were property. The disposal of property was then, as now, a matter of expediency, not of right and wrong. . . . There is as yet no ethic dealing with man's relation to land and to the animals and plants which grow upon it. Land, like Odysseus' slave girls, is still property. The land-relation is still strictly economic, entailing privileges but not obligations.

What Leopold is groping toward is a conception of justice that includes all of creation. Stone's essay, when it was published, seemed to herald a rapid change in the legal system whereby entities like the Mineral King Valley in the Sierra Nevada would be treated as morally considerable. However, there was no such rapid change. The seventies were followed by the eighties and (in North America) a decade of anti-environmental backlash. For better or for worse, it still is not possible to go to court representing the interests of a redwood tree.

But although the legal standing of natural objects has not changed substantially, the popular feeling that it is possible to treat nonhuman creatures unjustly has grown considerably. The animal rights movement, which in its extreme form opposes any human use of animals as though they were property, is evidence of what seems to be a growing conviction that animals, at least, are morally considerable. Recent concern about the rain forests (both tropical and temperate) suggests that ethical concern may be extending to plant communities as well.[1]

---

1. One of the greatest ironies of our time is the fact that as we have begun to extend justice to nonhuman creatures, we have withdrawn it from the human fetus. As animals, trees, and rocks have begun to be morally considerable, our society has determined that undeveloped humans should not be considerable. We cannot discuss this irony here, but it certainly implies a deep confusion about the human relationship to both creation and Creator.

Arguments have been advanced in support of a variety of criteria for moral considerability: some say a thing must be sentient in order to be considerable; others say it must be a living thing; still others say that simply being a part of the biosphere (rock, water, air) makes something morally considerable. We in Western culture are far from a concensus on the matter; indeed, it is likely that the whole debate has caused further polarization. But it is evidence of a widespread secular concern that our traditional concepts of justice leave too much out.

What Is "Due"?

If it is possible, at least in principle, to determine what creatures are "morally considerable" (and hence require justice), the discussion of distributive justice leaves us with a second set of problems. How do we distinguish what is "due" to a creature or a community? Within a human community (such as a nation), the central principle of distributive justice ("to each its due") requires that the benefits (and burdens) be distributed so that everyone receives the same degree of benefit and bears the same degree of burden, unless there are differences among the members which would justify different treatment. If there are such differences, justice demands that the benefits and burdens be shared in proportion to them. Thus the basic principle of justice allows for discrimination, but not arbitrary discrimination.

Clearly, however, before such a principle of justice can work it must be supplemented by a principle specifying which differences are indeed relevant. And here we find enormous disagreements, for there is little agreement in the world on what makes up "relevant" differences. Social status, contribution, effort, need — all of these have been appealed to, along with the ideal of complete equality.

But all of these criteria for justice are related to human beings. Are there any established guidelines which suggest how we might deal justly with nonhuman creatures (sentient, live, or not)? There is one of overwhelming importance: the notion of property. In the Roman-based law tradition which has shaped the West, ownership, whether it is of slaves, horses, trees, or rocks, has been understood to confer absolute right of treatment or disposal.

Property Rights

Nearly three centuries ago John Locke articulated the central value of property in Western thought by saying that all human beings were entitled to three things: life, liberty, and property. He was certainly recognizing the central importance of stewardship in the human task, but the tradition has tended to absolutize the idea of property. The discussion of property rights frequently proceeds as if they were an all-or-nothing proposition: either we have property or we have none; either we have fully private property or we have fully public property. As one recent writer puts it: If you own it, control it; if you don't own it, don't try to control it.

But this all-or-nothing approach seems to be a legacy of the Latin penchant for clarity over richness. Property rights are not absolute or single; they are actually a bundle of rights, perhaps not all equally valid. As Lawrence Becker has pointed out, the right of ownership deals with the right to use, the right to transfer, and the right to exclude others. There are still other rights associated with property: the right to manage, the right to destroy, the right to receive income, the right to the capital, and so on. Clearly "ownership" does not in itself clarify the question of just stewardship of creation. Considering created things to be our "property" raises as many questions of justice as it answers.

But at a more fundamental level, making property rights an absolute does not seem biblical. C. S. Lewis's ironic little book *The Screwtape Letters* makes plain (from the viewpoint of Hell) the biblical attitude toward property considered as an absolute right (remember, this is a Hell's-eye view of things):

> The sense of ownership in general is always to be encouraged. The humans are always putting up claims to ownership which sound equally funny in Heaven and in Hell. . . . It is as if a royal child whom his father has placed, for love's sake, in titular command of some great province, under the real rule of wise counsellors, should come to fancy he really owns the cities, the forests, and the corn, in the same way as he owns the bricks on the nursery floor. . . . [T]he joke is that the word "mine" in its fully possessive sense cannot be uttered by a human being about anything. In the long run either Our Father or the Enemy will say "mine" of each thing that exists. . . . At present the Enemy says "mine" of everything on the pedantic, legalistic ground that He made it.[2]

---

2. C. S. Lewis, *The Screwtape Letters*, rev. ed. (New York: Macmillan, 1982), pp. 97-99.

"Ownership," therefore, or "property rights," is not an adequate means for determining the just use of creation. For as "property" is understood in our tradition, it is a simplification of the crucial fact that what we call ownership is really stewardship: justice will not be done until we realize that the ultimate owner is God the Creator. Deliberations about justice which are based primarily on "ownership" (useful as that concept is in limited situations) are incomplete. Particularly if we are to talk about a biblical "ecojustice," we need to turn to the biblical picture of the wholeness of creation which is expressed in the peace or *shalom* of the Sabbath.

JUSTICE, *SHALOM*, AND SABBATH

As we suggested in the previous chapter, it is, above all, the Sabbath which reminds us of the full biblical view of justice. In Jürgen Moltmann's words:

> on the sabbath and through it, men and women perceive as God's creation the reality in which they live and which they themselves are. The sabbath opens creation for its true future. On the sabbath the redemption of the world is celebrated in anticipation.[3]

The Bible contains many glimpses of that redeemed world where justice and peace triumph:

> You will go out in joy
>   and be led forth in peace;
> the mountains and hills
>   will burst into song before you,
> and all the trees of the field
>   will clap their hands.
> Instead of the thornbush will grow the pine tree,
>   and instead of briers the myrtle will grow.
>   (Isa. 55:12-13, NIV)

As our understanding of ecological interconnectedness and moral considerability expands to include the whole planet, we find ourselves

---

3. Jürgen Moltmann, *God in Creation* (London: SCM Press, 1985), p. 266.

being led firmly back to this biblical picture of justice. But that this Sabbath for creation is connected with more conventional ideas of "doing justice" is made clear in Isaiah 58. This chapter begins with a vivid picture of the evil in God's marred creation and the travesty of all attempts at pleasing God which perpetuate such evil:

> On the day of your fasting, you do as you please
>   and exploit all your workers.
> Your fasting ends in quarreling and strife,
>   and in striking each other with wicked fists.
>
> (Isaiah 58:3-4, NIV)

The fasting which God urges on his people is of a very different sort. Rather than taking, the Creator of all counsels giving:

> Is not this the kind of fasting I have chosen:
> to loose the chains of injustice
>   and untie the cords of the yoke,
> to set the oppressed free
>   and break every yoke?
> Is it not to share your food with the hungry
>   and to provide the poor wanderer with shelter —
> when you see the naked, to clothe him . . . ?
>
> (vv. 6-7)

Clearly this is an action undertaken in a fallen world: poverty, quarreling, and injustice show that we are far off from the creation which God called good. Yet the goal is still the restoration of that created goodness. And it is a goodness which includes both God's earth and human worlds, in all their darkness and oppression. God calls us to work toward the Sabbath in which both earth and world rejoice before the Creator.

The conclusion of Isaiah 58 makes it clear that the invitation to "rebuild the ancient ruins" is a preparation for the Sabbath. And certainly one of the ruins which we are to rebuild is the degraded creation with which we began this book.

> If you keep your feet from breaking the Sabbath
>   and from doing as you please on my holy day,
> if you call the Sabbath a delight
>   and the LORD's holy day honorable,

and if you honor it by not going your own way
  and not doing as you please or speaking idle words,
then you will find your joy in the LORD,
  and I will cause you to ride on the heights of the land.

(vv. 13-14)

This promise is preceded and paralleled by even richer promises for those who undertake the task of justice:

The LORD will guide you always;
  he will satisfy your needs in a sun-scorched land
  and will strengthen your frame.
You will be like a well-watered garden,
  like a spring whose waters never fail.
Your people will rebuild the ancient ruins
  and will raise up the age-old foundations;
you will be called Repairer of Broken Walls,
  Restorer of Streets with Dwellings.

(vv. 11-12)

In this promise there is nothing of glory for the builder; there is only the promise of strength to keep giving, to be a "spring whose waters never fail."

This work of justice and restoration is clearly linked, in the biblical story, both back to the Sabbath and forward to Christ, underscoring that deep harmony between creation and redemption which is such an important part of early Christian theology.

The Sabbath is empty if we ignore the work of justice that needs to be done — especially the necessary work of rebuilding and reconciliation. But likewise justice is empty without the promise and hope of the Sabbath, a harmony of creation in which all creatures rest. Only a picture of justice as broad as this will enable us to think biblically about the rebuilding of creation. That biblical justice is not restricted to ideas about ownership, but neither does it leave out a concern for human needs. It is a picture of wholeness for earth — and for earth's keepers.

SECTION IV

WHAT SHALL WE DO?

CHAPTER 17

❧   ❧

Guideposts

This is what the LORD Almighty, the God of Israel, says to all those I carried into exile from Jerusalem to Babylon: "Build houses and settle down; plant gardens and eat what they produce. Marry and have sons and daughters . . . seek the peace and prosperity of the city to which I have carried you into exile. Pray to the LORD for it, because if it prospers, you too will prosper. . . . For I know the plans I have for you . . . plans to prosper you and not to harm you, plans to give you hope and a future."

— Jeremiah 29:5-11, NIV

The real work of planet-saving will be small, humble, and humbling and (insofar as it involves love) pleasing and rewarding. Its jobs will be too many to count, too many to report, too many to be publicly noticed or rewarded, too small to make anyone rich or famous.

— Wendell Berry, in "Out of Your Car, Off Your Horse"

WE KNOW NOW THAT WE ARE "IN CHARGE" OF GOD'S CREATION, THAT we are to serve the earth, and that we are to do so justly. Those who attempt to obey the will of God and to follow the mind of Christ are those who are to speak out, to be the new Isaiahs; they are also to act, to be the new Noahs.

But guidance is needed. How are we to be the new prophets and doers? In the present age we do not receive the Word of God as directly as the Isaiah and Noah of Old Testament times did. We must depend on the Word of God as it speaks to us through the Holy Spirit and as it has been set down in Scripture; and we must understand it in the context of a much fuller knowledge of God's works in creation.

But the Bible is not a textbook. It does not tell us how we in the twentieth century are to conduct our use of land and energy and our economic policies. It does, however, give us certain principles, relevant to all times, which we must seek to understand and apply to our own situations. We have presented some of those principles in Section III of this book.

In this concluding section of the book we turn to a discussion of the application of those principles to the situations outlined in Sections I and II. Here problems immediately arise. Proposing applications of biblical principles is difficult because we cannot see fully where they lead: they are like roads whose beginning we see, but whose course we have no way of knowing beyond the first bend. Suggestions about economic change are like this. Similarly, the proposed actions may be simple, just as diving off a cliff into deep water is a simple action, but it is that first leap which is difficult to take. Reducing our levels of food and resource consumption can be viewed in this way — most difficult to begin, though obviously quite necessary. We may also stall in our attempts to apply biblical principles to our life-styles and institutional structures — especially when we contrast the trickle of individual impact with the ocean of public apathy. Most attempts to recycle waste are difficult in this way. Finally, it is always hard — and potentially embarrassing — to take a definite stand and declare that we should (or should not) do one thing rather than another. It is easier to remain anonymous and uncommitted.

Nevertheless, we offer the following "guideposts," guiding principles for our use of energy, minerals, land, plants, and animals, as well as for our collective actions toward other nations. Caution is needed in using them, for guideposts are not permanent; they change the farther one gets along. Nor do guideposts hold any absolute authority; they are merely markers pointing out a path to a full human stewardship through the bewildering tangle of problems which affect the home of God's creatures and relations among them. It is up to each of us to actually pick a way

across the terrain of our times — and to discover, perhaps, that some guideposts are wrong, and to come back and set them right for other travelers. Yet knowing that they are imperfect and incomplete should not keep us from following them; at this point they seem to represent the best directions our actions might take as we read the map of our times in the light of biblical principles.

For those who wish even more practical suggestions, we include in Appendix A a list of specific areas requiring consideration and action on the part of Christian stewards. In Appendix B, we survey some of the more important and helpful books which can take you further in topics which this book introduces. Appendix C considers a specific stewardship issue: whether or not to use recycled paper. We hope the material in this last section — guideposts, suggestions, and readings — will further equip us all for earthkeeping: the high task of being stewards for the King of Creation.

🍂   🍂   🍂

THE GUIDELINES WHICH CONTEMPORARY WESTERN CIVILIZATION FOL-lows today in its use of creation are tangled and contradictory, for they come to us out of centuries of conflicting philosophical and religious ideas. In Section II of this book we explored those springs of action in some depth, for none of us in the modern world is entirely free from their influence. But those who have responded to the gospel of Christ (as we maintained in Section III) have a more certain guide for action rooted in the Christian revelation. It is difficult to distinguish completely those Christian principles from the tangle of other truths, half-truths, and errors by which we guide our action. As St. Paul said of the Christian gospel, "we have this treasure in earthen vessels" (2 Cor. 4:7).

Nevertheless, it is our purpose in this chapter to suggest some general guidelines for our treatment of creation. Rarely are these direct biblical principles; they are rather cultural insights which have been in-formed, corrected, and empowered by the Christian gospel. We receive the gospel not as disembodied souls but as living persons nested and entwined in a network of familial, cultural, political, economic, and eco-logical relationships. Some of those relationships and understandings are wrong and thus need to be corrected; many are correct but need to be empowered.

Sometimes these guidelines will conflict with, and sometimes they will correspond to, the wisdom of particular political and economic ideologies. When dealing with such ideologies we must move very carefully, guided by two important principles.

First, we must be careful lest we simply use the gospel as a tool to bring about a program which we have decided on other grounds deserves our attention. This is a strong temptation today: the magnitude of environmental problems is so great that it is easy to see them as the only important concern. Thus Green parties and "Deep Ecologists" cheerfully recruit Buddhist, Taoist, animist — and even Christian — ideas into the environmentalist cause if they will be useful. But our interest in the environmental movement should not be of this sort; it should proceed from the core of our faith, from the realization that "the earth is the Lord's" and that his kingdom should come (as we pray) "on earth."

The second principle which should guide our action seems almost to contradict the first. Not only should we not allow the gospel to be subordinated to an ideological agenda — in this case, an environmentalist one — but in addition we must not act as though there were any realm of creation or human action which lies outside the scope of the gospel, the new creation. Here it is helpful to reflect on Paul's words in Colossians which tie the gospel to creation in the strongest possible way:

> [Christ] is the image of the invisible God, the firstborn over all creation. For by him all things were created . . . all things were created by him and for him. He is before all things, and in him all things hold together. . . . For God was pleased to have all his fullness dwell in him, and through him to reconcile to himself all things. . . . This is the gospel that you heard and that has been proclaimed to every creature under heaven. (Col. 1:15-23, NIV)

In addition to beginning with "all creation" and ending with "every creature," this passage refers five times to "all things." The gospel is indeed for the whole creation, and we should not diminish it by assuming that it is irrelevant to environmental concerns. Thus at the conclusion of this chapter we suggest guidelines which touch on our eating, our use of energy, our recreation, and our politics — all are relevant to reconciliation with creation. But in the vast reconciliations which are required for creational healing, we should never forget that the fundamental reconciliation is the healing of the broken relationship between ourselves and our Creator. Only out of that reconciliation can we begin real "earthkeeping."

"What's the difference? It was a man-made lake in the first place."

From *American Scientist Magazine*.
© 1975 by Sidney Harris. Used by permission.

We have said that the gospel needs to inform, correct, and empower the various ideas about creation which we discussed in Section II, our historical survey of human thought and experience. But before presenting the more biblical guidelines for action which come out of such a sifting, it will be helpful to summarize those prevailing notions about creation which shape conventional environmental attitudes. We can do that quickly by reflecting once again on the various words we have used to refer to the object of our stewardship. In the Western world three names for creation in particular stand out, and they mark three attitudes toward the earth. Each of them captures important truths, but together they need to be harmonized and corrected by a full biblical doctrine of creation. Those names are "nature," "resources," and "environment," and they provide us with an outline for looking back at the history of our thought about the earth.

CREATION AS "NATURE"

"Nature" is an ancient name for the earth whose main import is captured in such common phrases as "Mother Nature" or "Nature's way." Since classical times the word has been used to describe the total of all existing things bound together in a fertile, quasi-personal divinity. This conception of nature is compatible with pantheism, the religious attitude which says that God and the universe are one. We encounter this divinized concept of creation in many Greek ideas — in Aristotle, for example, when he portrays the whole cosmos moving from potential to actual in fulfillment of its nature; we see it more clearly in Stoic conceptions of living in harmony with nature. We see it again in the vitality and organicism of the medieval worldview. The overall contribution of these ideas of nature has been the picture of the earth as something to be treated with reverence because it is divine. Carolyn Merchant laments the demise of this reverence for a divine nature in her book on the rise of modern science which is significantly entitled *The Death of Nature,* and much of ecofeminism and "Gaia" religion is directed toward an attempt to return to such a nature goddess.

Needless to say, "nature" is not a biblical concept: the Bible has no comparable word for "nature" and repudiates any notion of nature or natural process as divine. Nevertheless "nature," both then and now, gets at an important truth: that the earth is of great value, that it is mysterious and points to some kind of transcendent reality and purpose. We are mistaken in assuming that the only purpose is nature; but we are equally mistaken when we think (as recent generations have done) that what we once reverenced as nature can now better be mined and degraded as "raw material." And that brings us to the second influential — but misguided — set of ideas about the earth.

CREATION AS "NATURAL RESOURCES"

Two related ideas about creation gained strength in early modern times. Both are rooted in a creational understanding, but both, ironically, have worked against a full human stewardship of creation. The first of these ideas is that creation is something made by God, and hence it can be understood (in Kepler's phrase) by "thinking God's thoughts after him." Thus science was originally rooted in a faith in the goodness and rationality of creation — and ultimately in the character of the Creator.

The second idea — advanced most explicitly by Francis Bacon in his apology for the inductive method — is that human beings ought to have dominion over "nature": such dominion is the original state of things and ought to be restored. This too is rooted in a biblical understanding of creation and our place in it. Taken together, the two ideas combined to replace the medieval picture of nature as a kind of goddess with a mechanical picture of the earth as a great storehouse to be drawn on by human ingenuity and used to promote human well-being. Thus "nature" was replaced by "natural resources."

Contributing to this shift from "nature" to "resources" was a change in how natural processes were understood. In the medieval view of "nature," physical processes were seen as vital; even minerals and jewels were seen as "growing" in the womb of a fertile nature. This organic model of the operations of "nature" was replaced by a mechanical model. Every natural process (even the processes of life itself) could be reduced to and explained by the interactions of particles. The first form of such a mechanism was the atomism of the Epicureans in the ancient world, but the machine-like image of nature which it produced still dominates our explanations. Creation came to be understood more and more after the model of a great machine; the Creator came to be seen as a great machinist or inventor with no ongoing relationship with his creation. Not surprisingly, this mechanical understanding of creation encouraged not only the explanation but also the use of the earth as a supply of raw material and power (and also as a dump) for the processes of human industry. "Nature" has become only "resources." For several centuries — and nowhere more spectacularly than in the "New World" — human ingenuity has imposed a human world on the created earth. Only in relatively recent times have we begun to recognize that such treatment of the earth as a source of raw materials leads irreversibly to its degradation. This recognition has given rise to the "environmental" movement of the late twentieth century.

CREATION AS "ENVIRONMENT"

In the twentieth century we began to feel the consequences of treating creation simply as a resource. In North America careless agricultural practices caused topsoil to blow or wash away; heavy pesticide use produced unexpected mortality high on the food chain; air and water pollution became alarming. The insights of biologists like Rachel Carson and Aldo Leopold began to make us aware of the interconnectedness of life, and *ecology* became (in a double sense) a household word. We began to see ourselves as simply one more organism in a great web of living things, as a brief pulse in an evolutionary heartbeat. Creation was no longer "nature" or "resource" but a self-perpetuating cosmic process in which we were privileged (for at least a while) to be the eyes and ears — the "handiman for the universe," in Lewis Thomas's memorable phrase.

Yet there is a curious contradiction at the heart of environmental understanding. It has unquestionably been healthy for us to see ourselves as part of "the environment," nourished by the cycles of air, soil, water, and energy which sustain all other life. But a part of most environmental awareness is the implicit assumption that this network of living things marvelously adjusted to their environment is the result of evolution alone — and ultimately evolution is simply another name for chance. If all of "the environment," including humanity, is just a cosmic accident, then we have no reason to assume any particular responsibility for it; presumably the cosmic process will unfold as it will, and our actions are of no ultimate importance. But that is not at all the way that most environmentally aware people see their task as humans. Rather, they assume that we have a responsibility. It is wrong to diminish life's diversity; it is right to care for and nourish it. In short, we are best understood as stewards, and the word *stewardship* has been widely used to describe the human task.

But stewardship implies responsibility, and there can be no binding responsibility if we were produced by cosmic accident. What's more, stewardship implies not only responsibility *for* but responsibility *to*. Indeed, the concept of environmental stewardship points us back inexorably to a correct knowledge of our place in things: we are responsible creatures in a creation, and it is the Creator to whom we are uniquely responsible.

Obviously this recognition of our place in creation is crucial to a true understanding of stewardship. Let us then sum up the biblical principles (presented mainly in chapter 14) which define our stewardship:

a. God is Creator and Lord of the universe. He is thus both completely distinct from it (as any maker is distinct from his or her work) and thoroughly involved in it through Christ and the Holy Spirit, in whom all things are made, nurtured, and renewed.

b. The creation, in all its intricacy and diversity, is good. This goodness is not simply a declaration by God, but a recognition. And in the very independence of creation implied by God's acknowledgment of its goodness, we see the possibility that the goodness of creation might, in its freedom, come to be flawed.

c. Through both their nature and their task, humans are made to share in the care and sustaining of creation. Like the rest of creation, humans are made by God, and they depend on his gifts for their sustenance as surely as do beasts or trees. But unlike the rest of creation, men and women are made responsible to God. Thus they have a unique responsibility to demonstrate, to *image* the nature of their Creator in their actions.

d. The human relationship to God, to the rest of creation, and to other humans has become flawed. Though we have not lost all the goodness God intended us to show, even our best actions are likely to contain that which is self-centered and destructive, a grotesque caricature of divine lordship. Instead of understanding our unique gifts as a means to love and obey God, honor other humans, and care for creation, we humans have understood our dominion to be the occasion for increasing our own comfort and power at the expense of everything and everyone else.

e. Both the model and the means for a restoration of the right human relationship to God, to fellow humans, and to the rest of creation are in Christ. The Incarnation demonstrates the Creator's willingness to forsake lordship and dominion for the redemption of his creation. We mistakenly think that to act like God is to act like a tyrant; Jesus' actions show us just the reverse of our expectations.

f. Redeemed humanity is directed to exercise dominion, stewardship, and justice, guided by the mind of Christ. Redeemed humans are not to shun their powers of intellect, creativity, and technique. Rather, they are to use them for the wise and loving management of creation, developing the full potential of everything in creation — stone, beast, or human — and lifting all of that creation to share in their adoption as sons and daughters of God.

These biblical principles should underlie and direct any use we make of the earth, whether that use is for the praise of God, for the benefit of other humans, or for care of the earth itself. These principles also form a standard by which we can measure those twists and turns of human attitudes toward creation — both past and present — which we have been summarizing. And they also imply a number of general guidelines for our action in exercising stewardship over creation. To these guidelines we now turn.

1. The exercise of power inherent in our dominion must be rooted in wonder — that is, it must be humble. We should have and exercise power over creation. But our power comes from knowledge, and we need the humility to recognize that our knowledge is always incomplete. Wonder is the awed recognition of the limitations of our knowledge, and it is an important source of wisdom. Such humility would alter much of our education about creation; it might alter many of our habits of recreation; ultimately, it might change our industry and economics. Ecology (the study of the full, complex interrelationships among created things) should be an important part of every person's education — and especially it should be a part of the education of every Christian. Only out of the wonder and humility which come from such a deep knowledge of creation can we begin to exercise stewardship.

2. We have the responsibility to work toward a just human sharing of creation. The consumption of 40 percent of the earth's energy and mineral resources by 6 percent of the population is unjust. This does not necessarily mean redistribution, for wealth is not simply gathered from the earth; it is created by human action and ingenuity. But neither does it mean thoughtlessly increasing our wealth in the hopes that it will eventually benefit everyone. We need to share opportunities for wise stewardship of creation. And we also need to model a more stewardly use of creation ourselves. This would have a doubly beneficial effect. First of all, it would free more of the goods of creation for other peoples. Second, it would cease to hold before the peoples of the world a model of profligate and increasing consumption and would present instead a model of restrained use which is more nourishing of the health of the earth.

3. Stewardship implies responsibility for both human and nonhuman creatures. Human flourishing is not to be set *against* the rest of creation; we can only flourish *with* other creatures. (We should recall this threefold harmony — of Creator, human stewards, and all of creation — whenever we keep the Sabbath.) We can no longer assume that "environment" and "development" have conflicting agendas. When we destroy a forest, we not only eliminate habitat for wild creatures; we degrade the water, soil, and air which form our habitat as well. When we promote an agricultural or housing development which depletes the soil of its nutrients, strips the landscape of its trees, contours, and watercourses, and pollutes the air and water, we are depriving ourselves and other creatures of a place to be at home in creation.

4. We should use creation in a sustainable way, providing for future generations at least the same opportunities for stewardship of a healthy creation that we have had. We have no right to pass on to the future a planet impoverished of the diversity of its plant and animal life or of its non-renewable mineral wealth. An obvious implication of this principle is that we cannot simply use up fossil fuel "savings" as though there will be no more need for them when they (and we) are gone. (In fact, the only way in which we can really justify drawing on that fund of ancient sunlight is if we "reinvest" it to yield an equal or greater return — as in the construction of solar collectors.)

Another implication of this responsibility to future generations is that we should not use creation today so as to leave hazards for the future. Thus we need to exercise great care in our disposal or storage of toxic and radioactive wastes. Such an obligation does not necessarily mean that we should never create such wastes, but it does imply that we should do so only if we are sure of a safe method of very long-term storage.

Finally, this responsibility to the future means using our inheritance of mineral wealth whenever possible in such a way that it can be recycled.

5. Our planning horizon must be unlimited. As Christians, we believe that there will be an end to this world as we know it, but we "know not the day nor the hour" of that end. And since we have no way of knowing when it will be, we must proceed as though there will be no end to our need to exercise stewardly care.

6. *We need to know as fully as possible where the things which sustain us come from and how they are produced.* What is the source of the food we eat, the fuel we burn, the materials we use for shelter, clothing, and transportation? All are products of the earth and of human ingenuity, and it is important that we not simply take such things for granted. To know the forest that grew the beams in our house, the soil that grew the vegetables in our salad, the ore which was the origin of our automobile — all of these increase our knowledge of and participation in the production of what we use, as does growing or picking our own food, for example. Even a little of such an activity is a valuable reminder that we are participants in a wide community of life. (There is probably no stronger, more immediate, and more rewarding reminder of such participation than the cultivation of a small garden, even if it can be only a windowbox of herbs.)

7. *We should not undertake a process of agriculture, mining, transportation, energy generation, waste disposal, recreation, and so forth until we have evaluated its consequences for the household of life.* This does not mean that ecosystem-disturbing activities should be abandoned, but that they should continually be redesigned toward the ideal of an earthly creation which can meet human needs without being diminished in intricacy, vigor, and diversity. That we are, in most cases, unable even to conceive of such a use of creation need not keep us from maintaining it as an ideal toward which we can devote all the efforts of our reasoning, manipulating, and creative powers. It is enough that in almost all of our uses of creation we can imagine a way in which the process can be done better — not necessarily more cheaply in dollars, but with less cost to the ecosystem. Thus an agriculture in which crops are grown in a rotation which preserves and increases the fertile soil is closer to this ideal than the repeated single cropping of a soil-depleting plant like corn. We approach such an ideal with an energy network which uses energy income (various forms of solar power) rather than burning the "savings" of fossil fuels. And so forth. Our human goals should not be projected outside the limits imposed on us by the ecosphere and by our obligation as stewards to care for it.

8. *We should show particular concern for the animals we have brought into the human world through domestication and use.* It may be a painful necessity for us to butcher cows, keep chickens, and use monkeys for research. But if we do so we must never forget their worth as God's creatures, and when we make use of them we should do so with as little

pain as possible. In effect, this means we ought not to regard domesticated creatures only as resources. Each creature within our care, whether wild or domesticated, must be given room to develop its created nature.

9. *The lands which produce our food and provide important ecosystem functions must be protected from destruction.* We should develop policies which prevent the urbanization of the very lands upon which we ultimately depend for our well-being. Urban development should be directed away from the land that feeds us; it should be directed away from the wetlands that naturally cleanse the water running into our lakes and rivers; and it should be directed away from the floodplains which protect our homes from destruction. Above all, we should establish and support policies which encourage preservation of the soil. Such policies might include crop rotation, soil-building plantings, minimum-tillage agriculture, contour cropping, and the use of grassy drainage ways. When economic and policy incentives foster poor stewardship it is *everyone's* responsibility (not just the farmer's or logger's) to remove such adverse incentives.

10. *We must limit human population to a level which can be sustained within a healthy and diverse creation.* Human ingenuity and the harnessing of fossil fuels have encouraged us to forget that every environment has a carrying capacity. For some time now we have been increasing the earth's capacity to sustain humans by diminishing its capacity to sustain other creatures. But the real human population limit is one which allows sustenance not only for a flourishing human population but also for the full range of created life. We should not let the infinite worth of individual men and women lead us into thinking that the kingdom of God is necessarily enhanced by a mere increase in human numbers. When we see that redemption reaches to the whole creation, we also see that we must limit human numbers so that humans do not flourish at the expense of the degradation of the rest of creation.

11. *In planning for future energy needs, it is essential to consider the end use of energy and to determine an appropriate source for it.* Too often our energy planning has been done by considering all energy needs to be of the same sort, delivered in the same form. This assumption is carried out, in fact, in the increasing tendency to electrify our energy use, since electricity is the most easily transportable and transferable form of energy. But in order to achieve this ease, we often create great waste. In a house, for example, it is desirable to have an air temperature near 70 degrees Fahrenheit. To produce that temperature, it may be necessary to have a medium somewhat warmer — perhaps a 120-degree radiator. Yet to pro-

duce that low temperature heat (and as much as 35 percent of the energy used in heating in America goes to producing such low heat) we must burn coal, oil, or gas in a furnace at temperatures up to 2,500 degrees. Solar energy, on the other hand, delivers low temperature heat — somewhat below the boiling point of water — and thus is ideally suited for one of the main needs of such heat: space and water heating in homes. Such matching of end-use needs to appropriate energy sources requires some flexibility in the design of both homes and utilities, but the potential for saving, both economically and ecologically, is very great.

12. *We need to choose carefully those sources of energy which do the least damage to creation.* We must realize that some cost and risk is involved in making use of any energy source. Many good reasons have been advanced for opposing nuclear power, but such opposition is misguided if it assumes that any alternative — especially coal-fired power plants — is superior. The risks of increased coal burning (such as more acid rain and more carbon dioxide in the atmosphere) might be greater than the risks of nuclear power. But other alternatives — such as more conservation and various uses of solar energy — would be better than either. We also need to remember the *net* energy cost. The amount of energy that goes into building, maintaining, and dismantling any energy system — from nuclear to solar — may in the long run be so high as to render it environmentally unacceptable.

13. *Energy conservation is the single most important part of any energy program.* It has been shown conclusively that a determined and concerted effort to conserve energy can, at much less expense, have a greater impact on the energy problem than the development of any new energy source — including solar energy. Conservation is not just a stop-gap measure until other sources are discovered; it is a way of developing permanent habits of stewardship of this most basic resource. Energy conservation is not just an economic or patriotic act; it is an application of concern for the human and nonhuman life of the world. For the alternative to conservation is waste; and waste not only destroys some creatures directly (through various forms of pollution), but also keeps others from enjoying the goodness of creation.

14. *The fossil "fuels" — coal, oil, and natural gas — are a unique chemical treasure and, as much as possible, should not be burned as fuels but rather should be used as sources of synthetic material.* Oil, coal, and natural gas are our primary source of plastics. Yet currently we burn 95 percent of these hydrocarbons for fuel and use only 5 percent for synthetic ma-

terials, including medicines. Since there are many other potential sources for heat, but no comparable source for the chemical properties of these fossil materials, a stewardly use of these resources would be to stop using them for fuel and save them for these higher uses.

15. Since it is clear that we must rapidly shift from use of "savings" resources (fossil fuels) to use of "income" resources, we should give our greatest attention to the development and widespread use of solar energy conversion devices. Thus the order in which we must attempt to use our energy resources, and the order for our research and development priorities, should be something like this:

I. Income (and Short-Term Savings) Resources
   A. Solar-passive
   B. Solar-active
     1. Hydroelectric
     2. Solar thermal
     3. Biomass — e.g., wood, methane from wastes, alcohol or petroleum from plants or plant products
     4. Wind
     5. Solar electric
     6. Ocean temperature differential
   C. Tidal
II. Inheritance Resources
   A. Geothermal
   B. Nuclear fusion
   C. Nuclear fission
III. Savings Resources (Long-Term)
   Fossil fuels

16. Christians should seek to reform those societal structures which damage the ecosphere and produce injustice among humans. We referred earlier to our tendency to blame structures or processes for many of the problems mentioned in this book. We sidestep responsibility every time we begin a sentence with "Technology forces us to . . ." or "The economics of it require . . ." It is important to realize that structures and institutions are the creations of humans. Not only are we responsible for them, but we can, if we wish, change them. We participate in these larger structures in many different ways. As citizens, we are part of city, county, state or province, and nation. Obviously, we have an obligation to participate in those governments, even if our participation seems distant and peripheral. One kind of participation, of course, is to vote. Most candidates still say little about the issues discussed in this book, and Christian voters can perform a real service by bringing into public consciousness issues about land use, ecosystem preservation, solar energy, and so forth. We also have an obligation, when the opportunity and need arises, to participate more actively in government. If, indeed, the Christian gospel shows how power may be exercised, Christians should temper the widespread misuses of power — over nature and over humanity — by their presence in the "power structure."

There is yet another important way in which persons can affect the power structure. Many of us own stock in corporations and are, therefore, part of that corporate "body" which often treads so heavily on the earth and on human needs. We thus have an obligation to exercise whatever influence we have — financial and otherwise — to direct the action of that body to more stewardly practices.

17. We must maintain a clear distinction between price and value. Price is set by the market system and is a result of the available supply and of demands made on the basis of wants. Value, on the other hand, depends not on someone's cash-backed yearnings but on a quality intrinsic to the thing or to its function. To dispose of an object on the basis of price alone is to continue in that misunderstanding of dominion which says that humans are the only source of value and meaning on earth. Resources that are treated on the basis of *price* are dominated forcefully: their own selfhood is denied. Stewardship, on the other hand, recognizes *value* and seeks to enhance that value. It may even be that to recognize and steward properly the value of a thing will demand considerable sacrifice on the part of the steward. We may have to answer such questions as: What is the *value* of clean air, or a sparkling mountain stream? And what then are their prices?

This is not to say that the market system is an illegitimate or un-Christian means of using resources. But certainly the human-centered concept of price needs to be moderated by the more creature-centered concept of God-given value. And that value ought to be understood not only in terms of human utility, but also in terms of the thing itself — though again, human utility is one important value of things.

18. All people should be free to exercise stewardship over a fair share of creation. The commandment to exercise dominion was given to "the Adam": all humankind. Yet, because of the present inequities of the distribution of power over the earth's resources, vast numbers of people lack not only the basic means for sustenance, but also the very privilege to exercise stewardship. What this means is that we should regard "development" in Third-World nations not simply as giving, feeding, and clothing, but rather as making it possible for people to use — and misuse — their abilities as stewards. In a sense, the position of the wealthy, technologized nations in the West makes them "stewards of stewards." They do have power over Third-World peoples and their resources, but they should use that power as a means of helping those people attain their own independent selfhood and their own exercise of power. This may mean that we should remove trade practices which prevent self-development and encourage countries to process their own raw materials.

19. Our aid to developing nations should not impose Western ideas of development, but should encourage and enhance both the cultural uniqueness of the peoples of those nations and the diversity of creatures within them. The Christian view of humanity, it could be said, combines both that active manipulation in which the West has excelled and that selfless passivity with which the East has been preoccupied. Thus the Christian gospel has within it the ability to let both aspects of humanity develop together in their uniqueness, balancing each other rather than conflicting with each other. We must avoid the arrogance of aid, and learn stewardship and life-style practices from other peoples in their own integrity.

Westerners in general, and we North Americans in particular, must not encourage those in poorer nations to model their development on features of our own development. In many countries, pollution and labor-eliminating agriculture are encouraged as signs of progress. In order to convince these nations that the Western version of progress is not the best one, we must put into practice here ideas of progress which are revised according to the principles of stewardship and justice.

Whenever we have dealings with developing nations, we ought to avoid the *arrogance* of aid that forgets that many of the problems currently experienced by those countries have resulted from their wish to attain the standards of overconsumption and overproduction which are exhibited in our life-styles and institutions.

20. Our lives as stewards should make clear that the achievement of the central purposes of life is not directly proportional to our level of consumption. Our way of life, as well as our educational institutions, our businesses, and our churches, should make clear that quality of life does not necessarily improve with increased consumption. Western statistics on divorce, suicide, and drug and alcohol abuse make it plain that trying to "have it all" leads to misery. Given the unhappy consequences of that ideal of affluence, we ought to live by the guideline stated by Jesus at the beginning of the parable of the rich fool: "Watch out! Be on your guard against all kinds of greed; a man's life does not consist in the abundance of his possessions" (Luke 12:15, NIV). Paul implies the same in 1 Timothy 6:6: "Godliness with contentment is great gain."

These twenty guidelines are an attempt to apply biblical principles to our understanding of how to live on the planet in these last years of the twentieth century. They are, obviously, incomplete, imperfect, and tentative. But they are both a starting point and a goal for us as we continue to learn how to be better keepers of this troubled but beautiful earth.

A STEWARD'S HYMN

TALLIS' CANON

Calvin De Witt, b. 1935

1. Cre- a- tor Word by whose great power The
o- ceans roar and plants do flower, Cre- ate in us a
love for Thee, the Earth, all life, the sky, the sea.

2. O Word of God Who Earth did frame, Who
gives to man all things to name; Grant us the know- ledge
of Thy ways to care for Earth, to bring Thee praise.

3. Redeemer Lord who Earth did save,
Who lifted mankind from the grave;
Imbue us with redeeming grace
To heal the Earth, its blighted face.

4. Creator Word, by whose great power
The oceans roar and plants do flower,
May we, thine heirs, Thee emulate,
Our lives as stewards consecrate.

APPENDIX A

⋇   ⋇

What You Can Do

MUCH OF THIS BOOK HAS BEEN THEORETICAL AND GENERAL; ITS concern has been to provide an overview of human stewardship of creation, and (drawing on biblical principles) to provide general guidance for that stewardship. But we do not see theory as the opposite of practice, nor generalities as being opposed to specifics. Rather, theory and practice, generalities and specifics, work together; they ought to be viewed as parts of a continuum rather than as disjointed, fundamentally different elements of human thought and behavior.

Thus, as Christians, we are confronted with problems in both spheres: we must act against environmental hazards and profligate, unjust consumption patterns as well as against attitudes which encourage those hazards and patterns. Theory is not relegated to thinking about attitudes, nor is practice shunted toward recycling waste and riding bicycles. We must *act* in theoretical matters and *think about* practical matters; we must, for instance, organize our voices so that we may speak out strongly against ingrained habits of mind, and we must, in another instance, think out carefully the complicated matters of changes in our way of life.

What this comes down to, then, is that this book, with its emphasis on theory (what we think), would be incomplete without specific suggestions for practice (how we act). At the same time we recognize — without apology — that this book is largely general and theoretical and as such cannot aspire to being a handbook for action. (Not that the book ought to be considered impractical; its practicality, however, lies precisely in its

361

attempt to promote a theoretical understanding of the problems and to encourage action in response.)

Why, then, do we include this appendix on what you can do? For two reasons: first, because of the need to show how theory can lead directly into practice; and second, to show that there are good theoretical reasons for many commonly advised actions (such as insulating your home).

We have divided this appendix into levels of participation: first, the individual and family; second, political and economic structures; third, educational structures; and finally, the church. Such an organization stresses that the changes and (tentative) solutions to the problems we have described result neither from individual "change of heart" alone nor from massive "change of structure" alone. Rather, both individual and world-wide behavior — including all the gradations in between — must change. We should not view either individuals or structures as the determinants of the paths followed by the world as we know it. To assert that individuals control the direction that our planet takes is to be blind to the immense power of structures, but, at the same time, to call the power of structures determinative is to deny the responsibility of the individual.

One final word to put this appendix into context: we have to answer the question of *why* we must examine and change our life-styles and *why* we must urge governments and structures to examine and change their practices. The overriding motivation for such action rests, for Christians at least, in *responsible stewardship* — the task of caring for God's creation. We must act out of obedience to that task, not out of self-interest or even out of altruism. Non-Christians may indeed act out of such motivations; some (as is often the case and as Christians have often been slow to emulate) act out of genuine love and concern. But Christians have an added urgency and richness to their participation in stewardship and justice, and they also have less excuse for their lack of such participation. Self-interest and concern for the wider realm of human and nonhuman life are spurs to action of only secondary — though significant — impor-tance.

Responsible stewardship means that Christians may not be uncon-cerned or inactive in regard to their care of creation. These options of complacency are not open to them. Yet the call to a stewardship which is responsible to God and obedient to his Word entails a tremendously broad range of freedom. As specific as we would like to be, therefore, the possibilities for stewardship listed below cannot be understood to be binding in all cases or for each Christian. What is binding is responsible stewardship; how that stewardship might be worked out varies from situation to situation.

INDIVIDUALS AND FAMILIES

Care of Nonhuman Creation

Perhaps the most important way in which we can exercise good stewardship over creation is by making such stewardship a central concern of our own families. The most important focus for such care may be the training of children. But since children have a nearly infallible way of reminding parents of their own inconsistencies, these suggestions are as much for parents as for children.

1. It is important to be continually open to the wonder and beauty (as well as the complexity and the bewildering pain) of nonhuman creation. Make sure that your family does not live in an entirely synthetic world. This can be accomplished in the city as well as in the suburbs or in the country, but in all cases such openness to wonder requires a conscious and deliberate effort. To see and begin to understand the seasonal growth of plants, the passing through of migratory birds, the kinds of insects on the screen at night, the changes in the weather, the planets and the phases of the moon; to recognize in the hills, valleys, and plains of today the moraines, uplifts, and lava flows of the past — all these are ways of learning to live in wonder and curiosity at the marvel and diversity of creation.

2. Gardens are — in addition to being an important supplement to diet and budget — an excellent way of learning (and teaching) lessons about the basic processes of life. Particularly if the garden is nourished by the composting of vegetable wastes, a family has the opportunity to observe and nurture photosynthesis, growth, and decay. In addition, eating lettuce and tomatoes from our own garden is a good way of reminding us that any food (homegrown or not) has to come from natural processes — it is not manufactured in the dairy, freezer plant, or supermarket.

3. Although pets eat food which could be eaten by people, their presence in a household is good, for they make people more prone to empathize with nonhuman life. Caring for a dog, a cat, or a goldfish is a good way of learning how to care for living things generally. And most important, living with animals helps to nudge us a little way from anthro-

pomorphism by exposing us to a very different kind of created life which yet has value in itself.

4. In addition to these things which can all be done at home, it is important for a family occasionally to range more widely into places where the processes of life have proceeded with little human interference. Such excursions can range from a backpack trip in a wilderness area to a walk through a marsh. Such contact with relatively wild areas serves as a reminder that creation proceeds with great vitality quite apart from our involvement in it.

5. There are a variety of books, magazines, and films which can greatly enrich a person's — or a family's — depth of appreciation for creation. *Ranger Rick* and *Owl* are excellent magazines for teaching children environmental awareness. For adults, perhaps no magazine accomplishes such education so well as the beautifully written and gorgeously illustrated *Audubon* magazine. On a more popular level, *National Geographic* does a superb job of keeping its readers in tune with the earth and our treatment of it.

6. It is essential that the sensitivity to the material world generated by these activities be not just a private pleasure. They need to be channeled into action to preserve the possibility for future generations to develop a similar sensitivity. This usually involves the advocacy of causes — often defensive causes against development projects (industrial or residential) which threaten a natural habitat. Advocacy of such causes is an excellent way of building a child's understanding of the importance of stewardship of all life, not just human life and well-being.

Use of Creation

As was suggested above, our concern to care for nonhuman creation and our habit of using creation as a resource often conflict. This conflict will lessen when we adopt stewardly and conserving approaches to resource use such as the following:

1. Revise the habits we have adopted in moving ourselves and our goods from place to place — in other words, depend more on foot and pedal power, driving (less often) smaller cars and using public transit as much as possible.

2. Reduce the energy we consume for space heating and cooling by adequately insulating our homes, maintaining our furnaces at top

efficiency, "dialing down" at night and during extended periods away from the home, installing alternative heating and cooling systems such as heat pumps and solar-heating devices, turning on furnaces and air conditioning only when really needed, and appropriately designing new homes to allow for maximum "passive" use of solar energy.

3. Do without labor-saving but energy-consuming (and often simply unnecessary) appliances, and buy energy-efficient models of necessary appliances.

4. Install light fixtures which give maximum light per watt, and turn lights on only when necessary.

5. Recycle tin cans, glass bottles, newspapers, and whatever else your recycling center will accept (and whenever you have a choice, buy goods made from recycled material).

6. Reduce consumption of prepackaged and overpackaged goods.

7. Examine leisure-time activities. Begin vacationing nearer home, thus saving gasoline. Picnic in the parks nearest your home rather than traveling thirty miles to a marginally nicer park. Substitute swimming for water skiing, snow skiing for snowmobiling (even cross-country skiing for downhill skiing), bicycling for motorcycling, and jogging for going to a fitness club. An evening spent in the backyard with family or friends is often more enjoyable than an evening spent traveling to a distant place for amusement.

8. Encourage churches, neighborhood supermarkets, and so forth to set up recycling centers on their parking lots to receive cans, bottles, and newspapers.

9. Work with municipal officials to develop comprehensive recycling programs for both materials and energy recovery.

10. Encourage employers to set up car- or van-pooling programs for getting employees to and from work.

11. Avoid drive-in facilities, such as drive-in banks. When stuck in severe traffic jams or slow queues, turn off the ignition if you think that you will stand for more than twenty seconds without moving.

12. Try to conserve materials by buying good-quality products and using them as long as possible. For example, buy (for non-growing feet) good shoes and resole them regularly rather than continually buying new shoes.

13. Avoid use of disposable items as much as possible. Take reusable shopping bags to the supermarket. Avoid plastic forks, spoons, and knives (they are made from petroleum) and other disposable goods. Get beverages in returnable bottles. Avoid paper towels.

Other Life-Style Considerations

Responsible stewardship requires more than care for nonhuman creation. We must act with our fellow earthkeepers in mind. Thus we must search for ways to eliminate the blocks to stewardship possibilities encountered by a large part of the world's population.

1. Exponential population growth is one of those blocks. As individuals we cannot do much to stop this growth in the developing nations, but even in Western society zero population growth has not been achieved. Accordingly, those of us who would like to raise children ought to consider the size of the world population in determining how many children to bring into the world. And because a North American child places far more strain on the fabric of creation than a child in a poorer nation, we have an extra responsibility to bring our children up as earthkeepers.

2. Family size also bears on the economic problems outlined earlier in this book. The more children we Westerners have, the more our consumption will increase. But families and individuals must keep other things in mind as well when examining consumption patterns: we must, for example, (a) ask ourselves whether our buying habits satisfy real needs or whether they satisfy wants; (b) be aware of the fact that our "development" needs are often fulfilled at the expense of other people's subsistence needs — the check that is used to pay for a new piano could also go toward helping a village in India install a new well for fresh water, even though a new piano may be necessary for promoting our child's or our own musical talents; (c) support more strongly those agencies which work toward alleviating the causes of poverty and hunger; (d) understand where and how we get the products we consume — do they waste creation, and thus take away from those resources available to the poor? Do they support agricultural practices which allow the rich to hold and buy huge sections of land, forcing small farmers to overcrowded and underemployed cities? Does boycotting bring about the results we want, or does it create new problems of its own?; (e) learn more about political and economic structures so that we may wisely use our influence to help the poor and hungry (this is a suggestion which is also applicable in the contexts of care for nonhuman creation and resource use).

And So Forth

There are many more ways in which individuals and families can help in alleviating the problems with which we are here concerned. And though we may despair, thinking our efforts do not help, we must remember that careful examination of our way of life and of appropriate changes is good — first of all because it is *right* to do so; second, because such changes provide examples to others and set new trends; and third, because if we all stopped worrying about our insignificance and set to work, the total of our efforts would be enormous. In the meantime, individuals and families seeking to understand and alleviate the problems of environmental degradation, natural resource shortages, population growth, poverty, and hunger (among others) ought to provide themselves with "support bases," perhaps by:

1. Finding ways to live in a more intentionally communal way — *sharing* through communities which can be organized along various lines and to different degrees.

2. Joining or (where there is none) setting up study groups and action groups which direct themselves to the problems discussed in this book.

3. Becoming active agents in local, national, or international political, economic, educational, and ecclesiastical structures.

4. Arranging hunger awareness dinners to raise group consciousness about world hunger and profligate consumption patterns.

5. Supporting through prayer and finances the work of agencies which implement programs of greater stewardship and justice — for example, Bread for the World, the Christian Reformed World Relief Committee (CRWRC), and the Mennonite Central Committee, to name just a few.

POLITICAL AND ECONOMIC STRUCTURES

As we said earlier, individuals and families are not the only determining factors in these problem situations. Governments and business corporations make decisions which have far greater effects than our own individual or family decisions can have. These structures have created such complex systems of behavior that we often wonder whether anyone is "in control."

Yet it would be misleading to think that structures are moved by a dynamic separate from individuals. No one individual has much chance of changing structural problems, even from within the structure itself; but groups of individuals, with the aggregated power they would wield, can change the direction of those structures. We must, therefore,

1. Understand the complex systemic mechanisms of structures which waste resources, contribute to environmental problems, and treat the poor and developing nations unjustly.

2. Elect leaders (or become leaders ourselves) in politics and business who are aware of systemic malpractices and injustices and who will use their power to implement solutions to those problems — for example, to improve public transit systems, encourage energy conservation measures, set up food reserves, and promote equitable trade agreements.

3. Work toward equitable distribution of power. The argument is frequently used that entities such as business corporations, labor unions, or governments must be very big in order to be efficient or effective. This argument is frequently incorrect, but even where it may be correct, consideration must be given to the imbalance in power that large size creates. The same holds true for the distribution of wealth and education. One reason to avoid having too great a disparity in wealth or educational levels is that the wealthy and highly educated have a disproportionate influence on society.

4. Participate carefully. Systems require participation. Unjust systems, even when powerful, can be weakened by the failure of people of conscience to go along with them even when it is to their own selfish advantage to do so. Work for equitable taxes, fairer consumption patterns, adequate worker safety, and so on, even when it means the products we buy will cost more.

5. Be ready to protest. If everyone remains quiet, things will stay as they are. When people have the courage to raise their voices, sometimes in various forms of public assembly, their cause is noticed.

6. Support collective efforts to study, understand, and act to improve economic and political structures. We need to use insight, sponsor research, and show strength in order to get the job done. Individuals feel — and frequently are — impotent in the face of systemic problems. Collective effort is essential to the task.

EDUCATIONAL STRUCTURES

Our educational institutions are important "behind-the-scenes" structural determinants of our local, national, and international societies. Their indirect influence often means they can hide behind the more "up-front" political and economic structures. This societal institution which influences the direction of government, business, and labor must be called to responsibility. We can begin to do this if we:

1. Participate in school board decisions (attend meetings, secure positions of authority).

2. Support alternative educational institutions which teach children to treat the earth and its creatures with care, respect, and love.

3. Examine curricular materials for the presence of attitudes which promote poor stewardship and/or injustice, and provide alternatives.

4. Determine whether or not adequate attention is paid in the curriculum to (a) the philosophy and theology of our treatment of creation — be prepared to point out that stewardship is not compatible with pantheism, but points instead to theism; (b) the philosophy and theology of technology and technique; (c) practices which degrade creation and produce hunger and poverty; (d) the need for remanufacturing and repairing to curtail wasteful practices such as throwing things away as soon as they become slightly damaged.

5. Set up environmental studies programs.

6. Set up alternative food lines in the cafeteria, combining balanced diets, foods produced and prepared with less energy than usual, little waste, and concrete learning and discussion about food production and distribution.

7. Organize school or club projects such as: (a) raising money for organizations promoting and engaging in proper stewardship and just practices; (b) setting up a school vegetable and fruit garden for practical instruction in simplified food production; (c) setting up school recycling stations and remanufacturing shops; (d) experimenting with solar, wind, and other alternative energy sources; (e) planting hedgerows and establishing sites off-limits to humans to make it possible for wild animals to live on institutional grounds.

CHURCH

Individuals and families can effect tremendous change if enough of them work for it, and educational, political, and economic structures have enormous powers which can be directed toward good purposes. But the best intentions and efforts must find direction and unity of purpose. It is here that Christians are especially equipped to lead the calls to and efforts for good stewardship and justice. Christians, while acknowledging the shortcomings of their own insights and the lessons to be learned from non-Christians, must take up positions of leadership in the areas of scholarship, education, politics, economics, and the family. The church, as the community of Christians, must take up a courageous role and work for the establishment of Christian principles of stewardship and justice in the lives of individuals, families, and structures. It may begin to do so by:

1. Awakening its own membership to an awareness of the problems outlined in this book and the task and principles of stewardship and justice.

2. Raising the awareness of non-Christians to those same problems and principles.

3. Serving as a model in its own use of resources and care of God's human and nonhuman creation.

4. Performing its priestly and prophetic duties of praying for all of God's people and proclaiming all of God's Word.

5. Urging worship committees and pastors to regularly schedule services which focus, especially in the preaching of the Word, on stewardship of creation, theology of the natural world, justice in the use of resources, and the call to obedience in *all* human activities.

6. Encouraging the use and discussion of church school materials which focus on issues of stewardship and justice in the use of resources.

7. Viewing the church building as usable for more than just Sunday worship services.

8. Building new facilities only when necessary, and then with special attention to resource use.

THERE IS SO MUCH MORE WE MUST DO, SO MUCH MORE WE MUST LEARN. We must seek out those things by keeping our eyes and ears open and our minds alert to what goes on around us. The range of problems we have discussed makes an exhaustive list of "What You Can Do" untenable.

Every reader, therefore, in whatever station of life he or she occupies, with whatever talents he or she has, must join with others in determining problems — local, national, and international — and in matching themselves to those problems. Outlining areas crying out for consideration is the best we can do in this book; we can also direct you toward other books which may help to provide more specifics. We invite you, therefore, to make use of Appendix B.

APPENDIX B

✺   ✺

For Further Reading

THIS ANNOTATED BIBLIOGRAPHY IS INTENDED TO DIRECT READERS TO works which might fill in some of the gaps inevitably left by our overview in *Earthkeeping*.

In the past decade the number of books on environment-related subjects has multiplied rapidly, making it harder to draw up a representative list. A particular difficulty is the growing number of books which recognize that environmental issues are ultimately religious issues (which is good), but which adapt a sub-Christian or anti-Christian stance (which is unfortunate). There have also been a number of "backlash" books which object to what the authors perceive to be shallow or erroneous thinking within the environmental movement. We have included some books in both categories; they contain valuable insights but need to be read discerningly. We think it is important that our readers know something of the wide range of religious thinking on this subject (even if they disagree with it).

What follows is only a sampling; it is not intended to be exhaustive, but it should provide guidance for further reading in most of the areas we have discussed.

ON "THE STATE OF THE PLANET"

Brown, Lester, et al. *State of the World* [current year]. New York: W. W. Norton. These yearly reports, published in book form since 1984 by the Worldwatch Institute, provide invaluable, well-supported overviews of key environmental problems and solutions. Based on thorough research and surveys of the pertinent technical literature, they contain very reliable information. They are notable too for giving considerable attention to what is being done to alleviate problems. The Worldwatch reports are translated into most major languages and are used in hundreds of college and university courses.

Leopold, Aldo. *A Sand County Almanac and Essays on Conservation from Round River.* New York: Oxford University Press, 1962. This is arguably the most important single book in the modern "environmental movement." In the Almanac, Leopold brings us to appreciate the dynamic beauty of life month by month through the seasons; in the essays on conservation, he makes important contributions to an ecological view of the world, particularly in the essay "The Land Ethic," in which he provides a basis for altering our view of humankind from conqueror of the land community to harmonious member of the biosphere.

Lovins, Amory. *Soft Energy Paths: Toward a Durable Peace.* Cambridge, MA: Ballinger Publishing Company, 1977. This is undoubtedly one of the most important books written about energy policy during the past two decades. When it was published it provoked extensive debate about national energy policy, and the intervening years have tended to confirm the general accuracy of the analysis. Lovins argues that a complete rethinking of national energy policy is required, and strongly advocates phasing out nuclear and fossil fuel energy generation, making a transition to a network of various forms of "energy income" (supported by much more thorough energy conservation).

McHarg, Ian. *Design with Nature.* Garden City, NY: Natural History Press, 1969. In this impassioned, eloquent, and highly influential statement, McHarg not only analyzes the main problems with our shaping of the landscape, but also outlines (in considerable detail) the principles of a more enlightened "design with nature." The book is abundantly illustrated and is rich in historical example.

Miller, G. Tyler. *Living in the Environment.* Belmont, CA: Wadsworth Publishing Company (get the most recent edition, but all editions are valuable). This is by far the most inclusive textbook on environmental issues, including a wealth of well-presented data on basic ecology and issues of human impact as well as discussion of ethical response. It is an expensive but invaluable source of information, lavishly illustrated with photographs and graphics.

Our Common Future: The World Commission on Environment and Development. Oxford: Oxford University Press, 1987. This superb study is the result of a special UN commission looking into the relationship of environment and development. Based on interviews with thousands of people (from all walks of life) in countries on five continents, it makes an inescapable case that the health of human communities depends upon the health (increasingly threatened) of the natural systems that support them. The book contains a wealth of data, humanized by hundreds of eloquent statements from the people interviewed by the commission.

ON HISTORICAL BACKGROUND

Barbour, Ian, ed. *Western Man and Environmental Ethics.* Reading, MA: Addison-Wesley Publishing Company, 1973. This collection of essays comprises a seminar-type response to Lynn White's influential thesis in "The Historic Roots of Our Ecologic Crisis": that Christianity bears "a huge burden of guilt" for current environmental problems. Many of the articles address White's article directly, but all consider, from a variety of perspectives, the implications of Christian civilization for the treatment of the earth. (White's article can be found in *Science* 155 [1967].)

Berry, 'Wendell. *The Unsettling of America.* San Francisco: Sierra Club Books, 1977. Berry describes and attacks the takeover of agriculture in America by large-scale, impersonal methods, and laments the replacement of husbandry by technique and the consequent loss of cultural values. (See other, more recent books by Berry listed in the "Getting Down to Work" section below.)

DeVall, Bill, and George Sessions. *Deep Ecology: Living as If Nature Mattered.* Salt Lake City: Peregrine Smith Books, 1985. Written by two California philosophy professors, this is one of the best overviews of the religious dimension of the environmental movement as it emerged in the 1980s. In addition to describing basic movements and attitudes, it includes many extensive and illuminating excerpts.

These excerpts range from Christian to Buddhist to pagan, and like most works dealing in "environmental spirituality" they need to be read discerningly.

Glacken, Clarence. *Traces on the Rhodian Shore: Nature and Culture in Western Thought from Ancient Times to the End of the Eighteenth Century.* Berkeley: University of California Press, 1967. A careful, exhaustive, and impressive study of Western ideas about the relationship of humans to nature. The main theme is that three ideas have dominated Western thought: (1) the earth is specially designed for human habitation; (2) the earth — through its climate, topography, and so forth — creates a significant influence on human character and on culture; and (3) humans may or ought to modify the earth in certain ways — for example, by bringing order into nature on behalf of God.

Merchant, Carolyn. *The Death of Nature: Women, Ecology and the Scientific Revolution.* San Francisco: Harper & Row, 1980. This is the most scholarly and substantial of several books dealing with environmental issues from a feminist perspective. Merchant argues persuasively that the scientific revolution was accompanied by a major shift from seeing the earth as a beneficent mother (to be honored) to seeing the earth as a mistress (to be used).

Nash, Roderick. *Wilderness and the American Mind.* Third edition. New Haven: Yale University Press, 1982. This is the most comprehensive book on the idea of "wilderness," particularly as it developed in North American experience. It is clearly written and thoroughly researched, and it provides a good guide to the changes which have taken place in the last several centuries in the Western attitude toward "nature." (The third edition includes important new material.)

ON THEOLOGICAL PRINCIPLES

Austin, Richard Cartwright. *Hope for the Land: Nature in the Bible.* Atlanta: John Knox Press, 1988. This thorough study of the role of the created world in the Old and New Testaments has excellent insights, though it is somewhat too much influenced by the perspective which regards the Bible as more a record of human religious experience than God's revelation. This is the most substantial of several works of "environmental theology" by Austin, including a sympathetic biography of John Muir called *Baptized into Wilderness* (Atlanta: John Knox Press, 1987).

Beisner, E. Calvin. *Prospects for Growth: A Biblical View of Population, Resources and the Future.* Westchester, IL: Crossway Books, 1990. This is a good example of one Christian response to environmental concerns, which is (mostly) to dismiss them as ideologically influenced hysteria. Beisner proposes instead a greater emphasis on ownership and the free market, suggesting that such an emphasis would solve most environmental "problems" if governments and well-intentioned ideologues would not interfere. Beisner seems to ignore, misunderstand, or deny most of the ecological principles discussed in the opening chapters of *Earthkeeping,* but he represents a large Christian constituency which needs to be heard and understood.

Faricy, Robert. *Wind and Sea Obey Him.* Westminster, MD: Christian Classics, 1988. This is a brief but eloquent statement of a thoroughly sacramental (and Catholic) understanding of Christ as Lord and caretaker of creation — and of the implications of this for our own stewardship. It is one of the best and most theologically sound of a spate of recent books attempting to present an "environmental theology."

Fox, Matthew. *The Coming of the Cosmic Christ.* San Francisco: Harper & Row, 1988; and *Original Blessing.* Santa Fe, NM: Bear & Company, 1983. These two books are the most important works of an influential Dominican theologian whose concern is to turn the church toward a "creation-centered spirituality." Unfortunately, though Fox makes many valid criticisms of the Christian tradition and uncovers many rich resources within it, he reduces Christ to an impersonal principle of cosmic connectedness and rejects salvation through faith in the historical Jesus as "Christo-fascism." Fox's attempt to merge Christian thought with a generally New Age agenda cannot be ignored, but it must be read very critically.

Granberg-Michaelson, Wesley. *A Worldly Spirituality.* San Francisco: Harper, 1983. This is a solid outline for both a theological and an experiential relationship to God in Christ which does not leave creation behind.

————, ed. *Tending the Garden: Essays on the Gospel and the Earth.* Grand Rapids: Eerdmans, 1987. A very rich and varied collection of Christian viewpoints on "earthkeeping," including one on New

Age influence, several on biblical perspectives, an Eastern Orthodox view, and a remarkably eloquent statement from India by physician Paul Brand called "A Handful of Mud."

Gregorios, Paulos. *The Human Presence: An Orthodox View of Nature.* Geneva: World Council of Churches, 1978. A dense but theologically profound laying-out of the important Eastern Orthodox understanding of creation and the "human presence" in it. It was deliberately written as an answer to less careful — and less Christian — theological statements made in the 1970s by the World Council.

Hall, Douglas John. *Imaging God: Dominion as Stewardship.* Grand Rapids: Eerdmans, 1987. This important study reexamines the notion of the image of God and concludes that it is to be understood primarily as involving the activity of caretaking or stewardship.

—. *The Steward: A Biblical Symbol Come of Age.* Revised edition. Grand Rapids: Eerdmans, 1990. As the title suggests, this is a thorough assessment of the biblical concept of stewardship. In it Hall considers how we have diminished this concept and how we need to recover its biblical depths in a variety of contexts, including social and environmental.

Linzey, Andrew. *Christianity and the Rights of Animals.* Lexington, NY: Crossroad Publishing, 1987. This careful, biblical theological study by an Anglican priest avoids the inconsistencies and excesses of much of the "animal rights" movement and succeeds in setting forth a good foundation for thinking Christianly about our relationship to animals.

Moltmann, Jürgen. *God in Creation.* London: SCM Press, 1985. This is one of the more profound and far-reaching recent theological reflections on the doctrine of creation. It is especially helpful on the Trinitarian and specifically Christic dimensions of creation and on the creational implications of the Sabbath. Based on the 1984 Gifford lectures, it is written in clear awareness of the seriousness of ecological problems.

ECONOMICS AND TECHNOLOGY

Ellul, Jacques. *The Technological Society.* New York: Alfred A. Knopf, 1964. Ellul remains the severest and most profound critic of an unthinking modern acquiescence to "technique," and this is his earliest and most influential book. He argues that our civilization's commitment to rational efficiency is irreversible and irresistible. He has published many more recent studies on the same subject, including *The Technological System* and *The Technological Bluff,* and several more explicitly theological works such as *The Meaning of the City* and *The Subversion of Christianity.* Like most prophets, Ellul is prone to overstatement and is easily misunderstood and misapplied; but his message must be heard, especially by Christians.

Grant, George. *Technology and Empire.* Toronto: Ananzi Books, 1966. George Grant, influenced by Ellul, provides a powerful critique of North American society, all the more powerful because of his Canadian perspective. The book is a collection of loosely related essays, of which "In Defense of North America" is perhaps the most important.

Monsma, Stephen, ed. *Responsible Technology.* Grand Rapids: Eerdmans, 1986. Like *Earthkeeping,* this book is the result of an interdisciplinary attempt to develop a definitive Christian statement on technology, and it is one of the most comprehensive and balanced of such statements available.

Sagoff, Mark. *The Economy of the Earth.* Cambridge: Cambridge University Press, 1988. This is a thoughtful evaluation of the way in which economic considerations influence environmental decisions. Sagoff argues that we want, and will support, a policy which protects public goods above private self-interest; this work is a good corrective for those abundant arguments that all environmental problems would be solved through unfettered private ownership and unhindered working of the free market.

GETTING DOWN TO WORK: ACTION BOOKS

Berry, Wendell. *What Are People For?* San Francisco: North Point Press, 1990. This is one of several works by Wendell Berry which combine a thorough and profound critique of contemporary culture with hints of a way out — largely through paying more attention to the wisdom embodied in agricultural societies. Also helpful is his *Home Economics* (Berkeley, CA: North Point Press, 1987).

In the past few years dozens of environmental "how-to" books have been published. Most of them contain good advice, though sometimes they oversimplify the issues and write from a confused theoretical and ethical base. Here are some of the better books in this new genre of "practical earthkeeping":

The Canadian Green Consumer Guide, prep. by Pollution Probe Foundation. Canada: McClelland and Stewart, 1989.

The Earth Works Group. *50 Simple Things Kids Can Do to Save the Earth.* Berkeley: Earthworks, 1990.

—————. *50 Simple Things You Can Do to Save the Earth.* Berkeley: Earthworks, 1989.

—————. *The Recyclers Handbook: Simple Things You Can Do.* Berkeley: Earthworks, 1990.

MacEachern, Dianne. *Save Our Planet: 750 Everyday Ways You Can Help Clean Up the Earth.* New York: Dell, 1990.

Wilkinson, Loren and Mary Ruth. *Caring for Creation in Your Own Backyard.* Ann Arbor: Servant Publications, 1991. (Covers many of the specific suggestions found in the other books, but out of a more thorough biblical background.)

APPENDIX C

※ ※

A Case Study — Recycled Paper

As WE HAVE POINTED OUT IN THIS BOOK, MAKING STEWARDLY DECIsions is often a most difficult process. Answers are not always clear, and issues are complex. An excellent example of this occurred when the authors and publishers of this book were deciding whether or not to print it on recycled paper. Perhaps it seems self-evident that any book dealing with stewardly use of natural resources should, at least by way of example, be printed on recycled paper. After all, paper is made from trees, and shouldn't we recycle paper to save our forests? However, the issue is not that simple; perhaps a brief examination of the factors involved will reveal the complexity.

In making this decision, several factors must be considered. First, how does the *quality* of recycled paper compare to that of virgin materials? Secondly, how much *pollution,* of both water and air, is caused by the recycling process as compared to the virgin-materials process? How does the *energy* consumption of the two processes compare? And finally, how does the *economic* factor enter in — i.e., how do the *prices* compare?

The quality of recycled paper is certainly different than that of virgin-material paper, but this is not to say that either one is better than the other. Quality can be defined in terms of many different factors. In general, virgin paper yields a higher tear and fold strength, while recycled paper has added opacity and a certain feel of suppleness. Recycled paper also tends to be more dimensionally stable and have better performance generally, but it does have a disadvantage in terms of appearance if it is made of 100 percent recycled fibers. (Paper made only partially of recycled fibers can be made to look very much like "virgin sheet.") Overall, although there are differences in quality between virgin and recycled papers, it is more a matter of matching the paper used to the features desired than it is a matter of simply determining that recycled paper is superior to virgin paper (or vice versa).

Pollution has always been a major problem with paper manufacturing. For years paper mills have had the reputation of being major polluters, particularly of water, but also of air. Paper made of recycled fibers also results in pollution. Paper manufacturing is a very water-intensive process and substantial amounts of pollutants enter the waterstream. Formerly, because recycled paper requires de-inking and bleaching, the pollution generated in the recycling process was often greater than that for virgin paper. However, with environmental controls currently imposed upon discharge to waterways, both processes have become environmentally acceptable. Furthermore, with recent advances in production of recycled paper, it is possible to produce recycled paper with less air and water pollution than that produced during virgin-paper production. Although the issue is once again complex and not readily determined, it appears that, based on air and water pollution factors, recycling paper can be considered a more stewardly practice than using virgin paper. This conclusion is reinforced by major studies recently completed by both the United States Environmental Protection Agency and the Solid Waste Management Branch of Environment Canada.

Another pollution factor is the amount of waste paper disposed of in landfills. This paper decomposes in the soils and can release undesirable materials into the groundwater if the landfill does not have environmental protection devices built into it. Currently, recycling used paper is clearly a better alternative than landfilling it.

Energy is another factor to be considered. Many cities are now constructing large incinerators to burn solid waste and extract energy from it, and solid waste consists of about 50 percent waste paper. While it is clearly better to recycle paper than to landfill it, it is not obvious that it is better to recycle paper than to burn it and recover the energy. Once again, the analysis is complex. One must consider not only the energy recovered from burning the waste paper, but also the energy used in processing recycled paper in the plant. That net energy balance must then be compared to the energy used in producing new paper in the paper mill, including the energy consumed in chopping down additional trees, transporting them to the paper mill, pulverizing them, etc. If a careful analysis is performed, it appears that, from the energy standpoint, recycling paper is marginally better than burning it to extract the energy. As petroleum shortages increase and energy costs become higher, the energy issue becomes more important; indications are that higher energy costs will favor increased recycling of paper. In addition, we must recognize that as the population increases more wood must be devoted to the housing industry, rather than for the production of paper.

One final consideration: economics. Recycled papers are available in a wide variety of grades and qualities, just as are virgin papers. The variations of price depend more upon current market conditions for wood, waste paper, and finished paper products than they do upon the question of whether the paper is recycled or virgin. Thus, the price factor is a minor one, and depends very much upon the economic situation at the moment that the purchase is made. By and large, it appears that the prices are approximately equal for the two types of paper.

In summary, the use of recycled paper appears to be only slightly more stewardly than the use of virgin materials. However, since the use of recycled paper is rather new in the publishing industry, and since new manufacturing processes are likely to be developed with increased use of recycled paper, it appeared to the authors and publishers that printing this book on recycled paper would not only be a more stewardly use of resources, but would also encourage increased use of recycled paper in other instances.

Index of Names and Subjects

Index of Scripture References

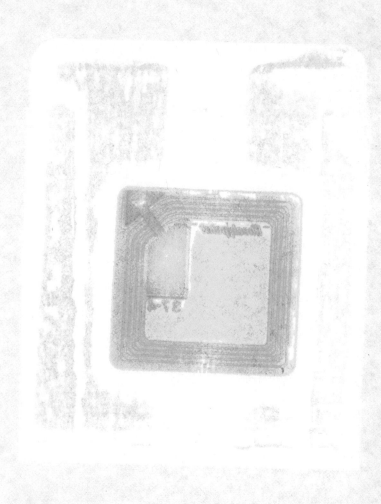